W9-CUW-545

This volume provides a comparative study of the problems and prospects of reform in modern Russian history. Drawn from contributions to a conference sponsored by the Kennan Institute for Advanced Russian Studies, the book raises important methodological and historiographic questions regarding the content, scope, and significance of various reform efforts, ranging from the Great Reforms of Tsar Alexander II to attempts to salvage the Soviet system undertaken by Khrushchev and Gorbachev.

One of the key issues raised is whether various attempts to modernize the political and social system were a series of cyclical failures or demonstrate a pattern of progressive development. *Reform in Modern Russian History* favors the second mode of interpretation and provides an excellent background for all who want to understand the Gorbachev era and contemporary Russian politics.

WOODROW WILSON CENTER SERIES

Reform in modern Russian history

Other books in the series

Michael J. Lacey, editor, *Religion and Twentieth-Century American Intellectual Life*

Michael J. Lacey, editor, *The Truman Presidency*

Joseph Kruzel and Michael H. Haltzel, editors, *Between the Blocs: Problems and Prospects for Europe's Neutral and Nonaligned States*

William C. Brumfield, editor, *Reshaping Russian Architecture: Western Technology, Utopian Dreams*

Mark N. Katz, editor, *The USSR and Marxist Revolutions in the Third World*

Walter Reich, editor, *Origins of Terrorism: Psychologies, Ideologies, Theologies, States of Mind*

Mary O. Furner and Barry Supple, editors, *The State and Economic Knowledge: The American and British Experiences*

Michael J. Lacey and Knud Haakonssen, editors, *A Culture of Rights: The Bill of Rights in Philosophy, Politics, and Law—1791 and 1991*

Robert J. Donovan and Ray Scherer, *Unsilent Revolution: Television News and American Public Life, 1948–1991*

William Craft Brumfield and Blair A. Ruble, editors, *Russian Housing in the Modern Age: Design and Social History*

Nelson Lichtenstein and Howell John Harris, editors, *Industrial Democracy in America: The Ambiguous Promise*

Michael J. Lacey and Mary O. Furner, editors, *The State and Social Investigation in Britain and the United States*

Hugh Ragsdale, editor, *Imperial Russian Foreign Policy*

Dermot Keogh and Michael H. Haltzel, editors, *Northern Ireland and the Politics of Reconciliation*

Joseph Klaits and Michael H. Haltzel, editors, *The Global Ramifications of the French Revolution*

René Lemarchand, *Burundi: Ethnocide as Discourse and Practice*

James R. Millar and Sharon L. Wolchik, editors, *The Social Legacy of Communism*

James M. Morris, editor, *On Mozart*

Reform in
modern Russian history

Progress or cycle?

Edited and translated by
THEODORE TARANOVSKI
with the assistance of
PEGGY McINERNY

WOODROW WILSON CENTER PRESS

AND

Published by the Woodrow Wilson Center Press and
the Press Syndicate of the University of Cambridge
The Pitt Building, Trumpington Street, Cambridge CB2 1RP
40 West 20th Street, New York, NY 10011-4211, USA
10 Stamford Road, Oakleigh, Melbourne 3166, Australia

© Woodrow Wilson International Center for Scholars 1995

First published 1995

Printed in the United States of America

Library of Congress Cataloging-in-Publication Data
Reform in modern Russian history: progress or cycle? / edited and
translated by Theodore Taranovski; with the assistance of Peggy
McInerny.
    p. cm. — (Woodrow Wilson Center series)
Papers from a conference entitled "Reform in Russian and Soviet
History—Its Meaning and Function," held May 5–May 7, 1990,
organized by the Kennan Institute for Advanced Russian Studies of
the Woodrow Wilson International Center for Scholars.
Includes index.
ISBN 0-521-45177-9
1. Russia—History—1801–1917—Congresses. 2. Soviet Union—
History—Congresses. 3. Perestroïka—Congresses. I. Taranovski,
    Theodore. II. McInerny, Peggy. III. Series.
DK221.R44 1995
    947.07—dc20   94-12807
                                            CIP

A catalog record for this book is available from the British Library.

ISBN 0-521-45177-9 hardback

WOODROW WILSON INTERNATIONAL CENTER FOR SCHOLARS

BOARD OF TRUSTEES

Joseph H. Flom, Chairman; Dwayne O. Andreas, Vice Chairman.
Ex Officio Members: Secretary of State, Secretary of Health and Human Services, Secretary of Education, Chairman of the National Endowment for the Humanities, Secretary of the Smithsonian Institution, Librarian of Congress, Director of the United States Information Agency, Archivist of the United States.
Private Citizen Members: James A. Baker III, William J. Baroody, Jr., Gertrude Himmelfarb, Carol Iannone, Eli Jacobs, S. Dillon Ripley.
Designated Appointee of the President: Anthony Lake.

The Center is the living memorial of the United States of America to the nation's twenty-eighth president, Woodrow Wilson. Congress established the Woodrow Wilson Center in 1968 as an international institute for advanced study, "symbolizing and strengthening the fruitful relationship between the world of learning and the world of public affairs." The Center opened in 1970 under its own presidentially appointed board of trustees. In all its activities, the Woodrow Wilson Center is a nonprofit, nonpartisan organization, supported financially by annual appropriations from Congress and by the contributions of foundations, corporations, and individuals.

WOODROW WILSON CENTER PRESS

The Woodrow Wilson Center Press publishes the best work emanating from the Center's programs and from fellows and guest scholars, and assists in the publication, in-house or outside, of research works produced at the Center. Conclusions or opinions expressed in Center publications and programs are those of the authors and speakers and do not necessarily reflect the views of the Center staff, fellows, trustees, advisory groups, or any individuals or organizations that provide financial support to the Center.

Woodrow Wilson Center Press
Editorial Offices
370 L'Enfant Promenade, S.W., Suite 704
Washington, D.C. 20024–2518
telephone: (202) 287–3000, ext. 218

Contents

Acknowledgments and editor's note   *page* xi

1 The problem of reform in Russian and Soviet
  history   1
    Theodore Taranovski

PART I. TRADITIONS OF REFORM IN
LATE IMPERIAL RUSSIA

2 *"Revolution from Above" in Russia*: reflections on
  Natan Eidel'man's last book and related matters   27
    Terence Emmons
3 Russia falls back, Russia catches up: three
  generations of Russian reformers   55
    Valentina G. Chernukha and Boris V. Anan'ich
4 From reform "from above" to revolution "from
  below"   97
    Larisa G. Zakharova
5 Reforms and political culture in prerevolutionary
  Russia: commentary   125
    Daniel Field

PART II. AUTOCRACY AND THE CHALLENGE OF
CONSTITUTIONALISM

6 The social problem in Russia, 1906–1914:
  Stolypin's agrarian reform   139
    Avenir P. Korelin

Contents

 7 Agricultural reform and political change: the case
   of Stolypin   163
   David A. J. Macey
 8 United government and the crisis of autocracy,
   1905–1914   190
   David M. McDonald
 9 Russia's parliament of public opinion: association,
   assembly, and the autocracy, 1906–1914   212
   Joseph Bradley
10 The reforming tradition in Russian and Soviet
   history: commentary   237
   Alfred J. Rieber

                PART III. THE UNCERTAIN INTERLUDE

11 The evolution of Bolshevik cultural policies during
   the first years of Soviet power   247
   Peter Kenez
12 Local power in the 1920s: police and
   administrative reform   265
   Neil B. Weissman
13 The antibureaucratic campaigns of the 1920s   290
   Daniel T. Orlovsky
14 The inconsistency of NEP: commentary   311
   Ben Eklof

        PART IV. THE CHALLENGE OF PLURALISM FROM
                KHRUSHCHEV TO GORBACHEV

15 Khrushchev and the crisis of the regime of the
   Marxian prince   319
   Carl A. Linden
16 Khrushchev's reforms in the light of perestroika   342
   Vitalii S. Lel'chuk
17 Perestroika: a revival of Khrushchevian reform or
   a new idea of socialist society?   366
   Giulietto Chiesa

18 Khrushchev and Gorbachev—similarity and
difference: commentary 384
 Robert V. Daniels
19 The reformer's dilemma—damned if it's reform,
damned if it's revolution: commentary 388
 William Taubman

PART V. THE PAST, THE PRESENT, AND THE FUTURE

20 Perestroika and the role of representative
institutions in contemporary Soviet politics 395
 Sergei B. Stankevich
21 Glasnost in Russia and the USSR: the 1860s and
the 1980s 401
 Iurii M. Baturin
22 Reform and revolution: commentary 407
 Blair A. Ruble
23 The fifth Russian revolution: commentary 412
 Robert C. Tucker
24 The return to normalcy: commentary 419
 Theodore Taranovski

About the editors and authors 425
Index 429

Acknowledgments and editor's note

The conference entitled "Reform in Russian and Soviet History: Its Meaning and Function," which was held from May 5 to May 7, 1990, was organized by the Kennan Institute for Advanced Russian Studies of the Woodrow Wilson International Center for Scholars. Both the conference and the volume that has come out of it were made possible by grants from the Woodrow Wilson Center Federal Conference Fund, the Ploughshares Fund, the W. Alton Jones Foundation, the Smith Richardson Foundation, and the Kennan Institute General Fund, all of whose generous financial support is hereby gratefully acknowledged. The success of the conference as an intellectual enterprise is due to the participants themselves, both those whose papers and comments are included in this volume and those whose contributions and insights do not appear here but nevertheless enhanced the level of discussion and analysis. Special thanks are owed to my friends and former colleagues from the Kennan Institute. They are the two program directors with whom I had the privilege of working—Peter Reddaway, who encouraged the initial proposal, and Blair Ruble, whose intellectual enthusiasm, moral support, and practical advice made the conference possible—and the members of the staff who worked very hard on the logistics—Daniel Abele, Stephen Deane, Monique Principi, and Nichelle Spears.

Many individuals have helped in the preparation of this book. I thank all the contributors, especially my Russian colleagues and Giulietto Chiesa, for their patience and cooperation and for the editorial liberty—indeed, the license—they afforded me. I am very grateful to Peggy McInerny, the Kennan Institute's editor, who assisted in the preparation of this volume. She skillfully crafted summaries of six of the chapters (the contributions by Alfred Rieber, Ben Eklof, Robert Daniels, William Taubman, Blair Ruble, and Robert Tucker) from tapes and verbatim transcripts of the proceedings for the authors' review and approval, and she provided other editorial expertise. I thank the Kennan Institute interns—Aaron Smith, Jennifer Leslie, and Mark McEuen—who prepared the texts of those transcripts. I would like to acknowledge support for manuscript preparation from the University of Puget Sound. I am greatly indebted to Florence Phillippi, whose typing and computer skills, good cheer, and imperturbable demeanor were of inestimable help. Finally, I thank Gisela, Tania, and Sasha for their love and their patience.

Six of the chapters (the contributions by Larisa Zakharova, Valentina Chernukha and Boris Anan'ich, Avenir Korelin, Vitalii Lel'chuk, Sergei Stankevich, and Iurii Baturin) were translated from the Russian by me, and I assume responsibility for any errors arising therefrom, as well as for editorial lapses elsewhere in the book. My editorial clarifications within the text are enclosed in brackets, and footnotes added by me are so identified and also enclosed in brackets. Terminology used in the translations (Russian titles, institutions, historical terms, and concepts) is, as far as possible, uniform throughout the volume for the sake of consistency and cross-reference. The transliteration of Russian names and terms follows the modified Library of Congress system. As is usually the case, Russian names presented a problem, and the solution adopted here was what might be termed commonsense inconsistency. The names of prominent people that have usually been anglicized in Western historiography or have a generally recognized spelling have been retained in that form (Alexander II, but Elena Pavlovna; Leon Trotsky and Michael Speransky, but Mikhail Gorbachev; Constantine, Peter, and Dmitry, but Sergei and Vitalii; Reutern, Witte, and Plehve, but Rittikh). Patronymic initials have generally been used only at the first appearance of a name. In cases where a person is identified only by initials and surname, both initials, if available, have been retained for purposes of proper identification. One editorial idiosyncrasy in the translations should be noted. The term "nobility" is used primarily with reference to the estate of the nobility, generically speaking (*potomstvennoe dvorianstvo*), whereas the term "gentry" is applied whenever it is clear that noble landowners (*pomeshchiki* or *pomestnoe dvorianstvo*), whether before or after 1861, are being discussed.

The chapters and commentaries reflect the basic structure and sequence of papers and commentaries at the conference, except for the addition of the editor's introduction and the omission of six contributions that were published elsewhere or were not submitted for inclusion in this volume. The papers were revised by the authors after the conference ended, and the volume's content took final shape by mid-1991.

Then, some fifteen months after the conference had ended, a series of momentous events marked a new departure in Russian history: the abortive coup of August 1991, the collapse of Soviet power, and the dissolution of the Soviet Union. The contributors were not asked to reconsider their papers in the light of these events, for any revisions would have given a false cast to the conference proceedings. I edited the papers to avoid obvious anachronisms, usually involving little more than changes of tense or references to Gorbachev and his policies. In the summer of 1992, the commentators were provided with the transcripts of their original remarks, which allowed them to make minor adjustments, but they did not change the substance of their commentaries. The introductory chapter, drafted in 1992, was revised in the spring of 1993, when the manuscript, after review by outside readers, was submitted for publication.

Given the extraordinary pace of change in Russia since 1991 and the uncertainties that still bedevil Yeltsin's regime, one might suspect that the proceedings of a conference held in the spring of 1990 would have been overtaken by events. The question of the nature, scope, and content of reform in contemporary Russia, however, is still very much on the political and research agendas. The synoptic and historical perspectives adopted by the conference's participants make its findings and conclusions still germane for scholars and commentators alike.

THEODORE TARANOVSKI
Tacoma, Washington
July 1994

1

▰◗▰

The problem of reform in
Russian and Soviet history

THEODORE TARANOVSKI

The twentieth century ended in December 1991 with the resignation of Mikhail Gorbachev as president of the Soviet Union and the decomposition of the Soviet Union into a conglomerate of independent states. No matter what the rest of the decade brings, barring the unlikely eventuality of a thermonuclear war, an era has drawn to a close. Our brief but traumatic century began in June 1914 and neared its end during the late 1980s, with the collapse of Communist power in Eastern Europe and the Soviet Union, the reunification of Germany, and the demise of the cold war. The Soviet Union, having exhausted all the potential of its economic and political system, imploded, and its empire fell apart. The revolutionary experiment begun by Lenin and institutionalized by Stalin expired in August 1991 as ingloriously as did the order that it overthrew in October 1917.

Given the dizzying kaleidoscope of changes in the former Soviet Union over the past decade, it should come as no surprise that although the August 1991 coup had been rumored about in the press, its denouement was no more expected than the import of Gorbachev's policies when he assumed power in 1985. On the contrary, Gorbachev's course of reforms—which some have called the "fifth Russian revolution"— had not been anticipated by either the academic community or professionals in government, many of whom even refused to recognize that fundamental change was in the offing until it could no longer be plausibly denied. And yet by 1988, if not earlier, it was becoming obvious that there was a widening gap between the conventional wisdom about the Soviet Union and the emerging realities.

1

This gap had important implications not only for scholarship but also for government policy, and it gave rise to two sets of questions that dominated the debates of the late 1980s. The first dealt with foreign policy and the nature of U.S.-Soviet relations. What should be the nature of the U.S. response to Gorbachev's "new thinking"? Could he be trusted? Was he worth "helping"? How long was he going to survive? The other set was a more fundamental one pertaining to the nature of the Communist system itself. Even if Gorbachev was intent on improving relations with the West, the outcome largely depended on a significant reorientation of Soviet internal politics. What was the intent and content of Gorbachev's reform program, with its succession of slogans and approaches—acceleration, glasnost, perestroika, democratization? How far was he willing to go? What were his chances of success? In short, was any "real" change possible in the underlying structure of the Soviet system?

The Kennan Institute for Advanced Russian Studies, whose mission is to promote scholarship and interaction between the academy and government, has always provided a forum for raising such questions. To organize another meeting on one of the topical issues of the late 1980s, however, appeared redundant and unproductive. Given the pace of change in the Soviet Union, the conventional wisdom promised to have a short shelf life. At the same time, the growing international rapprochement, new information unveiled by glasnost, and developments in Western and Soviet scholarship encouraged a fresh look at some key issues in Russian and Soviet history and offered an opportunity for renewed collaboration between Soviet and American scholars. A meeting that would approach contemporary affairs from a historical perspective without subordinating one to the other held the promise of new intellectual insights and of conclusions with practical implications. In 1988, the Kennan Institute began planning a major interdisciplinary conference, involving both Soviet and American participants, to analyze the role of reform in Russian and Soviet history.

The conference brought together thirty-three scholars, mostly historians and political scientists but including some experts from journalism and government as well. It examined the reforms of five periods: the 1860s; 1906 to 1914; the 1920s; the Khrushchev era (1956 to 1964); and 1985 to 1990. These periods were chosen as representative of evolutionary and moderate tendencies in Russian and Soviet history, as periods of relatively peaceful change and growth, in contrast, for example, to the Stalinist 1930s, when the system underwent severe disruption, or the revolutionary years of 1905–6 and 1917–21, when the aim was to overthrow the existing order. Contributors were not asked to deal with periods earlier than the 1860s, in the belief that to extend the coverage too far back—for example, to the Petrine or Catherinian epochs—would impede precision of analysis. The organizers also sought to avoid extensive consideration of Stalinism or of the revolution of 1917 because of the historiographic baggage involved.

There was no attempt to prescribe a formal definition of reform, but the unspoken assumptions were that reform is more than mere change, that it involves a conscious attempt at gradual transformation and improvement of state and society on the part of the political leadership, and that it addresses the needs of the governed and the defects of the existing state of affairs. Indeed, as Peter Kenez points out in his contribution, this was a normative definition. It reflected both the traditions of liberal Russian historiography and contemporary developments in the Soviet Union. The questions that the participants were asked to consider in planning their contributions included: What conditions gave rise to the consciousness of the desirability and necessity of reform? What was the historical range of reform alternatives and why were some chosen and others rejected? What were the intentions and goals of the reformers, whether explicit or implicit? What were the results of the reforms and what did they presage for the future? What were the lessons, if any, that could be drawn for the present?

The conference focused on political and social developments and Russian political culture, loosely defined. No papers were solicited on topics such as the economy, foreign policy, and the nationalities question, although these are significant issues, and they cropped up in the discussions. Given the role of central government and political leadership in Russian and Soviet history, it was seen as appropriate to maintain this focus but to examine the subject from a particular perspective.

The key objective of the conference was to increase our knowledge of the periods in question. At the same time, the conference was designed to serve a more general purpose. What was needed to comprehend the contemporary developments in the Soviet Union was not just new research findings or methodologies but also a reevaluation of the assumptions and interpretations in Russian historiography and Sovietology that have dominated the outlook of several scholarly generations. To conduct such a reevaluation from a purely theoretical and methodological point of view would more likely than not produce mostly abstruse generalizations. To do so on the basis of concrete historical material might result in some new conclusions.

Much of Western thought and policy concerning Russia and the former Soviet Union has been predicated on the assumption that they manifested profound patterns of stability and continuity. This general outlook reflects certain traditions of prerevolutionary historiography and has recently found favor among some Russian intellectuals. At the risk of oversimplification, it can be argued that the paradigm of Russian historical continuity, sometimes verging on historical determinism, has two variants. Social scientists tend to focus on the recent past. For them, the Soviet system is a manifestation of Marxist totalitarianism rooted in the heritage of tsarist autocracy and the utopianism of the revolutionary Russian intelligentsia. Historians and students of culture, on the other hand, are inspired mainly by the nineteenth-century statist school of Russian historiography, the sociological approach of Kliuchevsky, and the concept of "oriental despotism," which had been applied to Russia by Western observers beginning in the sixteenth century. In this version, Russia and, mutatis mutandis, the Soviet Union are perceived either as a form of Eastern tyranny or as a historical system sui generis. In practical terms, what this usually entails is the generalization and abstraction of mature Muscovite and early imperial (i.e., 1500–1750) sociopolitical and economic norms to posit a quintessential and unchanging Russian "tradition."

Both these approaches combine theoretical modeling with historical evidence to arrive at constructs that properly belong to the field of historical sociology, with all the strengths and weaknesses of that heuristic approach. All of these constructs served well the exigencies of the cold war and, curiously enough, they were mirrored and reinforced by Soviet Marxist denunciation of the Russian past (except in certain respects where history was equally distorted to serve the purposes of Soviet patriotism).

Thus, Russia emerges as the heir to the traditions of Byzantine caesaropapism and Mongol despotism. The culture of Eastern Orthodoxy; the autocratic service state and society; a serfdom that corrupted both lord and peasant; the absence of a bourgeoisie and of the commerce and industry that were its hallmark: all those characteristics doomed Russia to follow an essentially non-Western path. The revolutions of the twentieth century ultimately changed nothing, as tsars were replaced by commissars, and Russian autocracy by Soviet totalitarianism. The present was merely the continuation of the past in a different guise and, given this historical record, not much could be expected of the future. Many an observer of the Russian and Soviet scene has subscribed to the principle of *plus ça change, plus c'est la même chose.*

For present purposes, the important issue is the relation of historical continuity to the problem of reform in Russian history. The usual argument is that in an autocratic polity that dominates an inert society, change, when and if it comes, is wrenching, cataclysmic, and usually counterproductive. It may come as a "revolution from above," a violent imposition of the state upon the people. It evokes the images of Ivan the Terrible, Peter the Great, and Joseph Stalin, who pursued their goals with ruthless disregard for the needs and desires of their subjects. Conversely, change may be the result of the anarchic upheaval from below directed against the very foundations of state and society, the classic Russian rebellion—in Pushkin's immortal phrase, "senseless and merciless." Doomed to failure when led by Razin or Pugachev, it succeeded when guided by Lenin and his cohorts. In either case, the historical process moves in an uneven, jerky, and ultimately cyclical pattern. Promethean drive exhausts and overreaches itself and is followed by retrenchment and lassitude, which prepare, in turn, the soil for a new effort to challenge the gods of history.

These tendencies, as many conference participants noted, may be discerned in patterns of reform in modern Russian history, and, indeed, as Terence Emmons remarks, reform for one historian is a revolution from above for another. Reform either was never completed or was followed by its rejection and reversal: Alexander II, an unwilling innovator at best, was succeeded by the era of the counterreforms under his son; Nicholas II, equally vacillating, withdrew support from both Witte and Stolypin; the tactical retreat of the New Economic Policy (can reform be a retreat?) was followed by Stalin's leap forward (or was it backward?); and Khrushchev was deposed by Brezhnev. Progress, if there has been such a thing in modern Russian history, came in fits and starts, with periods of stagnation alternating with attempts to catch up with the West.

However, as the events of 1991 demonstrated, the wheels of Russian history have not stayed in the predetermined rut—or perhaps there is more than one rut to follow. The era of Gorbachev is, indeed, over, but one may conclude, paradoxically enough, that his very failure is evidence of the success of his reforms. Gorbachev's attempt to change the Soviet system was relatively peacefully transmuted into the overthrow of the system itself without lurching, at least until now, into either reactionary or revolutionary utopianism. It would be dramatic to claim that the scholars who met in May 1990 foretold this sequence of events, but they did not. In fact, as could be expected in a meeting dominated by historians, they were quite loath to draw any "lessons" for the present. The participants, however, did successfully navigate the passage between the Scylla of historical determinism and the Charybdis of failed prognostication.

The conference, by concentrating on reform in general, did not focus on Gorbachev's program in particular, although that was a leitmotif informing much of the discussion. It also did not treat reform eras as cumulative historical phenomena, each contributing to the burden of the past. Rather, each reform period was viewed as having its own dynamics and its own potential for realization. The focus on the specific and the particular, and the prevalence of the historical method in the papers, discouraged thinking in terms of a single chain or uniform pattern of causation. At best, there was recognition of structural congruence within a variety of historical cause and effect. Indeed, it was curious to note that the historians of the nineteenth century, while questioning the ability of tsarism to reform itself, were more optimistic about contemporary developments than were the Sovietologists, who saw reform potential in the past but tended to be more skeptical of the present.

The conference's fresh look at the past and the present led to two major conclusions. First, the pattern of failure or, at the most, of the partial success of past reform efforts illuminated the radical character of contemporary events. Second, the significance of the social dimension of reform in modern Russian history was underscored. The changing character and growing complexity of Russian society over the past century and a half played a crucial role in this process. As a consequence, the conference papers and comments collected in this volume have lasting scholarly value. They may also help explain why the reforms of Gorbachev, the coup that failed, and the revolution that is continuing have taken the course they did.

The first seven papers in this collection and the commentaries on them by Daniel Field and Alfred Rieber demonstrate the historical coherence of the period from 1861 to 1917. (Several participants found it necessary to reach further back into the past in order to place the period within a broader historical context.) Terence Emmons's contribution is a wide-ranging essay, raising both substantive and methodological issues, that takes as its point of departure Natan Eidel'man's provocative book *"Revolution from Above" in Russia*. One may note somewhat enviously that this slim paperbound volume, a work of popular history containing Eidel'man's musing on the shape of Russian history from the Mongol era to the 1920s, was published in an edition of 100,000 copies. Emmons's analysis is a fitting tribute to a late colleague and friend, who had accepted an invitation to participate in the conference but suddenly and tragically died of a heart attack late in 1989. Eidel'man sees Russian history as a progressive spiral, in a continuum from tsarism to Communism, in which autocracy and serfdom (the Asiatic path) represented impediments to modernization (Westernization), symbolized by the forces of democracy and the market economy. Although a series of revolutions from above had made substantive gains over time, none of them was successful, a fact that did not prevent Eidel'man from hoping the present might prove an exception.

Emmons uses Eidel'man's book to investigate several interpretative approaches, including the notions of "alternativity" and continuity in Russian history, and he points out the pitfalls of historical analogy and of reading the past into the present, or for that matter the present into the past. Emmons also tosses some pointed barbs at the conceptualization of the reform conference itself, which the editor hereby ruefully acknowledges as reasonably well aimed. Finally, he engages in a wide-ranging overview of the preconditions, objectives, and consequences of the era of the Great Reforms that nicely complements other contributions. He is echoed in his concerns by Daniel Field, who is skeptical about the notion of the "civic duty" of the historian and who doubts the comparability of the tsarist and Soviet periods and of their respective political subcultures. This conclusion is also implicit in Rieber's outline of the structural components of the reform process. He condemns Stalinism as a deviation from the normal pattern of Russian history and a departure from the reform tradition.

Valentina Chernukha and Boris Anan'ich also undertake a sweeping survey of what they characterize as the three generations of Russian reformers, from the reign of Alexander I to the revolution of 1905. In their view, the need to reform the system of political and social relations was already apparent in the early nineteenth century, and the failure to undertake it inevitably led to the revolutions of the twentieth. They focus on the programs and roles of the individual reformers, with most attention devoted to the reign of Alexander II. Perhaps the authors' most intriguing conclusion is that the scope and ambition of reformers' efforts declined over time. While Speransky could entertain notions of reshaping autocracy, Alexander II's rejection of any form of representation limited reformers' options, and after the counterreforms of the 1880s, statesmen such as Witte focused their energies on the economy. This approach, however, by stressing the significance of political institutions, neglects the importance of, for example, the judicial reform of 1864, which was probably the most radical and the most successful of the Great Reforms and which had clear constitutional implications.

Larisa Zakharova, on the other hand, concentrates on the emancipation of the peasants and its economic and social consequences in relation to other reforms of the 1861–74 period. Hers is a nuanced and perceptive account of the twists and turns of the reform process and of the motives that propelled it. Especially interesting is Zakharova's linkage of reform to the desire of the tsar and his closest advisers to maintain national prestige and Russia's position as a great power, which made them pay close attention to European public opinion, a situation that is not without its parallels today. On broader issues, Zakharova reaches many of the same conclusions as her colleagues. The state's refusal to undertake substantive political reform and to implement the program of the liberal bureaucracy, which was itself mesmerized by the ideal of the "reforming monarchy" and suspicious of social initiatives, led to the counterreforms of the reign of Alexander III and to the revolutions of the twentieth century. In turn, these revolutions revealed the "utopianism" of the reformers' objectives.

The agrarian question, along with autocracy, has probably been the key problem in prerevolutionary Russian history, and it is treated extensively by Avenir Korelin and David Macey, whose thoughtful contributions provide both complementing and contrasting interpretations of the Stolypin reform. Korelin succinctly summarizes the provisions of the 1861 emancipation and the socioeconomic conditions of the Russian countryside at the turn of the century and analyzes Stolypin's agrarian policy, starting with the debates of the period from 1902 to 1905. He argues that the government gradually ceased trying to solve the agrarian problem by measures improving the peasants' legal status and realized that economic steps were needed to alleviate their land hunger and to create a prosperous and politically reliable class of smallholders. He treats the economic and social consequences of the reform in some detail and concludes that the commune manifested considerable vitality, despite administrative pressure on it, and that the economic effects of the reform are still open to dispute. In any case, the reform failed to save the monarchy.

Two conclusions may be drawn from Korelin's study. The first is that, given the nature of tsarist state and society, there were limits to the extent that the government could engage in social engineering, limits that were reached by Stolypin's reforms. This, of course, would change after 1917. Second, the government constantly vacillated and delayed necessary change because it could not transcend the limitations of its own political culture, an observation applicable to other reform periods as well. For example, paternalistic tutelage over the peasantry was an article of faith for many government officials. Zakharova noted that the emancipation not only extended governmental power over the economy but also undermined the principle of private property by imposing restrictions on peasant disposition of the redemption land, and Emmons pointed out that the state infringed on the gentry's property rights in 1861 as well. Korelin illustrates how difficult it was for the state to abandon its support for the commune or to recognize the concept of peasant private property even some fifty years after 1861. The terminology of Russian legislative acts and of the political culture that they reflected is a translator's nightmare; opaque and inchoate as this terminology may be, however, it is evidence of significant realities and the values that underlie them, and its import must be carefully analyzed by any student of Russian political culture. For example, in tsarist Russia, the concept and the privilege of private property ownership (*chastnaia sobstvennost'*) was reserved for the landowning elite and urban social groups; the peasant still lived in the communal world and for the most part could aspire only to personal (individual) proprietorship (*lichnoe vladenie*).

In turn, these observations raise the question of continuity between the tsarist past and the Russian present, not just because collectivization may be viewed as a second enserfment, but also because widespread resistance to private property, especially in land, is often attributed to the persistence of a collectivist popular mentality. Indeed, peasant emancipation under tsarism could be compared favorably with agrarian reform in today's Russia, where the question of private ownership of land still hangs in the balance. Of course, the interests and aspirations of the peasantry and the ruling elite are different from those of their predecessors, but this does not necessarily close the case. Two other factors should be taken into consideration. First, the continuity of a single feature of a political culture, even an important one, does not signify continuity of the system as a whole. Second, as Macey points out, by 1916 "about 50 percent of peasant households had requested some form of government assistance in reorganizing their holdings." Apparently, they, too, were willing to see their world change when and if it was to their advantage (and they supported the commune for the same reason). From that perspective, one might well argue that the Russian Revolution resuscitated features of traditional peasant mentality, which collectivization later on reinforced, rather than being inspired by them.

In general, Macey takes a more sanguine view of Stolypin's reforms than does Korelin. He argues that a perceptual revolution was a necessary precondition of the reform, an observation applicable to the 1980s as well as to the 1860s, and he traces it to the turn of the century. (Interestingly enough, policy proposals that Korelin considers legal steps, Macey sees as economic measures.) Stolypin put these new ideas into legislation. Macey focuses on the politics of the reform process and sees the agrarian reform as part of a larger political scheme that Stolypin was never given the opportunity to implement. Stolypin failed politically because he and those who supported his outlook were unable to maintain the consensus necessary for the continuation of reform. As far as the agrarian reform itself is concerned, Macey gives high marks to Stolypin, especially for his "essentially democratic, voluntary, and legal methods," which stand in contrast both to what preceded him and to what followed him. In Macey's view, the overthrow of tsarism was "largely independent" of the promising processes of change in the countryside.

David McDonald analyzes the reasons for Stolypin's political difficulties. He reviews the attempt to strengthen the Russian autocracy, in the aftermath of the revolution of 1905, by creating a form of "cabinet" government (the United Government) under a "prime minister." The issues that McDonald addresses are crucial to our understanding of the nature of the imperial government, and elements of his analysis are to be found in other contributions. McDonald explores the dynamics of autocracy and the role of the sovereign in the system of Russian government during the reign of Nicholas II. Witte's attempt to become a powerful prime minister failed because Nicholas mistrusted him and because rationalization of the imperial government meant a weakening of the principle of autocracy. Stolypin's success in dominating other ministers was largely due to Nicholas's decision to rely on him to provide political leadership. Stolypin, however, could stay in power only so long as he maintained the confidence of the emperor, and once that was lost, his effectiveness precipitously declined. By 1910, Nicholas apparently decided to reassert his role in government, and Stolypin's successors, such as Kokovtsev, never managed to exercise similar influence. The problem with Nicholas's action, however, was that reassertion of autocratic power was dysfunctional and undermined the monarchy itself.

In fact, the dilemma of maintaining both a personalized autocracy and an efficient bureaucratic machinery bedeviled former occupants of the throne as well and with much the same results. Alexander II, for example, did not want to institutionalize the Council of Ministers. One can plausibly argue that the ministerial resignations in April 1881, when the new course of Alexander III's policy was announced, represented the first "cabinet" crisis in the history of the Russian autocracy. Nicholas's mentality was a systemic characteristic of Russian absolutism, and Stolypin should have anticipated his fate. The institutionalization of tsarist autocracy had proceeded too far for bureaucrats such as Witte or Stolypin to play the role of a traditional royal favorite, after the model of Potemkin or Arakcheev, but not far enough for them to function as prime ministers in charge of a cabinet.

This observation raises the issue of whether there is a cyclical pattern in Russian history, especially during the period from 1861 to 1917. The contributions discussed thus far portray a political and social system that needed reforming. They also support the view that there was a powerful wing within the imperial civil service that favored more or less integral reform and that only such reform could have successfully modernized tsarist Russia and saved the Romanov dynasty. The liberal bureaucrats won many battles but lost the war within the councils of the Russian government. Not only was the government divided, at times to the point of paralysis, but the basic stumbling block to successful reform remained the institution of autocracy. The mystique of autocracy and the obstinacy of the autocrats stood in the way of transforming Russia into a constitutional monarchy and a Westernized society, something that is also increasingly recognized in contemporary Russian historiography as the ultimate goal of the reformers.

However, the circularity of reform efforts in the 1861–1917 period, as Emmons contends, is only apparent, because the period is a continuous, and perhaps even progressive, whole. One should not forget that individuals who started their service in the bureaucracy in the 1840s under Nicholas I could still be found in institutions such as the Council of State or the Senate in the 1890s and the early 1900s. At the risk of exaggeration, it can be said that essentially the same dilemmas, the same options, and the same issues and arguments confronted the imperial polity during this entire period. This debate on Russia's future came to an end in 1917, as did the political culture, the institutions, and the social milieu that engendered it.

At least some reasons for this outcome are suggested by Joseph Bradley in his detailed study of the national congresses of various professional and civic organizations from 1906 to 1914. In his view, these congresses provided an outlet for social elements inadequately represented in the Duma. Although freedom of assembly was circumscribed and the government regulated these societies, their congresses, partially in response to this situation, became politicized and by 1914 served as a "parliament of public opinion," competing with autocracy in setting the political and social agenda of the country. They represented a new and powerful force for "reform from below."

Bradley's work clearly illustrates the vitality of civil society in prerevolutionary Russia in the early twentieth century. Until then, the sphere of public life was reserved for the servants of the state and the gentry elite, with the intelligentsia carving out a rival domain starting in the 1850s. The new civil society, reflecting the quickening pace of social evolution, encompassed a growing number and variety of social elements that could be regarded as middle class, elements actively seeking their own political and social place in the sun.[1] Bradley documents class, regional, and gender differences among groups that reflected social cleavages within Russian society. His work illustrates the social frustration and the alienation from the state that precipitated the revolution of 1905 and contributed to the revolutionary politics that led up to 1917. In this sense, Bradley's research straddles prerevolutionary and postrevolutionary Russian history.

Many conference participants expressed doubt whether the 1920s fit any reasonable definition of reform, especially if one conceives of reform

---

[1]See, for example, Edith W. Clowes, Samuel D. Kassow, and James L. West, eds., *Between Tsar and People: Educated Society and the Quest for Public Identity in Late Imperial Russia* (Princeton: Princeton University Press, 1991).

as change within an already established system. The tactical retreat of NEP did not signify the abandonment of the revolutionary goal of creating socialism. Indeed, as Weissman argues, in such a context reform may well mean attainment of "revolutionary ends through evolutionary means," an argument that has considerable merit when one contrasts NEP with War Communism or the 1930s. Ben Eklof, however, goes further and raises the intriguing question of whether NEP does not manifest as much, if not more, affinity with prerevolutionary as with Soviet history.

On the other hand, there is no escaping the import of 1917 for Russian history, and it cannot be gainsaid that a political *and* a social revolution did take place in that year. It brought about a new ruling class, a new socioeconomic order, and a newly dominant political culture that, like its tsarist predecessor, was a Western import. As Blair Ruble perceptively suggests, these differences are manifest both in the reality of the Soviet order and in the way scholars have approached it, especially in recent historiography. The revolution marked a shift in the balance between the political and the social dimensions of reform in modern Russian history, with the latter gaining prominence. It began an era of mass politics and social mobilization, which stood in considerable contrast to the elite and paternalistic character of the tsarist system, especially before 1900. The continuities with the prerevolutionary world, other than the obvious ones of population and geography, remained those of social and economic backwardness and the difficulties of effective governance of a multinational empire.

The three chapters dealing with NEP illustrate the complex and indeterminate nature of the period, which increasingly appears as a transitional stage, ill-suited to serve as an "alternative" model of reform for either Gorbachev or his successors. Peter Kenez argues that Soviet utopian goals required constant experimentation and that this constituted, in a sense, a permanent reforming urge. However, he contends that the considerable degree of cultural freedom in the 1920s was both relative and transient. Cultural pluralism was, in the final account, unacceptable to Marxism-Leninism, which admired the power of ideas and was convinced of its own monopoly on truth. Equally important, Kenez observes that, judging by the experience of NEP, there is no necessary correlation between economic liberalization and freedom of expression.

Neil Weissman and Daniel Orlovsky explore relatively specialized topics that provide considerable insight into the complexity of early

Communist politics and political culture. Weissman observes that the police represented the main point of contact between the state and the people, both before and after 1917. His comparison between the tsarist police in the post-1905 period and the Soviet militia in the 1920s is judicious and informative. While the two forces were designed to serve different political purposes, both of them adopted the ethos of professionalism, both operated in debilitating conditions, and both were employed for all sorts of administrative tasks in addition to law enforcement because the state lacked human and material resources with which to develop specialized agencies at the local level. Weissman, however, warns against an easy assumption of continuity. For example, while both proclaimed respect for the law in theory and abused it in practice, the tsarist view of legality was not likely to be inspired by "revolutionary consciousness of the interests of the laboring masses." In fact, one may well ask whether official perception of reality through Marxist spectacles and the solutions proffered did not aggravate the traditional problems of government in Russia.

One of the favorite solutions of the Soviet regime in the 1920s to the problems that were often self-created was to attack "the bureaucracy." In Orlovsky's view, the language of antibureaucracy and the various campaigns in the 1920s to overcome the evils of a mushrooming apparatus constituted a potent political weapon that played a role in Stalin's rise to power, though not in the way that they have usually been portrayed in scholarly literature. The language of antibureaucracy was used to demonize the political enemy, but it also served to coopt the growing class of white-collar workers into the proletarian "commonweal" and to legitimize the emerging Soviet social and political system.

The shadow of Stalin's quarter-century of terror, however, falls both on the 1920s and on the four decades that followed his death. The general tendency is to treat the period after 1953 as one of attenuated but recognizable totalitarianism. The heirs of Stalin may have abandoned his tactics of mass terror, but they maintained the cardinal features of his political and socioeconomic, now often referred to in Russia as the "administrative-command," system. However, as the contributions by Carl Linden, Vitalii Lel'chuk, and Giulietto Chiesa suggest, the eras of Khrushchev's reform and Brezhnev's stagnation increasingly appear less as a continuation of Stalinism than as a prelude to the downfall of the system itself.

The American political scientist, the Soviet scholar, and the Italian journalist agree that the crisis of the Soviet regime began in the late 1950s. Lel'chuk, for example, views Khrushchev's victory over the anti-Party group in 1957 as the effective end to his reformist efforts, and Chiesa dates the onset of the structural crisis of the economy, as reflected in declining rates of growth, to 1958. All three also agree that Khrushchev was unable to escape the ideological and structural constraints of the Soviet system that brought him down once his actions endangered the power and privilege of the ruling elite. Nevertheless, Khrushchev's attack on Stalinism and the concrete steps that he undertook to put an end to mass repressions and to improve the lot of the Soviet people undermined the foundations of the system and prepared the ground for Gorbachev, who himself came of age during the thaw of the 1950s.

Carl Linden asks the crucial question of whether a political leader can transcend the system that propelled him to power and the political culture that nurtured him. As chapters dealing with the tsarist period amply demonstrate, this was something that the last Romanovs proved incapable of doing and that was a key factor in the overthrow of the dynasty. Linden concludes that Khrushchev was unique among his colleagues in his moral revulsion against Stalinism and that his character is crucial to understanding his behavior. Linden's emphasis on the role of personality in history, however, must be balanced by Lel'chuk's and Chiesa's contention that Khrushchev's environment, as much as any personal flaws, placed limits on his freedom of action. Lel'chuk, in particular, is less sure about Khrushchev's motivations, and his work grapples with new sources and new ideas in an effort to approach objectively the totalitarian past.

The three authors further agree—and are echoed by Robert Daniels, with William Taubman gently demurring—that by 1990 Gorbachev had gone beyond mere reform of the system. Chiesa, an astute observer of the Soviet scene, claims that Gorbachev, although he started as essentially a Khrushchevian reformer, realized by 1987 that significant change in Soviet society and economy was impossible without political reform, and that this realization led to a vision of a new order incompatible with the principles of the Soviet system. Not just Stalin and Khrushchev but even Lenin had to be brought into question. In turn, Gorbachev's actions unleashed autonomous processes of political evolution and conflict that could no longer be controlled by the center. Chiesa concludes that the

Gorbachev era marked a new departure in Soviet and Russian history. The underlying processes that resulted in this outcome, in his view, still need to be elucidated, but their significance is already clear.

The contributions by Iurii Baturin and Sergei Stankevich are of equal interest although for different reasons. Although not formal papers, they have been included both for the force of their arguments and as historical documents in their own right, reflecting the ideas and concerns of two active participants in Russian public life at the time when perestroika was entering its crisis. Baturin, the author of draft legislation on freedom of the press and on the archives,[2] is a legal scholar and a protagonist of glasnost, whose comparison of the 1860s and 1980s, whatever its merits as scholarship, is an example of contemporary political discourse in Russia and of the role that history plays in it. His claim that the two eras paralleled each other was an effective political argument against Communist control over the media, which exposed the hypocrisy of the official ideology. It also manifests a polemical edge and an aesopian mode of argument that is traditionally Russian.

Sergei Stankevich, who at the time of the conference was a deputy of the Supreme Soviet and deputy mayor of Moscow, declared that a revolution was taking place in his country, and his analysis was as much descriptive as programmatic in content. Stankevich saw the Soviet regime at the point of moving from mere modernization to transformation, which was another way of saying that the Communist party would have to give up its monopoly of power and that the country needed democratization and reform in the direction of a market economy. He claimed that perestroika had wasted time, that Gorbachev had lost momentum and credibility, and that a coalition government was needed to get the reform moving again. Stankevich stressed the significance of the Supreme Soviet for the reform of Soviet state and society, and he anticipated that the newly elected urban soviets, especially in Russian cities where the coalition called Democratic Russia had just made major electoral gains, would serve as engines to push the process of democratization along.

Stankevich is still active in Russian politics. His views have evolved

[2]See Iurii M. Baturin, M. A. Fedotov, and V. L. Entin, *Zakon o pechati i drugikh sredstvakh massovoi informatsii: Initsiativnyi avtorskii proekt* (Moscow: Iuridicheskaia literatura, 1989); Iurii M. Baturin, B. S. Ilizarov, A. B. Kamenskii, M. A. Fedotov, E. I. Khan-Pira, O. V. Shchemeleva, and V. L. Entin, *Zakon ob arkhivnom dele i arkhivakh: Initsiativnyi avtorskii proekt* (Moscow: Iuridicheskaia literatura, 1990). See also Iurii M. Baturin and R. Z. Livshits, *Sotsialisticheskoe pravovoe gosudarstvo: Ot idei k osushchestvleniiu* (Moscow: Nauka, 1989).

since then, and a good portion of what he said has been overtaken by events, but several features of his presentation are still quite pertinent. The first is that his concept of modernization is functionally equivalent to the notion of reform under tsarism. The second is his emphasis on the role of *legislative* power for the proper functioning of the political system. The realization that "reform from above" is inadequate without input from below in the form of representative institutions, as demonstrated elsewhere in this volume, was a key motif in the reformist thinking and political history of late imperial Russia. Stankevich also endorsed the need for a firm legal order based on recognition of civil rights that was a cardinal principle of prerevolutionary liberalism as well.

Finally, Stankevich's presentation is especially significant for the student of Russian political culture in terms not only of what he said but also of how he said it. His speech is representative of a newly emerging vocabulary of Russian political discourse. For Stankevich, the Supreme Soviet was an embryonic parliament (*parlament*) at the federal (*federal'nyi*) level of government, contributing to the evolution of a system of "checks and balances"; the new city soviets were in charge of "municipalities"; and, of course, Gorbachev was no longer chairman but president (*prezident*). Even a cursory review of the Russian press discloses to the attentive reader evidence of wholesale adoption of Western political vocabulary as well as a revival of some prerevolutionary terminology: references to dumas, mayors, prefects, leaders (*lidery*), and entrepreneurs (*predprinimateli*) abound.

Stankevich, trained as a historian of the United States, was probably quite deliberate in what he was saying, but the appearance of a new vocabulary of political culture is nevertheless characteristic of most periods of change in modern Russian history. There is a direct linkage between such linguistic borrowing and the extent of acquisition of Western technology, institutions, and values. One need only think of the Petrine era or even the early Soviet period and contrast them with, let us say, the 1860s. The judicial reform of 1864 and the institutions of self-government of the same period were also inspired by Western examples, but foreign nomenclature was only rarely adopted or adapted (one instance was justice of the peace—*mirovoi sud'ia*). It was mostly coined anew, often with historical or nativist overtones: *prisiazhnyi poverennyi* instead of the equally acceptable *advokat* for "lawyer"; the zemstvo (officially, *zemskie uchrezhdeniia*); the city duma, and so on. Tsarist officials paid attention to such matters. For example, in 1889, Dmitry

Tolstoi expounded at length to the Council of State as to why the new agent of the Ministry of Internal Affairs should be called a "land commandant" (*zemskii nachal'nik*): so that by his very title he could properly impress his peasant charges.

This, of course, is a topic worthy of much more systematic analysis. What is being suggested here is that the vocabulary of Russian public discourse not only is indicative of the explicit content of Russian politics and political ideology.[3] It may also tell us something about culture and society as a whole. The predilection for linguistic borrowing is but one element in a continuous process of interaction between Russia and the West that involves material civilization and high and popular culture alike. Many of these elements may well have much greater societal significance than adoption of foreign words. Nevertheless, the vocabulary of political culture also reflects issues of national pride and self-definition, of status and power, of distance from or affinity with other peoples and civilizations.

The Petrine era, for example, which adopted the terminology of Western political discourse as well as Western institutions, manifested—and the present, which is doing the same, manifests—a sense of cultural uncertainty and national insecurity as well as receptivity to foreign models greater than was the case during, let us say, the reigns of Catherine II, which was also open to Western cultural influence, and of Nicholas I, which was not. This reflects both objective and subjective evaluations of Russia's standing vis-à-vis its Western rivals. In times of crisis, sizeable segments of the sociopolitical and cultural elites (there may well be important differences in outlook within and between the two, but that is another, although equally significant, issue) have sought adoption of European models to correct the situation. The reformers of the 1860s, however, while firmly committed to Russia's European orientation, possessed a level of national self-confidence and of cultural and psychological distance from the West that permitted them to adopt and adapt creatively but not indiscriminately. While this made for stability, continuity, and considerable success, it also had its negative side. The absolute monarchy successfully circumvallated the reformist impulse, with results that are well documented in this volume. Some of the reforms of Peter

[3]This vocabulary may consist of explicitly political, legal, or institutional norms and terminology or of a general outlook and behavior reflective of a political culture more broadly defined. For a succinct discussion of this issue, see Robert V. Daniels, *Is Russia Reformable?* (Boulder, Colo.: Westview, 1988), 39–40.

the Great survived until 1917, and the consequences of his cultural revolution are still with us. The limited reforms of the 1860s and much of the outlook that spawned them lasted but six decades. From that perspective, the historical potential of the present seems more open-ended, and the willingness to break with the past may present a greater range of alternatives than did either the 1860s or, for that matter, the 1920s.

The concept of reform in Russian and Soviet history remains complex and elusive. Blair Ruble has encapsulated the key themes and questions that came out of the conference, and Robert Tucker has limned the Gorbachev era and the Soviet experience as a whole on the broad canvas of Russian history. What remains for the editor is to make a few remarks reflecting on the contributions contained in this volume and to consider recent events.

To begin with, there is compelling evidence in favor of greater complexity and variety in Russian history than is usually assumed. Russia's rulers have striven over the past three centuries to emulate the material and cultural attainments of European civilization, even when ostensibly rejecting them. Success was ever elusive. It may well be true that, to quote Eidel'man, a historian sees "farther from the top," and that one should search for underlying structures and recurring patterns in order to explain the failure of various reform efforts in Russian history, by, for example, stressing the dichotomy between Russia and the West or the persistence of the autocratic tradition on Russian soil. It is also true that "God is in the details" and that the closer one examines a particular historical event, whether the peasant emancipation, Khrushchev's anti-Stalinist campaign, or Gorbachev's policy, the less preordained and the more fortuitous it appears. The chances of success or failure for any reform effort are indeterminate when viewed through the magnifying lenses of time, place, and circumstance. In retrospect, each one is only more or less probable as a unique historical phenomenon. Moreover, reforms or, for that matter, revolutions are usually perceived as failures or successes less in and of themselves—that is, in terms of the reformers' goals and accomplishments—than in relation to what follows them. The reforms of the 1860s may or may not be causally linked with the revolutions of 1905 and 1917, depending on how one evaluates the reforms themselves, the intervening events, and the causes of those revolutions, but for many historians the very fact that they did occur in a proximate future tends to discount the historical significance of the reform effort.

Second, it is political more than social or economic reform that ultimately matters and that determines the reform's degree of success. This was true for the 1860s and the post-1905 period, and it proved to be the precondition for the success of perestroika. Particular social and economic problems, even major ones, may be resolvable in the short run, but permanent adjustment to the process of social and economic evolution is not possible without political mechanisms that are able to respond to new circumstances. Any reform has a social dimension and involves a process of both inclusion and exclusion as new groups seek access to power and prestige while older elites are forced to relinquish their former preeminence. This was as true for tsarist Russia, where public-minded civil servants, zemstvo activists, or urban professionals sought input into the formulation of state policy, as for the erstwhile Soviet Union, where a variety of disaffected groups resented the Party's monopoly of power. The pattern of interrupted reform that is observed in both prerevolutionary and Soviet history is largely due to the absence of avenues that would readily have permitted political accommodation to social tension. This was recognized by reformers as disparate as Speransky, Valuev, Loris-Melikov, and Gorbachev, all of whom sought to institutionalize some form of political representation.

Third, successful reform must involve some unity of purpose at the top. It can be contended that a significant proportion of the Russian bureaucracy favored fundamental reform during the entire period from the 1850s to 1917 and that it failed to achieve it primarily because the autocrats refused to sanction diminution of their sovereign power. On the other hand, both Khrushchev and Gorbachev favored significant reform, only to fall afoul of the Party-state apparatus, which stood fast in defense of its privileges and its monopoly of power. Quite different circumstances produced the same outcome: the rejection of the reform course. In both cases, however, opponents of the reform, whether the tsars or the Party apparatchiks, recognized that the logic of the reform program transcended the parameters of the existing system and would involve its fundamental transformation. In that sense, reform would become revolution, and they refused to sanction that eventuality. Consequently, the student of Russian political history must analyze the interplay between the system and the ideology, between institutional structures and the goals and motives of the actors. This is true for both tsarist and Soviet periods and was recognized by many of the conference participants. Internalization of a new political culture appears to be a necessary precondition for any substantive effort to transform obsolete laws and institutions. This phenomenon is best illustrated and analyzed in the history of the Great Reforms, which were drafted and implemented by a new generation of "enlightened bureaucrats." The process is an interactive one, because the new outlook, in turn, informs and reinforces the functioning of the new "system," as shown, for example, in the reformed administration of justice after 1864.

Fourth, the most successful reform efforts in Russian history involved episodes when there was a relative congruence of interests and objectives if not between the rulers (*verkhi*) and the masses (*nizy*) then at least between the political leadership and "educated society" (*obshchestvo*). The most significant reform efforts in Russian history invariably involved tacit acquiescence or substantial elite support for the reformers. This was the case at least partially under Peter I, more so for the era of Catherine II and the 1860s, and markedly so during the 1980s. The breakdown of the connection between state and society, on the other hand, produced the Decembrist revolt in 1825, the terrorism of the 1870s, and the revolution of 1905. The 1980s and the early 1990s, however, were exceptional in that the process of reform engaged both the elites and the masses. A similar situation existed in the years preceding the 1905 revolution, but in 1905 and 1917, of course, the involvement of the masses in the political process produced a revolutionary outbreak. On the more recent occasion, in contrast to the early twentieth century, the political leadership was not only willing to respond to the pressure from below but actually worked to engender and manipulate it. Both the intelligentsia and the masses supported Gorbachev, at least during the late 1980s, in the hope that his efforts would produce economic prosperity and greater freedom. This relatively widespread social support acted as a powerful impetus for change and provided Gorbachev with freedom to maneuver. This interrelationship tends to be somewhat obscured in the various discussions of "revolution from above," "reform from above," "revolution from below," "reform from below," counterreform, and so on.

These observations permit us to arrive at a hypothetical ideal type of successful Russian reform. To begin with, the sovereign authority must possess adequate autonomy of power and be willing to undertake the process of reform *and* to accept its consequences, something that has rarely been the case in Russian history. Secondly, the ruler must have sufficient support within the government to draft and promulgate the

reform or at least be willing to provide political backing for the reformers within the bureaucracy. Conversely, there must be receptivity on the
part of the subjects, especially among the social elite, in order to guarantee successful implementation as well as a certain amount of pressure
from below to impress the political leadership with the reform's necessity. As a consequence, the ruler attains power to overcome resistance
from within the government itself and from the social elite and the
masses when their interests come into conflict, as they often do, and to
maintain the course. The closest that this concatenation of circumstances
came to being realized was during the 1860s and the 1980s. Any per-
turbance in this equilibrium that undercuts the ruler's will or his autonomy of power leads either to retreat, as under Alexander II and
Khrushchev, or to revolution, as under Nicholas II and Gorbachev. Once
the reform course is compromised, a counterreform that challenges the
political culture that inspired the reform in the first place may well follow, as happened under Alexander III and Brezhnev.

These observations are pertinent to an analysis of the Gorbachev era.
At one level of argument, the abortive coup of August 1991 supports
the notion that the Soviet Union was not reformable, that communist
totalitarianism, no matter how moribund, was unable to surrender its
monopoly of power. The coup also demonstrated that there were limits
to Gorbachev's willingness to envision an extension of reform to the
point at which "socialism," however defined, would be brought into
question. His forlorn hope, upon his return to Moscow from the Crimea,
that the Communist party was redeemable bears final witness to the
essentially reformist cast of his mind and character.

On the other hand, neither the August coup nor its immediate aftermath is worthy of being called a "revolution" in the classical sense of
the term—i.e., the overthrow of a political system accompanied by significant transformation in the social order. Many newly minted "democrats" are products of the Party apparatus itself, and much of the Soviet
institutional, legal, social, and economic structure, especially at the lower
levels and in the provinces, is still firmly in place. While this is likely to
change over time, and it is premature to pass final judgment, December
1991 is not even February 1917, much less October. Is it possible that
the weakness of a revolutionary drive today, unlike the situation in 1905
or 1917, is due to the fact that the masses have been coopted into the
system and have a stake in it to the extent that they did not in prerevolutionary Russia? And if this is true of the masses, it must be even

more so of what for lack of a better term could be called the "Soviet middle class."

What we have been witnessing since 1985 is something unique in Russian and Soviet history, something that a number of the conference participants did anticipate—a relatively peaceful, at least for now, transition from change within the system to change of the system itself. This transition from reform to revolution distinguishes the Gorbachev era from all other reform efforts in Russian and Soviet history and marks a successful breakout from the apparent cycle of unfinished reform.

The collapse of Communism and the demise of the Soviet Union, at least to this observer, suggest the need for a reconceptualization of the shape of Russian history, perhaps even for a historiographic "revolution." Until now, Russian and Soviet history of necessity had to be seen as sequential formations, one of which was completed and the other of which had a terminus a quo but no terminus ad quem. Until the Soviet period was over, its evolutionary potential and historical significance could be evaluated only provisionally. This is not to argue for historical relativism or "presentism" but simply to observe that distance in time, periodization, and taxonomic classification of historical phenomena affect our interpretation. In fact, they *are* a substantial part of interpretation.

The Soviet period, now that it is over, appears less as an independent historical formation than as an interlude or a stage in the course of modern Russian history. Indeed, not just 1917–21 but the entire Soviet era, to follow up on Robert Tucker's suggestion, may be thought of as a modern Time of Troubles. The revolutionary impulse of 1917 has played itself out, and an equilibrium is being reached between the Soviet utopia and the Russian heritage. The Soviet Union has collapsed, but it has produced a modern, urbanized, industrialized, and educated society that has now fallen upon hard times but that has also outgrown the Communist system. The post-Communist society is floundering in the wreckage of Soviet institutions and ideology and is seeking inspiration both in the contemporary West and in Russian history. This should not be surprising. A thousand years of Russian civilization, in itself a product of considerable interaction with the West, were not likely to be eradicated by seventy years of the Communist regime.

From that perspective, the reform efforts of the past no longer appear as a cumulative series of cyclical failures and abortive successes, but neither are they a linear sequence or some sort of a spiral. The shape of modern Russian history assumes a zigzag pattern. The 1920s were a prelude to ascendant Stalinism, while Khrushchev and to a lesser extent Gorbachev tried to salvage the unsalvageable. Their efforts were turned toward the past. The reforms of the 1860s and the constitutional era that followed the revolution of 1905, on the other hand, point less toward 1917 than toward the present. The prerevolutionary past and the post-Soviet present share the continuing integration of Russia into Europe.

Part I

Traditions of reform in late Imperial Russia

2

●━■●●

"Revolution from Above" in Russia: reflections on Natan Eidel'man's last book and related matters

TERENCE EMMONS

Uncertainty, like gout, cannot be cured, only treated symptomatically—or dropped into a footnote.

Edward Gibbon

The most important thing in science-fiction novels was radio. The happiness of mankind was expected from it. Well, we got the radio, but we haven't got happiness.

Ilya Ilf

SUMMARY OF THE BOOK AND ITS "LESSONS"

Ranging as it does over the length and breadth of Russian and Soviet history, with constant reference to the crisis of its time, Natan Eidel'man's book *"Revolution from Above" in Russia*[1] may perhaps be considered the author's *profession de foi* as engaged historian, man of letters,

[1] [Although the contributors to this volume analyzed developments in Russia and the former Soviet Union since the middle of the nineteenth century, the methodological and historiographic issues they raised obviously transcend these chronological limits and have relevance beyond the subject of reform. Two recurrent themes, or rather assumptions, inform many contemporary conceptualizations of Russian history. The first is that the shape of Russian history manifests a pattern that is circular in form and continuous in structure, and the second is that the reason for this pattern is that Russia is always trying to catch up with the West and never quite succeeding. These themes have a long intellectual pedigree, and they have recently been provocatively formulated by Alexander Yanov in *The Origins of Autocracy: Ivan the Terrible in Russian History* (Berkeley: University of California Press, 1981). Yanov traced "the cycles of Russian history" back to the middle of the sixteenth century, and the contemporary relevance of his work served as the inspiration for another scholarly conference on Russian and Soviet reform, held in 1986, with an approach and coverage that

and member of the Russian intelligentsia par excellence.[2] The work is
divided into two long parts and two short epilogues, which follow a
basically chronological order, although methodological and evaluative
comments, "lessons," and what might be called narrative asides are scattered throughout the text, in keeping, as it were, with the author's own
designation of its genre: "notes" (*zametki*). The stated aim of the book
is to examine precedents in Russian history for the current "great reforms, transformations of a revolutionary character begun on the initiative of the country's supreme leadership, 'a revolution from above.' "
This exercise is undertaken to suggest answers to such questions as:

Why from above . . . ?
Are there some kinds of general rules or repetitive patterns for such trans-
formations at various turns of the historical spiral?
What are the laws of behavioral dynamics of the popular masses in such a
revolution?
What are the forms of resistance to and types of danger for such changes?
What are the prospects?

differed from those of the conference that was the basis for this volume; see Robert O.
Crummey, ed., *Reform in Russia and the USSR* (Urbana: University of Illinois Press, 1989).
Eidel'man's book is a somewhat more sanguine treatment of the same themes, and his perspective can be viewed as part of a continuing dialogue on the shape of Russia's past and future. For that reason, Emmons's extensive analysis of Eidel'man's conception, along with
the excursus into the first half of the nineteenth century by Chernukha and Anan'ich (see the
next chapter), forms an appropriate bridge between broader historiographic concerns and
the specific findings of this volume.—Ed.]
[2] "*Revoliutsiia sverkhu*" *v Rossii* was first published serially between October 1988 and
March 1989 in the popular-science magazine *Nauka i zhizn'*. It appeared as a book in
the late summer of 1989. Following some introductory material, Part I (pp. 21–109) deals
with Russian history from Ivan IV (the Terrible) to 1855; Part II (pp. 110–58) focuses on
the epoch of the Great Reforms in the 1860s; Epilogue I (pp. 159–64) gives a coup d'oeil
at the following decades up to 1917; and Epilogue II (pp. 165–72) does the same for the
first years of the Soviet period up to Stalin's revolution from above and ends with a
recapitulation of the lessons.
    Eidel'man died suddenly of heart failure on November 29, 1989, at the age of fifty-
nine. While his views on Gorbachev's "revolution from above" surely evolved over the
last year of his life, I doubt that any major changes occurred in his overall interpretation
of Russian history or in his understanding of its lessons regarding the prospects for progressive change in his homeland.
    [Natan Eidel'man was a prolific scholar as well as a popular historian, who concen-
trated on the cultural and political history of the eighteenth and the first half of the
nineteenth centuries, the era of the formation of the Russian intelligentsia. He wrote
extensively on Alexander Herzen, the Decembrists, and Pushkin. His many books include
Tainye korrespondenty 'Poliarnoi zvezdy' (1966); a biography of the Decembrist Michael
Lunin (1970); *Gertsen protiv samoderzhaviia: Sekretnaia politicheskaia istoriia Rossii
XVIII–XIX vv. i Vol'naia pechat'* (1973); and, among several studies of Pushkin, *Pushkin
i dekabristy* (1979) and *Pushkin: Iz biografii i tvorchestva, 1826–1837* (1987).—Ed.]

In sum, says Eidel'man, "we intend to give a brief sketch not of all of Russian history, to be sure, but of those of its sections or 'subjects' that involve revolutions from above and that may help us to distinguish something new in the circumstances of today and tomorrow."[3]

We shall leave other remarks of a methodological character for later, noting for future reference only two items: first, the allusion to a "historical spiral" just quoted; and secondly, the remark in the last sentence of this introduction in which Eidel'man describes the book as "discussions of revolutions *and reforms*" (my emphasis).[4]

The centerpiece of the author's conceptual framework is the Great Reforms of Alexander II.[5] Eidel'man dates the beginning of the epoch at the death of Nicholas I in 1855. Similarly, he places the beginning of the current crisis at the death of Stalin in 1953, "ninety-eight years and three days" after the death of Nicholas I.[6] Then as now, the situation of the country demanded serious changes in the economic and political spheres, toward a market economy and democratization.[7] In the earlier period, the two central institutions of backwardness, which was characterized by "lack of feedback mechanisms" (these were, according to Eidel'man, the free market in the economy and democracy in the political system), were, of course, serfdom (*krepostnoe pravo*) and autocracy (*samoderzhavie*), and it is to an explication of the genesis, character, and persistence of those institutions that the remainder of Part I is devoted.

The root cause of Russia's backwardness vis-à-vis its Western neighbors, says Eidel'man, was the Mongol yoke: "In our opinion, the Mongol invasion was to a large extent responsible for the 'Asiatic principle' that manifested itself in Russia through serfdom and cruel autocracy."[8] From the devastation of Mongol rule, Russia emerged an economically and socially backward country, lacking a money economy and a middle class. Uniting the country in the fourteenth and fifteenth centuries, at about the same time that this was happening in its more developed neighbors, Russia's rulers mobilized resources in the struggle for national

---

[3]*"Revoliutsiia sverkhu" v Rossii*, 25 (hereafter cited as *RSVR*).
[4]Ibid., 26.
[5]Ibid., 26.
[6]Ibid., 27.
[7]Ibid., 28.
[8]Ibid., 31.

survival by "the non-economic, administrative means of direct extraction," which led directly to despotism and serfdom.[9]

Directly, but not inevitably. The second great tragedy of Russian history after the Mongol invasion was perhaps the first of the revolutions from above: that of Ivan the Terrible,[10] which wiped out the elements of Europeanization that had been developing (or recovering?) in Russia over the preceding century or more of national sovereignty ("Russian towns with European features, and liberties, and peasants who had to pay but could not be sold"). Russia's "first great alternative was: either serfdom plus autocratic supercentralization or 'ameliorated' feudalism with a growing bourgeois element plus absolute monarchies with certain elements of popular representation and judicial liberties."[11] Ivan's choice of the former path (itself a response to the backwardness engendered by the Mongol yoke) produced accelerated, threatening backwardness, which led in turn to "another great alternative, a new choice of the main path," that faced by Peter I.

The revolution from above of Russia's "crowned revolutionary" set the course of Russian history for the next 150 years. Peter's revolution, Eidel'man argues, evoked profound ambivalence among later commentators (after several generations of pure panegyrics) because of its mix of new European and traditional Asiatic elements: in economics, industrial development, but no bourgeoisie and the perpetuation of serfdom; in politics and culture, introduction of European values of "honor" and "justice" for the new nobility, but perpetuation of autocracy and its traditional use of fear. "The cudgel and honor in politics and morality

---

[9]Except for its emphasis on the effects of the Mongol invasion, this is a view of the dynamics of hypertrophy of state power in Russia that can be traced back to the nineteenth-century "state school" of Russian historiography. The classic statement of this proposition in terms of the interrelationship of military, fiscal, and institutional development is P. N. Miliukov, *Ocherki po istorii russkoi kul'tury. Chast' pervaia*, which first appeared in the mid-1890s. It has been echoed widely ever since, by such diverse writers on Russian history as Leon Trotsky and Richard Pipes.

[10]In Part I, Eidel'man does not use the specific term "revolution from above" to describe Ivan the Terrible's *oprichnina* and related developments, but it is clear from his concluding remarks that he believes the term is applicable. See *RSVR*, 169.

[11]*RSVR*, 48. The theme of the "absolutist" alternative in the fifteenth and sixteenth centuries has been developed recently in Yanov, *Origins of Autocracy*. The criticism that was leveled at that book for idealizing or "Europeanizing" Rus' in the century or so preceding the oprichnina could in some measure be applied to Eidel'man's interpretation as well. See the review of Yanov's book by Nancy Shields Kollmann in *Russian History* 10 (1983): 94–95. See also Crummey, *Reform in Russia and the USSR.,* 12–27.

stood in relation to each other approximately as did forced labor and the market in economics."[12]

In some respects, as a consequence of the Petrine reforms, Russia on the eve of the French Revolution and before the onset of the industrial revolution in Britain resembled the West more than at any time since the late fifteenth century. Russia had a reasonably competent army, competitive technology and industrial output, and a Europeanized culture of the elite. The nobility had considerably advanced the concept of honor and had achieved definite rights; the cudgel had been put aside for the most part. On the other hand, serfdom was in full force and had even been extended to a greater portion of the population, and such rights as the nobility had were not guaranteed by constitution or an independent judiciary. Autocracy, in short, was unlimited ("except by strangulation"), and in terms of technology and productivity, Russia was living on borrowed time.

Thus, at the end of the eighteenth century, serfdom and autocracy were on the agenda for another revolution from above, which was then— especially after the revolution in France—increasingly perceived as an alternative to a revolution from below: "The famous formula that was loudly proclaimed in 1856—'to liberate from above before they liberate themselves from below'—was in essence more or less understood by Catherine II, and then fairly clearly understood under Alexander I."[13]

Eidel'man sees the revolution from above developing during the reign of Alexander I simultaneously within the government and among the educated minority of the nobility. The failure of the reform plans of Michael Speransky and Nicholas Novosil'tsev and of the Decembrist movement are attributed by Eidel'man in large measure to the tsar's unwillingness to take La Harpe's advice to turn to the educated minority for support in overcoming the resistance of the conservative majority of nobles who occupied most of the offices in the administration.[14] There is a lesson here, Eidel'man concludes, "regarding those tsars who win by finding sufficiently broad, active, intellectual support, and those who lose by failing to do so."[15]

---

[12]RSVR, 59.
[13]Ibid., 78.
[14][F. C. La Harpe was a Swiss radical who was hired by Catherine the Great to be Alexander I's tutor and whose teachings imbued his pupil with romantic humanitarianism and vague constitutional sentiments.—Ed.]
[15]RSVR, 91. The contemporary implication is obvious.

The Decembrists' attempt at revolution from above was at the same time the first revolutionary attack from below, and it ushered in the "thirty-year counterrevolution" or "unenlightened despotism" of Nicholas I. In fact, Nicholas "for some time tried to assume the role of the 'revolutionary from above,' constantly emphasizing his Petrine heritage," but, fearing what might be called glasnost and faced with the "powerful and growing egotistical, zoological resistance of the apparatus, the upper bureaucracy, and the nobility," he temporized.[16]

What broke the aristocratic-bureaucratic resistance to reform and the fear of "strangulation" (*udavka*)—that is, assassination—that lay behind it? It was a combination of growing fear of the revolution from below, aroused by the European revolutions of 1830 and 1848, and of the 'capitalist encirclement' (the inverted commas are Eidel'man's) produced by the industrial revolution in the West and brought home by Russia's defeat in the Crimean War.

In Part II, Eidel'man concentrates on the reform era of 1855–66 (actually, extending into the early 1870s, when the last of the "bourgeois reforms" were carried through on the inertia of the first decade of the revolution from above). The agenda was the old one, dictated by serfdom and autocracy. The reforms fell into three groups, as they do "in various times and under various regimes, for there are no other reforms that encompass the entire life of a country":[17] economic reforms, emancipation of the peasants above all; political reforms—the zemstvo and town statutes and reforms of the judiciary and the military; and reforms of the educational system and censorship.

Eidel'man's views on the ideological aspect of the reforms and on their consequences will be touched upon in a later section; here, we will simply take note of several of his general remarks about the character of the process: (1) The simultaneity of reforms in all three spheres was unavoidable, because they were all interconnected. (2) "Once started, the reforms found their executors." Eidel'man is referring to the senior bureaucratic dignitaries (*sanovniki*), who had the tsar's ear and advocated change: not so much the junior technocrats, such as Nicholas Miliutin, the Semenovs, and Sergei Zarudnyi, but their patrons who made their work possible—Sergei S. Lanskoi, Dmitry N. Bludov, Dmitry N. Zamiatnin, Iakov I. Rostovtsev, and Modest A. Korf, the "turncoats"

---

[16]Ibid., 102.
[17]Ibid., 110.

left over from the previous regime. (3) Alexander II persevered because Lanskoi and his colleagues convinced him that the threat from the "left" (that is, "from below") was greater than that from the "right," for Prince Pavel Gagarin and others of his ilk would not dare organize a coup in such threatening circumstances. (4) The role of glasnost in the reform process was to gain supporters for the reforms, thereby freeing the executive authority to some extent from its own apparatus.

If Peter's reforms endured for 150 years, the reforms of the 1860s endured for 40 or 50—no mean achievement in those more rapidly changing circumstances. The limitation was not that little was given; it lay rather in the "lack of historical flexibility" of those who did the giving. The reforms stimulated civic activity, which should have been encouraged as a means of laying the foundation for continuation of the reform process. Instead, the regime retrenched and in so doing made revolutionaries of those who wanted the reforms to work. There had been a coming together of the regime with progressive elements in the country, but there then followed their gradual isolation from each other.

Eidel'man's main conclusion is that, in order to attract, or at least not to alienate, such people, the conservative nobility and the government should have made further concessions, should have allowed at least an elementary constitution, and—this is the main thing—should have shown flexibility, developing and perfecting what had been granted rather than cutting back on it. In other words, reforms from above, even in such a "statist" country as Russia, demanded reinforcement from below in the stages that followed. Otherwise, the house would remain without a foundation, or, more precisely, with an inadequate, "poorly designed" foundation, and such a building could easily collapse if pressure from below or from above were increased.[18]

In Epilogue I, Eidel'man first of all evaluates the revolutionary movement, which, as he sees it, was the product of retrenchment. The Bakuninist-populist strategy of stimulating a revolution from below having failed, the movement to some degree returned to the Decembrist tactic of revolution from above, an inherent characteristic of a revolutionary movement in a highly centralized political system. The tragedy of the People's Will terrorists was that they were unable to respond positively to the governmental concessions that they had extracted (that is, the Loris-Melikov "constitution" and the peasant and other reforms that were

[18]Ibid., 157–58.

being planned in connection with it); they went too far and provoked reaction, "a counterrevolution from above."[19]

At the same time that it was engaging in carrying out this counterrevolution from above, the regime stimulated industrial growth, but it did not extend rights to the new groups that appeared with it. Thus, even the liberals were made revolutionaries (witness the Union of Liberation). In these conditions, the counterrevolution from above soon gave rise to opposition from below, which burst out in the revolution of 1905–7. That revolution did not get rid of the autocracy, but it did bring significant improvements—in wages, in political and civil rights, and in the creation of the Duma, "ninety-five years after Speransky and forty-four years after the emancipation of the peasants."[20] In the wake of the revolution (there was no counterrevolution this time, and the "coup d'état" of June 3, 1907, does not qualify as one), there was one more attempt to carry through a revolution from above—the Stolypin reforms—in order to avoid an explosion from below and to create a new mass basis of support. The reform strategy was simple: "to enrich some peasants at the expense of others." Stolypin was hated by the left and by the right: by the former for being "bourgeois," by the latter for his designs on the political power of the nobility. Once again the time-worn method of "strangulation" was used, but it was applied this time not to the monarch but to his prime minister (thus demonstrating, incidentally, the significance of the ministerial reforms). The opposition to Stolypin, and Stolypin's fate, reflected the seriousness of his alternative. Its rejection precipitated the revolution from below in 1917.[21]

In Epilogue II, Eidel'man argues that, even after the 1917 revolution from below, the traditional role of the state and the apparatus was retained. The Bolsheviks won, partly because of their considerable support in the army and a favorable disposition in the countryside, but chiefly because they could take the capitals and the major centers of trade and industry. In introducing the New Economic Policy, an attempt to marry the "socialized-command heights in the economy with a market base, and centralized power with democracy and self-government," the Bolsheviks showed themselves to be more flexible than the last several emperors in their maneuvering to maintain mass support. Nevertheless,

[19]Ibid., 159–60.
[20]Ibid., 161.
[21]Ibid., 163–64.

despite Lenin's attempt to forestall it, the bureaucratic-centralizing tradition won out—in part, paradoxically, because of the thoroughness of the destruction of the old order, including such elements of civil society as "the zemstvos, dumas, bourgeois courts, freedom of the press, and so on." The failure of NEP provokes thoughts not only about the concrete correlation of forces in the 1920s, but also "about the centuries-long tradition of supercentralization and 'lack of commodity relations' (*netovarnost'*)."[22] This observation introduces the recapitulation of the "lessons." (In the interest of economy and clarity of exposition, the following enumeration departs somewhat from the presentation in Eidel'man's text.)[23]

1. "A high proportion of changes of both a revolutionary and a counterrevolutionary character in Russia since the fifteenth and sixteenth centuries has come from above, from the state, or from a relatively small group aspiring to take power." The ultimate cause of this "non-European" path was the low level of urban development and the "weakness of the third estate," intensified by the Mongol invasion "and other inhospitable factors."

2. "The role of the people has been enormous, as everywhere, but in Russia it shows up differently than in countries with developed commodity relations and bourgeois democracy: There is great energy, but independence and initiative are far less [in evidence] than obedience to the will of the elite."[24]

3. Historically, the people have aligned themselves with the tsar in the hope of uniting with him against the ruling stratum, the bureaucracy. Naive as this reliance has been, it had a historical foundation, and such an alliance has occurred in various forms.

4. "The bureaucracy, the apparatus, has been a powerful force in Russian history in the conditions of centuries-long centralization and the absence of democratic 'counterbalances' and traditions. This apparatus should not be simply identified with the supreme power; while this may be true in the general economic scheme of things, it is inadequate for concrete political analysis." The two may come into conflict because "one can see farther from the top" (*iz dvortsa chasto vidnee*). This is

[22]Ibid., 167–68.
[23]Ibid., 169–72.
[24]There is some ambiguity of meaning in the last phrase. The Russian is "*ogromnaia energiia, no samostoiatel'nosti, initsiativy kuda men'she, chem ispolneniia voli verkhov.*" *RSVR,* 169.

the source of resistance by the bureaucrats and the rich even to those reforms that are designed to save their own skins.

5. The various forms of bureaucratic resistance to revolution and reform from above included sabotage, provocations, scare tactics, white terror, and coups d'état. "Attempts are not infrequently made to bring about a superficially democratic limitation of 'initiative from above' through active involvement of the middle strata." This is a concealed form of conservative reaction.

6. "The forms of overcoming this resistance were no less varied: outright retributions; frightening the bureaucracy with internal and external dangers; a certain amount of reliance by the throne on the masses; moving the capital; and creation of a parallel apparatus."

7. It is in the nature of the situation that revolution from above combines a relatively decisive break (required in part by the absence or inadequacy of adaptive mechanisms) with intricate maneuvering and tacking, which are required for noncatastrophic percolation of change downward.

8. By the same token, the absence of theory and of historical experience dictate the method of trial and error to the "revolutionary state" (*gosudarstvo-revoliutsiia*) in its search for the best forms of action.

9. The habitual argument of the conservatives that proponents of reform are lacking is not justified: Fundamental reforms begun after periods of stagnation (*zastoi*) quickly find "reformers" in the ranks of the young, part of the "elders," and even "turncoats" among the dignitaries of the old order.

10. Revolutions from above often produce significant, if insufficiently guaranteed, changes over a relatively short period, usually ten to twenty years. The ensuing ebb tides and even "counterrevolutions" rarely return things to the status quo ante, so that the next attack begins from an advanced line.

11. "The best foundation for fundamental reforms from above is their continual extension and expansion, the creation of more or less reliable feedback systems (*sistemy, obratnoi, sviazi*) (market, glasnost, democracy) that permit effective coordination of life and politics." The progressive intelligentsia plays an immense role in this process.

At the very end of his text, Eidel'man turned to the chances of success for the revolution from above that was going on at the time. What follows is a loose translation of these final sentences:

Since the sixteenth century, Russia has several times faced the alternative of taking the "European" or the "Asian" path. Sometimes the [European path of] market economy and self-government [tovarnost' i samoupravlenie] was chosen, at other times it was a compromise, but often it was corvée [barshchina] and despotism that won out.

Every such victory was a historical tragedy for the people and the country that cost the lives of hundreds of thousands, even millions, of people, and through fear and slavery humiliated, robbed, and corrupted the souls of the survivors.

The latest great attempt is taking place before our eyes.

In the event (God forbid!) of failure and another fifteen or twenty years of stagnation . . . I think the country will be doomed to the fate of such "unreconstructed" [neperestroivshikhsia] powers as Ottoman Turkey and Austria-Hungary; it will be doomed to irreparable changes, and after experiencing terrible crises and enormous sacrifices, it will all the same be compelled to introduce a market and democracy.

One of the advantages of the present revolution is the enormous historical experience that has been accumulated over the centuries of tsarism and the decades of Soviet power.

We believe in success, not a one-time gift of fortune, but a difficult progress—ebbing and flowing, yet ever moving forward.

We believe in success: there is no other way.

METHODOLOGICAL ISSUES

To any reasonably attentive reader of Soviet Russian highbrow journalism (publitsistika), much of this rummaging in the national past for "lessons for the present and future" would seem familiar, certainly by late 1987. The search for "alternativity"—that is, for historical junctures of choice—came to perform an almost talismanic or incantational function in the political discourse of the late 1980s. At first, the search focused on the 1920s—on NEP and the Bukharinist alternative to Stalinism. Next, it reached beyond the Soviet period to the history of prerevolutionary Russia, focusing especially on the Great Reforms of Alexander II, to which many parallels have been found, implicitly or explicitly, with the reform program of Mikhail Gorbachev (according to the principle: the more parallels, the greater the contemporary relevance of alternativity).[25]

[25]"Recognition of the existence of choices in history [osoznanie variantnosti istorii] is of great significance for one's orientation in the present. For alternativity is not just 'either-or'—it is also a matter of constant choice." Iu. N. Afanas'ev, "Perestroika i istoricheskoe znanie," in Iu. N. Afanas'ev, ed., Inogo ne dano (Moscow, 1988), 492. The exploration

Two things in combination, I would argue, distinguish Eidel'man's essay from others in this genre and make it particularly pertinent to our concerns: the breadth of his inquiry over the entirety of the eighteenth and nineteenth centuries (and even earlier) up to the 1920s, using as his guide or selective principle the notion of revolution from above as a *process;* and the explicitness of the "lessons" for today that he draws from the exercise.

The notion of revolution from above. As Eidel'man defines and applies the concept, it appears to be in many respects identical with "radical reform" and similar terms used by many other writers. It is probably safe to say that none of the three main episodes that are paradigmatic for his generalizations—the establishment of the oprichnina by Ivan IV, the activities of Peter I, and the Great Reforms of Alexander II—would qualify as "revolutions" according to the generally accepted view that the term ought to be reserved for changes in regime.[26] Of the three, only Peter's transformation might be regarded as meeting that criterion, because the changes he wrought in the character and ideology of the political system were so profound as to overshadow the preservation of dynastic continuity.[27]

Indeed, in regard to the reforms of Alexander II it may be that their assimilation to the ranks of revolutions from above comes from the Pe-

of "alternativity" in Russian history has occupied considerable space in the pages of the "thick journals," such as *Novyi mir, Znamia, Oktiabr',* and *Druzhba narodov,* as well as in such mass-media publications as *Ogonek, Moskovskie novosti, Nedelia,* and even *Pravda* (in the occasional special Friday history columns), not to mention the professional historical journals. Many other writers in the genre have called attention to the reforms of Alexander II, including A. Tsipko, I. Kliamkin, G. Popov, and, of course, the leading specialist on the history of the peasant emancipation, Larisa Zakharova (see her "1861: reforma i reformatory," *Nedelia,* 1989, no. 5). In Zakharova's opinion, interest in the reforms of Alexander II has been running higher than at any other time in the 125 years since they occurred: L. G. Zakharova, "Samoderzhavie, biurokratiia, i reformy 60-kh godov XIX v. v Rossii," *Voprosy istorii,* 1989, no. 10: 3–24.

Apparently, Gorbachev himself has compared his own reforms to those of Alexander II; see Mikhail Geller, "Tovarishch defitsit," in *Russkaia mysl'* (Paris), February 23, 1990, p. 5, reporting on an interview with Gorbachev by James Billington in the summer of 1988.

[26]See, for example, the discussion of this issue in the editor's introduction and elsewhere in Crummey, *Reform in Russia and the USSR.* Eidel'man does treat the Decembrist revolt and the People's Will movement as revolutions from above manqués and the Bolshevik Revolution as a successful revolution from above, but this does not alter the point.

[27]As Nicholas V. Riasanovsky points out, Peter was considered a "revolutionary" *avant le mot* (literally) by his contemporaries, even though it was apparently Herzen who first called him a (crowned) "revolutionary": *Riasanovsky, The Image of Peter the Great in Russian History and Thought* (New York: Oxford University Press, 1985), 138–39.

trine reforms by way of recent Gorbachevian transformations.[28] As we know, Gorbachev himself used the term "revolution from above" to describe perestroika. The precedent for this kind of usage by a Soviet leader in describing his own policies was set by none other than Stalin, who called collectivization, and the 1928–38 decade in general, a "revolution from above."[29] To my knowledge, however, the reforms of the 1860s had never been described as a revolution from above before the advent of perestroika.

This apparently trivial point raises the not-so-trivial problem of historical feedback: the possibility that perceptions formed by current events are being projected onto past events. Does perestroika resemble the Great Reforms, or vice versa? This question needs to be kept in mind whenever the subject of history and the present is engaged. A few comments about Eidel'man's interpretation of the Great Reforms from this perspective will be made later.

It is clear that Eidel'man chose the term "revolution from above," rather than mere "reform," however modified, to identify what he saw as a recurrent pattern of far-reaching, state-initiated changes in Russian *and* Soviet history; that he defined the pattern in terms of origins, or causes, and process, rather than results; and that by doing so he found it possible to treat such diverse episodes as the reign of Peter the Great, the reforms of Alexander I, the reforms of the 1860s, the Stolypin reforms, the Stalin revolution, and perestroika as belonging, in some important respects, to the same order of phenomena. Is there indeed such a degree of continuity?

The problem of continuity. This is not the place to review the concept of continuity either as a general problem of historical epistemology or in terms of the "Russia-USSR" controversy; the literature on both subjects is vast.[30] Here I want only to make a couple of points about Eidel'man's use of the concept and then to add a few comments about the

---

[28]Zakharova uses the term (in quotes) in her popular historical writings but avoids applying it directly to the Great Reforms.

[29]It was so described in the *Short Course* of the history of the Communist party (1938); see Robert C. Tucker, "Stalinism As Revolution from Above," in Robert C. Tucker, ed., *Stalinism: Essays in Historical Interpretation* (New York: W. W. Norton, 1977), 77–108.

[30]Some sensible and erudite remarks on these issues can be found in Alexander Dallin, "The Uses and Abuses of Russian History," in Terry L. Thompson and Richard Sheldon, eds., *Soviet Society and Culture: Essays in Honor of Vera S. Dunham* (Boulder, Colo.: Westview, 1988), 181–94.

problem of continuity in relation to the theme of the meaning and function of reform in Russian and Soviet history.

On the face of it, Eidel'man's notion of continuity, like many other
views of recurrent patterns in Russian history, may appear to be nothing
more than what Alexander Gerschenkron called "the periodicity of
events," the view that "present—or, at any rate, subsequent—experience
is understood as a reiteration of past experience . . . the causal mechanism of propulsion remaining essentially unaltered from rotation to rotation."[31]

While no serious writer on Russian history has subscribed to this
notion of *corsi e ricorsi* in its pure circular form, some have come much
closer than others.[32] Eidel'man's view of continuity in Russian history,
I submit, is quite far removed from any "myth of eternal return," and
this is so in regard to two ideas in particular.

The first is the idea of typological or structural comparison:

We are not speaking of the concrete content of the Russian changes of those
days or of their results or lack thereof, but only about *a common type of transformations;* in that sense, we can find much in common among reformers separated by centuries and class affiliation—let us say, in ancient Greece, in Russia
at the end of the nineteenth century, and in the Soviet Union at the end of the
twentieth century.[33]

Elsewhere Eidel'man observes: "We are not playing at comparisons [i.e.,
drawing direct parallels], but if the country finds itself faced with ty-
pologically comparable tasks 100–125 years later in completely different
conditions, this is something worth thinking about very seriously."[34] In
other words, his approach is in fact a comparative approach.

The second idea, or image, is that of spiral development. Eidel'man

[31]Alexander Gerschenkron, "On the Concept of Continuity in History," in Alexander Gerschenkron, *Continuity in History and Other Essays* (Cambridge, Mass.: Belknap Press
of Harvard University Press, 1968), 21–23.
[32]See especially Yanov, *Origins of Autocracy,* chap. 1. Yanov describes the Soviet system
before perestroika as *"a medieval political system*—an autocracy," *tout court* (p. 65;
emphasis in the original). See also his table of two virtually identical columns comparing
the characteristics of the regimes of Ivan the Terrible and Stalin (pp. 59–60). For a much
more sophisticated view, emphasizing recurrent patterns going back to Ivan the Terrible
and describing the Stalin revolution as "archaization," see Tucker, "Stalinism As Revolution from Above." Both Yanov and Tucker, incidentally, put much weight on Stalin's
well-known affinity for the historical image of Ivan IV.
[33]*RSVR,* 111. Emphasis in the original.
[34]Ibid., 28.

uses this idea to account for the apparent repetition of long-past experience—for example, the apparent return of serfdom and autocracy under Stalin ("although no Russian autocrat ever had so much power").[35] The notion seems to be based on a genetic analogy or metaphor; indeed, Eidel'man even uses the term "social genetics," which he describes, however, simply as a matter of "historical tradition, continuity, accumulated over centuries, even millennia, that is less susceptible to change (although it does of course undergo change) than the technical, external side of life."[36]

Straightened out, then, Eidel'man's spiral turns out to be a way of conceptualizing cultural continuity, the persistence of certain attitudes over long periods of time. If we add to this Eidel'man's reading of Russian history as a story of progress measured in terms of overcoming backwardness or of Westernization (the market and democracy), the essential elements of his methodology are in place.

To be sure, his idea of progress is not teleological, linked to a belief in the inevitability of a happy ending. It is, however, based on the view that, overall, there has been advancement in history, albeit with detours and periods of regression. This, I believe, is how we should read his remark about "the next attack begin[ning] from an advanced line" (point ten in my enumeration of lessons above). Such a view is not simply deduced from the study of revolution from above in Russian history; it derives from a broader historical perspective, one "rooted in a perception of history as a continual movement from the realm of necessity to that of choice, and a belief that the growth and diffusion of knowledge increasingly equips us with the opportunity, and the capability, to make those choices."[37] It seems to me that these words, though written by a British historian without any direct reference to things Russian, evoke precisely the enlightenment tradition of the "progressive Russian intelligentsia" to which Eidel'man assigned an enormous role in the cause of reform and to which he himself belonged completely.

It would be wrong to end the discussion of Eidel'man's historical

---

[35]Ibid., 24.

[36]Ibid., 24. It may be noted that Yanov also uses the image of the spiral ("the political spiral"), but it is nothing more than an adaptation of essentially circular motion that is meant to allow for increasing complexity. See *Origins of Autocracy*, 59.

[37]Michael Howard, "Structure and Process in History," *Times Literary Supplement*, June 23–29, 1989, p. 689.

views with the impression that his last book is of value only for his intellectual biography, a *profession de foi,* politics projected into the past, or what have you.

To be sure, concepts like revolution from above or continuity are mental constructs that do not exist in nature. As Gerschenkron reminds us, "It is the historian who, by abstracting from differences and by concentrating on similarities, establishes the continuity of events across decades or centuries filled with events that lack all pertinency to the continuity model."[38] Historians have written books evoking a tradition of revolution from below or of democratic institutions in Russian history that, in terms of epistemological criteria, are probably neither more nor less arbitrary than books that focus on the tradition of centralized political authority and revolution from above.[39]

Of course, the use of any selective criteria in writing history involves arbitrary decisions; such arbitrariness is obvious in the case of Eidel'-man's book, as it is in this volume. But to quote Gerschenkron once more: "It is the arbitrariness of the process of cognition. . . . Concepts are plans for action; they are programs of research . . . and they will be known by their fruits, that is to say, their usefulness in organizing empirical data in such a fashion as to obtain meaningful and interesting, though not necessarily positive and final, results."[40]

The problem of reform. These remarks about Eidel'man's methodology and the concept of continuity in general provide, I believe, a useful perspective on the theme of reform in Russian and Soviet history. This conference is focused on five historical episodes designated as manifestations of reformist and moderate tendencies in Russian history since the 1860s. It has been suggested that the chronological framework could have been extended deeper into the past to include the Petrine and Catherinian epochs. But in any case, the aim, in part at least, was to provide a corrective to the idea that Russian history moved only by cataclysmic leaps, whether instigated from above or from below.

---

[38]Gerschenkron, "On the Concept of Continuity in History," 38.
[39]A recent example is Sergei Pushkarev's posthumously published *Self-Government and Freedom in Russia* (Boulder, Colo.: Westview, 1988), but the search for such traditions has been characteristic of Russian historiography since well before the revolution of 1917. There is a discussion of this aspect of academic historiography in the late nineteenth century in my article, "Kliuchevskii i ego ucheniki," *Voprosy istorii,* 1990, no. 10: 45–61.
[40]Gerschenkron, "On the Concept of Continuity in History," 38.

In the comparativist spirit of this enterprise, it would seem worthwhile to confront its program with the continuity question posed above. What is immediately noticeable in light of the preceding discussion of Eidel'man's book is that all but one of the reform episodes being considered here were treated by Eidel'man as manifestations of the phenomenon of revolution from above (the exception being the era of NEP).[41] If we further consider that a classic revolution from above in Eidel'man's (and not only Eidel'man's) view, the reign of Peter I, could have been fitted into the conference's survey of reform, are we not led to think that it is all a matter of labels?

I think not. The criteria for selecting our particular set of reform episodes for comparison apparently were (1) the absence of violence, and (2) their "evolutionary," "moderate" character. It would be problematical, to say the least, to qualify Peter's transformations as "reform" by either criterion. Moreover, even the emancipation of 1861 and the Stolypin agrarian reforms entailed a certain level of violence: violations of gentry property rights, "cut-offs" of peasant allotments, and forced acceptance of the statutes in the first case, and forced dissolution of communes in the second. (Even the widespread use of violence in the usual sense of the word by Stolypin and his associates in the pacification of the countryside in 1906 and early 1907 might be considered part of the same overall "reform" episode.)

If, on the other hand, we accept all the aforementioned episodes as meeting the criteria of peacefulness and moderation, then what are we left with, before the Bolshevik Revolution and Stalin's revolution from above, as major examples of "violent state-imposed change from above" in modern Russian history?

It is easy to find examples of cataclysmic revolt from below in Russian history before 1917, although there were no instances of it in the entire nineteenth century. One could argue that the revolution of 1905 combined elements of the traditional Russian rebellion (*bunt*), particularly in the agrarian sector, but even there one sees a mixture of old forms of protest and new ones, such as strikes and political mobilization, that had only very recent or no precedents in Russian history. But that is another subject.

---

[41]Eidel'man discusses twentieth-century developments only very briefly in his epilogues, but it is clear to me that he sees the entire period from 1917 to 1932 or so as a single revolution from above during which a moderate, "mixed variant," akin to NEP, was a possibility for a while.

The point is that there are numerous examples of "state-imposed change from above" in modern Russian history, but it is not always violent; or, more precisely, the degree of violence varies considerably from case to case. In other words, even the most peaceable and moderate transformations have been "state-imposed changes from above," and using the element of violence as a sorting principle tends to obscure this central fact.

The same point can be made about "moderation." For example, while there are a number of beguiling similarities between the reforms of the 1860s and those of the 1980s (as noted by many authors, including Eidel'man), and the reformers of both the 1860s and the era of perestroika have eschewed violence as an instrument of reform policy, the fact is that the Great Reforms were indeed gradualist in intent and presented no systemic threat to the regime.[42] Whatever might be said about the original intent of Gorbachev and his confidants, there can be no doubt that what followed involved a challenge to the system, whether one chooses to describe it as the dismantling of the totalitarian state or of the Stalinist system, or as the confrontation of dictatorship and democracy. The question, therefore, is the extent to which a direct line of continuity or comparison can be drawn between the reforms of the 1860s and perestroika if the guideline is the idea of moderation or reformism. We shall do well, in any event, to keep in mind Eidel'man's focus on the *processes* of state-initiated change, which he called "revolution from above," and on the structural underpinnings, or lack thereof, that conditioned their outcomes.

As a pragmatic matter, the analysis of the historical incidents of reform identified for this conference should surely yield meaningful and interesting results, considering the collection of scholars that has been assembled. Even the inclusion of NEP as an era of reform—whatever one may think of its viability as an alternative to the party-state system that began to take shape immediately after the Bolshevik seizure of power—makes good sense: References to the "late Lenin" and to the ideas and economic experience of the 1920s became part of the language of political discourse in the late 1980s.[43] Whether the results of our

---

[42]Eidel'man, it will be recalled, described both serfdom and autocracy as being on the reform agenda of the 1860s, but this should be understood as a broad, evolutionary agenda in which the introduction of a modicum of self-administration represented only a first step. The institution of the autocracy was never under direct threat at that time.

[43]In January 1990, the debate over the "Leninist tradition" in Soviet politics reached the

inquiry prove meaningful and interesting is not a matter to be resolved by appeals to an outside authority, be it the rules of logic or of metaphysics. The discovery of patterns in history, and historical explanation in general, owe a great deal to cognitive psychology and cultural history.[44] As Robert Tucker has perceptively remarked, "cultural patterns out of a nation's past do not repeat themselves in the present simply because they were there," nor do circumstances carry their own self-evident meaning, "[for] what people and political leaders *act upon* is always the circumstances *as perceived and defined by them,* which in turn is influenced by culture."[45]

The "enormous historical experience" that Eidel'man saw as one of the advantages for the present is not "simply there." It has to be deliberately found and explained. In the final analysis—as the Marxists used to say—the elucidation of reforms and of the possibility of alternatives existing in the past may of itself be the most important lesson for the present.

SUBSTANTIVE REMARKS ABOUT THE REFORM PROCESS FROM 1865 TO 1914

I want to conclude with a few remarks concerning (1) the preconditions, (2) the intentions and goals, and (3) the consequences of reforms in Russian history. The point of departure is the Great Reforms of the 1860s, but insofar as the fundamental elements of the reform program, embracing the agrarian question, political institutions, and legality, that came to the fore at the time remained on the agenda until the fall of the old regime—and awareness of this fact is a basic prerequisite to an understanding of the fluctuating pattern of reform and reaction over the last decades of the old order—there is no need to limit discussion to the reforms of the 1860s.

On preconditions. The problem of the preconditions for the reforms of

point where a prominent member of the Democratic Platform group warned that an appeal to Leninism had become an identifying characteristic of the conservative Communist party apparatus—the contemporary Soviet equivalent of "the last refuge of scoundrels." Iu. N. Afanas'ev, speech at the All Union Conference of Party Clubs, held in Moscow, January 20–21, 1990, as quoted in *Russkaia mysl'* (Paris), January 26, 1990, p. 6.

[44]Paul A. Roth, "Narrative Explanations: The Case of History," *History and Theory* 27 (1988): 1–13.

[45]Tucker, "Stalinism as Revolution from Above," 102; emphasis in the original.

the 1860s is in the first place the problem of the causes of the emancipation of the serfs—which is not to deny the interconnectedness of all the reforms of the 1860s or to imply that the other reforms were merely adjustments required by the emancipation. On the contrary: The emancipation was the key to the reforms; it was not accidental that it came first.

The problem of the preconditions for the emancipation, or rather the treatment of that subject in the literature, constitutes something of a reductionist's nightmare. For an entire generation, beginning in the 1930s and lasting into the 1970s, Soviet historiography was virtually dominated by the "revolutionary situation" view of the origins of reform: The penetration of the "feudal-serf system" by money-commodity relations over the decades preceding the 1850s created a "systemic crisis"; the main manifestation of the crisis was a deterioration of the material conditions of life for the enserfed peasantry that led to a rising level of peasant disorders; and the higher level of disorders finally produced a "revolutionary situation" of which the emancipation was the main "by-product" (*pobochnyi produkt*). At its most extreme, this theory led to the view that the progressive radicalization of the reform in the course of its preparation was at each step due to a marked rise in the level of peasant violence.[46]

I have indulged in this slight departure from my vow to avoid historiographical excursions for two reasons. The first is that this "model" has had repercussions on the interpretation of the entire subsequent history of agrarian legislation. Subsequent activity in the area of agrarian legislation in the early 1880s and following the revolution of 1905 tended to be interpreted as reflexive reactions to short-term situations of stress. The fact is that "revolutionary situations" in the late nineteenth and early twentieth centuries served only to precipitate action on legislative projects long in the works. There is a strong line of continuity between the emancipation of 1861 and all subsequent agrarian reform proposals under the old regime, just as there was continuity linking the 1861 reform to earlier legislation and reform projects going back at least as far as 1803. The same could be said about other areas of administration and legal reforms.

---

[46]This view was most closely associated with Academician M. V. Nechkina and her Group for the Study of the Revolutionary Situation of 1859–1861. On the historiography of the emancipation, see Peter Scheibert, *Die russische Agrarreform von 1861: Ihre Probleme und der Stand ihrer Erforschung* (Cologne and Vienna, 1973).

The second reason is that the rise and decline of this effort at causal reductionism points up the fact that the explanation of the preconditions of the reforms of the 1860s has in many respects returned in recent years to what it had been before 1917. To put it in a nutshell, the predominantly liberal prerevolutionary scholarship followed closely the perceptions of contemporaries of the reform in attributing the reform ultimately to the rise of abolitionist sentiment grounded in both moral and economic arguments. This movement was due, in the end, to the growing influence of education and "European" values among the nobility. And this return to the perceptions and values of contemporaries seems to be characteristic of recent scholarship: One of the most recent works on the reform declares that, by the middle of the nineteenth century, "the question that remained to be determined was not whether emancipation would occur, but when and how."[47]

The catalyst that impelled the regime—that is; Alexander II and his confidants—to overcome the fear of disorder, even, as Eidel'man suggests, of assassination, as well as bureaucratic resistance, was Russia's defeat in the Crimean War, the country's first major military setback since the early years of the reign of Peter I. It called into question Russia's status as a great European power and brought to the fore as at no time, perhaps, since Peter came to the throne, the issue of overcoming Russia's backwardness. (The "lessons" of the Crimean War were, of course, being drawn by contemporaries in a substantial underground literature even before the final defeat.) From the beginning, the issue of reform was linked to the idea of Russia's modernization and Europeanization.

This matter of evolving mentalities touches on what might be called the cadre question. Eidel'man's answer to that question was, "*Nuzhno reformy nachat', a liudi sami naidutsia*"[48]—"get the reforms going" and the people needed to carry them through will show up by themselves. But it seems to me that this answer amounts to a kind of self-fulfilling prophecy, retroactively applied. The fact is that all the reforms of the 1860s were the work—in terms of both the details of the legislation and the overall spirit that informed them—of a generation of "enlightened" or "liberal" bureaucrats that had emerged in the ministries of Nicholae-

[47]Peter Kolchin, *Unfree Labor: American Slavery and Russian Serfdom* (Cambridge, Mass.: Belknap Press of Harvard University Press, 1987), 363. See also Zakharova, "Samoderzhavie, biurokratiia, i reformy."
[48]*RSVR*, 89.

van Russia in the 1840s. Many, perhaps most, of them were of service gentry backgrounds with little or no land or serfs, and all were products of the interlocking systems of ministerial government and higher education that were crafted, to a large extent, by Speransky at the beginning of the nineteenth century and were brought into full operating order, so to speak, under Nicholas I. Most of them were acquainted with each other and regularly met and exchanged views on such occasions as the meetings of the Imperial Russian Geographic Society: "With the exception of Prince V. A. Cherkasskii and the specialists who drafted the Judicial Reform of 1864, every government official who helped to draft and support the Great Reform legislation took an active part in the Geographical Society between 1850 and 1857."[49] The reform ethos took shape inside the unreformed ministerial bureaucracy during the thirty-year "period of stagnation" that was the reign of Nicholas I. Although we still know relatively little about this element in the bureaucracy, it must be considered an essential precondition to the reforms of the 1860s.[50]

Two points should be made about the question of pressures for reform "from below." The first is that, although the regime in no way confronted a "revolution from below" either immediately before or during the reform era, the *perceived* threat of popular violence increasingly occupied the minds of the elite over the decades preceding the reform. The acuity of the perceived threat was undoubtedly linked to changing values and the "lessons" refracted through those values from the revolutionary experiences of Europe since 1789—most recently, the events of 1848.

That is not to deny the probability that a growing expectation of emancipation, linked to rumors generated by nearly half a century of secret government deliberations and projects for peasant reform, yielded

[49]W. Bruce Lincoln, *In the Vanguard of Reform: Russia's Enlightened Bureaucrats, 1825–1861* (De Kalb: Northern Illinois University Press, 1982), 100. On the formation of a cadre of reformers in the Ministry of Justice, see Richard S. Wortman, *The Development of a Russian Legal Consciousness* (Chicago: University of Chicago Press, 1976), especially chap. 8, "The Emergence of a Legal Ethos."

[50]Systematic study of the enlightened bureaucrats of the 1860s is a fairly recent development; see the works by Lincoln and Wortman cited in n. 49, by Field and Zakharova in n. 53, and by Zakharova in n. 25. These bureaucrats were the heroes of the first generation of historians who strove to keep "the spirit of the Great Reforms" alive in the age of counterreforms under Alexander III. See, for example, G. A. Dzhanshiev, *Epokha velikikh reform*, which went through at least nine editions between the 1880s and 1900.

reduced tolerance among peasants for their bondage.[51] By the same token, and this is the second point, the reports of a sharp increase in incidents of peasant disorders beginning in 1858 and continuing into 1862 were, to the extent that they reflected reality and not just increased governmental nervousness, responses to the reform preparations by the administration, rather than their cause.[52]

Finally, one should consider the range of options or alternatives that were available once the general decision to abolish serfdom had been taken. The touch-and-go history of the reform program of the "liberal bureaucrats," up to and including its being rammed through the Main Committee with a majority of one vote and its emergence from the State Council on the eve of promulgation as a minority position, is now well known.[53] However, I would argue that more or less this program— emancipation of the peasants *with land,* but for redemption, with various restrictions on the peasants' movements and on their right to dispose of their land, and with retention of communal landholding—was the only viable option open to the government.

Given the government's desire to effect a gradual transition, avoiding both radical dislocation of the peasantry and ruination of the gentry, it had no choice but to emancipate the peasants with some land for redemption. By and large, the gentry were not absentee landowners, insofar as they generally retained demesne land and depended on estate income rather than being true absentees collecting some kind of generalized "feudal dues," but neither were they actively involved in cultivation. The peasants worked all the land, and with their own inventory. Since this "economic knot" of serfdom was still very much intact when the state intervened, its undoing would have to be a slow and complicated process involving the solution of complex problems of labor supply and capital.[54]

---

[51]This point is made in Kolchin, *Unfree Labor,* 362.

[52]A fuller argument about peasant behavior around the time of the reform is presented in my article, "The Peasant and the Emancipation," in Wayne S. Vucinich, ed., *The Peasant in Nineteenth-Century Russia* (Stanford, Calif.: Stanford University Press, 1968), 41–71.

[53]Daniel Field, *The End of Serfdom: Nobility and Bureaucracy in Russia, 1855–1861* (Cambridge, Mass.: Harvard University Press, 1976); L. G. Zakharova, *Samoderzhavie i otmena krepostnogo prava v Rossii, 1856–1861* (Moscow, 1984). See also Lincoln, *In the Vanguard of Reform,* and Wortman, *Development of a Russian Legal Consciousness.*

[54]Alexander Gerschenkron, "Agrarian Policies and Industrialization, Russia 1861–1917," in *Cambridge Economic History of Europe* (Cambridge: Cambridge University Press, 1965), 6, Part 2: 712–13.

In other words, landless emancipation was out of the question (although the emperor, for one, was probably brought to this realization only well after the reform process was under way), and therefore the dissolution of the complex economic relations of serfdom could be brought about only gradually, while legal administrative restrictions were retained. The legislation of 1861 was meant only as a first step, resurrecting in some measure civil and legal rights for the peasants and removing the direct, slaveowner-like authority of the landlord.[55]

To varying degrees, the same gradualist, transitional approach can be seen in all the other reforms of the 1860s that impinged on the existing system of social stratification: They were *first steps* in the direction of breaking down estate distinctions and creating a unified citizenry. This brings us to the matter of intentions and goals.

On intentions and goals. The reforms of the 1860s have with considerable justification been labeled "bourgeois reforms" in Soviet historiography. The goal of their planners—the enlightened bureaucrats such as Nicholas Miliutin and the enlightened gentry minority that was variously drawn into the preparation of the reforms and then took an active part in manning the new institutions issuing from them, as arbiters of the peace (*mirovye posredniki*), justices of the peace, zemstvo deputies, and so on—was to effect the country's transition to a modern class society in which political rights would be linked to individual property ownership and equal civil rights would be provided for all.

Gentry landownership would be preserved and communal tenure would give way to private household farming among the peasants. Local self-government and representative institutions at the center would be established, and the autocracy would in time become a limited monarchy. Russia, in short, would become a modern, European state, a constitutional monarchy, and a state ruled by law. Many writers have seen a direct line of continuity connecting the reforms of the 1860s with the 1809 reform project of Michael Speransky.[56]

[55]As Peter Struve pointed out long ago, "serf law" (the legalized enthrallment of the serf to his master) was abolished in 1861, while much of the "serf economy" (the system of agrarian relations that had developed under serfdom) survived long after 1861, being too vast and complex a matter to be dealt with by a single legislative act. P. B. Struve, *Krepostnoe khoziaistvo* (St. Petersburg, 1913), 156. See also Kolchin, *Unfree Labor,* 374–75.

[56]The vision of the enlightened bureaucrats, especially Nicholas Miliutin, is described in Zakharova, *Samoderzhavie i otmena krepostnogo prava.* The reform program of the

To be sure, the reforms of the 1860s did not of themselves realize that vision. For example, the emancipation's economic provisions gave title to the land kept by the peasants, not to individual householders but to the villages collectively, with joint fiscal responsibility (*krugovaia poruka*) of its members for redemption and tax payments; the administrative statutes left the peasants as a kind of an order apart, with separate peasant courts and a separate system of administration; and the principle of property-based representation in the new zemstvo institutions of local self-governance was seriously compromised by the establishment of a special curia for the peasants that left them seriously underrepresented.

These "shortcomings" of the reforms are well known, and, as Eidel'man remarks, they have tended to overshadow in Soviet historical memory the very real achievements of the reforms.[57] But the reformers believed in progress and the European model. They were clear on the intent and direction of the reforms, and they thought the impediments to the transformation left in the legislation, with the aim of avoiding disorder and financial disaster (and here communal tenure was the key institution), would be removed in due time by the play of natural forces, supplemented by renewed spurts of government intervention. It is clear that Miliutin and his colleagues thought of the emancipation statutes as only the first step in a long-term government intervention in agrarian relations, whose aim was to transform the communal peasantry into a class of independent smallholders—the aim that was revived by Stolypin in 1906.[58]

Recent writing on the reforms of the 1860s has emphasized their interrelatedness, which was also a characteristic of prerevolutionary liberal historiography, but so far the other reforms of the 1860s (that is, other than the peasant legislation) have received rather little detailed attention.

enlightened gentry is described in my work, *The Russian Landed Gentry and the Peasant Emancipation of 1861* (Cambridge: Cambridge University Press, 1968). Eidel'man clearly accepts the idea of Speransky's "constitutional legacy," but not all modern scholars are in agreement on that issue. See, for example, the views of Nicholas V. Riasanovsky, *A Parting of Ways: Government and the Educated Public in Russia, 1801–1855* (Oxford: Clarendon, 1976), and Marc Raeff, *Understanding Imperial Russia: State and Society in the Old Regime* (New York: Columbia University Press, 1984).

[57]*RSVR*, 143. See, in particular, the rueful comparison of the judicial system established in 1864 and the Soviet judicial system (pp. 141–44).

[58]Zakharova, *Samoderzhavie i otmena krepostnogo prava*, 234 and passim. For an overview of the history of agrarian legislation to 1914, see Alexander Gerschenkron, "Russia: Agrarian Policies and Industrialization, 1861–1914," in Alexander Gerschenkron, *Continuity in History and Other Essays*, 140–248.

It does seem clear, however, that the interrelatedness of the reforms involved not only the ramifications of the emancipation in other spheres of life and administration, but also a pervasive guiding ideology, whose main features have been alluded to above and which was reflected throughout the reform process to one or another degree. This point can be illustrated by the reforms affecting the church and the clergy in 1867 and 1869. These are almost never mentioned in the context of the Great Reforms, yet they clearly conform to the general pattern: Their aim was to transform—gradually—the clergy from an estate into a profession.[59]

On the consequences. As far as the reforms' consequences were concerned, the reformers' expectations, particularly in the area of agrarian relations, were of course massively frustrated. For a couple of decades, beginning with the counterreforms of the 1880s, the state actually got into the business of trying to shore up the economic and administrative foundations of the communal peasantry as part of a social-monarchist strategy that endured into the revolution of 1905 but did not survive it. The result was, among other things, stagnation of agricultural productivity in conditions of rapid population growth, hardly, as Gerschenkron has pointed out, an ideal basis from which to launch the campaign of rapid, state-sponsored industrialization commenced by Witte in the 1890s.[60]

Such was the operation of what Hegel called the irony of history in late nineteenth-century Russia. The struggle between the forces of "reform" and "reaction"—or more accurately, to borrow a phrase from Theodore Taranovski, between liberal reform and the traditional ethos of the *Polizeistaat*[61]—in postemancipation Russia has been more or less thoroughly studied and is the subject of another paper in this volume,[62]

---

[59]Gregory L. Freeze, *The Parish Clergy in Nineteenth-Century Russia: Crisis, Reform, Counter-Reform* (Princeton: Princeton University Press, 1983), Part 3.

[60]Gerschenkron, "Russia: Agrarian Policies and Industrialization," 211.

[61]Theodore Taranovski, "Sudebnaia reforma i razvitie politicheskoi kul'tury tsarskoi Rossii," in L. G. Zakharova, Ben Eklof, and John Bushnell, eds., *Velikie reformy v Rossii, 1856–1874* (Moscow, 1992), pp. 301–17.

[62]See the next chapter. A coauthor of that chapter, Valentina Chernukha, is also the author of two excellent monographs that describe in detail the fate of the reform initiatives of the 1860s in regard to the peasant commune, institutions of representative government, and related matters up to the end of the reign of Alexander II: *Krest'ianskii vopros v pravitel'stvennoi politike Rossii (60–70 gody XIX v.)* (Leningrad, 1972); and *Vnutrenniaia politika tsarizma s serediny 50-kh do nachala 80-kh gg. XIX v.* (Leningrad, 1978).

so I shall not take it upon myself to explore that subject at any length here. I will limit myself to two observations.

The first is that we need to be very circumspect in speaking of the consequences of the reforms of the 1860s, because the program that had its first great successes in the reforms of those years remained on the agenda and, in fits and starts, was further implemented over the following years up to the outbreak of World War I; indeed, elements of that program in the area of local self-government were still being applied by the Provisional Government in 1917. To my mind, the abortive Loris-Melikov projects of 1879–81, the Bulygin constitution of 1905, the State Duma legislation of 1906, and the Stolypin reforms all fit into the same ragged continuity in the evolution of the Russian polity. In asserting this view, which was something like an article of faith with the liberal Russian intelligentsia before the widespread demoralization that overcame its ranks in the wake of 1905, I am not arguing that Russia would have become a modernized constitutional monarchy were it not for the accident of World War I; the crisis of the Russian body politic and social was indeed grave by the early years of the twentieth century. At the same time, it cannot be entirely excluded that historians of the twenty-first century will look back on the reform processes of the 1980s and 1990s as the resumption and continuation of a process of political and social development begun in the middle of the nineteenth century, if not earlier.

The historian cannot ignore, in any case, the fateful and persistent resistance of the Russian old regime to yielding any of its monopoly on power to the bitter end. Eidel'man and others have noted the failure of the state to find "reinforcements from below" as a crucial factor limiting the advance of state-sponsored reforms, and the constitutional struggle of the early twentieth century is known to all of us.[63]

My second and final point is more by way of an agenda for research than an observation. Pondering the fate of reform in late imperial Russia inevitably gives rise to questions about the nature of bureaucratic resistance to public participation in governance, for the resistance, as we know, did not come only from the person of the autocrat. To explain this resistance solely in terms of a struggle between liberal reformers and a conservative majority of bureaucrats steeped in the traditions of the *Polizeistaat* would be, I think, a gross simplification. After his abrupt,

---

[63]*RSVR*, 157–58; Zakharova, "Samoderzhavie, biurokratiia, i reformy," 24.

Othello-like dismissal immediately after promulgation of the reform, Nicholas Miliutin, the liberal reformer par excellence, wrote to his brother, who was then the war minister, of the need of the monarchy to rely on the liberal gentry in regaining the reform initiative.[64] But at the time of his ascendancy during the work of the Editorial Commissions (1859–60), he had been intent on reducing gentry participation in the preparation of reform to the barest minimum, suspicious of the motives of even the most liberal gentry activists and in general jealous of the bureaucracy's monopoly in the reform initiative:

Never, never, so long as I am in power, will I allow any pretensions whatever on the part of the gentry to the role of initiators in matters concerning the interests and needs of the entire nation. Concern for them belongs to the government; to it and it alone belongs the initiative in any kind of reforms for the good of the nation.[65]

No doubt he was sincere in his insistence that relaxation of the government monopoly would be used only for selfish gentry interests, but his close collaborator and fellow bureaucrat, P. P. Semenov, disagreed with him.[66]

The point is that even the most liberal of bureaucrats, nobles themselves, may have been deeply in thrall to the myth of the centralized state as the sole engine of progress in Russian history. Stories of similar import could be recounted from the biographies of such later prominent progressive statesmen as Witte and Stolypin. (The latter uttered the famous remark in 1907, after the State Duma had been in existence for more than a year, "Thank God Russia has no parliament.") But the fact is that, although a number of good studies of the bureaucracy dealing with the estate background, education, age and rank structure, and other characteristics of the upper levels of officialdom have been produced in recent years, we still know relatively little about the bureaucratic ethos.[67]

---

[64] As cited in Zakharova, "Samoderzhavie, biurokratiia, i reformy," 21.

[65] As quoted in Zakharova, *Samoderzhavie i otmena krepostnogo prava,* 189. See also W. Bruce Lincoln, *Nikolai Miliutin: An Enlightened Russian Bureaucrat* (Newtonville, Mass.: Oriental Research Partners, 1977).

[66] Katherine Jolluck, "P. P. Semenov-Tian-Shanskii as Emancipator" (unpublished paper, Stanford University, 1989).

[67] A recent significant enlargement of our knowledge of this subject is Dominic Lieven, *Russia's Rulers under the Old Regime* (New Haven: Yale University Press, 1989), which is devoted, despite its title, to explicating the world views of several representatives of the bureaucratic elite under the last tsar.

3

Russia falls back, Russia catches up:
three generations of Russian reformers

VALENTINA G. CHERNUKHA and
BORIS V. ANAN'ICH

The reforms of the 1860s and of the late nineteenth and early twentieth centuries must be viewed as successive efforts by the tsarist government to resolve historical problems that confronted Russian society since the reign of Alexander I. With the reforms of Peter the Great, the Russian Empire had become part of European civilization, and the French Revolution, which had an immense impact on Western society and politics, inevitably left its mark on Russia as well. The Russian autocracy had to take into account developments elsewhere in Europe if it wanted to maintain its prominence in the European community. Moreover, the Russian Empire had expanded during the reign of Alexander I to the point where its system of government required modernization. The defects in the administration of the borderlands and the need to reform national-religious policy were becoming apparent. Early in the nineteenth century, the tsar and his advisers realized that both state and society required significant change. As General M. F. Orlov put it: "The era of the French Revolution was a great era . . . I see a marvelous lesson for nations and kings arising from the depths of this immense catastrophe. An example like this is given so that it should not be followed."[1]

The reform proposals commissioned by Alexander I adumbrated the path that Russia had to follow in order to keep up with Europe. Russia had to be transformed into a constitutional monarchy and a legal state

---

[1] M. F. Orlov, *Kapituliatsiia Parizha: Politicheskie sochineniia. Pis'ma* (Moscow, 1963), 55–56.

(*Rechtsstaat* or *pravovoe gosudarstvo*) with separation of powers, basic elements of legality, civil rights, and freedom of the press. The country needed a cabinet government headed by a prime minister responsible to representative institutions. The system of estates, serfdom, centralization, and government interference in economic and financial affairs represented significant obstacles to the progress of industry, trade, and culture.

These obstacles could have been removed either by reform or by revolution. Russian society spent the entire nineteenth century struggling to overcome them but failed to resolve the problem in its entirety. Three generations of Russian revolutionaries fought to transform Russia during that time; concurrently, three generations of Russian bureaucratic reformers drafted a variety of proposals for changing the socioeconomic system and the state administration. The reform process in the nineteenth century appears cyclical in character. Periods of active consideration and implementation of reform were followed by periods of stagnation. Russia alternately fell behind the progress of Western countries and then strove to make up for lost time.

THE FIRST GENERATION: M. M. SPERANSKY, N. N. NOVOSIL'TSEV, P. A. VIAZEMSKII, N. I. TURGENEV

Tsar Alexander I (1801–25) entertained many reform plans, and his intimate circle consisted of men who shared his views and who were capable of drafting them into law and putting them into effect. Although the Alexandrine epoch had many aspiring statesmen from the aristocracy, its most prominent reformer was Michael M. Speransky, the first important official to come from the raznochintsy. A gifted, well-educated, hard-working, and skillful codifier, Speransky drafted the broadest and most detailed reform program. His swift rise began in 1803, and for a decade he was the tsar's confidant. He has left a rich documentary archive, but his most important projects, undertaken on instructions from the emperor, were the proposals for judicial reform and the draft of a Russian constitution. They were not fated to be implemented, but they anticipated both the judicial reform of 1864 and the establishment of the State Duma in 1905–6.

Speransky's works embody an array of legal and political ideas derived from contemporary European jurisprudence.[2] In his "Memorandum on the Organization of Judicial and State Institutions in Russia" (1803), Speransky, developing his notion that the executive power must be responsible to the legislative, stressed the dominant role of public opinion and identified two conditions under which it could guarantee adherence to law: "public character of all governmental actions" (i.e., glasnost) and "liberty to print" (i.e., freedom of the press).[3] Thus, already in 1803 Speransky postulated the necessity of separation of powers, supremacy of the legislative authority, subordination of the executive power to the legislative (which was rejected fifty years later in the reign of Alexander II), control of the executive by public opinion, and public functioning of the ministers and of the government as a whole.

Speransky's draft constitution, which he prepared in 1809 at Alexander's request and called an "Introduction to the Code of State Laws," amounted to a proposal for transforming Russia from a despotic into a constitutional state, with legislative barriers against the revival of arbitrary rule. The grant of a constitution, in Speransky's opinion, would serve to forestall a revolution from below. Like many Russians of the early nineteenth century, Speransky believed that the grant of a constitution from above would be much less problematic than the abolition of serfdom. After all, a constitution would involve only an extension of the rights of society, whereas emancipation of the peasantry would curtail the liberties of the numerous and influential serfowners. Hence, Speransky thought that his proposal for a constitution could be implemented immediately but that emancipation was best postponed. In writing his "Introduction," Speransky was guided not only by existing European constitutional norms, especially those of England, but also by European historical experience. Considering the history of European states, Speransky noted: "How many disasters, how much bloodshed, could have been avoided if the rulers, more closely discerning the progress of the spirit of society, had based the principles of government on it, and did not try to conform the people to the government but the government to the state of the people."[4]

---

[2] N. V. Minaeva, *Pravitel'stvennyi konstitutsionalizm i peredovoe obshchestvennoe mnenie Rossii v nachale XIX veka* (Saratov, 1982), 103–4.
[3] M. M. Speranskii, *Proekty i zapiski* (Moscow, 1961), 109.
[4] Ibid., 109.

Speransky proposed the creation of a State Duma, a legislature composed of deputies elected from the provinces, with the franchise based on property qualifications. Its chairman would be elected by the deputies, subject to confirmation by the emperor. The Duma would be divided into several specialized commissions that would review various measures and legislative proposals submitted by the ministers in the name of the monarch or the Council of State. The latter was to be established as a kind of counterweight to the Duma, in order to maintain the emperor's power.[5]

Although Speransky's plans were sympathetically received by Alexander I, most of them were not implemented. However, the Council of State was established, with power to review bills and pass legislation, although any measures that it enacted obtained the force of law only upon confirmation by the emperor. This purely bureaucratic institution survived until the revolution of 1905, when it was transformed into the upper chamber of the parliament. On the eve of the war of 1812, Speransky was suddenly exiled from St. Petersburg, and the initial period of his career in government came to an end.

The first half of Alexander I's reign is usually perceived as having been more liberal than the second. Nevertheless, even in this latter period, the emperor commissioned, in 1819, work on a "Statutory Charter of the Russian Empire"—that is, a constitution. P. I. Peshar-Deshan [Pechard-Deschamps—ed.] was invited from France to draft it, and the poet and bureaucrat Peter A. Viazemskii translated it into Russian. Nicholas N. Novosil'tsev, by then in charge of the Russian administration in Poland, was the organizer of the whole enterprise. The provisions of the charter were to be extended to the entire Russian Empire. This would have also meant the repeal of the Polish constitution of 1815, but the charter was largely modeled on it and had a decidedly liberal character.

This draft constitution called for the creation of a bicameral parliament (State Sejm or State Duma) and proclaimed the inviolability of property, judicial independence, accountability of officials, equality of citizens under the law, and freedom of the press and of emigration. The issue of serfdom was skirted, although its significance had long been recognized. Early in his reign, Alexander I had raised the issue of eman-

---

[5]See Marc Raeff, *Michael Speransky: Statesman of Imperial Russia, 1772–1839* (The Hague: Martinus Nijhoff, 1957); S. A. Chibiriaev, *Velikii reformator: Zhizn', deiatel'nost', politicheskie vzgliady M. M. Speranskogo* (Moscow, 1989), 215.

cipation, and it was placed on the agenda of the so-called Unofficial Committee (*Neglasnyi komitet*) in 1801. In 1820, upon the initiative of a group of aristocrats including Viazemskii, an effort was made to found a society of noble landowners to advocate abolition of serfdom and to take the initiative on this question. Both Novosil'tsev, a partisan of the English parliamentary system, and Viazemskii hoped that the new constitution would lead to the realization of their long-held aspirations. Viazemskii, in particular, viewed his involvement in the project as one of the most important events of his life and was greatly dismayed when Alexander I failed to approve it.

If Speransky was just a bureaucrat, an armchair statesman, and Viazemskii a civil servant and a Decembrist sympathizer, Nicholas I. Turgenev represented quite a different type. He had participated actively both in government politics (he was an assistant state secretary in the Council of State after 1816 and an official of the Ministry of Finance after 1819) and in the Decembrist movement. He also knew and was influenced by the Prussian reformer Baron Heinrich Friedrich vom Stein.

In June 1816, Turgenev drafted a reform plan spanning a quarter of a century, or five quinquenniums. The first step on the road to a free Russia with a parliamentary government was to be the training of competent reformers. Between one hundred and two hundred young men were to be sent abroad for four years, mostly to study jurisprudence. During the first quinquennium, three-person committees were to draft legislative proposals for a new law code and the reform of finances and state administration, which were to be promulgated during the second period. The chief task of the third period, according to Turgenev, was the creation of a political estate of "peers" from among the nobility who did not own serfs. They were to function as the mainstay of the tsar's power during the process of reform and peasant emancipation. The abolition of serfdom was planned for the fourth period, and introduction of popular representation for the fifth. Turgenev thought that the power of the monarchy should be limited in Russia, though not to the extent that it was, for example, in Great Britain. He proclaimed that "everything in Russia must be accomplished by the government, nothing by the people itself."[6]

Autocracy confronted organized political opposition for the first time in the second half of Alexander I's reign. The Decembrists, like the re-

---

[6]*Dnevnik N. I. Turgeneva za 1811–1816 gody* (St. Petersburg, 1913), 2:333–34.

formers, considered Russia a European state. They opposed despotic rule and serfdom and championed civil liberties. They accepted the tactic of the military coup d'état, but they strove to keep violence to a minimum and viewed it as an imposed step, made necessary by the government's delay in introducing reform. The gentry revolutionaries were an elite and privileged social group, which could have provided support for the monarchy because its political program in many respects resembled the reform proposals that the government considered but failed to enact.

The second quarter of the nineteenth century seems to have been an opportune time for the implementation of these grandiose plans for reform, and to this day historians wonder why Alexander I had set them aside. However that may be, Alexander's successor, Nicholas I (1825–55), had no intention of acting on them. Instead, he settled accounts with all critics of the Russian reality. There were few impressive political figures during his reign, with the exceptions of P. D. Kiselev and S. S. Uvarov, the latter an intelligent and educated man who deliberately adopted the goal of delaying progress. Uvarov's task was "to push back Russia for fifty years from what the future was preparing for it."[7] His formula of "Orthodoxy, Autocracy, and Nationality" became the slogan of an official ideology that proclaimed that autocracy was unshakable and represented a unique, traditional, and immutable form of government to which the Russian people were devoted.

The thirty years of "deadly stagnation," as the reign of Nicholas I was called even by contemporaries such as Peter Chaadaev,[8] had pernicious consequences for the Russian economy and society. The period gave rise to a new generation of revolutionaries as well as to a new generation of reformers.

THE SECOND GENERATION: P. A. VALUEV, GRAND DUKE CONSTANTINE NIKOLAEVICH, P. A. SHUVALOV, N. I. LORIS-MELIKOV

The model of the 1860s reform era. Societies often need a powerful shove to lift themselves out of stagnation, and Russia's defeat in the Crimean War in 1856 provided it. The defeat demonstrated Russian military and economic backwardness. It threatened Russia with the loss

---

[7]A. V. Nikitenko, *Dnevnik* (Leningrad, 1955), 1:174.
[8]P. Ia. Chaadaev, *Stat'i i pis'ma* (Moscow, 1989), 43.

of European great-power status and forced the autocracy to initiate change in order to restore its position. Internal developments also put pressure on the next tsar, Alexander II (1855–81): peasant discontent, growing gentry opposition, and economic disorganization. An analysis of the internal political crisis of the period of the late 1850s and early 1860s and the reforms that followed permits us to construct a model of "the era of reform" in Russian history.

The initiative in favor of reform and against the era of stagnation was taken by the liberally inclined gentry intelligentsia. By early 1855, K. D. Kavelin, B. N. Chicherin, N. A. Mel'gunov, and N. A. Zherebtsov had drafted memoranda analyzing the state of the country and proffering their own solutions. This period was also characterized by the leftward movement of the conservative intelligentsia, as best illustrated by M. P. Pogodin. Next came the consolidation of democratic forces: Nicholas Chernyshevsky, who had been putting out *The Contemporary* (*Sovremennik*), was joined by Nicholas Dobroliubov in 1857. *The Russian Word* (*Russkoe slovo*), whose contributors included Dmitry Pisarev, became prominent only in 1860. The conservatives organized themselves even later; they adopted a wait-and-see attitude until November-December 1857, when Alexander's rescripts proclaimed his intention to intervene in landlord-peasant relations. The founding of the provincial gentry committees helped to unite the conservatives, and the appearance of the *Journal of Landowners* (*Zhurnal zemlevladel'tsev*) was the earliest indication of their mobilization.

As far as the government was concerned, the bureaucratic elite, conditioned by Nicholas I to act as mere executor, proved inert and manifested no interest in reform. Even Alexander II's attempts to advance the peasant question in the Secret Committee, founded on January 3, 1857, and presided over by A. V. Orlov, were paralyzed. That is why Alexander II began to reshuffle ministers and top administrators. First, he had to remove the most odious and patently incapable individuals and then find replacements capable of drafting and implementing reforms. Personnel turnover continued well into 1861–62, by which time the individuals who implemented the major reforms of the 1860s were in charge of the ministries: P. A. Valuev, A. V. Golovnin, D. A. Miliutin, A. A. Zelenyi, D. N. Zamiatnin, M. Kh. Reutern. The only ministry favoring reform in the mid-1850s was the Naval Ministry, headed by Grand Duke Constantine Nikolaevich; in fact, it was intended to serve as a model for the reorganization of other institutions.[9] It was Baron E. V. Wrangel, the Naval Ministry's jurisconsult, who early in 1856 drafted the instruction on rationalizing the operations of government institutions and the relations of superiors to subordinates in the bureaucracy. Even, however, if there were no reforming statesmen among the ministers in 1856–57, the officials of the "second layer" of the ministerial bureaucracy, such as assistant ministers and department directors, were actively involved in the process. One need only recall Valuev's controversial memorandum, "Thoughts of a Russian," Iu. A. Gagemeister's report on finances,[10] the activities of A. I. Levshin, who initiated the emancipation, and the work of N. A. Miliutin and V. P. Bezobrazov. These individuals were the core of a group of bureaucratic reformers who were in charge of various committees and commissions.[11]

There were no other choices at the time. The only question was the one of how to transform a serf-owning Russia into a capitalist Russia, with the countries of Western Europe serving as models. Indeed, the contemporary press was replete with accounts of how Europe resolved such issues as the agrarian reform, self-government, and the administration of justice. Moreover, every reform in modern Russian history began with the preparation of an official memorandum on the state of affairs in the West. But the forms of transition to capitalism (the reform "package" and the consistency, speed, and timetable of changes) were in the hands of the legislators and of the social elements that were pressuring them. Different groups were interested in realizing their own program of reform.

In any reform era, the role of social institutions and public organizations that reflect collective and class interests grows immeasurably. Russia had neither political parties nor experience with broadly organized social and political activity, but Russian society learned quickly. At first, likeminded individuals gathered in the traditional salons and circles of friends (e.g., the circle of K. D. Kavelin in St. Petersburg and the Moscow circle of the Korsh brothers and M. N. Katkov). The St. Petersburg salon

---

[9]A. P. Shevyrev, *Russkii flot posle Krymskoi voiny: liberal'naia biurokratiia i morskie reformy* (Moscow, 1990), 184.

[10]Gagemeister's report, "O finansakh Rossii," was published in *Istoricheskii arkhiv*, 1956, no. 2: 100–125.

[11]L. G. Zakharova, "Samoderzhavie, biurokratiia, i reformy 60-kh godov XIX veka v Rossii," *Voprosy istorii*, 1989, no. 10: 3–24; W. Bruce Lincoln, *In the Vanguard of Reform: Russia's Enlightened Bureaucrats, 1825–1861* (De Kalb: Northern Illinois University Press, 1982).

of Grand Duchess Elena Pavlovna became the place where the bureaucratic elite met reform-minded candidates for civil-service jobs. Between 1858 and 1859, provincial gentry committees provided a forum for both liberal and conservative viewpoints. The nobility ascribed great importance to the St. Petersburg convocation of representatives of these committees in 1859–60, hoping that they could dictate to the government the conditions of emancipation. Both this convocation and the provincial committees themselves were new forms of sociopolitical activity in Russia. The assemblies of the nobility also served as political platforms, and it was there that "constitutional" petitions were composed in the 1860s. Public banquets, which were completely legal means of public gatherings, allowed large groups of individuals freely to expound their views. Some of these banquets, such as the annual one held by the framers of the Emancipation Act, became traditions.

The scholarly intelligentsia used their learned societies, committees on political economy, and literacy groups for these purposes. The history of the political economy committee of the Geographic Society is a good example. In 1859, a group of economic liberals—including V. P. Bezobrazov, N. Kh. Bunge, P. A. Valuev, and I. V. Vernadskii—founded a committee, attached to the society's statistical section, which they intended to transform into an independent Political Economy Society, like one that existed in Paris. They brought together scholars, entrepreneurs, and officials with the aim of influencing government policy by analyzing the most important economic issues and making recommendations concerning them. The committee's members gave public lectures and contributed to a journal, *A Guide to Political Economy* (*Politiko-ekonomicheskii ukazatel'*). The Chess Club and the Petersburg Union of Agriculturalists became centers of activism. A Society for Mutual Land Credit was founded in 1866 to serve both as a credit institution and as a surrogate for a conservative gentry party.

The Russian press provided the most consistent form of public pressure on government. That is why glasnost invariably appeared in Russia during a crisis situation. This phenomenon is the result of an increase in social activism, on the one hand, and, on the other, confusion on the part of the government, which is aware of its lack of popularity. But there is another circumstance to consider: The government has no reform program after an era of stagnation and is therefore interested in receiving input for the formulation of one through the press. That is the reason for the relaxation of censorship. In the 1860s, the relaxation of censorship was complemented by the widespread circulation of manuscripts and the use of émigré publishing houses, which allowed the smuggling into Russia of the works of such authors as Alexander Herzen, P. V. Dolgorukov, and P. L. Bliummer. The late 1850s were characterized by an extraordinary flowering of a variety of periodical publications and by growth in readership.

This, however, is but one side of glasnost: the relative freedom for the expression of public opinion. Its other side is the manifestation of glasnost in the actions of the state. Albeit unwillingly, the government began to publish information about the establishment and activities of legislative commissions, guidelines for reform, the texts of legislative drafts, and so on. This was done to pacify public opinion and to demonstrate the efficacy of autocracy. Moreover, the authorities actively sought public input in regard to the content and character of proposed reforms. Such was the case, for example, in 1862, when the press, solicited by the minister of education, A. V. Golovnin, carried on a lively discussion of the principles of the censorship reform.

How radical the reform program is and how completely it is realized depend on circumstances. Society cannot maintain a prolonged effort, and eventually fatigue sets in. Furthermore, the first reforms, as a rule the most pressing ones, lower social tensions and reassure both the government and society, weakening the government's reformist drive. On the other hand, the radicalism of the revolutionary democrats in the 1860s and the Polish revolt of 1863, which frightened the moderates, made the liberals less demanding of government and more patient in regard to reform. Finally, in contrast to the first quarter of the nineteenth century, when constitutionalism was on the political agenda, the reform "package" of Alexander II did not include this plank. The refusal to create a mechanism for public participation in political decision making inevitably prepared the ground for a new crisis.

Finally, the reforms of the 1860s demonstrate that the state sanctions new departures only in the initial stages, while new laws are being drafted. As soon as the effects of the reforms manifested themselves, the autocracy clearly indicated that it was not ready to engage in a dialogue with society, to cooperate with it. This was obvious in the cases of censorship, the zemstvo, and judicial reforms. The government initially attempted to "correct" the reforms, to modify or ignore the laws in its reaction to the consequences of the reforms. By the 1880s, the autocratic monarchy went further and decided to review the basic principles of the reform era itself.

Formation of the government's program. The student of nineteenth-century Russian politics is constantly faced with the question of whether the government had any sort of general program for either its short-range or its long-range policy. The fact that there is no document approved by a high state organ as a guiding policy statement would seem to answer this question in the negative. Nevertheless, neither the policies of Alexander II nor those of Alexander III give an impression of purposelessness. The reforms of the 1860s were integrated and coordinated. The 1880s have been called "the era of the counterreforms," because they were guided by the two general objectives of increasing state control over the institutions of self-government and of replacing the principle of "noncorporatism" (*bessoslovnost'*) in Russian society by the traditional principle of corporatism (*soslovnost'*). [For an explication of the issues involved in this question, see footnote 15 in the next chapter, by Zakharova.—Ed.]

If one considers the fact that Russia lacked cabinet government and legal political parties until the revolution of 1905, it becomes apparent that the supreme authority could have had no fixed, general program. In fact, as the nineteenth century progressed, the country was increasingly being undermined by institutional divisiveness (*vedomstvennost'*). Periodically, the heads of key institutions submitted policy statements upon the monarch's request. For example, the Ministry of Finance submitted major policy memoranda in 1857, 1860, 1866, and 1880.[12] A. V. Golovnin presented the program of the Ministry of Education in 1862.[13] D. A. Miliutin repeatedly submitted proposals for the reorganization of the army.[14] Even when considered together, these institutional programs at best only partially substituted for an integrated and coordinated government policy. Nevertheless, the autocracy possessed a number of mechanisms that tied together institutional plans and actions into what can be conditionally viewed as a general state policy. It is as

[12]L. E. Shepelev, *Tsarizm i burzhuaziia vo vtoroi polovine XIX veka* (Leningrad, 1981), 17, 57–63, 100–108, 135–40.
[13]Iu. I. Gerasimov, *Iz istorii russkoi pechati v period revoliutsionnoi situatsii kontsa 1850—nachala 1860-kh godov v Rossii* (Moscow, 1974), 133.
[14]P. A. Zaionchkovskii, *Voennye reformy 1860–1870-kh godov v Rossii* (Moscow, 1952).

legitimate to refer to "the state policy" as it is to speak of "the government" in Russia, although neither the Committee of Ministers nor (after 1905) the Council of Ministers would qualify as a true government.

The monarch, as the sovereign, coordinated the actions of Russian state institutions. All draft legislation and important administrative measures were prepared and promulgated with his sanction, although only a portion of them received his personal imprimatur. Measures that required coordination of or input from several institutions were usually discussed by the tsar with a group of top officials and were sometimes reviewed later by a group of specially chosen ministers. Guiding principles for the administration as a whole were periodically issued in imperial manifestoes and rescripts (for instance, the document announcing Alexander II's accession to the throne; the rescript of May 13, 1866, rallying the conservatives; the manifesto of Alexander III of April 29, 1881, reaffirming the principle of autocracy; and the manifesto of Nicholas II of February 26, 1903, and the decree of December 12, 1904, both of which promised comprehensive social and administrative reform). Interagency policy formulation and coordination were aided by the practice of establishing legislative commissions that included officials from all the institutions that had a jurisdictional stake in the issue, by discussions of administrative affairs in the Committee of Ministers, and through the legislative process of the Council of State. Finally, the Council of Ministers, established in 1857 and chaired personally by the tsar, was supposed to coordinate state policy as a whole.

State and society represented two opposing forces, and the government's program was usually the result of a compromise between the two. Ideas emanating from society, whether expressed in manuscript form or published in newspapers or journals in Russia or abroad, were widely circulated throughout the bureaucracy, even at the top levels. Alexander II read Herzen's journal *The Bell* (*Kolokol*), and many memoranda were addressed to him personally (for example, the letters of M. P. Pogodin) or to his ministers. In short, during the 1850s and 1860s and later as well, there was a shared domain of reformist ideas. The extremist views, either from the right (the conservatives) or the left (the revolutionary democrats), only made the ideas of moderate liberals that much more attractive to the government. The moderately liberal program of Russian society, in fact, may be viewed as the provisional general program of the state. Widespread involvement of society's representatives in legislative activity, most obvious in the case of the Editorial Commissions, helped the government elaborate its policy.[15] The liberal press also had influence in some specific instances. As is well known, a compilation of press reports on the question under consideration was an integral step in the drafting of many legislative proposals. This happened in the case of the judicial, censorship, and tax reforms.

The initial version of the government's reform program was formulated in 1859; indeed, all the Great Reforms of the 1860s were in the pipeline by then. Merely to list the acts that were promulgated, however, does not do justice to the reform program as envisaged in the period from the late 1850s to the late 1860s. A Tax Commission was established in 1859 to prepare a radical reform of the system of taxation. Another commission was charged in that year with reform of the passport system. In the late 1860s, the attempt to allow free convertibility of paper currency into gold failed, and for this reason it has been little discussed by historians. The adoption of the gold standard was postponed until the late nineteenth century. At the same time (1869), a law on peasant migration was being considered, but nothing was done during the reign of Alexander II. It should also be noted, however, that the reform program never contemplated reorganization of the state structure, although several reformers wanted to accomplish this objective as well.

Approaches to reform. The late 1850s and early 1860s gave birth to Russian revolutionary democracy and the ideology of utopian peasant socialism. This ideology advocated the overthrow of autocracy by a peasant revolution, followed by a republican form of government and communal socialism. In opposition to it within the government was a group of reformers who aimed to avoid a jacquerie by establishing a resilient economic, social, and political system. If the differences between the revolutionaries and the reformers of the first generation were relatively minor, the gap between the two was much greater half a century later. Moreover, there were significant differences between the reformers of the first and of the second generation. The former simply adopted Western models and planned to introduce a constitution and a constitutional regime. The latter no longer proposed a constitution and only

[15] L. G. Zakharova, *Samoderzhavie i otmena krepostnogo prava v Rossii, 1856–1861* (Moscow, 1984); Daniel Field, *The End of Serfdom: Nobility and Bureaucracy in Russia, 1855–1861* (Cambridge, Mass.: Harvard University Press, 1976).

proffered elements of representation in order to strengthen the autocracy; they carefully emphasized the "unique" nature of the Russian state. To be sure, they were not always sincere, for they held responsible posts in government and had to accommodate their plans to the emperor's wishes. Alexander II, in contrast to Alexander I, made no constitutional promises or overtures and, on the contrary, always spoke against such innovations in no uncertain terms. Indeed, this attempt to separate socioeconomic from political reform was one of the reasons why the government's economic program ultimately failed.

It was difficult to develop broad policy initiatives of national significance within the ministerial milieu between the 1860s and the early 1880s because each state agency was institutionally isolated from the others and concerned only with its own sphere of jurisdiction. That there were statesmen with wide-ranging programs was due at least in part to the fact that there were institutions with a "broad" profile, such as the Ministry of Internal Affairs or the Third Section, responsible for "order" in the country as a whole. Of course, not every minister of internal affairs or director of the Third Section had or proposed a broad program; one needed special qualities for this, but such officials had both the opportunity to raise general policy considerations and a rationale for doing so. During this period, two ministers of internal affairs, Peter A. Valuev and Michael T. Loris-Melikov, the chairman of the Council of State, Grand Duke Constantine Nikolaevich, and the chief of gendarmes, Peter A. Shuvalov, were statesmen of vision who saw the need to complement various socioeconomic reforms with popular representation on the national level. They were otherwise men of quite divergent outlooks, but it is remarkable that they all tried to create some sort of a Russian variant of a national representative body, conjoining autocracy and representation.

Valuev held important state posts throughout the twenty-five-year reign of Alexander II and had major influence on internal policy, taking part in all the great and lesser reforms of the 1860s and 1870s. He was a well-educated hereditary bureaucrat without landed estates and was thus dependent on state service. He was a "Westerner" by intellectual persuasion, who often, however, had to trim his proposals to suit the theory of Russia's historical particularity. "The institutions without which Europe cannot exist are not alien to Russia," he declared in 1881. "Russia cannot go back and must follow the path predestined for all nations in the history of mankind. But if we aim to domesticate European civilization among us, we must take as a model not the despotism of the Orient, but European institutions."[16] He often simply copied European practices, adopting, for example, the contemporary French press law as his model for censorship reform. But his true idol was England. He was known as "the Russian Lord Beaconsfield," his favorite newspaper was the *Times* of London, and he often referred to his own "English manners." When he proposed in late 1861 to introduce representatives of the clergy and the Holy Synod into the Council of State, Valuev was using the British parliament as his model.[17]

The beginning of the reign of Alexander II found Valuev in the post of the governor of Courland. He began immediately to engage in advocacy writing (*publitsistika*), which contributed to his speedy transfer to the Ministry of State Properties in St. Petersburg. However, even while serving in the Baltic, Valuev, apparently preparing for a more significant role, sketched out the programs that he believed the Russian government should follow in order to escape its crisis. In his "Thoughts of a Russian" (September 1855), he formulated an idea that many shared and expressed at the time: "During our gigantic struggle with half of Europe, it could no longer be concealed under the canopy of official self-praise how much we have fallen behind our enemies."[18] Valuev maintained this awareness of the dangers of stagnation and of the need for timely reform throughout his life. He was one of the best-prepared and intellectually most European of the reform era's statesmen, and he fully realized the obvious shortcomings of what had been accomplished.

The idea of a national representative body was central to Valuev's program. With its aid, he hoped to make peace with the gentry, to lay the foundation for the cooperation of state and society, to curtail the excesses of autocracy (to put limits on "expressions of imperial will"), to resolve the nationalities issue, and to improve the legislative process. His program had a moderately liberal character and was fully in tune with the spirit of the time. Viewing the gentry as the estate closest to the throne, he took its interests into account and to a certain extent reflected them, but he never granted those interests supremacy. Attuned

---

[16]*Russkii arkhiv* 7 (1906): 448.

[17]Gregory Freeze, "P. A. Valuev and the Politics of Church Reform (1861–1862)," *Slavonic and East European Review* 1 (1978): 69. See also Gregory Freeze, *The Parish Clergy in Nineteenth-Century Russia: Crisis, Reform, Counter-Reform* (Princeton: Princeton University Press, 1983).

[18]*Russkaia starina* (May 1891): 349.

to the needs of the time and having no links to the landed magnates, he was not in sympathy with their oligarchic (aristocratic) demands. He reached the height of his influence on internal policy between 1861 and 1868. For a brief time in 1861, he was director of the chancellery of the Committee of Ministers and of the Council of Ministers, and then he began a seven-year tenure as minister of internal affairs. Following a forced retirement, he served for four years in the Council of State, and he was appointed minister of state properties in 1872, in which position he showed that one could demonstrate breadth of vision even in a specialized agency. In April 1872, he appointed the first postreform commission to study the needs and problems of Russian agriculture. His hope somehow to link the work of the commission with the idea of establishing a national representative assembly failed to materialize, and his dreams were revived only in 1880–81, when the internal crisis once again sharply intensified.

Valuev considered Austria as the country whose state system was closest to that of Russia, and his reform proposal took the Austrian Reichsrat as a model. Valuev started from the premise that it is best to modify existing institutions as little as possible, and for that reason he focused on reforming the Council of State, an advisory legislative body. The council, retaining its advisory function, would become the upper house. A Congress of State Deputies would be the lower house, consisting of representatives from zemstvos, towns, and borderlands without zemstvo institutions. The emperor was to appoint one-fifth of the deputies to the congress. The congress was to be convened once a year, in contrast to the council, which was intended to be a permanent body. A link between the two houses was formed by sixteen deputies from the congress who participated in the council's deliberations.[19]

Most reform-minded statesmen at the time considered it absolutely necessary to take some initial step toward popular representation, to create a precedent, to institutionalize in some practical way the idea that society should participate in the affairs of government. Valuev was an exception in that he considered it important to make such a step not merely symbolic but a significant one that could be trusted by society and serve as the basis for cooperation. Here his position sharply differed from that of Alexander II, who preferred to make any concession as small as possible and only if it was absolutely necessary. Four times

[19]*Vestnik prava* 9 (1905): 235–69.

Valuev tried and failed to realize his vision: in 1861–63, in 1866, in 1872–74 (when he supported the proposals of the chief of gendarmes), and in 1880–81.

Valuev's second key idea was to reorganize the apex of the administration into a "cabinet." He did not dare even to suggest a major reform on this issue and only tried to get approval for "special conferences" of ministers to discuss the most important policy problems. Only those matters on which the heads of the executive agencies failed to reach agreement were to be transferred to the Council of Ministers. However, even this feeble effort to approximate European forms of government met with failure. The autocrat had no desire under any circumstances to relinquish even a small part of his prerogatives.[20]

The narrowness of Valuev's program is apparent if one considers that he did not envisage the introduction of civil liberties, such as freedom of speech and the press, personal inviolability, or freedom for political parties. He acted as a classical bureaucrat, striving to retain in his hands the means of controlling society. He argued for and won extensive powers over the press for the Ministry of Internal Affairs during the discussion of censorship reform. In 1865–68, he did everything possible to subordinate the courts to his ministry in press trials.

Valuev also wanted to reform the tax system and increase state revenue by introducing an income tax, graduated according to ability to pay. He favored a more active fiscal and economic policy to increase revenue, and on this ground he criticized the minister of finance, Michael Kh. Reutern, who always considered it his primary objective to lower costs and to cut the budgets of various institutions. Valuev also favored encouragement of private peasant landownership. He considered communal landholding a convenient means for the government to deal with the village but also an institution patently harmful to the development of productive forces and of village agriculture. The agricultural commission of 1872 was supposed to give the peasant an opportunity to leave the commune.

Valuev considered the landed gentry the most important social group in Russia because it controlled the sources of wealth in an essentially agrarian society and because it was educated, and he wanted to give it its due place in the new order. (In this he differed with Alexander II and

[20]V. G. Chernukha, *Vnutrenniaia politika tsarizma s serediny 50-kh do nachala 80-kh gg. XIX veka* (Leningrad, 1978), 155–98.

Grand Duke Constantine, who saw the peasantry as a conservative mainstay against the political aspirations of the nobility.) For this reason, Valuev wanted the government to become more solicitous of the economic needs of the gentry and to provide it with financial support. He contended that this could be achieved by government subsidies to private mortgage banks.

Valuev's program was obviously both moderate and reasonable. And yet it was realized—or more precisely, its principles were realized—only at the beginning of the twentieth century, when the autocracy confronted a real revolution and not just a potential one. That is why his 1863 memorandum was included in the papers of the government commissions considering the establishment of the State Duma in 1905.

Another proposal for a national representative body came from Grand Duke Constantine Nikolaevich, a member of the ruling family but an acknowledged leader of the liberal bureaucracy. He earned his reputation while heading the Naval Ministry in the second half of the 1850s and by his truly immense efforts on behalf of the emancipation. Nevertheless, his liberalism was of a Slavophile variety, which gave rise to differences with, among others, Valuev. At a time when many landlords were bitterly opposed to the emancipation and the assemblies of the nobility were presenting "constitutional" demands, Constantine Nikolaevich considered it expedient for autocracy to counterpoise peasant conservatism to gentry political aspirations. The grand duke's influence on internal policy was diminished by his appointment as viceroy of the Kingdom of Poland in the summer of 1862. His prolonged absence from St. Petersburg accounts for his lack of involvement in the preparation of some of the most important reforms, such as those affecting the zemstvos and the administration of justice. Constantine Nikolaevich returned to the political arena of the capital in January 1865, when he was appointed chairman of the Council of State. The nature of this appointment shaped the character of the political role that he could play; he could exert considerable influence on legislative drafts, but he could not exercise legislative initiative. The chief exception was a proposal he made in 1866 to establish and attach to the Council of State two elective representative assemblies of deputies from the nobility and from the zemstvos, to be convoked at the discretion of the emperor and charged with a predetermined agenda. Tsar Alexander II unequivocally rejected this extremely modest proposal from his brother.

The third major figure in this generation of reformers was Count Peter A. Shuvalov. In contrast to Valuev, who represented a noble-bureaucratic point of view, Shuvalov espoused the outlook of the milieu to which he belonged by birth and status, the landowning court aristocracy. His mother was Polish, and this was often cited to explain his Westernism and "cosmopolitanism." Having graduated from the Corps of Pages, Shuvalov opted for a military rather than a civil-service career. The Corps of Pages was poor preparation for statesmanship, but it was not training that determined appointments to government office in tsarist Russia. Shuvalov's father held high posts at the court of both Nicholas I and Alexander II, and his son served in the imperial retinue of Alexander II, where he was eventually promoted through all three of its ranks: wing-adjutant, major general of the retinue, and finally adjutant-general. The energetic officer was appointed in 1857 as chief of police in St. Petersburg in order to bring order to the police force and to elevate its prestige in the eyes of the inhabitants. His training for office took place in France.

After three years of supposedly successful police service, Shuvalov briefly became director of the Department of General Affairs of the Ministry of Internal Affairs but soon afterward was appointed assistant chief of gendarmes in 1861. Shuvalov accepted the post without enthusiasm and began his tenure with a memorandum proposing the abolition of the secret police, an idea which he continued to entertain, planning in the 1870s, for example, to merge the Department of Police with the Third Section. At the time, he greatly feared for his reputation, and he asked Herzen, via S. S. Gromeko, a well-known liberal Russian journalist, to treat him gently [in his publications]. In a conversation with M. L. Mikhailov, who had just been arrested, he persuasively portrayed himself as a "liberal," and in late 1861 he submitted his resignation. His last position before attaining ministerial rank (and the post of chief of gendarmes was equivalent in status to that of a minister) was as the governor-general of the Baltic region. In April 1866, after Karakozov's attempted assassination of Alexander II, he was appointed to head the Third Section, at which point his eight-year tenure as de facto prime minister began. He assumed the role of leadership among the ministers, gathered a group of like-minded colleagues around himself (A. P. Bobrinskii, S. A. Greig, K. I. Pahlen, and D. A. Tolstoi), and together with them worked to formulate and realize his program. He also had connections with Field Marshal A. I. Bariatinskii, an old friend of the emperor's, who decided in the mid-1870s to resume his career as a statesman.

Whereas Valuev was interested in modernizing the state structure, Shuvalov's concern was to strengthen the political role of the landed gentry. He declared that he favored the West European pattern of development, and he categorically rejected the aims of the so-called Russian party, at the time understood to refer to followers of Slavophilism and nationalist believers in Russian autochthony. Shuvalov wanted to develop local self-government, but he intended to strengthen gentry representation there by including large landowners, who would not be elected but would be seated as delegates on the basis of property qualifications. These reconstituted zemstvos would then work to replace communal by private peasant landownership. Shuvalov also supported the idea of an all-estate canton, but in its conservative variant, in which the head (*volostel'*) of the canton was to be a noble landowner.[21] Justices of the peace would no longer be elected but instead would be appointed from the gentry ranks. Here his model was England, where the landed gentry played a key role in local affairs.

As is demonstrated by his memorandum regarding a "Society for Workers' Welfare" and his conversation with B. A. Markevich, Shuvalov was anticipating the appearance of the proletariat in Russia.[22] He proposed a policy of state paternalism and the building up of social-insurance capital that could be used for welfare benefits and, in the final account, even for pensions. This policy was intended to reduce the acuity of the workers' question.

According to Shuvalov's plans, the influence of the landed gentry, which would have by then assumed key positions in the counties and provinces, was to be strengthened by its representation at the national level. It is characteristic that during his service as chief of gendarmes, Shuvalov never admitted to his constitutional and parliamentary intentions. However, in 1881, once out of power, he proclaimed that "an advisory assembly can bring no benefit whatsoever. One must openly introduce a constitutional system by establishing two houses and giving them a decisive voice. If this cannot be done immediately, one must, at

[21]V. P. Meshcherskii, *Moi vospominaniia* (St. Petersburg, 1898), 2: 152–55.
[22]*Istoriia proletariata SSSR* (Moscow, 1932), 10: 50–90; Otdel rukopisei Gosudarstvennoi biblioteki imeni Lenina, *fond* 120, *papka* 27, *delo* 3, *list* 16.

the least, erect a foundation upon which real representative government could eventually arise."[23] In order to accomplish this, he was willing to use Valuev's 1863 proposal.

In 1874, Shuvalov, a Westerner and Anglophile whose strategic goal was a constitution and a bicameral parliament, nevertheless chose very modest tactics, inviting representatives of society to discuss draft legislation for only one particular issue at a time. Valuev's agricultural commission was convoked to deal with agrarian problems. Valuev and Shuvalov then planned to have representatives of zemstvos, gentry, and towns either draft their own legislative proposals or evaluate those prepared by the ministries. This was a far cry from either a parliament or any sort of permanent representative assembly. Shuvalov, the adherent of European ways, was compelled to engage in purely Russian inventiveness.

Shuvalov was the only statesman during the reign of Alexander II who made some progress on this issue. In April 1874, the Committee of Ministers approved, as an experiment, a commission formed of representatives of zemstvos, gentry, and towns to discuss an already drafted bill on the hiring of agricultural labor. This decision, confirmed by the emperor, was not published and was utilized only once, in 1875. The unwillingness of the autocrat to permit change in the legislative process and a consequent redistribution of authority was so great that Shuvalov's attempt cost him his job as chief of gendarmes and resulted in his appointment as ambassador to London, far away from matters of internal politics.[24]

After Shuvalov resigned, there was no strong statesman with a wide-ranging program in Russian politics, and it was only a new societal upsurge that brought another such leader to power. Michael T. Loris-Melikov, a "fighting general," was a man without much political experience and a newcomer to the bureaucratic elite. Although he was at the helm of state only a bit longer than a year, he is much better known than his predecessors, however unjust that may be. In 1880, at the height of the revolutionary crisis, he was appointed head of the Supreme Executive Commission and then minister of internal affairs. Alexander II, increasingly insecure and fearful of the terrorism of the People's Will, charged Loris-Melikov with prosecuting the revolutionaries, but also in-

---

[23]E. A. Peretts, *Dnevnik (1880–1883)* (Moscow, 1927), 53.
[24]Chernukha, *Vnutrenniaia politika*, 67–117.

structed him to take steps "to meet insofar as possible the lawful demands and needs of the people."[25]

Loris-Melikov quickly took stock of the situation, surrounded himself with individuals of moderately liberal persuasion (A. A. Abaza, N. S. Abaza, N. Kh. Bunge, M. S. Kakhanov, D. M. Sol'skii), and formulated a program of reforms. This was not difficult to do. For more than twenty years, the popular and scholarly press, the zemstvos and the assemblies of the nobility, and the congresses of landowners had been advocating progressive reforms, and a long list of proposals had been drafted by various legislative commissions. Two main ideas lay at the base of Loris-Melikov's program. The first was to cooperate with the liberal elements of society in order to transform them from opponents to allies both in the struggle with the revolutionary movement and in passing new reform legislation. The second was to promulgate economic measures to help the peasantry. This was intended to undercut revolutionary propaganda and to remove the threat of a mass peasant movement.

The most important concession to the liberal public was to include representatives of the estates in various commissions charged with drafting reforms, approximately in the same form as attempted by Shuvalov a few years earlier. In 1880–81, this was one of the chief demands of the liberal forces in society. By this time, the institutions of local self-government had taken root, and the liberals thought that representation on the national level would not deteriorate into oligarchy. A properly structured legislative process was viewed as a guarantee of progressive policies. At the same time, Loris-Melikov was ready to meet another significant demand of the liberals: extension of freedom of the press. To be sure, the aim here was merely to complete the censorship reform of 1865 by transferring all cases dealing with the press to the jurisdiction of regular courts. This would put a stop to the administrative arbitrariness that was provoking such discontent within society and in the press. A commission on the press was established to alleviate the problem. As far as his other proposals were concerned, Loris-Melikov did not hide the fact that they were based on statutory drafts buried among the papers of various commissions and offices. "Improvement in the moral level of the clergy" and "granting of rights to schismatics" were other parts of his policy that were derived from the programs of his predecessors.

[25]"Konstitutsiia grafa Lorisa-Melikova: Materialy dlia ee istorii," *Byloe* 4–5 (1918): 164.

The two greatest agrarian problems of the time were the shortage of land and the peasant tax burden, and Loris-Melikov focused on them. He proposed to aid peasant emigration from overpopulated provinces to less populated territories, in order to alleviate land hunger, and a fiscal reform to lower the tax burden, including the taxation of all estates— that is, extending taxation to the gentry—on a "just" basis. Loris-Melikov succeeded in implementing only one of all his proposed agrarian measures: the abolition of the salt tax. All five congresses of landowners had urged this step in the past but had been disregarded; now, however, when autocracy was facing a dangerous moment, the government acted quickly.

Alexander II supported Loris-Melikov's program both in principle and in particulars. The emperor also approved in principle the proposal for elected deputies but with the proviso that this step be reviewed one more time by the Council of Ministers. A meeting for this purpose was scheduled for March 8, 1881, but Alexander's assassination on March 1 changed the situation. His successor, Alexander III (1881–94), decided to reestablish control by harsh measures. Loris-Melikov's plan for a national representative body, which he had put forth as strengthening rather than weakening the autocracy, cost him his office. Alexander III's response to this plan is well known: "Thank God that this criminal and hasty step toward a constitution was not taken, and that this whole fantastic proposal was rejected in the Council of Ministers by a very narrow margin."[26] There are reports that, in a conversation with E. T. Baranov, Alexander voiced his sentiments even more clearly: "Constitution? That a Russian tsar would swear allegiance to some sort of herd of cattle?"[27] It was in such an atmosphere that the third generation of Russian reformers ascended the historical stage.

THE THIRD GENERATION: N. KH. BUNGE, S. IU. WITTE, P. D. SVIATOPOLK-MIRSKII, P. A. STOLYPIN

Soviet historiography has conventionally viewed the 1860s and 1870s as an era of reform, and Alexander III's change of course as ushering in an era of stagnation and counterreforms. This interpretation gives insufficient weight to the facts that, in the earlier decades, the liberal re-

[26]Ibid., 162.
[27]A. S. Suvorin, *Dnevnik* (Leningrad, 1927), 166.

formers and their opponents were locked in constant conflict and that, on the other hand, even in the late 1880s, the state could not completely abandon reformism, especially in matters of economic policy.

The primary reason that the opponents of the Great Reforms won out in the early 1880s was that the government rejected constitutional reforms on a European model. Instead, it revived the theory of the autochthonous evolution of Russia, and internal policy became more nationalist in character. Issues of foreign policy also played a role. The Polish uprising of 1863, which derailed the monetary reform that had been initiated by the government, had caused a nationalist reaction in certain circles of Russian society; and the Russo-Turkish War of 1877–78 and events in the Balkans promoted Pan-Slavic sentiments. Finally, one must take into account the spread of protectionist notions in Europe itself, under the influence of Friedrich List and his conception of the national economy.

The nationalist course proclaimed by Alexander III was prepared while he was still heir apparent and was nourished within his entourage by the vigilant tutelage of his mentor, Constantine P. Pobedonostsev. In the late 1870s, two members of this circle, the well-known publicist General Rostislav A. Fadeev and Adjutant-General Illarion I. Vorontsov-Dashkov, elaborated a conservative program and had it published as *Letters on the Contemporary Condition of Russia (April 11–20, 1879—April 6, 1880)*. The *Letters* first appeared anonymously in Leipzig and were then reprinted four times in Russia in 1881–82.[28]

The *Letters* sharply attacked Western constitutionalism and contrasted it with "vital popular autocracy" and a zemstvo that would incarnate "the idea of the union of tsar and people" and acknowledge "the tsar as tsar, and not as the head of the executive branch." The authors criticized the "excessively huge bureaucratic mechanism" as being infected with nihilism and called for restoration of pre-Petrine institutional forms, in particular the assembly of the land (*zemskii sobor*). These ideas were also supported by some Slavophiles, especially Ivan S. Aksakov.

In contrast to Fadeev and Vorontsov-Dashkov, Pobedonostsev and

---

[28]See B. V. Anan'ich and R. Sh. Ganelin, "R. A. Fadeev, S. Iu. Vitte i ideologicheskie iskaniia 'okhranitelei' v 1881–1883 gg.," in *Issledovaniia po sotsial'no-politicheskoi istorii Rossii* (Leningrad, 1971); V. G. Chernukha, "Bor'ba v verkhakh po voprosam vnutrennei politiki tsarizma (seredina 70-kh godov XIX v.)," *Istoricheskie zapiski* 116 (Moscow, 1988): 167–84.

Michael N. Katkov rejected outright the idea of restoring the assembly of the land and insisted on the need to strengthen the autocratic power. This thesis was officially proclaimed in the Manifesto of April 29, 1881, written by Pobedonostsev, which set the new course of government policy. The supporters of reform, Loris-Melikov, A. A. Abaza, and D. A. Miliutin, resigned in May. Their successors, upon Pobedonostsev's recommendation, were N. P. Ignat'ev as minister of internal affairs, Nicholas Kh. Bunge as minister of finance, and P. S. Vannovskii as minister of war.

In August 1881, Vorontsov-Dashkov was appointed minister of the court. According to A. N. Kulomzin, director of the chancellery of the Committee of Ministers, the program of the *Letters* was supported by Ignat'ev, M. N. Ostrovskii (minister of state properties), and Bunge, and the three ministers adhered to it until the spring of 1882. Ignat'ev included "experts" from society in the groups that were drafting legislation for reform of internal migration and the liquor trade. Upon Ignat'ev's initiative, commissions were established to review laws pertaining to local government (under M. S. Kakhanov), service in provincial administration (E. A. Peretts), the civil law code (N. I. Stoianovskii), and government contracts and deliveries (V. D. Filosofov).

Although Alexander III hated the principle of representation, he was reluctant to oppose the proposal for convocation of the assembly of the land immediately after his accession, and he permitted Ignat'ev to work on a manifesto for almost a year.[29] The minister's zeal only weakened his standing in the eyes of the emperor, and in late May 1882, Ignat'ev was replaced by Dmitry A. Tolstoi. This put an end to any discussion in ruling circles of the topic of representation, and the course of internal policy became openly nationalist and pro-gentry. "Again it became fashionable," wrote F. I. Rodichev in reference to the early 1880s, "to wear gentry caps with red bands. . . . A new, so-called 'gentry' era began. But the flatterers called Alexander III a peasant tsar and a peacemaker."[30] Less than a year before his appointment, Tolstoi's candidacy in zemstvo elections was rejected by the landowners' curia of the county of Zaraisk in Riazan province because he was the author of a memorandum submitted to Alexander II that "defended serfdom."[31] In the 1850s, Tolstoi

---

[29]P. A. Zaionchkovskii, *Krizis samoderzhaviia na rubezhe 1870–1880 godov* (Moscow, 1964), 460.
[30]F. I. Rodichev, "Iz vospominanii," *Sovremennye zapiski* 3 (Paris, 1933): 287.
[31]Ibid., 286.

was a "confirmed *konstantinovets*," that is, a charter member of a circle of liberally inclined civil servants around Grand Duke Constantine Nikolaevich. However, while the emancipation statute was being drafted, he switched sides.[32] When he became minister, Tolstoi chose as director of his chancellery A. D. Pazukhin, the marshal of nobility of Alatyr county in Simbirsk province, "a conscientious partisan of serfdom" and a man "of selflessly gloomy inclinations."[33]

Pazukhin set forth his philosophy in a book entitled *The Contemporary Situation in Russia and the Estate Question,* published in Moscow in 1886. It relied on ideological constructs elaborated by Pobedonostsev and Katkov. Pobedonostsev was a supporter of a "restoration of firm autocratic authority" and in favor of "perestroika of peasant administration, of the 'zemstvo soapbox,' of 'powerless courts,' of 'the lying press,' and of education."[34] In January 1895, Pobedonostsev, striving to retain his position as the court ideologist, submitted to Nicholas II a memorandum on the general direction of internal policy. Extolling autocracy, Pobedonostsev denounced Western parliamentarianism as completely inapplicable to Russia. By adopting it, the Russian government would turn into a "government of parties" and become "the fount and principle of oppression, conflict, and destruction, undermining all values on which rest the moral convictions" of the Russian people.[35]

Katkov, who in the late 1850s and early 1860s had been a Westernizer and an Anglophile, supported Pobedonostsev during the 1880s. He praised autocracy as the most perfect and progressive form of government and proclaimed Russia to be "more Westernized than the most Western country in Europe."[36] The nationalist orientation of the official ideology of the 1880s and 1890s, however, was fully compatible with recognition of Western authorities in politics or philosophy. Pobedonostsev, for example, happily relied on Thomas Carlyle and Max Nordau

---

[32]P. A. Zaionchkovskii, *Rossiiskoe samoderzhavie v kontse XIX stoletiia* (Moscow, 1970), 59.

[33]Rodichev, "Iz vospominanii," 286–87.

[34]S. L. Evenchik, "Pobedonostsev i dvoriansko-krepostnicheskaia liniia samoderzhaviia v poreformennoi Rossii," *Uchenye zapiski Moskovskogo gosudarstvennogo pedagogicheskogo instituta im. V. I. Lenina,* no. 309 (Moscow, 1969): 232–33.

[35]Iu. B. Solov'ev, "Nachalo tsarstvovaniia Nikolaia II i rol' Pobedonostseva v opredelenii politicheskogo kursa samoderzhaviia," *Arkheograficheskii ezhegodnik za 1972 g.* (Moscow, 1974), 316–17.

[36]V. A. Tvardovskaia, *Ideologiia poreformennogo samoderzhaviia (M.N. Katkov i ego izdaniia)* (Moscow, 1979), 230–31.

in his criticism of West European parliamentarianism,[37] and Katkov urged Russians to follow the example of Bismarck in his struggle with the socialist and labor movements.[38]

The program of the counterreforms was the result of a collective effort, but Katkov and Pobedonostsev played a decisive role in shaping it. Their nationalism affected their outlook on foreign policy as well; they supported the extension of Russian influence in Asia and imperial expansion in the borderlands, Pan-Slavism and liberation movements among the Slavs, and entente with France. Their economic policy was based on national industrial development as a means of strengthening the autocracy. They called for subsidies to branches of industry that were of interest to the government, protectionism, paper money, strict state control over stock-exchange operations and private entrepreneurship, use of state monopolies in liquor and tobacco for purposes of taxation, and economic support for gentry agriculture (by means of Gentry and Peasant Land Banks). Development of the national economy was to go hand in hand with support for communal landownership in the villages.

This program was expounded in the pages of the *Moscow News* by I. F. Tsion (Cyon),[39] Katkov's mouthpiece on economic and foreign-policy issues, and in the polemical writings of the assistant procurator general of the Holy Synod, N. P. Smirnov, which were directed against Bunge's economic policy and inspired by Pobedonostsev.[40] Thus, "the party of the counterreform," basing itself on clear ideological principles, elaborated a political program for the autochthonous development of Russia and proceeded to implement it, gradually overcoming the resistance of the liberal bureaucracy. By the 1880s, the Council of State and the Senate had become "refuge[s] for the old reformers." By no means did all the newspapers welcome "the gentry era" and "the rule of the politically reliable."[41] Some liberal organs of the press, such as *Herald of Europe* (*Vestnik Evropy*), *Russian News* (*Russkie vedomosti*), and

---

[37]V. V. Vedernikov, "Krizis konservativnoi ideologii i ego otrazhenie v pechati (1895–1902 gg.)," *Vestnik Leningradskogo gosudarstvennogo universiteta* 8, no. 2 (1981): 104–7.
[38]Tvardovskaia, *Ideologiia poreformennogo samoderzhaviia*, 231.
[39]B. V. Anan'ich and R. Sh. Ganelin, "I. A. Vyshnegradskii i S. Iu. Vitte—korrespondenty 'Moskovskikh vedomostei'," *Problemy obshchestvennoi mysli i ekonomicheskaia politika Rossii XIX–XX vekov* (Leningrad, 1972), 12–34.
[40]Shepelev, *Tsarizm i burzhuaziia*, 145–46.
[41]Rodichev, "Iz vospominanii," 286–87.

Russian Thought (Russkaia mysl'), supported the existing zemstvo institutions and opposed social corporatism.[42]

The most powerful voice in Russian journalism of the 1880s, however, was that of Katkov himself. Writing in 1886, Katkov attacked Bunge as belonging to the party that had "suffered defeat on April 29, 1881," but had refused to lay down its arms and had continued to oppose the course of government policy. "This is the party," wrote Katkov, "that had formerly rested its hopes on [the ministries] of education, justice, and finance, then on the latter two, and now only on the last one, which controls the vital resources of the country."[43] By that time, Bunge was the last influential figure in the executive who supported the ideals of the 1860s. The minister of education, A. I. Nikolai, was dismissed in March 1882 and replaced by I. D. Delianov, making it possible for the government to revise the university statute in 1884. In November 1885, the minister of justice, D. N. Nabokov, was succeeded by N. A. Manasein, and the attack on the judicial reform commenced. At about the same time, Pobedonostsev and Katkov opened a press campaign against Bunge that ended with his resignation on December 31, 1886, and his replacement by the candidate of the *Moscow News*, I. A. Vyshnegradskii, a professor of mechanics at and director of the St. Petersburg Technological Institute and a man well known in the Russian business community.

Bunge's resignation was a blow to the party of liberal reform. He was a major figure within its ranks, and he had elaborated his own program of state reform. He had been appointed assistant minister of finance under A. A. Abaza in August 1880, and although he of course shared the views of his reform-minded colleagues, he was a man prone to compromise. After becoming a minister, he supported the views of Fadeev and Vorontsov-Dashkov, but when they were defeated by Katkov and Pobedonostsev in the summer of 1882, he managed to survive in his post.

In September 1880, Bunge submitted a memorandum to Alexander II in which he advocated a series of steps to improve the Russian national economy. He argued that "to aid industry and manufacturing and commercial enterprises, what is needed from the government is . . . not so

---

[42]L. G. Zakharova, *Zemskaia kontrreforma 1890 g.* (Moscow, 1968), 85.
[43]M. N. Katkov, *Sobranie peredovykh statei "Moskovskikh vedomostei" za 1886 god* (Moscow, 1889), 117. See also Zaionchkovskii, *Rossiiskoe samoderzhavie*, 84–89.

much material aid as the enactment of laws that would establish a system that can be applied to the development of a modern economy. In this regard, Russia has fallen behind all of Western Europe by half a century." Russian industrial progress was "inhibited" because the country "lack[ed] modern factory legislation." Bunge initiated its development.[44]

He also supported reform of stock-market legislation and creation of a widespread network of joint-stock commercial banks.[45] Between 1882 and 1886, Bunge implemented the repeal of the poll tax. He supported the principle of social equality in matters of tax policy, the repeal of joint fiscal responsibility, a review of the passport system and introduction of a uniform passport for all estates, encouragement of free peasant migration, and, ultimately, replacement of communal by individual landownership. In his view, Russian industrial progress mandated the development of productive forces in the village. He envisaged organic industrial growth and the development of capitalist relations in the countryside. Bunge also tied national economic progress to reform of the administration and creation of a "united" government.

In contrast, the key objective of both Vyshnegradskii and his successor, Witte, was to adapt economic policy to the political doctrine prevailing during the reign of Alexander III. This was reflected in their endorsement of conservative agrarian policy during the late 1880s and early 1890s and of greater government intervention in the national economy. The introduction of land captains in 1889 increased gentry control over the institutions of peasant self-administration. The commune was to be upheld, and laws strengthening communal landownership were passed in 1893. Government interventionism was also manifested in Vyshnegradskii's and Witte's protectionist tariff policy, culminating in the tariff of 1891. Vyshnegradskii initiated regulation of grain freight tariffs in 1889, and additional legislation under Witte during the middle 1890s greatly increased the government's role in the grain trade. "Only state power may dispose of the economic destinies of the country," Vyshnegradskii proclaimed.[46]

The reforms of the third generation. The retreat from liberal reform and the nationalist-chauvinist policy pursued by the government in the 1880s

---

[44]V. Ia. Laverychev, *Krupnaia burzhuaziia v poreformennoi Rossii* (Moscow, 1974), 59. Bunge's memorandum was published by A. Pogrebinskii in *Istoricheskii arkhiv* 2 (1960).
[45]L. E. Shepelev, *Aktsionnernye kompanii v Rossii* (Leningrad, 1973), 120.
[46]T. M. Kitanina, *Khlebnaia torgovlia Rossii v 1875–1914 gg.* (Leningrad, 1978), 95.

retarded the economic and social evolution of the country. The last decade of the nineteenth century began with a tragic famine that disclosed to the whole world the deep crisis of the imperial system of government. Harvest failures and famines were not uncommon in Russian history, but the vast human and territorial extent of the 1891–92 disaster testified to its deep social causes. Just as the Crimean defeat had done, the famine aroused Russian society, reminded it of the country's backwardness, and influenced the growth of both revolutionary and reform movements.

By the middle 1890s, two reform proposals were attracting the attention of Russia's ruling circles. One was authored by Bunge and the other by Witte. This marked the beginning of the third stage of the reform process in the nineteenth century. Its distinguishing characteristic was a compromise between West European and national-chauvinist ideas. This was reflected in the personal cooperation between Bunge and Witte, in the eclectic character of their programs, and in the evolution of their views.

Bunge had taken the first step toward a compromise with nationalist ideology when he sided with Fadeev and Vorontsov-Dashkov, and he was compelled to continue along this path. He presented his views in the form of a political testament, the so-called Posthumous Memorandum, which encompassed the totality of his outlook. This memorandum was printed in a limited number of copies [for internal government circulation—ed.] soon after Bunge's death in 1895 and had influence on state policy during the early years of Nicholas II's reign.[47]

Bunge's program represents a distinctive bridge between the outlooks of the second and third generations of reformers, and Bunge himself, taking into account a certain evolution of his views, can be seen as belonging either to the former or to the latter. His tendency to compromise assured him bureaucratic longevity and allowed him to remain in the post of chairman of the Committee of Ministers until his death. He also had ties to the imperial family. Bunge was invited to St. Petersburg in the early 1860s as a tutor to Grand Duke Nicholas Aleksandrovich, the oldest son of Alexander II, and he also taught both Alexander III

[47][N. Kh. Bunge], *1881–1894: Zapiska naidennaia v bumagakh N. Kh. Bunge.* See also George E. Snow, trans., *The Years 1881–1894 in Russia: A Memorandum Found in the Papers of N. Kh. Bunge* (Philadelphia: American Philosophical Society, 1981).

and Nicholas II when they were heirs apparent.[48] The dualistic character of Bunge's political testament has earned him a very contradictory reputation in historiography, on the one hand as a "Westernizer" and moderate liberal,[49] and on the other, as a "dyed-in-the-wool reactionary" and a Russifier.[50]

Despite its nationalist coloration, Bunge's memorandum is in many ways unique among reform proposals of the nineteenth century. It was very broad in scope and addressed many issues of government policy, including the nationality question. Moreover, it represented an attempt to analyze the process of reform itself, starting with the reign of Nicholas I, and it suggested ways to counter not just the revolutionary movement but also socialism as an ideology. Bunge condemned the politics of the "thirty years of stagnation" under Nicholas I and criticized the failure to complete the process of reform under Alexander II and Alexander III. He opposed the view, widely shared in bureaucratic circles, that revolutionary ideas had been imported into Russia from abroad, and he believed that the main cause of the political crisis of the autocracy lay in Nicholas I's refusal to undertake reform, especially the emancipation. Portraying Alexander II and "his closest associates" as reformers and supporters of the awakening of "the life of society," Bunge nevertheless accused them of "falling into the other extreme." "They thought that everything would turn out all right if society were given as great a degree of independence and freedom as possible, without infringing on the foundations of the political system (the autocratic monarchy)."[51] This was a veiled reproach to the reformers, not because they had granted too much autonomy to the localities but because the reforms did not go far enough and did not affect "the foundations of the political system."

However, Bunge himself did not raise the question of radical change in the system of government. He approved of Ignat'ev's attempts to involve "experts" in policy formulation. He proposed to reform and augment the Council of State by annually appointing one or two noble zemstvo deputies to it. He urged that experts from various parts of Rus-

[48]N. I. Anan'ich, "Materialy lektsionnykh kursov N. Kh. Bunge 60–80-kh godov XIX v.," *Arkheograficheskii ezhegodnik za 1977* (Moscow, 1978), 304.

[49]B. B. Glinskii, "Period tverdoi vlasti," *Istoricheskii vestnik* (August 1912): 689.

[50]I. F. Gindin, *Gosudarstvennyi bank i ekonomicheskaia politika tsarskogo pravitel'stva (1861–1892 gg.)* (Moscow, 1960), 56–57.

[51]Bunge, *1881–1894*, 8.

sia be more frequently invited to participate in the Council's deliberations and that they be given the right to vote, even if only in the departments [and not in the plenary session—ed.]. He wanted to simplify the legislative process and to speed up the passage of bills. Bunge did not directly address the issue of united government, though he did criticize ministerial disunity.[52]

His proposals for reform of local government were more definite. Bunge wanted the governor to be not just an agent of the Ministry of Internal Affairs but a representative of the central government, and he proposed introducing a special "provincial council," consisting of civil servants from various ministries (Internal Affairs, War, Finance, State Properties, and State Control) and representatives of the zemstvos, municipalities, and village communities. This council was to replace the numerous institutions and boards chaired by the governor and to consider provincial affairs but without intervention into "purely executive, administrative, and police" matters. Analogous institutions were to be created at the county level, but with a narrower jurisdiction. In this way, Bunge was striving to create something resembling a united government at the local level. He strongly supported broadening the competence of local self-government (zemstvo, municipal, and rural), but under the supervision of central authority. Bunge also called for providing the canton and the village with a system of administration that would reflect the already existing mix of different estates, a system in which all estates would bear equal burdens and be under the same institutions of self-government.[53]

The issue of a reasonable relationship between public and private principles in the economy was central to Bunge's thinking about the development of the cultural and material resources of the people. He wanted to promote popular education, raise the standard of living, and improve the fiscal system. He advocated expansion of "private land-ownership among the peasants"—that is, replacement of communal landholding by private landed property—but he also wanted smallholders protected from losing their land to pay off debts, and he cited the United States as an example of how this could be done. He favored short-term credit institutions and migration to help the peasantry.[54]

---

[52]Ibid., 78–82.
[53]Ibid., 85–88.
[54]Ibid., 104–8.

Bunge viewed equitable factory legislation, participation in profit-sharing, and establishment of closer relations between entrepreneurs and employees as the best methods for improving the condition of the working class. He viewed the spread of socialist ideas as dangerous, and he urged the Russian autocracy to promote legal and economic conditions that would improve "the material status of each and every one, both of the propertied and of the working classes." The government was to encourage private property and to make it easier for everyone to accumulate capital and to attain credit. Bunge warned against replacement of a "free" private economy by a "compulsory state or public economy," and he opposed government intervention into those branches of the economy that were "successfully managed by private entrepreneurship."[55] His solution to the appeal of socialism was to create in Russia a certain kind of "people's" capitalism under the aegis of autocratic power, a system ready to share profits with the workers and to function within the parameters of the legal state.

Of particular interest in Bunge's program is the segment dealing with nationality policy. Bunge argued that the nationalist orientation of Alexander III's policy was a manifestation of a universal phenomenon, the abandonment of the "cosmopolitan views of the end of the eighteenth and first half of the nineteenth century" in favor of nationalism, whose theoretical foundation was Friedrich List's *The National System of Political Economy.* "Hungary wants to Magyarize the Slavs, Germans, and Rumanians, Germany to Germanize the French in Lorraine, the Danes in Schleswig, and the Poles in Poznan. Poles aim to Polonize Little Russians in Galicia; we also try to Russify our borderlands," Bunge wrote.[56] He declared himself an enemy of "rootless cosmopolitanism" and "egotistic nationalism" alike. He favored the dominion of Russian state authority and Russian institutions but argued that the way of life of the minorities and the particularities of the borderlands had to be taken into account. The Russian language was to be the official language, but with retention of local languages and dialects, and the dominance of the Orthodox church was not to limit the religious freedom of the minorities or even of sectarians.[57]

A special section of the Posthumous Memorandum was devoted to

[55]Ibid., 133, 136–37.
[56]Ibid., 6, 16.
[57]Ibid., 17–22.

the Jewish question, and it contained numerous anti-Semitic sentiments. The profound anti-Semitism of both Alexander III and Nicholas II was no secret; Bunge thus had to consider the imperial prejudices, and he knew that any proposal for a radical change in the government's policy toward the Jews had no chance of success. What Bunge meant when he urged reform of Jewish legislation is not always clear and was beset with contradictions. He seemed to suggest an improvement of the Jewish situation in the Pale of Settlement and granting to the Jews limited rights that would assure them of a "lawful means of existence."[58] Bunge's program was bitterly attacked, but many of his proposals were ultimately adopted by prominent officials, including his erstwhile opponents.

In the late 1890s, Sergei Iu. Witte and his Ministry of Finance became the main advocates of reform, and for a while, Finance played a special role among the ministries. Witte originally saw the *Letters on the Contemporary Condition of Russia* as a revelation and participated in the press campaign against Bunge in 1886. However, once he assumed the post of minister of finance in the early 1890s, Witte set out to promote the capitalist industrialization of Russia and not only accepted many of Bunge's views but put them into practice. Witte's program was elaborated during the 1890s and attained its final form by the end of the decade. It was not presented in any single document, but we can reconstruct it on the basis of his writings and various memoranda submitted to Nicholas II.

Under Bunge's influence, Witte had changed his view of the commune. He came to support the repeal of joint fiscal responsibility, new passport legislation that would assure the free migration of the peasantry, and the dismantling of communal landownership. Following Bunge's advice and rejecting Katkov's economic doctrine, Witte introduced the gold standard. He began actively to seek foreign capital and pursued a policy of accelerated industrial growth. Once again, the slogan of catching up economically with the more advanced industrial powers of Europe came to the fore. Witte hoped to attain his objectives over roughly a ten-year period, at the cost of placing a heavy burden on the taxpaying ability of the population.

Whereas Bunge had called for broad development of private initiative, Witte relied on government intervention in the economy. Accordingly, he reformed the State Bank at the outset of his tenure as finance minister

[58]Ibid., 41.

in order to have it serve, as much as possible, the needs of his economic policy. Witte also increased government control over private banks and stock-exchange operations. Along with attracting foreign capital, he mobilized internal resources by using the state liquor monopoly and indirect taxation, and he provided tariff protection for Russian industry from Western competition. Witte's program also anticipated the peaceful economic penetration of the markets of the Near, Middle, and Far East, with government help, in order to secure them for the developing Russian industry.

Witte wanted to prove that Russia was able to progress economically without any changes in its system of government, and that a monopoly of political power could be successfully utilized to accelerate capitalist industrialization. As a result of the industrial surge of the 1890s, Russia did indeed narrow the gap with the economically advanced European countries, but Witte's system was rent by the profound contradiction of attempting to use the methods and instruments of an antiquated political system to promote the development of capitalism.[59] Moreover, Witte's dream of catching up economically with the progressive European countries was undermined by the Russo-Japanese War and the revolution that followed. The liberal circles of Russian society perceived Witte's policies as a "grandiose economic diversion of autocracy" from the kind of political and social reform they favored.[60]

Witte saw his general policy as also applicable to the management of the local economy. In his view, the precedents of the liquor monopoly and state ownership of the railroads gave promise of successfully replacing the zemstvo institutions with civil servants in the provinces. With this expectation in mind, Witte joined forces with Pobedonostsev to oppose I. L. Goremykin's proposal, inspired by Bunge's memorandum, to extend the zemstvo to the western provinces. After winning that battle, Witte founded in 1902 the Special Conference on the Needs of Agriculture to work out new peasant legislation. However, the Special Conference relied on the work of local committees that often reflected the point of view of liberal zemstvo members, and by this time Witte's views had undergone further evolution. D. N. Liubimov reported in his memoirs that Witte, in a conversation with the minister of internal affairs, Via-

[59][Compare also Theodore H. von Laue, *Sergei Witte and the Industrialization of Russia* (New York: Atheneum, 1969)—ed.]
[60]*Osvobozhdenie* 2 (1903): 24, as cited in B. V. Anan'ich et al., *Krizis samoderzhaviia v Rossii, 1895–1917* (Leningrad, 1984), 43.

cheslav K. Plehve, in the fall of 1902 questioned the very principles of government policy that had been enunciated at the beginning of Alexander III's reign, regretted the fact that the reforms of the 1860s were not completed, and urged reconsideration of the question of popular representation.[61] In that same year, the Ministry of Internal Affairs took over direction of agrarian policy from Finance. By 1903, Witte's influence had waned and, like Bunge before him, he was kicked upstairs to become chairman of the Committee of Ministers. Plehve thereupon became the most influential figure in the Russian government.

On the whole, Plehve was a partisan of stagnation. Although he recognized that the political system was in crisis and needed change, he was perfectly willing to "freeze" the existing state of affairs. At the same time, he was not averse to portraying himself as a reformer. The result of this stance was the Manifesto of February 26, 1903, written jointly by himself, the emperor, and V. P. Meshcherskii, which promised to help the peasantry, to expand local self-government, and to strengthen the influence of the Orthodox church. Plehve also proposed what came to be called the Plehve constitution: a Council for the National Economy attached to the Ministry of Internal Affairs and with the inclusion of specially invited "local leaders." Nevertheless, Plehve's policies meant growing reaction, persecution of zemstvo leaders, and an increase in the power of governors. Plehve was assassinated in July 1904.[62] His successor, Prince Peter Sviatopolk-Mirskii, was the last bureaucratic reformer before the revolution of 1905.

The Russo-Japanese War, especially the first Russian defeats, intensified the already growing revolutionary crisis in Russia and forced the government to reconsider the issue of reform. In many respects, Sviatopolk-Mirskii was a follower of Bunge. A. N. Kulomzin has said that he read his own copy of Bunge's [posthumous—ed.] memorandum to Sviatopolk-Mirskii and "told him all about its contents and that the imperial decree of December 12, 1904, was its complete fulfillment."[63] The prince apparently lacked a program of his own and to a certain

---

[61]"Otryvki iz vospominanii D. N. Liubimova (1902–1904 gg.)," *Istoricheskii arkhiv* 6 (1962): 81–83.

[62]For more on Plehve, see Edward H. Judge, *Plehve: Repression and Reform in Imperial Russia, 1902–1904* (Syracuse: Syracuse University Press, 1983).

[63]See Kulomzin's archival memoirs, *"Perezhitoe,"* Tsentral'nyi gosudarstvennyi istoricheskii arkhiv, f. 1642, *opis'* 1, d. 195, *list* 83.

degree became a reformer despite himself. "They attack me from all sides," he wrote to his relative D. S. Sheremetev in November 1904,

and, I think, they do not take into account the difficulty of my situation. Is it my fault that Russia has turned into a barrel of gunpowder?! . . . I beg you not to believe anyone who slanders me [by claiming] that I want a constitution. I so badly do not want a constitution that I recognize the need for reform lest we be soon forced to grant the kind of constitution that will be demanded. I assure you that we are not far from it, if we maintain the existing system of rule that has brought Russia to the boiling point.[64]

Sviatopolk-Mirskii attempted to include in his program the proposal, previously made by Loris-Melikov, to add elected representatives from local institutions of self-government to the Council of State, but it was rejected. The tsar clearly indicated that he did not favor any form of representation whatsoever. In a conversation with the Moscow marshal of nobility, Prince P. N. Trubetskoi, Nicholas II declared:

I recognize that in the case of today's Russia, the constitution would produce the same results as in Austria. Given the lack of culture among the people, our borderlands, the Jewish question, etc.—only autocracy can save Russia. Moreover, the peasant will not understand the constitution; he will understand only one thing, that the tsar's hands have been tied, and then—well, congratulations to you, gentlemen![65]

The decree of December 12, 1904, promised to observe legality, to develop self-government, to sponsor state-funded workers' insurance, to repeal many legal constraints on the minorities, and to grant greater freedom of the press. The issuance of this decree exhausted the "normal" peaceful reform potential of the Russian bureaucracy. However, it had no major impact on the evolution of Russian society. It became an example of reformism that came too late.[66]

Reform during revolution. With the outbreak of revolution in January 1905, the period of sluggish reformism ended, and the process of reform took off at a gallop, driven by events taking place no longer in the

---

[64]As quoted in K. F. Shatsillo, *Russkii liberalizm nakanune revoliutsii 1905–1907 gg.* (Moscow, 1985), 311.
[65]Ibid., 309.
[66]The peculiarities of the reform process and the issue of delayed or interrupted reforms or counterreforms are not discussed here. This theme is raised in the American historiography; see, for example, Richard Robbins, "Russia's Famine Relief Law of June 12,

chancelleries but in the streets. The era of drafting position papers was left behind, and the leaders of the Russian bureaucracy became reforming pragmatists. In less than a year, by October 1905, Russia acquired a united government in the form of a Council of Ministers and a representative institution in the State Duma. As Witte declared in the Council of State on May 30, 1907: "We had lived not a year between December 12, 1904, and October 17 of the following year, but perhaps half a century. From the perspective of October 17, the decree of December 12 was nothing but a historical document, and it is impossible to view it otherwise than as a historical document."[67]

In the revolution of 1905, Witte and Peter A. Stolypin were, so to speak, rival reformers. Witte's task was to arrest the spread of the revolution during its ascending phase. Once this was done, he was succeeded by Stolypin, whose function was to make sure that autocratic power and popular representation in the form of the new State Duma could coexist and work together. Both of them, however, championed liquidation of the commune and development of peasant entrepreneurship. Both Witte and Stolypin sought to complete the reforms of the 1860s at different stages of the revolution, but this objective was never attained. Witte drafted the Manifesto of October 17—which, it may be said, was issued a century too late—and participated in planning for the State Duma. He headed the first united government in Russia and made an effort to include representatives of society in it. Nevertheless, this united government failed to become a cabinet government, nor did the State Duma become a parliament, in the West European sense of these terms. Witte was forced to resign when the revolutionary wave retreated, because he was too radical a reformer.

In order to preserve the tsar's prerogatives and to secure the coexistence of his power with the united government and the Duma, Stolypin had to change the electoral law to assure a more compliant Duma. He also broke off the negotiations with Duma deputies and representatives of the public about a coalition or Cadet ministry. Stolypin's agrarian reform greatly affected the Russian village by 1914, but it did not make the peasant economically free, either within or outside of the commune,

1900: A Reform Aborted," *Canadian-American Slavic Studies* 10 (1976): 25–37, and Theodore Taranovski, "The Aborted Counter-Reform: Murav'ev Commission and the Judicial Statutes of 1864," *Jahrbücher für Geschichte Osteuropas* 29 (1981), 2: 161–84.

[67]*Stenogramma Gosudarstvennogo soveta,* May 30, 1907, Tsentral'nyi gosudarstvennyi istoricheskii arkhiv, f. 1148, o. 10, d. 3, l. 180.

and it was characterized by the compulsion typical of Russian reformism. Witte's ambitious agenda for catching up with the economically developed European countries was no longer on the table after the economic crisis of 1900, and especially after the Russo-Japanese War and the revolution of 1905. In 1913, V. N. Kokovtsev declared in the Duma that Russia was incapable of attaining this goal for at least the next twenty years.[68] The idea of accelerated industrialization was abandoned in favor of a harmonious evolution of agriculture and industry that would take into account Russian traditions and peculiarities.

CONCLUSION

Throughout the nineteenth century, the Russian autocracy was trying to maintain itself with the help of reforms that were intended to avert revolution and to prevent Russia from falling behind Europe. There were three stages in the evolution of Russian autocratic reformism. The first came in the early nineteenth century, during the reign of Alexander I. The French Revolution and the Napoleonic wars influenced the views of the emperor, the revolutionaries (the Decembrists), and of the reformers. Alexander I envisaged the evolution of Russia in purely European terms and planned to establish a constitutional regime and to abolish serfdom. His advisers turned to Western prototypes of reform and drafted legislation according to the emperor's instructions or reflecting his inclinations. Alexander's vacillations and delays in implementing reform contributed to the emergence of the first generation of Russian revolutionaries, who planned a bloodless coup d'état in order to achieve the same goals that the bureaucratic reformers had in mind.

The opportunity was lost, however, when Nicholas I ascended the throne during the Decembrist revolt and proved to be concerned only with shoring up his own regime. His entire policy was opposed not only to revolution but even to reform, which he considered too radical. Pursuing an active foreign policy, Nicholas I rejected constitutionalism and postponed emancipation, even as the need for it was becoming obvious. Nationalist themes appeared in the ideology of "official nationality"; the stress was laid on the historical peculiarities of Russia, particularly on the autocracy as the distinctive characteristic of Russian statehood. Au-

---

[68]*Stenograficheskii otchet IV Gosudarstvennoi dumy* (St. Petersburg, 1913), Part 2, p. 1944.

tocracy supposedly required no modernization; on the contrary, it represented the best method for safeguarding the rights of the imperial subjects. In the end, the country that for half a century had been perceived as the arbiter of Europe suffered a crushing defeat in the Crimean War and entered a state of profound crisis.

The second stage of both revolutionism and reformism occurred in the reign of Alexander II, during the 1860s and 1870s. Alexander became a reformer under the pressure of circumstances, and the times brooked no delay. A Westernizer in his general outlook, he nevertheless had to rely on a "national," or what might be called a Slavophile, doctrine to create a certain hybrid reform that would permit modernization of Russian society. He resolved only one of the two fundamental problems confronting Russia since the early nineteenth century: the abolition of serfdom. As for the other, the introduction of constitutional government, he was not willing to go any further than local representation in the form of zemstvos. He allowed the drafting of proposals to create a national representative body with advisory powers only under pressure from reformers and more likely than not merely as a tactical step.

The reforms of the 1860s and 1870s in some respects were a step back in comparison with the proposals for the transformation of Russia that had been elaborated in the reign of Alexander I. If the reformers of the first generation approached their task by asking what was the best political structure for the empire, the reformers of the second generation, though differing greatly among themselves in outlook, sought to attain only what would be agreed to by the emperor. This resulted in attempts to find some form of representation that would retain control over legislation in the hands of the crown and not impair the principle of autocracy. All such proposals, with the exception of Valuev's, entailed advisory legislative commissions with limited jurisdiction.

The reformers elaborating these proposals were faced with Russian revolutionary democrats whose radical demands they had no hope of assuaging. Moderate political reform, however, could have strengthened the monarchy and broadened its social appeal by gaining support from the liberal social elements. The refusal of the tsarist regime to permit any change in the political system not only fueled the growth of revolutionary sentiment but also distorted the liberal character of the reform process and gave encouragement to its opponents, who were inspired by the ideology of Slavophilism.

The third period of Russian reformism occurred in the 1890s and the early 1900s. It was preceded by the era of the counterreforms in the 1880s, during which some reform processes continued simply out of inertia but which also witnessed the triumphant reassertion of the principle of a powerful and immutable autocracy. This was a peculiar form of stagnation, which was marked not by inactivity but rather by strenuous efforts to reshape the reforms of the previous reign in line with conservative political and social principles. The counterreforms were designed to strengthen the principle of corporatism, to increase the power of the gentry in the provinces, and to maintain the peasant commune. The reformers of the third generation were permitted to devote their efforts only to the economy.

By this time, however, these efforts may well have been in vain. Political reform had to be introduced in the early stages of industrialization, as had happened in many European countries, for Russia to develop a capitalist society and economy. Russia, however, embarked late upon the path of industrialization, and the process was characterized by leaps driven by state interventionism. One must not, of course, minimize the significance of the reforms of the 1860s and 1870s. Serfdom was abolished, trial by jury was introduced, a new financial system was created, impetus was given to the evolution of local self-government, and glasnost became widespread. One should also not underestimate the changes in the economy produced by the policy of industrialization in the 1890s. Nevertheless, Russian society continued to lack political liberty. This huge, multinational empire had to either evolve into a constitutional, legal state or maintain itself through powerful authority. The Russian emperors preferred the second option and justified their choice ideologically by allusions to historical and national particularities and to the autochthonous character of the Russian political system. At the same time, they constantly underestimated the dangers of revolution.[69]

[69][The discussion brought out additional obstacles to the successful transformation of the Russian autocracy into a constitutional and law-based state. Terence Emmons noted that, although some sort of constitutional structure might have been possible in the eighteenth century, when the nobility was the only political class, this became progressively more difficult during the nineteenth, with the continued existence of serfdom and the increased political mobilization of other social elements. Both he and Ben Eklof commented on the inherent contradiction of an activist state pursuing a policy of social reform and yet infringing upon fundamental rights, such as those of property (not only those of the nobles, granted in 1785, but also, as noted by Zakharova, those of the peasantry after 1861) and violating the principles embodied in the idea of a constitutional order, a civil society, and the rule of law. The rule of law in particular, by its protection of individual rights, could also have been used to uphold the vested interests of the social elite that the state was intent on undermining. This tension was painfully obvious during

Russian society inexorably marched toward revolution during the course of the nineteenth century. The crisis of authority manifested itself above all in the autocracy's inability to adopt a consistent course of reform that would resolve in a timely fashion the problems that confronted the state and in its disdain for the reforms proposed by its own statesmen. The crisis of authority inevitably drove society down the path toward revolution and imposed its own imprint on the character of the Russian liberation movement. The three stages in the evolution of this movement were organically linked with the failures of the government's reform policy in the early nineteenth century, in the era of the Great Reforms, and at the beginning of the twentieth century. Each of these periods produced remarkable representatives of Russian reformist thought. Nevertheless, most of their proposals were not destined to be fully realized, and partial reform only paved the way for revolution.

the 1850s and 1860s in the case of individuals, such as Nicholas Miliutin, who mistrusted the gentry and relied on authoritarian means in order to attain reformist ends. Finally, Alfred Rieber stressed the difficulty of introducing constitutionalism in a multiethnic empire with a number of distinct religious traditions and a great variety of legal and administrative patterns and institutions, such as existed even under tsarist autocracy.— Ed.]

4

From reform "from above" to revolution "from below"

LARISA G. ZAKHAROVA

The peasant emancipation of 1861 and the acts that followed and were made necessary by the abolition of serfdom were the most important and radical reforms in Russian history between the eighteenth and early twentieth centuries. These reforms provided a new point of departure for the course of Russian history and determined the future path of Russia's historical evolution. They defined the essence of the agrarian problem that threatened, by the early twentieth century, to produce a revolutionary upheaval. Thus, the reforms "from above" that were promulgated between 1861 and 1874 largely determined the revolutions "from below" in 1905 and 1917.

It is fitting that a conference on reform in Russian and Soviet history take as its point of departure the year of 1861 and end with recent events. Indeed, perestroika has aroused unprecedented interest in the era of the Great Reforms, and much has been written about them in specialized periodicals and popular press alike. Public interest has been evident, and it is important that amid this cacophony one hear the authentic voice of the professional historian. Public opinion and various political ideologies and parties had found the history of the Great Reforms directly relevant also at other times, during other sharp turns in the history of Russia—for example, at the onset of the era of reaction in the 1880s and during the revolution of 1905. This is again the case today. The difference between 1861 and the present, between emancipation and current events, is a matter not only of years elapsed but also of two different historical epochs. And yet, despite this fundamental qualitative difference, the problems of the 1860s were similar to those of today. On the eve of the peasant emancipation, Russia, then as now, was choosing among alternative paths for its historical evolution.

THE PRECONDITIONS OF THE REFORM AND
THE DRAMA OF THE HISTORICAL SITUATION

The state's initiative in abolishing serfdom and promulgating other reforms manifested itself only after its defeat in the Crimean War and was prompted by the war's outcome and consequences. This is neither a new nor a controversial idea, but it has been presented in the historical literature one-sidedly. The government's actions have traditionally been viewed as outgrowths of the weakness of Russia's economic system, which was based on servile labor and had been in crisis throughout the second quarter of the nineteenth century. Use of new sources, however, permits us to evaluate the role of the Crimean War in the history of the reform from a different perspective.

The most painful consequence of the war—the greatest concern of the ruling elite—was the fear it aroused that Russia might lose great-power prestige, suffer international isolation, and be revealed to the entire world as, in the contemporary phrase, a colossus with feet of clay. The most capable individuals in the government and, most important, Alexander II understood that the foreign policy of Nicholas I was bankrupt. They strove to overcome Russia's isolation and worried about European public opinion. These goals ran counter to the ambitious ideology of "official nationality."

The Russo-French entente was proof of the break with the traditions of the defunct Holy Alliance, and it was justly perceived by European public opinion as also marking a turn toward liberalism in the internal policy of Alexander II. This is reflected in the correspondence between Pope Pius IX and Alexander II in the first half of 1859; in the impressions of A. V. Golovnin during his visit to France in 1857–58; in the attention that Alexander II paid to Baron August von Haxthausen's views on the peasant question; and in the founding in Belgium, in the summer of 1855, of the newspaper *Le Nord,* which was sponsored by the Russian government and whose purpose was "to acquaint Europe with the real situation in Russia" and "to attempt to destroy baseless and false views about our fatherland." (It was *Le Nord* that disclosed the first document leading to the emancipation, the Nazimov rescript of

November 20, 1857, a month before it was published in Russia.)[1] The international situation, especially Russia's relations with the West, influenced the new direction of the autocracy's internal policy. It was no accident that the first, albeit nebulous, hint about the forthcoming reforms was contained in the Manifesto of March 19, 1856, which made public the ignominious terms of the Peace of Paris.

The economic necessity of reform also became apparent during the war. However, the economic factor manifested itself not so much in a crisis of the serf economy as in the state of Russia's finances. The budget deficit had been growing steadily since the mid-1840s, and it grew even more rapidly during the war, increasing from 52 million silver rubles in 1853 to 307 million in 1856. It was the war and the large-scale issuance of paper money that destroyed the balance between Russia's foreign obligations and her ability to meet them. The share of the state's income from liquor sales increased from one-third in 1845 to 43 percent in 1853–56. The monetary system and the credit institutions were in complete disarray. Gold backing for paper currency dropped by 50 percent. Bank deposits decreased from 150 million to 13 million rubles between June 1857 and June 1859, and a run on the banks would have produced immediate bankruptcy. M. Kh. Reutern, the minister of finance, saw this not just as the insolvency of the credit system but as the insolvency of "all of Russia," which was unproductively wasting capital.[2] The critical financial situation was worsened by the imperial policy of the autocracy that strained budgetary resources. The Caucasus alone, for example, consumed one-sixth of total state income in the late 1850s.[3] The impoverishment of the ancient provinces of Central European Russia was one disastrous consequence of such an allocation of resources. The problems of the fiscal and bank crises were constantly being discussed during the early years of Alexander II's reign in the Financial Committee and in the Council of Ministers, as well as in the correspondence between the tsar and his brother and closest political adviser, Grand Duke Con-

[1]Tsentral'nyi gosudarstvennyi istoricheskii arkhiv (hereafter cited as TsGIA), *fond* 1093, *opis'* 1, *delo* 336, pp. 7–8; f. 1882, op. 2, d. 1933, pp. 1–2; Otdel rukopisei, Gosudarstvennaia publichnaia biblioteka (hereafter cited as OR GPB), f. 37, op. 1, d. 162, pp. 34, 40, 49; Otdel rukopisei Gosudarstvennoi biblioteki imeni Lenina (hereafter cited as OR GBL), f. 169, *karton* 61, p. 34; P. A. Zaionchkovskii, "K voprosu o deiatel'nosti Sekretnogo komiteta po krest'ianskomu delu v 1857 g.," *Istoricheskie zapiski* 58 (Moscow, 1956): 338–39.
[2]TsGIA SSSR, f. 560, op. 14, d. 294, pp. 1–20; f. 563, op. 1, d. 851, pp. 108–10; f. 565, op. 14, d. 152, pp. 493–97.
[3]OR GBL, f. 169, kart. 61, *edinitsa khraneniia* 25, pp. 31–35; ed. 26, pp. 18–19.

stantine Nikolaevich. Beginning in 1857, references to "the catastrophic condition of finances" became prominent in their letters.[4]

The awakening of public opinion also acted as a powerful stimulus to reform. Manuscript literature was more widely circulated than ever before, and the publications of Alexander Herzen's Free Russian Press penetrated into Russia from London. Glasnost burst forth after the dark years of "censorship terror" between 1848 and 1855. "Glasnost" as well as "the thaw" are terms and concepts symbolizing the year 1856, the year of awakening, and the harbingers of things to come. Of course, glasnost was mostly critical of the existing state of affairs, but its real impact lay in the creation of constructive proposals and drafts, typical especially of liberal thought, and it moved the government to action. Glasnost began to dissipate fear, that characteristic attribute of the Nicholaevan system. The emancipation of the society's intellectual and spiritual energies was a necessary precondition of reform. The change of rulers coincided with an acute and spontaneous consciousness of the need for fundamental reform and with the crisis of the Nicholaevan system as a whole and of its ideological underpinning, the theory of official nationality. "The former system has outlived its time": that was the judgment pronounced by M. P. Pogodin three months after the death of Nicholas I.[5]

Although the government decided to take the initiative on the issue of emancipation, it still lacked a definite plan of action or a program of reform. Alexander II, who ascended the throne in his late thirties, was a man with fully formed character and without particularly liberal inclinations. He set out upon the reformist path not out of conviction but under the pressure of harsh circumstances that he soberly and accurately evaluated. This was a prominent virtue of his mind and character. His aim was to restore the shaken prestige of Russia and to maintain autocratic power—in other words, the traditional political system. The official reform program was elaborated only gradually, in response to the changing political situation in the country and the shifting balance of forces favoring and opposing change. All of these factors, as well as the social psychology, the historical tradition, and the experience of both Russia and Europe, were dynamically interconnected. Manifesting them-

[4]Tsentral'nyi gosudarstvennyi arkhiv oktiabr'skoi revoliutsii (hereafter cited as TsGAOR), f. 722, op. 1, d. 928, pp. 184–201, 221, 266–71; d. 681, pp. 61, 63–65.
[5]M. P. Pogodin, *Istoriko-politicheskie pis'ma i zapiski v prodolzhenii Krymskoi voiny* (Moscow, 1874), 315.

selves under conditions of glasnost and the thaw, new and unusual for Russia, they pushed the authorities in the direction of a liberal course of policy.

Starting in the 1930s, Soviet historiography greatly exaggerated the role of the peasant movement and of its impact on the emancipation. One must overcome this stereotype and yet recognize the profound truth and perspicacity of the generalization formulated by M. E. Saltykov-Shchedrin, probably the most socially aware Russian writer and himself a participant in the reform process. Saltykov-Shchedrin concluded in 1863 that the peasantry, despite its lack of organization and the weakness of its protests, "succeeded in imprinting its ineradicable mark on the reform."[6] There were no disturbances, but the peasantry eagerly anticipated liberation; in 1855, thousands left their villages, seeking to reach the tsar in response to rumors 'that emancipation would follow the conclusion of the peace, and in 1858–59, many joined the temperance movement. Although the elite recognized that there was no immediate threat of a peasant uprising, the memory of past jacqueries, of Pugachev and Razin and of peasant involvement in European revolutions, nevertheless greatly increased its fear of the masses.

Most of the gentry openly or covertly opposed the reform, even after they had been compelled, as loyal subjects, to reconcile themselves to the monarch's will. The liberal gentry that recognized the need for emancipation was in the minority. The initial steps in the reform process, the formation of opposing factions in the Provincial Committees that began to be organized in early 1858, the consolidation of a conservative majority and a liberal minority—all strengthened the role and the significance of the liberal gentry. They also enhanced the autonomy of state power vis-à-vis the ruling estate. The bourgeoisie and the urban social groups played hardly any role in this process.

Under conditions of the objective necessity of emancipation and the absence of a class capable of a conscious and organized struggle for it, or of social forces capable of sponsoring it, the state undertook the role of leadership in all emancipatory reforms from beginning to end. However, the state, embodied in the monarch and his bureaucracy, was not a uniform entity. Both the bureaucratic elite in St. Petersburg, which formulated policy, and the key provincial officials were products of the

---

[6]As cited in S. Makashin, *Saltykov-Shchedrin na rubezhe 1850–1860-kh godov* (Leningrad, 1972), 339.

Nicholaevan system, and most of them had no plans for any kind of reform. Nevertheless, already by the mid-1850s, a solid albeit small circle of individuals, who shared views, convictions, and a program for reform, had emerged within the bureaucracy. This liberal—or, in the terminology of American historiography, enlightened[7]—bureaucracy was the avant-garde of the reform.

The liberal bureaucracy was formed within the ministries and other state institutions not in isolation but in contact with liberal representatives of society—litterateurs, scholars, and journalists, many of whom also worked in the civil service. This collaboration attained organizational form in 1845 with the establishment of the Russian Geographic Society, headed by Grand Duke Constantine Nikolaevich, who agreed with and favored the liberal bureaucrats. The Russian Geographic Society was institutionally attached to the Ministry of Internal Affairs, where the liberal bureaucrats were especially active. Nicholas A. Miliutin, their generally recognized leader, served in the ministry first as director of the Economic Department and then as acting assistant minister from April 1858 to April 1861. The influence of the liberal bureaucracy within the government during the drafting and implementation of the reform was not static; it waxed and waned under the pressure of reaction, but there is no doubt that it had decisive influence on all the major reforms.[8]

---

[7][Richard S. Wortman, *The Development of a Russian Legal Consciousness* (Chicago: University of Chicago Press, 1976); W. Bruce Lincoln, *In the Vanguard of Reform: Russia's Enlightened Bureaucrats, 1825–1861* (De Kalb: Northern Illinois University Press, 1982)—ed.]

[8][Although the phenomenon of Russian liberalism is relevant to Zakharova's concerns, it transcends the scope of her article and would require extensive separate treatment. The existence of Russian liberalism in the prerevolutionary period, and, in particular, its manifestations during the era of the Great Reforms, have been recognized in scholarship both before and after 1917. See, for example, A. A. Kornilov, *Obshchestvennoe dvizhenie pri Aleksandre II* (Moscow, 1909); Viktor Leontovitsch, *Geschichte des Liberalismus in Russland* (Frankfurt am Main, 1957); George Fischer, *Russian Liberalism* (Cambridge, Mass.: Harvard University Press, 1958); Terence Emmons, *The Russian Landed Gentry and the Peasant Emancipation of 1861* (Cambridge: Cambridge University Press, 1968) and *The Formation of Political Parties and the First National Elections in Russia* (Cambridge, Mass.: Harvard University Press, 1983); and N. M. Pirumova, *Zemskoe liberal'noe dvizhenie* (Moscow, 1977). These works, while they view particular government officials or policies as liberal, conceive of liberalism as primarily an ideology of the landowning gentry and later on of urban middle-class and professional social elements in opposition to autocracy. Although references to the liberal bureaucracy can also be traced to nineteenth-century sources, attempts to discern and systematically treat liberalism as an intellectual and political current *within* the government have been few and sketchy. Soviet historians, starting with A. E. Presniakov—see his introductory comments in *Dnevnik E. A. Perettsa* (Moscow, 1927), iii–iv—and including such prominent students of tsarist politics as Zak-

Thus, the dramatic character of the historical situation was already inherent in the preconditions of the reform process. Radical reforms were objectively necessary, but the social forces, the classes, required to put them into effect had not as yet arisen. The autocratic monarchy was the driving force behind the reforms, and this circumstance threatened to subordinate the reforms to the interests of the existing state power. As a consequence, reform would be unable to change the traditional political culture of the country. On the other hand, there was also the danger that the bureaucrats, inadequately restrained by social forces, would get carried away with their own schemes and legislate controls and structures that would prove barren.

THE RANGE OF ALTERNATIVES

In planning the peasant emancipation, Alexander II and his government considered various options and arrived at their decision not at once but only at the end of 1858. Their choice, competing with alternative proposals, won out and became the core of subsequent legislation. The first official government program of emancipation was contained in the rescript of November 20, 1857, to the governor-general of Vilnius, V. I. Nazimov, and in the rescript of December 5, 1857, to the governor-general of St. Petersburg, P. N. Ignat'ev. These became prototypes for the other forty-six provinces of European Russia. Basically, the program was a combination of local reforms that had already been carried out: the southwest inventories of 1848 and the emancipation of the Baltic peasantry in 1816–19. In this alternative, peasant emancipation went

harova herself and P. A. Zaionchkovskii, have routinely referred to the liberal bureaucracy without attempting to provide a theoretical explanation of its genesis and outlook, other than to treat its representatives and their outlook as somehow "objectively bourgeois" in character. Western scholars, such as Richard Wortman and W. Bruce Lincoln (see n. 7), who have done pioneering work on the mentality of the imperial civil service, have been loath to view the bureaucratic reformers as nineteenth-century liberals—and with good reason, given the character of Russian officialdom and the dominant political culture of tsarist autocracy. An exception to this general approach is Theodore Taranovski, "The Politics of Counter-Reform: Autocracy and Bureaucracy in the Reign of Alexander III, 1881–1884" (Ph.D. diss., Harvard University, 1976), where bureaucratic reformism is viewed as a variant of Central European liberalism. See also Theodore Taranovski, "Sudebnaia reforma i razvitie politicheskoi.kul'tury tsarskoi Rossii," in L. G. Zakharova, B. Eklof, and J. Bushnell, eds. *Velikie reformy v Rossii, 1856–1874* (Moscow, 1992), 301–17. For an interpretation that stresses the diversity of political outlook within the bureaucratic elite by the early twentieth century, as well as its affinity with the European social and political milieu, see Dominic Lieven, *Russia's Rulers under the Old Regime* (New Haven: Yale University Press, 1989).—Ed.]

hand in hand with the preservation of the landlords' seigniorial author-ity. The allotment of ploughland in usufruct under undefined terms could well result in mass dispossession of the peasantry, with the gentry retaining all rights of landownership. However, the swift evolution of the sociopolitical situation in the country demonstrated the inadequacy of this compromise variant. When the Provincial Committees were or-ganized in the first half of 1858, it became obvious that the majority of the gentry favored the Baltic alternative of landless emancipation. This, in turn, strengthened the hand of those officials who supported landless emancipation and of the erstwhile partisans of serfdom, who were forced to accept it as the lesser of evils.

The proponents of the Baltic form of emancipation reached the height of their influence in the spring of 1858. In June, the Imperial Public Library announced that it had 108 books on the peasant question, of which 17 dealt with Russian provinces, 18 with both Russian and Polish territories, and 73 with the Baltic region. A number of journals, includ-ing the official organs of the Ministry of Internal Affairs and the Ministry of Education, published articles on peasant emancipation in Livonia, Estland, and Courland. Most members of the Chief Committee on Peas-ant Affairs—including its chairman, I. F. Orlov, who was also chairman of the Council of State and of the Committee of Ministers—and other prominent and powerful statesmen favored the Baltic model. A. S. Men-shikov, the inept general who had been commander-in-chief during the Crimean War, recorded in his diary for January 11, 1858: "I am learning from those involved that they want to apply to our Russian properties the 1856 statute on the Estland peasantry."[9] Greatly alarmed, Nicholas Miliutin conveyed the same information in a letter to his brother Dmitry on April 19, 1858.[10] It was just at this time that the Chief Committee had introduced modifications into the program of the imperial rescripts that increased the likelihood that the emancipation would follow the Baltic pattern. An entry in Alexander II's aide-mémoire testifies that he, too, was not averse to the idea.[11]

The fact of the matter, however, when evaluating the question of historical alternatives, is that Alexander II and his government ultimately

---

[9]"Dnevnik A. S. Menshikova," Gosudarstvennyi arkhiv russkogo flota, f. 728, op. 1, d. 2438a, p. 3b.
[10]Larisa G. Zakharova, *Samoderzhavie i otmena krepostnogo prava v Rossii, 1856–1861* (Moscow, 1984), 99–100.
[11]Ibid., 92–124.

rejected the Baltic variant, despite the support it received from most of the bureaucratic elite and landowning gentry. In October and November 1858, the government adopted a completely new approach, unprecedented in past Russian and European practice. This program was officially confirmed by the emperor on December 4, 1858, and thus carried greater legal weight than the previous rescripts. The radical change was a decision to permit peasant redemption of allotment ploughland as property, the end result of which would be to transform the peasants into petty landowners. In turn, this meant abolition of the landlords' seigniorial authority and an extension of civil rights to the peasantry. Only six months before, such ideas had been considered treasonable and were prosecuted by the censors. For instance, K. D. Kavelin was dismissed as tutor to the heir apparent and fell into disgrace when his memorandum upholding such views was published in *The Contemporary*.

The reasons for such a sharp turn in government policy are a separate issue, which I have analyzed in my other works. The causes were many, they were interconnected and cumulative, and they arose within a brief interval, the late spring and the summer of 1858. Among them were major peasant disturbances in Estland after the New Peasant Statute of 1856 was implemented in April 1858, an unexpected event that shook the government and deprived the Baltic model of its former attractiveness; the rejection by imperial peasants of personal emancipation without land, granted by the decree of June 20, 1858; the personal impressions of Alexander II, who visited the central provinces in August 1858 and returned convinced of the peasants' enthusiastic faith in the tsar's emancipatory mission and in their own approaching freedom from servile yoke; the emperor's belief that the gentry, even if discontented, would loyally obey him; the discussions in the Provincial Committees that showed growing conflict within the gentry; and finally, the personal influence on Alexander II of his closest and absolutely trusted adjutant general, Ia. I. Rostovtsev, who sided with the new reform program.[12]

THE CONCEPTUAL DESIGN OF THE EMANCIPATION AND THE LEGISLATIVE ACTS OF 1861–1874

The conceptual design that shaped the legislative acts of 1861–74 emerged gradually from the collaboration of liberal bureaucrats and lib-

[12]Ibid., 124–35.

eral representatives of society. Its final formulation took place in the Editorial Commissions, an unprecedented and unique institution in Russian history that functioned between March 1859 and October 1860 and crafted what became the Emancipation Act of February 19, 1861. The Commissions were exceptional in several ways: liberals were in the majority in them, the membership was relatively young and included representatives of both the bureaucracy and society, the tempo of work was very intensive, and new methods of governmental decision making were employed, including glasnost and the publication and wide dissemination of drafts. This framework is significant for understanding not only the emancipation and the other peasant reforms of the 1860s but also the zemstvo reform of 1864, which was closely linked with peasant affairs, and indirectly all other reform legislation. The conceptualization of the emancipation was generalized to all the reforms of Alexander II.

According to the design of the liberal majority on the Editorial Commissions, laid out in several programmatic memoranda, the peasant emancipation meant the inclusion in a single legislative act of a revolutionary process of transformation. Its first stage was the emancipation of the proprietary peasant from personal bondage, and its final stage, the transformation of all peasants into smallholding proprietors, while preserving, of course, gentry landholding and large-scale agriculture. This goal was to be attained peacefully, without the revolutionary upheavals that had characterized the countries of Western and Central Europe. As noted in the Explanatory Memorandum that introduced the Editorial Commissions' drafts, "Russia is more fortunate in this respect. It is given the opportunity to benefit from the experience of other countries . . . and to traverse at once the entire road that lies ahead, from the initial steps to the final abolition of obligatory relations [between lords and peasants—ed.] by redemption of allotments."[13] Using the experience of the agrarian reform in France (the creation of small peasant proprietorship) and in Prussia (redemption as the method), the men who drafted the emancipation legislation formulated an independent variant, based on Russian conditions and traditions, to resolve the agrarian problem. Its key was the retention of the commune and of communal landownership while allowing better-off peasants to leave it. This Russian

---

[13]*Pervoe izdanie materialov Redaktsionnykh komissii dlia sostavleniia Polozhenii o krest'ianakh, vykhodiashchikh iz krepostnoi zavisimosti*, Part 18 (St. Petersburg, 1860), 1–20.

version of a new agrarian order entailed the coexistence of two types of economy: peasant smallholding and large-scale gentry agriculture. It was designed to prevent dispossession of the peasantry, proletarianization, and the revolutionary upheavals that would result.

One can judge how Nicholas Miliutin and his closest collaborators envisaged the future competition of these two types of agrarian economy by some of their comments and actions. When, at the height of the Polish revolt in 1863, Alexander II was compelled to recall Miliutin, whom he had sent into retirement, and to entrust him with reform of the rebellious provinces, the leader of the liberal bureaucracy, together with his old collaborators from the Editorial Commissions, Iu. F. Samarin and V. A. Cherkasskii, drafted an agrarian program for Poland that de facto legalized previous peasant seizures of landed property. One should not automatically view this Polish variant of the liberal bureaucracy's conceptualization, directed as it was against the seditious Polish nobility (*szlachta*), as reflecting its general design for Russia as a whole. However, we know the opinion of Miliutin's closest collaborator, K. D. Kavelin. He was the author of the 1855 memorandum urging redemption of peasant land and the coauthor with Miliutin of the proposal to free Grand Duchess Elena Pavlovna's peasants on her Karlovka estate, a proposal that served as the model for the emancipation as a whole, and he lived long enough to witness the transition to compulsory redemption that completed the reform. In an article published in 1881 commemorating the twentieth anniversary of the emancipation, Kavelin wrote that the significance of "this great deed" was "the creation in Russia of smallholding peasant landownership on a colossal scale. This event . . . laid the foundation for a new civic consciousness (*grazhdanstvennost'*)"; it was a prologue "to a new era of world history," still hidden from the inquisitive gaze of contemporaries. With this act, "we were the first to open the door into the future, and we had already stepped over the threshold."[14] One way or another, for the liberal bureaucracy the ultimate end of the emancipation was the creation of smallholding landownership as the basis of a future agrarian order that would include all of the peasantry—not just the former proprietary serfs but also the state and imperial peasants, as well as all other categories.

This conceptualization of the emancipation conjoined real and concrete aims with utopias and illusions that were very characteristic of this

[14]K. D. Kavelin, *Sobranie sochinenii* (St. Petersburg, 1898), 2: 646.

era and of all strands of social thought. The liberal members of the Editorial Commissions believed in the possibility of guiding the historical process, of constructing a future system, and of shaping the evolution of the country, which stood "on the threshold of a new life." To implement their aims, the commissions drafted a law that, unlike what had happened anywhere else in Europe, strictly regimented future developments.

This strict regimentation can be largely explained by the fact that the liberal bureaucracy functioned within the confines of an absolute monarchy based on serfdom and that it confronted real obstacles to its goals. For example, Alexander II absolutely refused to make peasant redemption of allotment land compulsory for the gentry, and the monarch's prerogatives were untouchable. The Editorial Commissions created an inner mechanism of reform that assured progressive continuity of movement from the beginning, freeing the person of the peasant, through the state of temporary obligation, to the final goal, the transition to redemption. The peasant's usufruct over the allotment was recognized "in perpetuity" and the peasant's obligations, once determined, as "permanent." Given the terms of the emancipation, the changing market conditions for both land and grain, and the gentry's dire need for cash to reorganize their mortgaged and overmortgaged estates (which constituted more than 50 percent of the total number of estates), the permanent character of the usufruct and of the dues owed by the peasant to the landlord forced the landlord to begin the process of redemption. Redemption was the only solution to the web of circumstances woven by the state. The peasants had no freedom of choice, either. Afraid that the economic burden of acquiring landed property might result in significant dispossession of the peasantry, the legislators forbade the peasants to refuse allotment land. Retention of the commune, and impediments to departure from it (though not an outright prohibition: departures required approval by two-thirds of the village assembly), largely served the same purpose. Except for Samarin, the authors of the draft legislation were not convinced supporters of the commune. They felt compelled to retain it as "a fact of life," a tradition, and hoped that it would eventually become extinct. The system of redemption of allotment land, including the state's role as creditor, was a heavy burden on the peasantry; the difference between the price paid to the gentry by the government and the peasant redemption payments was immense, and the state reaped the profit.

The reform design was more principled and decisive in the sphere of legal relations. The abolition of personal bondage signified the loss of the gentry's seigniorial authority. Peasant self-government was introduced: the canton (*volost'*) and the village community (*sel'skoe obshchestvo*, based on the peasant commune), with elective officials and assemblies. This represented the basis for subsequent peasant participation in other new institutions, such as the zemstvo and trial by jury. However, while protecting the interests of the peasants from erstwhile serfowners, peasant self-government was controlled by local authorities, and this increased the role of state power.

One of the cardinal postulates of the liberal bureaucracy's conceptual design for emancipation was the "wager" on the monarchical initiative in the process of reform. Monarchical initiative was a kind of guarantee that the reforms would be brought to fruition. It presupposed, according to Nicholas Miliutin, "the continuity and consistency" of reform. Monarchical leadership was a symbol of faith for the liberal bureaucracy, its credo, its substitute for a constitution that at the given historical moment could not be put on the reform agenda. This circumstance also made the reform program acceptable to the monarchy.

The resolution of the peasant problem also impinged on the reform of local self-government and, in part, of the administration of justice. The creation of an all-estate (*vsesoslovnoe*) elective zemstvo was closely linked in Miliutin's program with corporate (*soslovnoe*) peasant self-government. Peasant representation in the county (*uezd*) zemstvos (regardless of whether peasants were under the redemption regime or acquired land as private property) was equal to that of the other estates (noble and urban), with each group electing one-third of the deputies. Similarly, the all-estate institution of trial by jury involved significant representation of the peasants through the elective officials of their self-government, who were eligible to serve. The social inclusiveness (*vsesoslovnost'*) of the most important new political institutions (the zemstvo and the jury) was attained by means of social corporatism (*soslovnost'*); the estate organization of the peasantry helped the former serfs to enter the as yet unknown realm of social inclusivity and to join civil society. The new was attained by transcending the old, not by a revolutionary break with it.[15] This approach entailed the risk of the continuing via-

[15][Zakharova raises some fundamental and very little studied issues of prerevolutionary Russian social history and political culture alike that are deeply embedded in Russian

bility of serfdom, perpetuating its norms, traditions, and customs under new sociopolitical structures. This risk was even greater because fundamental political reform, the promulgation of a constitution, was not a part of the liberal design. The autocrat and the supreme and central state institutions retained their former prerogatives.

The organic link between emancipation and the other reforms was most clearly reflected in the principles that the liberal bureaucracy introduced into the institution of the arbiters of the peace (*mirovye posredniki*), created by the Emancipation Act of February 19, 1861, as the chief mechanism for implementing the reform. The arbiters of the peace were an estate institution, consisting of gentry only; the questions of whether it would be elective, and of the peasantry's involvement in it, were raised, but they could not be resolved before emancipation and

social nomenclature, legal terminology, and the language of bureaucratic politics. In law, prerevolutionary Russian society right down to 1917 was comprised of "estates" (*sosloviia* or *sostoianiia*), each of which had clearly defined rights and privileges. All four of the main estates (the nobility, the clergy, the burghers, and the peasantry) contained distinct subcategories (for example, personal and hereditary nobility), but even aside from that, the character and dynamics of Russian social reality were much more complex than the official schema allowed for. That in itself is a significant historical problem. The issue is further complicated by the fact that one of the key objectives of the liberal bureaucracy was to modernize Russian society by introducing the principle of citizenship. The liberals wanted to dismantle the hierarchy of estates and to base social relations on the equality of citizens under law. The Great Reforms in their totality were to be an intermediate stage in this process. Unlike many old institutions—for example, the peasant commune, the assemblies of the nobility, and the lower-level courts introduced by Catherine II— which were estate (*soslovnye*) in character and had competence only over members of a particular social category, some of the new institutions, such as the zemstvo, had jurisdiction over society at large. They were "all-estate" (*vsesoslovnye*) in character in that the estates retained aspects of their social identity (the electoral curiae combined elements of property franchise and estate affiliation), but their competence and functioning transcended estate categories. The next step in the process of reforming Russia would be "noncorporate" (*bessoslovnye*) institutions, organs of government or civil society instituted on the basis of citizenship without reference to estate affiliation in terms of their membership or function. The reformed courts came closest to this ideal. On the other hand, Russian conservatives always strove to retain the hierarchical principle of corporatism (*soslovnost'*) in institutional and social structures, and they identified corporatism with the survival of autocracy, gentry privilege, and the continuing social isolation of the peasantry. It is impossible to understand the issues at stake and the import of policies fought over in postreform Russian government without paying close attention to the vocabulary of its political culture. This vocabulary, like the social and political reality it portrayed and the future it sought to conceptualize and institute, represented a mixture of the old and the new, and its sources were to be found in both the Western and the Russian intellectual and institutional heritage. It reflected both the complex process of the interaction of Russia and Europe and the changing character of the imperial state and society in the nineteenth century. A good introduction to the topic is Gregory Freeze, "The *Soslovie* (Estate) Paradigm and Russian Social History," *American Historical Review* 91 (1986): 11–36.—Ed.]

were postponed for three years. Nevertheless, the liberal bureaucracy embedded in it such principles of the future judicial reform as independence, irremovability, and publicity. Arbiters of the peace were subordinated neither to the local or central administration nor to the assemblies of the nobility. The majority of the gentry, supported by the conservative bureaucracy, eagerly sought this last provision as a substitute for lost seigniorial authority. Arbiters of the peace could be removed from office only by a decision of a court of law, confirmed by the Senate. The liberal bureaucracy hoped to see arbiters of the peace pave the way for the creation both of new local government institutions and of the lowest organ of the new administration of justice, the elective justice of the peace (*mirovoi sud'ia*). It is typical and symptomatic that draft legislation for both the arbiters of the peace and the zemstvo reform were prepared by a commission of the Ministry of Internal Affairs chaired by Nicholas Miliutin, just as the Editorial Commissions were beginning their work.[16]

The liberal conceptual design was quite coherent and embraced the full range of reforms. Miliutin believed that the emancipation, the introduction of local self-government, and the new judicial institutions had to be integrated with radical fiscal reforms. However, these dreams, as well as the efforts of his highly placed patrons to have him appointed as minister of finance, were never realized. That post was given to Reutern, who was, however, ideologically close to Miliutin and also belonged to the liberal bureaucracy. Reutern had received his education in the Naval Ministry under Grand Duke Constantine Nikolaevich, when it was known as "the Ministry of Progress," and underwent "training" (*stazhirovka*—another term characteristic of those years) in Europe and America between 1856 and 1858, after which he served as a member of the Editorial Commissions. He presented his plan of financial reform to Alexander II in 1866. "The Great Reforms," he wrote, "have found us in a situation of a decaying system of credit institutions, disordered circulation of money, and insufficient national capital—that is, without means of transportation [or] liquid capital." He argued that continuation of the reform effort was a key precondition of successful financial reorganization. In his view, "only growing confidence in the stability of

[16]N. F. Ust'iantseva, "Institut mirovykh posrednikov v sisteme gosudarstvennogo stroia Rossii (formirovanie i kompetentsiia)," *Gosudarstvennyi stroi i politikopravovye idei Rossii vtoroi poloviny XIX veka* (Voronezh, 1987), 24–33.

our political institutions, in the solid but gradual and unhurried grafting of already undertaken reforms onto our civil life, and the belief that we are unwilling to interfere in the political disputes of other countries" could halt the emigration of capital and, on the contrary, assure its accumulation and attract foreign investment. The resolution of the problems of the money market depended on a "reduction of government demand," so that savings could be directed into all branches of industry in order to increase the bullion backing for the ruble. Government borrowing should be reallocated from unproductive expenditures to productive uses, in the first place to railroad construction. The internal market should be opened to private interests and to the railroads. Reutern viewed large-scale railroad construction by private Russian and foreign capital, with government help, as the solution to the empire's difficult fiscal situation and saw in it "the present and future of Russia." A key element in this plan was the decrease in military expenditures and consequently in imperial ambitions. This last position was not shared by the liberal bureaucracy as a whole, and it ultimately ended Reutern's career.[17]

Bureaucratic liberalism may have had intellectual and programmatic coherence in its efforts to reform economic and social relations, create a civil society, and introduce new public and political institutions, but it was nonetheless lacking. As pointed out earlier, it was based on the notion of monarchical initiative instead of being true political reform, although one could surmise that in a distant future some sort of a constitution was seen as inevitable. V. P. Semenov-Tian-Shanskii (the son of Peter Petrovich, the scholar and a member of the Editorial Commissions) wrote that Miliutin "believed in a representative form of government. He viewed the reforms of Alexander II as preparing Russian society to accept the principle of popular representation within a monarchical form of government."[18] There is documentary evidence that Grand Duke Constantine Nikolaevich favored very limited public representation from zemstvo and gentry assemblies in the system of supreme state institutions in his proposal of 1866 (before Karakozov's assassination attempt). Even more relevant in this context was the link between Loris-Melikov's so-called constitution and the precedent of the Editorial

---

[17] TsGIA, f. 560, op. 14, d. 294, pp. 1–20; f. 563, op. 1. d. 9, pp. 1–8.
[18] V. P. Semenov-Tian-Shanskii, "Vospominaniia 'Stranitsy semeinoi khroniki': Fragment dopolneniia k gl. VII 'Osvobozhdenie krest'ian'," Bakhmeteff Archive of Russian and East European History and Culture, Columbia University, 57.

Commissions.[19] These, however, were only future perspectives, and the reform design of the late 1850s and the early 1860s was not crowned by the principle of constitutionalism. This was its tragic incompleteness.

An indirect piece of evidence that the liberal bureaucracy had a quite coherent view of reform is to be found in the integral nature of the programs opposing it. An alternative conception was most fully and clearly expressed within the bureaucracy by Peter A. Valuev in his memoranda and counterproposals regarding the peasant and zemstvo issues. Valuev was an eager and indefatigable critic of the Editorial Commissions, and he also succeeded Nicholas Miliutin as the official in charge of these two most important reforms. Valuev's basic positions were landless emancipation and the retention of gentry landownership and the privileges based on it; establishment of the zemstvo on the basis of assemblies of the nobility, practically without peasant participation; introduction of a limited and oligarchical national representative institution, based on the gentry zemstvo and subordinated to the Council of State; and complete rejection of the arbiters of the peace because they were not under gentry control. His reference to the arbiters of the peace as a product of the liberal bureaucracy is typical: "I do not like the friends of our enemies."[20] Moreover, the gentry as a whole, whether liberal, conservative, or reactionary, opposed the proposals emanating from the Editorial Commissions. Gentry views on emancipation were by no means uniform: The liberal gentry urged compulsory redemption of 50 percent of the allotment by the peasantry, abolition of gentry seigniorial authority, all-estate self-government, and a new justice administration, whereas the conservatives wanted landless emancipation and preservation of the legal privileges of the nobility. But all of them agreed on one issue: They were opposed to any great expansion of state power in the economic and social spheres. In fact, the design of the liberal bureaucracy produced increased state power over the economy and made the government function as the arbiter of relations between owners (or proprietors) of the land. The state played a key role in the establishment of new forms of property, and this could not but affect the emerging civil society in Russia.

The drafts of legislation, codified by the Editorial Commissions, were

---

[19]Larisa G. Zakharova, "Perepiska Ministra vnutrennikh del P. A. Valueva i gosudarstvennogo sekretaria S. N. Urusova v 1866 g.," *Istoriia SSSR,* 1973, no. 2: 115–27.

[20]See Larisa G. Zakharova, "Autocracy and the Abolition of Serfdom in Russia, 1856–1861," *Soviet Studies in History* 26 (1987).

based on the ideas of the liberal bureaucracy. Changes were introduced during the debates in the commissions by deputies from the Provincial Committees, and later on in the Chief Committee and in the Council of State. The most important ones were cuts in the allotment norms and increases in peasant obligations, which obviously had an impact on the ultimate goal of the reform, the redemption; the creation of a new category of "free allotment" [also known as "the pauper's" or "the beggar's" allotment, under which peasants could receive gratis one-quarter of their normal allotment in exchange for giving up claims to the rest—ed.], proposed by a supporter of the Baltic variant of emancipation, Prince P. P. Gagarin, which opened the way to dispossession and represented one of the main reasons that peasant landholding decreased in comparison with the prereform era; and the replacement of the permanence of peasant obligations by mandatory review after a twenty-year period. Although the liberal bureaucracy considered the permanence provision crucial, Miliutin viewed this last change as inconsequential and argued that by the early 1880s any minister of internal affairs would opt for compulsory redemption, as indeed proved to be the case. On the whole, the government operated on the principle that the two sides should "bargain over the terms of redemption" (*otkupnoi torg*).

Despite Miliutin's resignation soon after emancipation and the transfer of the zemstvo reform into the hands of his enemy, Valuev, the vision of an all-estate local self-government ultimately triumphed, in its basic conception if not in its original scope. Valuev did not succeed in excluding the peasantry from the zemstvos; peasant representation was relatively important at the county level, although the gentry was given the leading role (except in the peasant zemstvos of the northern provinces). Most important, the social composition of the zemstvo was not predetermined once and for all in the law, and the new institution would inevitably develop in response to postreform social and economic evolution. The promulgation of the 1864 zemstvo reform also made inevitable the introduction of elective and all-estate municipal self-government.

On the whole, the reforms incorporated the cardinal principles advocated by the liberal bureaucracy: separation of legislative, administrative, and judicial powers; property qualification for franchise; all-estate local self-government; the "noncorporate character" (*bessoslovnost'*) of the reformed justice administration; irremovability and relative independence of the judiciary; and glasnost in the operations of the new institutions. However, the radical financial reform envisaged by Reutern did not take place. Most important, the framework of the legal state (*pravovoi poriadok*) was being introduced without constitutional guarantees and with the retention of autocratic power, its bureaucratic apparatus, and the traditional political culture.

THE IMMEDIATE AND LONG-RANGE CONSEQUENCES OF THE GREAT REFORMS

Some consequences of the reforms manifested themselves very quickly. Redemption of ploughlands, despite its not being obligatory for the landlords, proceeded apace everywhere. By 1870 it embraced 45 percent of former serfs, and by 1880 it had reached 85 percent; in 1881 the government adopted compulsory redemption, as Miliutin had predicted in 1860. The process of redemption was large-scale and included all categories of the peasantry after the emancipation of the imperial family's peasants (1863) and the state peasants (1866). The liberal bureaucracy's goal of creating peasant smallholding on a scale previously unseen in any other country was largely realized by the late nineteenth century. As for gentry landownership, based on cultivation of large estates (in contrast to peasant smallholding), it gradually but irrevocably lost its position, comprising by 1905 only 62 percent of all privately owned land, and in 1916, less than 50 percent—half of which was rented out.

The coexistence of two agrarian economies, peasant farming and large-scale gentry agriculture, was at the core of the reform's design for the near future, and it continued to define the socioeconomic evolution of the postreform village and the character of the agrarian system. Emancipation resolved the peasant question but not the agrarian problem, which remained on the agenda and became very acute in the early twentieth century. It augured mass peasant disturbances and revolutionary upheavals that had not been anticipated by the legislators, who were convinced and sincere adherents of evolution and progress.

Although the legislators' "wager" on peasant acquisition of landed property by means of redemption became law, the long-range consequences of the reform sharply diverged from the original intentions. Cutting down on peasant landholding was initially allowed only in exceptional cases. However, as a result of changes introduced under pressure from the gentry and the majority of the bureaucracy, the total area of allotment land ultimately decreased by about 20 percent (and in a number of provinces the decrease was considerably greater). The resulting dispossession of the peasantry was precisely what the liberal bureaucracy had striven to avoid. Another reason for this undesirable development was demographic. Population in the core territory of the Russian state, as established by Peter the Great, increased by approximately 25 million in the thirty-six years following the emancipation, reaching a total in 1897 of 78 million, the vast majority of whom were peasants. The legislators had foreseen the effect of this growth. Miliutin, debating the deputies from the Tambov Provincial Committee in the Editorial Commissions, who wanted the gentry to be compensated for their losses by state-owned land, argued that treasury lands must be preserved, because natural population growth would produce a shortage of land among the peasants, and they would then need additional acreage.[21] As is well-known, the emancipation resulted in a decrease of peasant landholding and led to land hunger, and that prepared the ground for a mass peasant movement.

The acute land hunger of the peasantry was exacerbated by excessive and impoverishing redemption payments. By 1866, the ministry of finance declared that "arrears in redemption payments at least in some cases are due to the fact that the payments exceed peasant means."[22] The government did not react at once, but in 1883 it was compelled, despite the turn toward a policy of reaction that had taken place, to reduce redemption payments. Even so, what the peasants paid to the state as creditor was three times what the gentry had received for their land. The state not only failed to contribute its own resources but, on the contrary, made a fortune out of the peasantry. The revolution of 1905 put an end to this robbery. The system of redemption worked out in the Editorial Commissions failed to anticipate the extent of the impoverishment that the reform would produce as the price of redemption rose during the legislative process.

Moreover, the reformers' expectations that the commune would die out, that joint fiscal responsibility would soon be repealed, and that there would be an inexorable albeit gradual transition from communal to household and individual landownership proved completely unjustified.

[21] *Osvobozhdenie krest'ian v tsarstvovanie Aleksandra II: Khronika deiatel'nosti Komissii po krest'ianskomu delu N. P. Semenova* (St. Petersburg, 1890), 2: 72, 85–86.
[22] TsGIA, f. 560, op. 14, d. 294, p. 37.

This was not just the result of the policy of Alexander III's government, which, by legislative acts in 1886 and 1893, increased the power of the patriarchal head of the family over its members and shored up the commune by closing off even those opportunities for departure permitted by the Emancipation Act. The centuries-old tradition of the commune, founded on customary law, proved much more durable than had been anticipated by the reformers. When in 1870 the Chief Committee on the Organization of Village Society, chaired by Grand Duke Constantine Nikolaevich, investigated peasant attitudes toward the commune in several central provinces, it found that the vast majority supported complete preservation of the commune.[23] Communal landholding, which represented 85 percent of peasant landownership in European Russia, was not undermined until 1906, and it was not destroyed (or there was not enough time for it to be destroyed) even by the agrarian reforms of Stolypin. This distinguishing characteristic of Russia's agrarian system influenced not only the processes of socioeconomic change but also peasant social psychology, where notions of collectivism took precedence over those of individualism, just as the idea of equality prevailed over that of liberty. The family, the commune, and the state weighed heavily on the personality of the peasant.

It should be noted here, however, that the very conception of property was significantly changed by the peasant emancipation. In order to provide legal justification first for allotting arable land to the peasantry in permanent usufruct and later on for its redemption, Iu. F. Samarin introduced the concepts of "full" and "partial" landed proprietorship. In theory and in the letter of the Emancipation Act, all land was gentry property [whatever the peasants might have thought on the subject—ed.]. The landlords, however, could dispose at their discretion of only their "full" property—that is, their estate (*pomest'e*) and eventually those parcels (*otrezki*) of the allotment land that the law allowed them to keep.[24] "Partial" property—that is, the allotment land—was eventually

---

[23]M. N. Druzhinin, "Glavnyi komitet po ustroistvu sel'skogo sostoianiia," in *Issledovaniia po sotsial'no-politicheskoi istorii Rossii* (Leningrad, 1971), 275–80.

[24][The Emancipation Act dealt only with private landownership and proprietary serfs. The noble landlord was the legal proprietor of all ploughland, whether cultivated by himself or parceled out to his serfs, as well as of forests, meadows, etc. The assumption behind the idea of peasant allotment was that the peasant should be given enough arable land for economic self-sufficiency and that this would roughly correspond to what he had been cultivating before 1861. Various provisions of the Emancipation Act allowed the lords under certain conditions to cut down on peasant landholding as part of the final settlement between the two sides.—Ed.]

to belong to the peasantry, but as communal, not private, property. Thus, the 1861 reform as a whole did not strengthen the principle of private property but, on the contrary, undermined it. Furthermore, this redistribution of landed property between landlords and peasants gave the state the right to exercise control over the property rights of landowners and greatly strengthened its role in socioeconomic development.

The emancipation introduced millions of peasants to civil existence. The zemstvo and municipal reforms of 1864 and 1870 created all-estate representative organs of local self-government. Despite the numerical preponderance of the gentry in the zemstvo assemblies and of the privileged social orders (nobility and merchants) in the municipal councils of St. Petersburg, Moscow, and the provincial capitals, representation of peasants in county zemstvos and of small taxpayers in most town councils was not mere fiction. The first elections to county zemstvo assemblies in 1865–66 in the twenty-four provinces of European Russia produced the following average social composition of assembly delegates: gentry, 42.5 percent; merchants and burghers, 12.3 percent; peasants, 38.8 percent, and clergy, 6.4 percent. In the provincial zemstvo assemblies, delegates from the gentry were in an absolute majority, which they retained throughout the assemblies' existence. However, county zemstvo assemblies over a twenty-year period (up to 1886) manifested a tendency toward a decline in gentry representation in certain regions; for example, in the central industrial area, gentry delegates comprised 38.2 percent of the county delegates in the province of Kaluga, 37 percent in Vladimir, 35.6 percent in Nizhnii Novgorod, 34 percent in Iaroslavl, 32.7 percent in Kostroma, and 30.1 percent in Moscow. Apart from the northern regions, where there were zemstvos dominated by the peasants, Taurida in the Crimea stood out from other provinces, averaging only 25.5 percent gentry representation in county assemblies during the middle 1880s.[25] This decline in gentry representation reflected changes in the agrarian social structure resulting from the emancipation and was even more pronounced in the social composition of the electorate.

Analogous indicators can be seen in the social composition of municipal governments. A total of 27,834 delegates were elected to 613 town councils (63 provincial and 550 county and special ones) between 1887 and 1889. Some 23,400, or 84 percent, served in the councils of county

[25]Larisa G. Zakharova, *Zemskaia kontrreforma 1890 g.* (Moscow, 1968), 12–27, and appendix 5, pp. 170–71.

towns. In these towns, 51.1 percent of the delegates came from the non-privileged estates of petty burghers, artisans, and peasants. As far as property qualifications for the franchise were concerned, 53 percent of the delegates to the 613 councils were in the categories of small and very small urban taxpayers. The senatorial inspections of 1880–81 concluded that "municipal government is almost completely in the hands of the commercial class, primarily of petty and by no means well-off traders, who numerically overwhelm all other elements of the electorate."[26]

The representation of taxpaying, nonprivileged estates was even more pronounced in a completely new institution created by the judicial reform of 1864, the jury. In 1883, peasants made up 57.4 percent and burghers 18.6 percent of jurors in twenty provinces of European Russia.[27] The creation of a "new civic consciousness" that the reformers had incorporated into the legislation was becoming real in the process of the reforms' implementation. By virtue of the radical character of the reforms, this process was becoming largely irreversible.

The institutions created by the reforms were vulnerable not because of their social composition but because of their lack of independence, for these new, all-estate, elective bodies were incorporated into the old system of the autocratic monarchy. In the final account, they were subordinated to the state, and they functioned under the conditions of authoritarian power and the traditional political culture. The old administration, both in the center and in the provinces, retained its positions and was elevated above the new institutions. The entire system of supreme executive and legislative advisory organs was untouched by the reforms. Alexander II, having so resolutely supported the abolition of serfdom, stubbornly and consistently denied the necessity and possibility of a constitution for Russia or of any kind of direct limitation on his power. If one may speak of Alexander's convictions, they included first and foremost a faith in the autocratic monarchy as the best and most organic form of government for the Russian people.

While initiating the steps that led to emancipation, Alexander II also created the Council of Ministers, which he personally chaired. The council did not signify the acceptance of the principle of a collegial and united government; rather, it was designed to increase the unlimited power of

[26]L. F. Pisarkova, "Sotsial'nyi sostav gorodskikh glasnykh nakanune kontrreformy 1892 g.," *Istoriia SSSR*, 1989, no. 6: 152–60.

[27]A. K. Afanas'ev, "Sud prisiazhnykh v Rossii (organizatsiia, sostav, i deiatel'nost' v 1866–1885)" (author's abstract of candidate diss., Moscow, 1979), 13.

the autocrat. For its first few years, the council lacked defined institutional status and was convoked each time by the personal decision of the tsar. Its sessions were often adjourned in midsentence if the emperor became tired or bored, and no minutes were kept of the proceedings. It was this institution that symbolized the traditional principle of Russian statehood, not the Editorial Commissions, with their liberal program, unity of purpose, involvement of the public, and new government practices. It is also no accident that all the reforms, as soon as they became law, were subjected to limitations and distortions. The well-known "improvements" in justice administration, zemstvo and municipal self-government, censorship regulations, and education, constantly revising the legislation of the 1860s and 1870s, testified to the autocracy's hostility to the new political institutions and to the legal norms of contemporary Europe.

Even more threatening to the reforms was the autocracy's imperial policy, which ran counter to Reutern's program of fiscal recovery. Vast military expenditures were a heavy burden on the state budget. The dramatic confrontation between Reutern and Alexander II before the tsar declared war on Turkey in 1877 was the last straw. The autocrat took over, disregarding the conclusions of his minister of finance; Reutern immediately decided to resign once the war was over and regardless of its conduct and results, because he considered the cause of fiscal reform lost.

The autocracy's lack of consistency in following the liberal course once it had been adopted, the halfheartedness and incompleteness of the reforms, and the burdensome economic terms of the emancipation were all reflected in the political consequences of the reforms. Peasant dissatisfaction with the land settlement, widespread refusal to reach agreements with the landlords, and peasant demonstrations and massacres at Bezdna and Kandeevka paved the way for the appearance and spread of revolutionary democracy. Government persecution of the liberal arbiters of the peace, especially by the new leadership of the Ministry of Internal Affairs, weakened the liberal social elements that had only recently been involved in drafting the emancipation law. Delay in reforming higher education produced the student movement, even within military schools, and led to protests and resignations among the liberal professoriat, formerly completely loyal to the government. Political agitation spread to Poland and provoked the 1863 revolt, and noble assemblies in St. Petersburg and Moscow demanded political rights for the gentry.

Alexander II and his government failed to react adequately to the depth and danger of the impending confrontation with society. Late in 1861, Alexander wrote to his brother Constantine: "The roots of evil doubtlessly exist and have already penetrated rather deep, and that is why we are not dozing. To promote greater unity in the actions of the government, I have ordered strict compliance with the procedure already established in 1857 for the submission of all significant issues to the Council of Ministers."[28] These words show both the tsar's perspicacity in regard to the political consequences of the reform and his shortsightedness, his inability to understand that in the new Russian conditions there was no future in relying on the old methods and traditional forms of rule, rooted as they were in a serfdom that had just been abolished by the government itself. However, this outlook continued to be characteristic of Alexander for some twenty years and would become even more pronounced after Karakozov's assassination attempt in 1866.

Quite different was the reaction of Nicholas Miliutin, the leader of the liberal bureaucracy. Upon departing Russia in early May of 1861, he wrote to his friends and collaborators, Samarin and Cherkasskii, that "now all hope rests with the liberal gentry in the provinces" and with the arbiters of the peace, devoted to the cause of emancipation. In two letters to his brother Dmitry, the minister of war, written late in 1861 and early in 1863, he wrote of the urgent need to create a middle-of-the-road party (*le centre*) within society to support the reformist course within the government, and he declared that the state's loss of initiative in sponsoring progressive reform threatened the collapse of the cause of the peasant emancipation and of the creation of civil society.[29] Such apprehensions were expressed by many other reformers over the years, especially eloquently by Golovnin and Kavelin.

The active and passive confrontations of state and society were resolved by the events of March 1, 1881, when Alexander II, seemingly favoring new liberal concessions, agreed to convoke the Council of Ministers to discuss the "constitution" of Loris-Melikov and was assassinated by the populists within the hour. The tragic end of the reformer

[28]TsGAOR, f. 722, op. 1, d. 928, p. 270.
[29]OR GBL, f. 169, kart. 69, ed. 12, pp. 9–14.

signified also the end of the reform era. Instead of a "constitution," Russia received first the manifesto "On the Immutability of Autocracy" of April 29, 1881, and then, on August 14, 1881, the Regulation on Measures to Protect State Security and Public Peace. Not an assembly of elected representatives of zemstvos and towns, but an administrative "Special Conference" was to determine the character of Russian politics. According to this regulation, any locality could be declared to be under extraordinary protection, and any of its inhabitants could be arrested and exiled without trial for five years or could be turned over to a court-martial. The local administration was empowered to close schools and commercial and industrial establishments, to stop the activity of the zemstvos and town councils, and to shut down the organs of the press. This regulation, promulgated initially as "temporary," for a three-year period, was subsequently renewed periodically and remained in force until the revolution of February 1917. The leadership role of the auto-cratic monarchy in progressive reforms had been exhausted.

The traditional political system and its political culture were inextri-cably intertwined with serfdom, and they manifested vitality in the strug-gle with reformist innovations. Unlike the reforms of the 1860s, the counterreforms of the 1880s and early 1890s had neither a conceptual framework nor a coherent program. A. D. Pazukhin, until then an un-known marshal of the nobility of Alatyr county, was rescued from the provincial backwater of Simbirsk by D. A. Tolstoi, the minister of in-ternal affairs, and supported by M. N. Katkov, to provide ideological support for the militant elite with his primitive and destructive program. This was a fitting reflection of the intellectual level of the government that undertook the counterreforms. The simplistic design of the coun-terreforms was to strengthen the old order and the traditional state struc-ture as much as possible under the new circumstances. In order to attain this goal, one did not require the historical experience of Europe, thoughtfulness and learning, professional expertise, or the energy and élan of youth—all of which had been distinguishing traits of the re-formers.

The reform program of the 1860s took as its point of departure the premise that fundamental social and economic change was paramount. The counterreforms of the 1880s, on the other hand, focused first and foremost on the new political institutions: peasant self-government, the all-estate zemstvo, the new system of courts and judicial procedure, glas-nost, and university autonomy. What followed was the law on the land captains and the abolition of the justices of the peace in 1889, the legislation on the peasant family and the commune of 1886 and 1893, the University Statute of 1884, the zemstvo and municipal acts of 1890 and 1892, the intensification of censorship, and the shutting down of democratic and liberal publications.[30] The chief thrust of the counterreforms was not so much to restore social corporatism, although efforts were made to support the nobles' privileges, as it was to impose state dominance over society and its institutions: to strengthen the administrative system and to repress social initiative by state power; to preserve the commune and to subordinate peasant self-government to the bureaucracy by means of the land captains; to subject the peasants to the tutelage of the family and the commune rather than extend and develop their individual rights. As Katkov put it, "The government is advancing, the government is coming back."

However, in the socioeconomic sphere, the reform continued: compulsory redemption for the remaining 15 percent of the peasants under temporary obligation and reduction of the redemption payments in 1881–83; the founding of the Peasant Land Bank in 1883; transfer of the state peasants to the redemption regime in 1886—the whole economic policy of N. Kh. Bunge. Bunge had been an active member of the Editorial Commissions and had participated in drafting the redemption provisions of the Emancipation Act. After his resignation, the government initiated in the mid-1880s an economic policy with profound consequences for the country. This was the policy of I. A. Vyshnegradskii and S. Iu. Witte, designed to stimulate railroad construction and state-supported industrial development to a degree unprecedented in Russian history, and to accelerate the industrialization of the country while maintaining strictly conservative political arrangements. This wager on a powerful autocratic monarchy and the widespread development of modern industry in an agrarian and peasant society, without taking the social consequences into account and without adopting an appropriate social policy, produced great contradictions. Witte recognized that communal landownership and the entire peasant legal order resting upon it had to be reformed; his championing of private landownership by peasant smallholders prefigured Stolypin's reform. He attempted to garner public support through the local committees of the Special Conference on the

---

[30]See P. A. Zaionchkovskii, *Rossiiskoe samoderzhavie v kontse XIX stoletiia* (Moscow, 1970).

Needs of Agriculture. At that point, his ideas and policies encountered the resistance of the same autocratic monarchy whose proponent he had always been, and he was dismissed from office.

By the time that Nicholas II, the grandson of Alexander II, ascended the throne in 1894, the autocratic monarchy had become ossified. The state, refusing to abandon its imperial ambitions and having lost its ability to react in a swift and timely fashion to societal needs and to provide political solutions to crisis situations, was marching toward revolution. The words of G. V. Plekhanov upon the accession of the new tsar proved prophetic: "Alexander III sowed the wind, and it depends on Nicholas II whether a storm will rise." The reformers of the 1860s had envisaged, in contrast to revolutionary Europe, five centuries of peaceful evolution for Russia, as Kavelin had put it. Instead, three Russian revolutions following one upon another shook the world only fifty years after the era of reform. These three revolutions demonstrated what should have been obvious: the importance of the peasantry and of the agrarian problem and the undoubted weakness of the bourgeoisie and of the liberal forces. The three revolutions illuminated as well the utopianism of the reformers' ultimate goals.

5

Reforms and political culture in
prerevolutionary Russia: commentary

DANIEL FIELD

THE HISTORIAN AND CIVIC DUTY

The theme of this volume and the substance of the contributions by Emmons, Chernukha and Anan'ich, and Zakharova combine to pose the question of the civic duty of the historian. This is a pressing concern for our Russian colleagues, now that nonhistorians (often ill-informed and sometimes ill-intentioned) have taken up the search for historical alternatives; but it is also a concern for all historians, because every human being has a stake in the outcome of the ongoing political struggles in the [former] Soviet Union. Emmons has reminded us that the availability to statesmen and others of a truly usable past depends on the willingness of the knowledgeable specialists to participate in public discourse. I know he is right, but I am more comfortable engaging in discourse with other historians—or, failing that, with students. Reading the carefully crafted generalizations in the essay by Chernukha and Anan'ich, I was, so to speak, distracted by my memory of the masterful and detailed books and articles by the two authors that underlie their chapter, which is still too detailed for a popular outlet such as *The Week* (*Nedelia*). If detail must be sacrificed in the interest of "public discourse," mastery may be sacrificed as well.

Emmons has evoked the example of the late Natan Eidel'man, who was remarkable for his civic courage and civic consciousness, but also for his scrupulous and tenacious scholarship. It would be reassuring to believe that all of us can and must follow his example in all those respects, but his last book, *"Revolution from Above" in Rus-*

sia,[1] shows how difficult it is to combine these qualities. If we take *"Revolution from Above"* as a political document, as an expression of the author's hopes for Russia, I would sign it with both hands, and I hope it is still widely read there. Taken as a work of history, however, *"Revolution from Above"* arouses misgivings. For example, Eidel'man's treatment of the Mongol conquest as a blow that sundered Russia from the rest of Europe and from which she has been six hundred years in recovering does not, I believe, correspond to the findings of the best Russian medievalists, and his analogy between the conquest and an atomic attack prompts a comparison between the Muscovy of 1525 and Japan today. The proposition, which Eidel'man frequently endorses, that the development of cities and of a bourgeoisie is essential to the development of political and economic freedom is venerable but questionable.[2] More disturbing, although seemingly trivial, are instances of carelessness concerning sources by this matchless expert on sources. He refers several times to Alexander II's statement that reform from above is better than reform from below. But seventy-five years ago, Popel'nitskii took the trouble to find out what Alexander actually said. The quotation comes from a speech in which the tsar, speaking publicly from the throne twenty months before he set emancipation in motion, specifically renounced any intention of emancipating the serfs "at this time."[3] The speech, including its tortured syntax, can be placed in the overall context of Alexander's statecraft, but it is important to get things right. The same applies to Chicherin's speech; Eidel'man wonders (p. 155) how it served to provoke the government of Alexander III to remove Chicherin from his post as mayor of Moscow. In that speech, Chicherin encouraged his listeners to cooperate with the regime, stick to "small deeds,"

---

[1]N. Ia. Eidel'man, *"Revoliutsiia sverkhu" v Rossii* (Moscow, 1989).

[2]The data of the census of 1897 for the fifty provinces of European Russia show a significant and positive correlation ($r^2 = .347$) between urbanization and literacy but a stronger and negative correlation ($r^2 = -.461$) between literacy and Orthodox Christianity. Protestant tradition holds that every believer should be able to have unmediated access to Scripture; Roman Catholic and especially Orthodox Christians have relied on the rites of the church for salvation and have taken a utilitarian attitude toward reading. I would suggest that the vitality and durability of civil liberties and representative government in early modern and modern Europe have been more closely associated with literacy rates (and ultimately with religion) than with the proportion of city dwellers.

[3]A. Popel'nitskii, "Rech' Aleksandra II moskovskomu dvorianstvu 30 marta 1856," *Golos minuvshego* 5–6 (1916): 392–97. [An English translation of the relevant passage can be found in Terence Emmons, *The Russian Landed Gentry and the Peasant Emancipation of 1861* (Cambridge: Cambridge University Press, 1968), 51—ed.]

and wait for the government to reward them with a parliament; he was voicing what would soon be castigated as "senseless dreams."[4] These and other instances of ahistoricity are disturbing because they are so uncharacteristic of the author as we knew him. Did Eidel'man sacrifice something of himself as a "specialist" for the sake of "public discourse"?

"Revolution from Above" ends with a series of lessons Eidel'man draws from his survey. The lessons, although suffused with passion, were meant to reassure the leadership and the public of what was then still the Soviet Union. I hope that at least the leaders, both then and now, have not taken them too much to heart. The proposition that "one can see farther from the top" conveys very well the perspectives of Peter I, Alexander II, and Stolypin, but it also corresponds to the beliefs of despots from Herod to Ceausescu. The maxim that "complex maneuvering and 'tacking' " are necessary to every nonviolent revolution from above is unexceptionable, but it behooves us to recall how often in imperial Russia a strategic "tack" turned into a voyage lasting years or decades.

More generally, I do not find in the writings of the best historians (in Eidel'man's other books, for example, or in the publications of Zakharova, Chernukha, Anan'ich, and Emmons) anything resembling a lesson that lends itself to direct application, like a prescription or a formula. Indeed, the history of Russia provides many examples of persons and groups who drew knowledgeably on the lessons of history and suffered grievously as a result. The Mensheviks in October 1917 provide one instance; they knew, with the certainty that a botanist knows that a palm tree will not grow out of an acorn, that the Bolshevik seizure of power was "adventurism" that could only enhance the real threat to the revolution, Bonapartism.[5]

My examples suggest that when historians try to pass the baton of learning to policy makers, the transfer is usually bungled; the baton is not really what the historian is equipped to deliver, while the policy maker is likely to grab the wrong stick or to use it as a cudgel. Moreover, it has not been proved that a subtle and detailed understanding of past

[4]Text in B. N. Chicherin, *Vospominaniia Borisa Nikolaevicha Chicherina: Zemstvo i Moskovskaia duma* (Moscow, 1934; reprint, Cambridge, 1973), 234–36. Chicherin had failed to draw the appropriate lessons from reprimands for two previous speeches and from the appointment of Dmitry Tolstoi as minister of internal affairs.

[5]See, for example, Fedor Dan's speech of October 24, as quoted in S. P. Mel'gunov, *Kak Bol'sheviki zakhvatili vlast'* (Paris: La Renaissance, 1953), 85.

events makes a positive contribution to a discussion of policy. What if a historical myth (or half myth) provides crucial inspiration to the forces of light? What if the substitution of a nuanced and scholarly understanding of that myth would give courage to the enemies of promise? Where then does our duty as historians lie?

THE QUESTION OF SCALE

It may be that historians of imperial Russia can, in good conscience, evade those questions. In its scale, in its ambitions, and in the stakes involved, Gorbachev's revolution from above in the Soviet Union dwarfed all precedents, including even Peter I's. Consider the basic principles and premises of the Soviet polity that Gorbachev and his associates renounced [even before August 1991—ed.]:

1. "Russia one and undivided," a guiding maxim of both the tsarist and Soviet polities that was dear to their most ardent supporters.

2. Systematic absence of glasnost—the principle that debates and decision making must take place behind closed doors, which dates back at least to the Tenth Party Congress (1921) and took firm hold with the defeat of the "right opposition," permeating all forms of culture and all aspects of administration for sixty years.

3. "The leading role of the Party," which has prevailed in various forms since 1918, at the expense of representative institutions and popular sovereignty—at the expense, in other words, of all that was promised by the slogan, "All power to the soviets!"

4. Russian and Soviet exceptionalism, which dates back to Stalin's articulation of the (profoundly non-Marxist) concept of "socialism in one country" in 1926, and which had serious consequences for politics, culture, and the economy. By comparison, the tsarist statesmen who, as Chernukha and Anan'ich remind us, argued for Russian autochthony were only playing with words.

5. The command economy, which has been repudiated in principle, if by no means in practice, and which has prevailed (except during the period of the New Economic Policy) since 1918. Repudiation of this principle entails the substitution of market forces for dictation from above and, to a lesser extent, of incentives and rewards for terror.[6]

---

[6]On the tenacity of the command economy and the Party apparatus in the industrial city of Magnitogorsk, see Stephen Kotkin, "The Soviet Rustbelt," *Harriman Institute Forum*

6. No sacrifice by the peasantry, the public, and the regime is too great if it serves to maintain a socialist (or collective) form of agriculture. This principle goes back to the summer of 1930, when it turned out that "dizziness from success" was not a problem after all, and gained in strength with each change of leadership, culminating in the actions of the Brezhnev era, when massive investments in collective and state farms were accompanied by costly expenditure of convertible currency on foodstuffs from abroad.

These principles shaped every aspect of Soviet life, they were closely intertwined, and, until a relatively short time ago, they seemed unshakable. By comparison, the reforms of the 1860s, the 1890s, and 1905–11, momentous as they indeed were, seem to be timid or even largely cosmetic measures.[7] Insofar as perestroika represented a rebuilding from the ground up, it had no real analogues in the imperial period.

THE QUESTION OF POLITICAL SUBCULTURE

Even if the reforms and reform plans of the imperial period were commensurate in magnitude with those of the 1980s, we must establish whether they were also intrinsically comparable. We must consider the issue of political culture, which figures directly in Zakharova's paper and by implication in the papers by Chernukha and Anan'ich and by Emmons.

I maintain that the peculiarities of the environment from which reform legislation emerged and in which reform proposals were considered vitiate comparisons between the imperial period and the last years of the Soviet era. Even if there were substantial continuity between the national political cultures of the Russian Empire and the Soviet Union, as some have argued,[8] we have to reckon with the distinctive political subculture within which policy was framed under the last five tsars, a subculture

---

4 (1991), and Stephen Kotkin, *Steeltown, USSR: Soviet Society in the Gorbachev Era* (Berkeley: University of California Press, 1991).

[7] Emmons reminds us that the minimum definition of "revolution," from above or below, entails a change of regime. On this count, the events of 1987–91 surpassed even the Petrine revolution—although the Soviet leadership, like Peter in his time, relied to a significant degree on old cadres to do revolutionary work.

[8] Notably, Edward L. Keenan in "Muscovite Political Folkways," *Russian Review* 45 (1986): 115–81. See also the comments of Robert V. Daniels, Robert O. Crummey, Richard Hellie, and Richard Wortman in ibid., 46 (1987): 157–98.

borne by the monarch and the few dozen persons with access to him on matters of policy.

A statesman once acidly remarked that in Russia, ministers never resigned over matters of policy. The observation is substantially, although not literally, true, which is surprising, because a minister served only so long as he had the confidence of the autocrat. If his proposal on a major matter was rejected, there was no appealing to a higher instance or waiting for the next election; he had lost his mandate of confidence. If this logic had been strictly observed, however, the turnover of ministers would have been disquietingly rapid, and the continuity and stability that ordinary administration requires would have been gravely disrupted. The requisites of policy making, especially policy innovation, were in conflict with the requisites of administration. The autocrats and their associates developed means to minimize this conflict, all of which amounted to softening the hard edges of policy so as to prevent the full weight of autocratic power from crushing policy makers or policy options.

The simplest of these means was to divorce policy formulation from administrative responsibility.[9] Ia. I. Rostovtsev, for example, had no portfolio when he directed the drafting of the legislation abolishing serfdom—he had nothing going for him except the personal trust of the tsar—and the actual legislative work was carried out by men with secondary administrative responsibilities or with none. The policy-making activities of Shuvalov in the reign of Alexander II and of Pobedonostsev in the reign of his successor extended far beyond the jurisdiction of the agencies they headed.

Another of these means was the propagation of a peculiar variety of illusion that prevailed within the monarch's entourage. A minister whose policy initiative failed would console himself with the belief that he had been frustrated by a camarilla of obscurantists (or of "reds") surrounding the autocrat and temporarily obscuring the truth—for example, "The tsar wants it, but the boiars are resisting." The autocrat himself often encouraged these illusions; when he dismissed a minister, he would insist on his personal regard for the ex-minister and on his accord with him, explaining the dismissal by vague allusions to others whom he must, for the moment, accommodate. Kokovtsev's account of his dis-

[9] I would distinguish this technique from the related tendency to vest broad responsibility in favorites (Potemkin, Arakcheev).

missal sounds very much like A. I. Levshin's account of his dismissal sixty years previously.[10]

Another means was to minimize to the utmost the significance of a policy initiative and to wrap it elaborately in loyalist rhetoric. Loris-Melikov promised great things from the elective institution that he proposed, but he insisted that it was consistent with the institution of autocracy and even that it was not really an innovation, because it was modeled on the work of the Editorial Commissions and of the provincial deputies who had appeared before them.[11] Witte was a master of this technique; when his economic and fiscal policies came under challenge, he began his defense by declaring that he was dutifully pursuing policies launched by his predecessors.[12] A variation of this technique was to exploit the lack of cabinet ("united") government by keeping major initiatives within the confines of one's agency; judging from Polovtsov's diary, Witte's ministerial colleagues in 1899 had no conception of the overall policy the minister of finance was pursuing.[13] Another variation was to argue for a connection, often factitious, between a line of policy and the institution of autocracy itself.[14] Because of the use of these techniques, it is often hard to establish what a minister's real convictions were (as Chernukha and Anan'ich observe with respect to Loris-Melikov), and it is not certain whether we should speak (as they do) of the "evolution" of Witte's views concerning the commune and representative institutions or simply of his growing candor in the face of mounting political and economic difficulties.

[10]A. I. Levshin, "Dostopamiatnye minuty v moei zhizni," *Russkii arkhiv* 8 (1885): 475–558; V. N. Kokovtsev, *Iz moego proshlogo* (Paris, 1933; reprint, Paris, 1969), 1: 102.

[11]N. V. Golitsyn, ed., "Konstitutsiia grafa Loris-Melikova: Materialy dlia ee istorii," *Byloe* 4–5 (1918): 162–66. Loris-Melikov was on active military duty in 1859 and 1860 and apparently did not realize that the encounter between the deputies and the commission was completely unproductive in terms of policy and a fiasco in terms of public relations.

[12]See his personal report of early 1899 in N. F. Gindin, ed., "Ob osnovakh ekonomicheskoi politiki tsarskogo pravitel'stva XIX—nachala XX v.," in A. L. Sidorov et al. eds., *Dokumenty po istorii monopolisticheskogo kapitalizma v Rossii (Materialy po istorii SSSR, VI)* (Moscow, 1959), 175–76.

[13]A. A. Polovtsov, "Iz dnevnika," *Krasnyi arkhiv*, 1931, no. 3: 120–21. See also the discussion of ministers' relations with the emperor in Andrew Verner, *The Crisis of Russian Autocracy: Nicholas II and the 1905 Revolution* (Princeton: Princeton University Press, 1990), 46–64.

[14]Here the greatest virtuoso was N. A. Miliutin. In a series of memoranda prepared for S. S. Lanskoi to present to Alexander II, Miliutin successfully represented the attempts of his opponents to avail themselves of institutions and forums that the autocracy itself had provided as encroachments on the autocrat's prerogatives. See N. P. Semenov, *Osvobozhdenie krest'ian v tsarstvovanie Aleksandra II* (St. Petersburg, 1889–93), 1: 826–34, and M. A. Miliutina, "Iz zapisok," *Russkaia starina* 98 (1899): 113–17.

Apart from these "softening" devices, other aspects of the political subculture of the emperors, their ministers, and their court deserve consideration. Consider Zakharova's penetrating discussion of the impact of Russia's defeat in the Crimean War. For Russia's leaders, she says, "the most painful consequence of the war . . . was the fear it aroused that Russia might lose great-power prestige."[15] Zakharova is not seeking to invoke the simplistic concept of *Primat der Aussenpolitik;* rather, she is reminding us of an important aspect of the mental world of reformers, would-be reformers, and counterreformers—an aspect that is all the more important to recall because it was rarely directly articulated in connection with the reform agenda. In this world, diplomacy enjoyed pride of place. In the best edition we have so far of the memoirs of Witte (who was, among other things, a quintessential senior bureaucrat), a single chapter is devoted to the author's activities as minister of finance, while his dealings with foreign statesmen are described in loving detail.[16] At the very time that autocracy was facing its greatest domestic crisis, Nicholas II admitted to a confidant that he found his prime minister's memoranda on domestic politics too long and complicated to read through, and so he turned Witte's memoranda over to D. F. Trepov (!) [the governor-general of St. Petersburg—ed.] to summarize.[17] He would not have been so negligent if the documents had concerned relations with his crowned uncles and cousins.

In the latter part of Zakharova's paper and throughout Chernukha's and Anan'ich's, the issue of a national representative institution gets primary attention. This emphasis is appropriate;[18] the subculture with

[15]The discussion is all the more important because historians tend to oversimplify the connection between defeat and reform. The texts cited to demonstrate this connection— Pogodin's *Istoriko-politicheskie pis'ma,* Valuev's "Duma russkogo," and Aksakov's *O vnutrennem sostoianii Rossii*—fling recriminations at the administration and call for various kinds of renewal and glasnost but are virtually or completely silent on the subject of serfdom.

[16]S. Iu. Vitte, *Vospominaniia* (Moscow, 1960) contains seventy chapters (in three volumes). Of the thirty-seven chapters covering the period through Witte's dismissal as minister of finance, three are primarily devoted to domestic economic policy and thirteen to international relations.

[17]E. J. Bing, ed., *The Secret Letters of the Last Tsar: Being the Confidential Correspondence between Nicholas II and His Mother, Dowager Empress Maria Fedorovna* (New York: Longmans, 1938), 211.

[18]I cannot agree, however, with Eidel'man's facile assumption that a national legislature would necessarily have hastened Russia's modernization, mollified the revolutionary movement, and perhaps averted the crises of 1905 and 1917. Austria had a national legislature, yet by 1900 it had collapsed in the face of the competing claims of ethnic groups and the rise of working-class socialism.

which they are dealing was dominated by autocracy, and a national legislature was, so to speak, the obverse of autocracy, and the issue was on the minds of the autocrats and their ministers from the time of Speransky's scheme of 1809 to Minister of Agriculture Ermolov's plea to Nicholas II on the morrow of Bloody Sunday. Because of their focus on this issue, Chernukha and Anan'ich necessarily deal more with plans than with enacted legislation. In view of the jealousy with which the last five autocrats cherished their authority, why did the issue keep coming up (except during the reign of Nicholas I)? Why did insiders from Novosil'tsev to Ignat'ev come forward with proposals that were, it would seem, bound to fail?

One reason was that giving consideration to quasi-constitutional schemes was a kind of ritual within this subculture. With the example of the institutions of Western and Central Europe ever present in the minds of the tsars and their ministers, it was appropriate from time to time to soberly consider "crowning the edifice" in Russia, and then, no less soberly, to reaffirm autocracy.[19] Rituals come and go, to be sure. Loris-Melikov and Ignat'ev were summarily dismissed for their presumption, and this particular ritual was not in fashion in the period from 1882 to 1903. On the other hand, Valuev, one of the most intelligent and one of the touchiest statesmen of the nineteenth century, does not seem to have been much distressed by the periodic rejection of his plan for a national assembly.[20] He understood that he had played his part in a ritual.

Another reason is related to the rationale of national representative institutions. Shuvalov and Valuev (and probably Loris-Melikov) believed that the establishment of constitutional monarchy was essential if Russia were to match the economic and social progress of her neighbors to the west, but the reform was traditionally justified as a device for obtaining necessary information, which required bypassing the selfish and pettifogging bureaucrats who stood between the tsar and his people. "To disclose the whole truth to the tsar" was the slogan of moderate constitutionalists for a century. There were two problems with this rationale. First, it was, in most instances, a transparently insincere way of

[19]In the reign of Nicholas I, the object of ritual consideration was serfdom. Between 1826 and 1857, nine secret committees were convened to consider the reform of serfdom; each one concluded that any major legislation would be untimely or premature.
[20]We eagerly await Zakharova's forthcoming publication of Grand Duke Constantine's diaries to learn of his response in similar circumstances.

seeming not to encroach on the prerogatives of the autocrat. Second, there were ways of getting information from the nation at large, of conferring with informed persons from the localities, with no loss of political control or setting of unwelcome precedents. The commission on hired labor in agriculture mentioned by Chernukha and Anan'ich provides an example, as do various conferences held under the auspices of ministries (and within their walls) in the reign of Nicholas I. Indeed, the practice can be traced back to Patriarch Filaret, who in 1619 dismissed the assembly of the land (*zemskii sobor*) and for the next fifteen years of what was in effect his regency relied instead on conferences with representatives of particular occupations or regions. Many subsequent autocrats would resort to this safe and easily controlled source of "feedback" (*obratnye sviazi,* in Eidel'man's phrase).

Finally, if the political subculture of autocracy was as durable as I have indicated, how can we understand the emergence and intermittent success of genuine reformers? What is the basis for Eidel'man's optimistic assertion that, "once transformations are undertaken, they will find people to carry them out"? Part of the answer, for the imperial era, lies in the character of the periods of relative stagnation, when the values of "official nationality" were asserted. An unstated component of the basic "Orthodoxy-autocracy-nationality" formula was a commitment to military values and to maintaining or enhancing Russia's status as a great power. Neither autochthony (*samobytnost'*) nor nationality (*narodnost'*) corresponded to the values and mentality of the peasant or entailed a complacent acceptance of backwardness. The regimes of Nicholas I and Alexander III wanted trained, reliable personnel. To that end, they founded and patronized educational institutions, both civilian and military. Their ministers sought, by control of admissions and curricula as well as through censorship, to train a generation of technicians with no unwelcome values or loyalties attached to their expertise. The attempt was as hopeless as the attempt, in our own time, to dissociate computer technology from its illogically inseparable companion, rock music. The reformers and constitutionalists of the 1850s and 1860s emerged from the universities, the School of Jurisprudence, and similar institutions with new skills and new values; they were the necessary product of the Nicholaevan system, just as the members of the Union of Unions were the unwelcome but legitimate progeny of Alexander III. Neither Nicholas nor Alexander (nor Brezhnev) was willing to pay the price of thoroughgoing, systematic stagnation.

Zakharova also draws attention to the remarkable energy and capacity for work of the reformers of 1857–66 and to the tenacity and commitment, in different and less favorable circumstances, of Reutern. Bunge figures in much the same way in Chernukha's and Anan'ich's paper. Without these qualities—without, in a word, the immense self-assurance of the reformers—peasant and judicial reforms, in particular, could not have been enacted in the form they took. Conversely, at least in the second half of the nineteenth century, the opponents of reform and the advocates of counterreform were rarely able to make effective use of the high positions they generally occupied. It may have gratified Dmitry Tolstoi to forbid any celebration of the twenty-fifth anniversary of the abolition of serfdom, but Miliutin, Rostovtsev, and Iakov Solov'ev had altered the destiny of the nation, and he could not. Compared to their opponents, the counterreformers were inert, passive, and amateurish. A great part of the explanation of this pattern derives from the consideration that the reformers, from Kochubei to Witte, were consistent exponents of cosmopolitan culture and hence of the view that there was a single path of development that Russia must follow. The opposition of their rivals was grounded in the idea of Russia's special path, her particularism, her autochthony. Few educated Russians in the nineteenth century, and none with governmental responsibilities, could be consistent and thoroughgoing exponents of autochthony. Chernukha and Anan'ich have drawn attention to a basic contradiction in "national-chauvinist" doctrine: commitment to autocracy and hostility to the bureaucracy, which was simply autocracy at the retail level.[21]

Beyond that, the Fadeevs and Pazukhins were cosmopolitan in the very fabric of their lives and the structure of their discourse; such men could vent their nationalistic sentiments by creating unpleasantness for Jews and Finns, but they were as remote from the values of the village as were the Valuevs and Wittes, and much of what they professed had to be, in some measure, artificial or meretricious. The inconsistency of autochthony as a basis for policy making subtly eroded the morale and energy of its advocates, just as those who believed in a single path of development and took their orientation from the "sensible and solid civilization" of Western Europe drew energy and self-confidence from

---

[21]On this and related contradictions in nationalist, conservative, and reactionary doctrine, see the thoughtful essays in Hans Rogger, *Jewish Policies and Right-Wing Politics in Imperial Russia* (Berkeley: University of California Press, 1986).

the consistency of their doctrine and from its correspondence to the way they lived their daily lives.

The subculture of policy makers in the Soviet period has, of course, had its own rhetorical conventions, unstated rules, ideological determinants, pervasive myths, habits, and shibboleths. I listed some of the shibboleths above. Like its counterpart in the late imperial period, this political subculture shaped and may still shape the substance of policy by delimiting the range of possible options. The two subcultures, however, had relatively little in common, and only perhaps in the period from 1934 to 1953 did the Soviet subculture exhibit the kind of stability and tenacity that characterized its counterpart between 1801 and 1917. It follows that contemporary activists and policy makers may continue, as some of them and their counterparts also did during the Gorbachev era of the 1980s, to seek heroes and exemplars, if they find them useful, in the polity of the imperial period. They can also find reformers associated with very general and familiar ideas—legal order, glasnost, and property rights. And they and everyone else will derive a diffuse but genuine benefit from developing their understanding of their nation's past. More than that they should not expect to find. Problems of comparability and commensurability and the difficulties of packing historical scholarship in a directly usable form severely limit the possibility of finding valid alternatives for the present and future in the reform activities of the imperial period. By the same token, we historians have our duties as scholars and our duties as citizens; it is rarely possible effectively to combine these two kinds of duty.

Part II

Autocracy and the challenge of constitutionalism

6

The social problem in Russia, 1906–1914:
Stolypin's agrarian reform

AVENIR P. KORELIN

Russia entered the twentieth century with a varied, unbalanced, and polymorphous economy and a contradictory and explosive sociopolitical structure. The society was on the verge of revolutionary upheavals. The growing social tension burst forth in the spectacular class warfare of the three Russian revolutions. The key issue was the agrarian problem, which had remained unsolved for all practical purposes since 1861. But if the emancipation and its consequences have been treated with relative unanimity in historical and economic scholarship, the "second peasant reform" (the name contemporaries gave to the efforts of Peter A. Stolypin, prime minister and minister of internal affairs from 1906 to 1911, to modernize the Russian village) and especially its consequences continue to be disputed to this day. Indeed, arguments about Stolypin's reform plans recently became particularly heated.[1] The reasons for this are to be found primarily in the crisis situation in the country today, in the disappointment of certain social circles with the possibilities and potentialities of the system of collectivized agriculture, and in the desire to embark on an alternative approach in the form of individually owned peasant farms. This essay examines only several aspects of this broad theme, those that conditioned the reform and shaped its character and results.

---

[1] V. Seliunin, "Istoki," *Novyi mir*, 1988, no. 5: 185–86; P. N. Zyrianov, "Spasitel' russkoi derevni?" *Dialog*, 1990, no. 12: 69–78; *Literaturnaia gazeta*, July 26, 1989, p. 12.

THE FORM AND CONSEQUENCES OF EMANCIPATION

The factors conditioning Stolypin's agrarian policy were rooted in the reform of 1861. As is well known, the abolition of serfdom was a turning point in the socioeconomic modernization of Russia. However, the content and shape of the reforms promulgated "from above" by the absolutist polity were subordinated to a single objective: the preservation to the greatest extent possible of the economic and political positions of absolutism and of the old ruling class of landowning gentry. This imparted a complex, even contradictory character to the evolution of Russia toward a capitalist economy and bourgeois society.

The government did not dare to emancipate the peasants without land. To begin with, peasant farming was a major component of the agricultural economy, even in prereform Russia. Second, the noble estates were not prepared either financially or technically to operate under new conditions without the traditional object of exploitation: the peasant and his household inventory. Finally, the authorities were—with good reason—apprehensive of the sociopolitical consequences of landless emancipation, which would have amounted to peasant pauperization. The socially homogeneous, immobile, semipatriarchal village represented a base of broad social support for the autocracy, one that provided it with an immense, albeit relative, supraclass autonomy.

The state implemented the reform as a major credit operation, taking upon itself the initial peasant expenditures for the redemption of land from the gentry. The peasants got the land, but the size of their expensively redeemed allotments in most cases precluded prosperity. The landowners retained most of their estates and kept the best land. Under conditions of a predominantly natural economy and an acute need on the part of the peasants for cash to pay taxes and make the redemption payments, the village was condemned to remain dependent on its former lords. As a result, the landowners could readily avail themselves of the opportunity to use the transitional, so-called labor-rent, economy, where the peasant hired himself out for pay (in cash, in kind, or in land), using his own animals and equipment. Comprising elements of feudal corvée and capitalist hire, these arrangements grew into a system in which hired labor became the chief mechanism for the operation of the agricultural economy. Moreover, this system allowed the landlords to exploit the peasantry in conditions of near servitude over a prolonged period, with clear negative consequences for the economic development of the village and of the country as a whole. Under this system, the peasants were not only economically dependent on the landlords but were also subject to extraeconomic compulsion. The peasant commune, in part, served this latter purpose.

The government allotted land to the peasants not as private property but in communal landholding and substantively limited their right to dispose of it. The communes controlled more than four-fifths of peasant landholding. This solution was aimed at multiple objectives. To begin with, the commune was transformed into a guarantor of redemption payments to the treasury by making all of its members jointly responsible for both redemption payments and taxes. Second, having formally attained personal freedom, the peasants remained bound to the land; that is, they could not, without the commune's permission, abandon their allotment until all redemption payments had been made. This provision was used by the landlords to get cheap labor for their estates. Third, the government de facto excluded redemption land from the marketplace; the allotments could be sold only with the permission of the village community and only to individuals of the peasant estate, and they could not be mortgaged. By this means, and also by periodic repartition of the communal land as the population grew, the authorities hoped to prevent proletarianization of the peasantry and sharp economic stratification within the village. Fourth, the commune was also transformed into the lowest link in the system of courts and administration and thus could be used by the autocracy to regulate social relations in the village in the interest of the treasury and the landlords and to maintain mass social support for the regime.

CONDITIONS AND OPTIONS IN 1906

It is important to note that most of the property limitations established by law in 1861 were supposed to be only temporary. According to the design of the reformers, a member of the commune who had redeemed his allotment became a free peasant smallholder, able to demand to receive his land as a consolidated holding.[2] However, in the 1880s and 1890s, the government undertook a series of steps that had all the earmarks of a counterreform and that confirmed the legal inequality of the

[2]*Polnoe sobranie zakonov Rossiiskoi imperii*, 2nd ser., nos. 36650 and 36657 (hereafter cited as *PSZ*).

peasantry. The allotment and the peasant household inventory were declared family property, which limited the rights of the head of the family; the division of family property was restricted in order to prevent fragmentation of the allotment; peasant migration to new lands or departure to towns or other localities in search of work was made more difficult; and village self-government and peasant courts were subordinated to the land captains, who were crown officials selected from among the gentry. Finally, in 1893, peasants were forbidden to undertake early redemption and to leave the commune.[3] The tendency to favor economic leveling and to conserve the village commune had finally won out in the agrarian policy of tsarism. This goal was also supported by the policies of the Peasant Land Bank, founded in 1883. The bank resold gentry lands that were entering the market mostly to the village communities.

Despite the influence of these powerful retarding factors, a capitalist perestroika was taking place in the economy of both landlord and peasant, especially in the borderlands of the empire, where the vestiges of the feudal heritage were less burdensome. The total area of arable land, and the volume and value of agricultural production, were all rising. Russia was one of the largest grain exporters on the world market. The growth of agriculture under the influence of rapidly developing industry was becoming more apparent, but on the whole the modernization of the agrarian economy was proceeding very slowly. One of the reasons for this was the survival of almost medieval patterns in agriculture.

The landlords, who had by 1906 lost about 40 percent of their landholding despite governmental support, nevertheless still controlled some 53 million *desiatiny* (1 *desiatina* = 1.1 hectares, or 2.7 acres), which was more than 60 percent of total private landownership. Moreover, 80 percent of all gentry landholding consisted of large estates, ranging from five hundred to hundreds of thousands of desiatiny.[4] Many landlords were incapable of properly managing such large properties, and so they rented out much of their land to the peasants. By 1900, of 16,700 estates mortgaged to the Gentry Bank, only 29 percent were properly organized

[3]E. M. Brusnikin, "Krest'ianskii vopros v Rossii v period politicheskoi reaktsii (80–90 gg. XIX v.)," *Voprosy istorii*, 1970, no. 2: 34–47.
[4]Avenir P. Korelin, *Dvorianstvo v poreformennoi Rossii, 1861–1904* (Moscow, 1979), 54, 66, 131.

capitalist enterprises, 51 percent were rented out, and 20 percent were some sort of mixture.[5]

The vast majority of peasants suffered from land hunger. In 1905, 10 million peasant households (out of 12.3 million) controlled 75 million desiatiny—an average of 7.5 desiatiny per household. If we take into account the fact that at the existing level of agriculture and technology, a normal household economy required from eight to fifteen desiatiny (depending on the region and quality of the soil), then four-fifths of all peasant families lacked opportunity for increasing their production. In the postreform period, the average size of the allotment in the central regions of the country was practically halved, from 4.8 to 2.6 desiatiny, as a result of natural population growth in the village and the low rate of migration into the towns.[6] The peasants' situation was worsened by the burden of taxes and redemption payments, by the increase in rent and land prices, and by the prolonged fall in agricultural prices resulting from the world agrarian crisis, the consequences of which were felt in Russia until the early twentieth century.

The preservation of the vestiges of servitude in agriculture affected directly or indirectly all aspects of national life. The situation was assuming crisis proportions at the beginning of the twentieth century and threatened a revolutionary explosion. The autocracy's reaction was to establish a number of commissions and committees charged with analyzing the situation and finding ways to resolve the crisis. All of them pointed to the low level of the agrarian economy and the extreme land hunger of the peasantry. The problem could have been resolved by two means: either expansion of peasant landholding at the expense of state and private landownership or the adoption of measures that would sharply increase the efficiency of the agricultural economy.

The first method would have had its own financial and organizational problems, but it would have radically lowered the level of social tension in the village and opened the way for the peasants gradually to acquire the means for improving their economy. On this basis and by means of gradual natural selection, there would have appeared a layer of the most enterprising and capable farmers, who could later be integrated via cooperatives into the national economic system. Such a variant was per-

[5]Avenir P. Korelin, *Sel'skokhoziaistvennyi kredit v Rossii v kontse XIX—nachale XX v.* (Moscow, 1988), 28.
[6]M. S. Simonova, *Krizis agrarnoi politiki tsarizma nakanune pervoi russkoi revoliutsii* (Moscow, 1987), 135.

fectly feasible from an economic standpoint, for at the beginning of the twentieth century the peasants produced about 90 percent of total agricultural output and some 75 percent of its market share.[7] However, it would have required the transfer to the peasantry of almost all available state and private land merely to meet the elementary requirements of increasing the peasant allotments to the necessary size. Such an option was unacceptable to a regime closely linked with the gentry.

Consequently, the government focused its attention primarily on the second alternative, although under the pressure of the peasant demands it repeatedly granted concessions on the land issue as well. Nevertheless, the chief strategy for attaining its goals was to take not direct economic steps but legal measures. The commissions established to resolve the agrarian problem, although occasionally reaching diametrically opposing conclusions, all viewed the improvement of the legal order in the village as the best way to resolve the crisis. Changes in the legal status of the peasantry were, in their view, supposed to encourage peasant initiative, entrepreneurship, and economic independence. It was thought that such steps, in turn, would speed up modernization of the village economy and increase its efficiency, raise the level of peasant culture, and inculcate in the peasants the sense of private ownership, so that they would be not enemies but allies of the landlord. The issue of peasant land hunger would resolve itself, but the key problem was that of the commune. It was the commune that was proclaimed to be almost solely responsible for the impoverishment of the village. How justified was this accusation?

In 1905, there were 135,000 communes in the provinces of European Russia. Some 9.6 million peasant families (77 percent of the total) owned land communally and controlled 115 million desiatiny of allotment lands (83 percent of the total).[8] The role of the commune in the postreform village was contradictory. As an agrarian peasant union, reflecting the level of socioeconomic and agricultural development of the village, it performed, with some success, the functions of economic assistance and social protection for its members. Periodic repartitions of land and its division into strips of commensurate quality and condition were suited

[7]I. D. Koval'chenko, "Sootnoshenie krest'ianskogo i pomeshchich'ego khoziaistva v zemledel'cheskom proizvodstve Rossii," in *Problemy sotsial'no-ekonomicheskoi istorii Rossii* (Moscow, 1971), 174, 188–90.
[8]*Statistika zemlevladeniia 1905 g.: Svod dannykh po 50 guberniiam Evropeiskoi Rossii* (St. Petersburg, 1907), 174–75.

to the leveling principle of land use. Even in the early twentieth century, the commune to a certain extent continued to perform its function as the collective organizer of agricultural processes (rotation of cultivation, cultivation of grasses, improvements in animal husbandry, and so on). With the development of capitalism, however, it was becoming apparent that the commune could not prevent social stratification of the village and that the leveling principle of land use represented a brake on growth of the peasant economy. The property and legal disabilities of the peasantry and the administrative and fiscal functions of the commune, imposed on it by the state, had additional pernicious effects.

Despite the ever more obvious anachronism of the social isolation of the village, the autocracy, until the hour of the revolution, proved incapable of abandoning its traditional patriarchal tutelage in matters of agrarian and peasant policy. To be sure, it wavered as the revolutionary crisis progressed. On the one hand, while creating commissions to study the village and to propose solutions to the crisis, Nicholas II proclaimed, in the manifesto of February 26, 1903, and the decree of January 8, 1904, that immutability of the peasant estate and inviolability of the commune were to remain as the fundamental principles of government policy. On the other hand, these same acts proposed "to seek means by which individual peasants could leave the commune," to abolish joint fiscal responsibility, and to reform the Peasant Land Bank so that it would be easier for the peasants to acquire the land that they needed. The decree of December 12, 1904, promised to bring peasant legislation into line with general civil law.[9]

The vacillations and inconsistency of the supreme authority could not but affect the development of the new course of agrarian policy. Nevertheless, in their most general outline the contours of the future Stolypin reform were sketched out already in the years before 1905. This can be observed in the activity of the Editorial Commission for Review of Peasant Legislation (1902–4), established within the Ministry of Internal Affairs under the general direction of V. K. Plehve, and in the Special Conference on the Needs of Agriculture (1902–5), working under the aegis of the Ministry of Finance, headed by S. Iu. Witte.[10]

Both the commission and the conference took as their point of departure the proposition that the main cause of the agricultural crisis lay

---

[9] *PSZ*, 3rd ser., nos. 22585, 23860, and 25495.
[10] Simonova, *Krizis agrarnoi politiki*, 10–25.

in the inadequacy and incompleteness of peasant legislation, and that one of the chief problems necessitating review was the status of the commune. A step forward from the past perception of the commune as an autochthonous attribute of the Russian village was the recognition of the facts that communal forms of organization were not unique to Russia and that the commune merely reflected a definite and rather low level of socioeconomic development of the countryside as well as the backwardness of peasant society. The transition from a natural to a market economy was fundamentally changing the situation. The commune was increasingly seen as an impediment to farmers with initiative and entrepreneurship, who by then should have been granted the right to leave it. A proposal was also made to offer landless peasants the opportunity to acquire lands through the Peasant Land Bank or to aid their migration to Siberia and Central Asia. Even at that time, voices were raised favoring, even if only as an experiment, the establishment of consolidated holdings in individual proprietorship. A package of legislative proposals envisaged the reorganization of local administration, self-government, and the courts and bringing the legal status of the peasantry closer to that of other social groups in the empire. Nevertheless, the recommendations of both groups had the same main thrust: No compulsory measures should be undertaken to force the disintegration of the commune or of the peasant estate. The solution of this problem was to be left to the workings of time.

However, the goals pursued by the commission and the conference were diametrically opposed. Plehve, the conservatives, and the reactionaries were counting on strengthening the commune by these means, if only for the immediate future. Witte and his supporters from the liberal bureaucracy were convinced that the natural evolution of events would soon, and by itself, bring the demise of the commune and the widespread extension of private landownership to allotment land. But the allotment land was on the whole to retain its character as the property of a particular estate, lest the peasantry lose its chief means of subsistence.

Having vacillated, the autocracy failed to take any constructive steps toward the resolution of the problem and limited itself to half-measures: Joint fiscal responsibility was abolished (March 12, 1903), as was corporal punishment for the peasantry upon conviction in the canton court (August 11, 1904); the Temporary Regulations on peasant migration to unoccupied land, granting certain privileges to emigrants, and a law on small loans were enacted (June 6 and 7, 1904).[11] Even the onset of revolution did not, at first, affect this situation. True to his rigid principle of postponing solutions to acute problems until the last moment, Nicholas II reacted to the growing peasant movement by creating new commissions and conferences. Their recommendations did not go beyond what had been proposed, other than to provide more detail and additional rationale.

In the fall of 1905, however, as a wave of land seizures and attacks on gentry estates took place, proposals to transfer a portion of private and state-owned land to the peasantry were voiced within the government and in society. Under these circumstances, the autocracy was forced to grant concessions. The manifesto of November 3, 1905, while proclaiming the inviolability of gentry landownership, simultaneously announced a reduction of redemption payments by half in 1906 and their complete repeal as of January 1, 1907. At the same time, the Peasant Land Bank was authorized to purchase gentry lands without restriction and to resell them to the peasantry on easy credit terms.[12] In this way, economic measures, obviously forced upon the government, finally came to the fore. Nevertheless, the autocracy still did not abandon its perception of the peasantry as a conservative mass on which it could rely. This is evidenced by the electoral law for the State Duma, promulgated on December 11, 1905, which favored the peasants.[13]

Thus, the first outbreak of revolution was beaten back, and the government rejected the idea of the expropriation of gentry lands. But the abolition of the redemption payments brought closer the inevitable turnaround in agrarian policy. In January 1906, Witte, prime minister at the time, argued in a report to the tsar that the danger of a renewal of peasant disturbances had not passed. He proposed, as a follow-up to the manifesto of November 3, 1905, to recognize allotment land as the personal property of its proprietors and to establish a procedure for leaving the commune. This step, in his view, would have a salutary impact on the peasants' legal consciousness and would impart to them a healthier attitude toward other people's property.[14] A draft of a new agrarian reform, intended for submission to the Duma, was prepared. It

[11]*PSZ*, 3rd ser., nos. 22629, 2470, 24737, and 25014 (art. 1).
[12]Ibid., no. 26871.
[13]Ibid., no. 27029.
[14]*Agrarnyi vopros v Sovete ministrov (1906 g.)* (Moscow and Leningrad, 1924), 80.

outlined more decisive steps to equalize the status of the peasants and other estates in the area of civil and property rights, and it anticipated the gradual transformation of peasant communal landholding into individual holding and of family property into heritable personal property. Urgent and immediate steps were proposed to help needy peasants acquire land through the Peasant Land Bank, either from state properties or by purchase from private landowners, and to take more energetic measures in regard to migration.[15] Nevertheless, the government's agrarian policy proved insufficiently radical in a revolutionary situation. The idea of expropriating gentry lands in one way or another had wide support. The dissolution of both the First and the Second Duma were caused primarily by bitter political strife over the agrarian problem.

STOLYPIN'S PROGRAM

It was in such circumstances that Peter A. Stolypin entered the political arena, being appointed minister of internal affairs on April 26, 1906, and chairman of the Council of Ministers on June 8. It was natural that his agrarian program in many respects would coincide with previous proposals. Its outlines were disclosed for the first time in the draft statute, "On Agrarian Communities with Allotment Landownership," presented to the State Duma on June 6, 1906. The draft included provisions concerning the necessity of equalizing the rights of peasants and other social groups, replacing communal and family ownership by personal property, and creating consolidated holdings. Leaving the commune was to be purely voluntary. The commune, where it was retained, was to be transformed into a simple union of landed proprietors, which would be released from the tutelage of the local administration. The intention was to create "a mass of small and middle proprietors," who, as the authors of the proposal stressed, were everywhere "the supporters of the state order that protects their vital interests." Migration policy and the activity of the Peasant Land Bank would continue as before to focus on the poorer elements in the village, reflecting the traditional patriarchal policy toward the peasantry. Indeed, the proposal as a whole was not especially radical. The allotment lands were to remain the property of the peasant estate, with all the past limitations in the spirit of the manifesto of Feb-

[15]S. M. Sidel'nikov, *Agrarnaia reforma Stolypina: Dokumenty i materialy* (Moscow, 1973), 58–61.

ruary 26, 1903. What was new, however, was that sociopolitical rather than economic desiderata for changing the course of agrarian policy were now coming to the fore.[16]

In short, the basic features of the proposal were not original. Stolypin continued along a beaten path. Strictly speaking, he was not the author of a new agrarian policy, but he was not plagiarizing ideas, either. As the governor of Saratov, in a personal report to the tsar on the state of the province for 1904, he had expressed his opinions about the pernicious influence of the commune on the state of the countryside and pointed to peasant smallholding as the means to save the peasants from poverty and to strengthen "order in the state." Moreover, this new smallholder was not to be, in his view, a usurious kulak, exploiting his peasant neighbors, but an independent, cultured, and prosperous farmer.[17] Apparently, it was not only Stolypin's merciless treatment of peasant disturbances but also his positive program that attracted the attention of the supreme power. Once he became prime minister, Stolypin made his agrarian policy the axis of his general reform policy, calculated to modernize the socioeconomic and in part also the political system of the country. From a principle of "first pacification—then reform," he relatively quickly advanced to recognition of the necessity and inevitability of reform while the revolution was still in progress. He formulated this notion for himself early in 1907 in the following terms:

Reforms are necessary during the course of a revolution, since the deficiencies of internal order to a large degree gave birth to the revolution. If we engage exclusively in the struggle with the revolution, in the best case we shall remove its consequences but not its cause. . . . Furthermore, the path of reform has been triumphantly announced, the State Duma has been created, and one cannot turn back. This would be a fateful error; where a government has succeeded in overcoming revolution (Prussia, Austria), it prevailed not just by physical force but by assuming the role of leadership in reform, while relying on force. To direct all the creativity of government to police measures is a sign of the powerlessness of the ruling authority.[18]

And, finally, Stolypin was the first to go from words to deeds and to begin to implement a new course in agrarian policy.

As chairman of the Council of Ministers, Stolypin issued a govern-

---

[16]S. M. Sidel'nikov, *Agrarnaia politika samoderzhaviia v period imperializma* (Moscow, 1980), 84–85.

[17]Sidel'nikov, *Agrarnaia reforma*, 44.

[18]As quoted in V. S. Diakin, "Stolypin i dvorianstvo," in N. E. Nosov, ed., *Problemy krest'ianskogo zemlevladeniia i vnutrennei politiki Rossii* (Leningrad, 1972), 233–34.

mental proclamation on August 24, 1906, presenting the program of his cabinet. It opened with threats to settle accounts mercilessly with the revolutionary movement, and it announced the introduction of military field courts-martial. At the same time, the proclamation promised a series of reforms. Furthermore, the agrarian reform, the key plank of his platform, along with some other legislative proposals, was to be introduced immediately, as an extraordinary measure and without debate in the Duma.

Nevertheless, until the fall of 1906, the government continued its former and basically unsuccessful policy of partial concessions. The acts of August 12 and 17 and of September 19 transferred to the Peasant Land Bank parcels of state lands in Siberia and European Russia for resale to the peasantry. The decree of October 5, 1906, repealed a series of substantive limitations on peasant rights, which brought them closer in legal status to the rest of the population of the empire.[19] A peasant would now be free to enter the civil service and certain educational institutions, to obtain an internal passport, to choose a place of residence, and to leave the commune in order to seek employment elsewhere. Legislative restrictions on the division of family allotments were lifted, and well-to-do peasants owning purchased land could participate in zemstvo elections in the landowners' curia [rather than in the peasant curia—ed.]. Basic reform of local administration, self-government, and the judicial system was also promised.

Most of the decree's provisions had a direct bearing on the agrarian reform, but this became apparent only in the decree of November 9, 1906, whose promulgation fully revealed the character and direction of Stolypin's policies. This decree, which became law on June 14, 1910, after approval by the Duma and the Council of State, proclaimed that, in connection with the repeal of the redemption payments, allotment lands were being freed from restrictions imposed by the communal system, that the peasants were being granted the right of free departure from the commune, and that their allotment would become their personal property.[20] More than that, if at the time the peasant was cultivating communal land in an amount above the allotment norms, this additional land could be purchased from the village community at the relatively low prices of the 1860s. This seemingly insignificant point con-

[19]*PSZ*, 3rd ser., nos. 28315, 28357, and 28392.
[20]Ibid., nos. 28528 and 33743.

tained an insidious inner meaning: The government calculated that such peasants would be eager to leave the commune, which indeed proved to be the case. A formal request to depart from the commune now needed to be confirmed by a simple majority vote of the village assembly. But if the assembly took no action over the period of a month, the matter was transferred to the jurisdiction of the land captain, who, following the government's preferences, usually decided in favor of the request. In those village communities that had had no repartitions since the initial allotment of land, all members of the commune were declared automatically to be the proprietors of their allotments.

Thus, the basic purpose of this act was to awaken within the peasantry the instinct of private property and to initiate the destruction of the commune. However, this was merely the first stage in the realization of the new agrarian policy. From the economic point of view, the simple declaration that the allotment lands were personal property did not remove all the inconveniences arising from scattered strips, the open field system, mandatory crop rotation, joint use of the commons, and so on. The second step in the attack on the commune, then, was the [land settlement—ed.] law of May 29, 1911, which focused on the organization of landholding (*zemleustroistvo*).[21] The right of the peasant who became the owner of his allotment to consolidate his strips into a compact holding was anticipated by the decree of November 9, 1906. But the land settlement law itself now became the basis for recognizing allotment land as personal property. The main thrust was in the direction of creating farmsteads (*khutora*), where the peasant homestead was relocated onto the holding, and consolidated holdings (*otruba*), where the homestead remained in the village.

The promulgation of these laws changed the very basis of the patriarchal and tutelary orientation of traditional agrarian policy. Middle and well-to-do farms now became the focus of the government's concern. As Stolypin himself put it, a "wager" was being placed "not on the poor and the drunk, but on the strong and the powerful."[22] Agrarian reform acquired definite logic and coherence. In particular, the operations of the Peasant Land Bank (which by a decree of November 15, 1906, was empowered to mortgage allotment lands) and of the Migration Office were

[21]Ibid., no. 35370.
[22]*Sbornik rechei P. A. Stolypina, proiznesennykh na zasedaniiakh Gosudarstvennogo soveta i Gosudarstvennoi dumy (1906–1911)* (St. Petersburg, 1911), 75.

subordinated to the main goal of the reform: the nurturing of peasant smallholders.[23] The decree of October 5, 1906, was also integrated into the system of measures designed to transform the village. On the one hand, it facilitated departure from the commune and separation from the land of those elements whose link to the village was becoming attenuated. On the other, it strengthened the position and the legal and property status of the prosperous social elements in the village; it granted them the opportunity to become actively involved in the organs of zemstvo self-government; and it liquidated the antiquated functions of the commune.

However, devotion to the old ways was powerful enough to be reflected even in the new agrarian legislation. Its inconsistency and limited character were apparent first of all in its treatment of the status of the allotment land and of its proprietor. For example, ownership of allotment land retained attributes of peasant corporatism, and the owners of allotments continued to be limited in their right to dispose of them. As Stolypin declared when discussing the agrarian question in the Third Duma: "The state, in order to provide the agrarian population with a fund of landed property, limits [the right of] disposition over this property; the allotment land may not be alienated to individuals belonging to other estates; it may not be mortgaged except to the Peasant Land Bank; it may not be sold for debt, and it may not be devised."[24]

Besides, the tutelary tendency in government policy apparently had a certain basis in reality: The agrarian population, despite its relative decrease within the total population of the empire, continued to increase in absolute numbers and to present employment problems. It was also obvious that the government was not interested in promoting the creation of large peasant farms that could compete with the gentry; a temporary limit of not more than six allotments was established on the concentration of landed property in the hands of one individual. All these restrictions decelerated the process of mobilization of peasant land and contributed to its devaluation. To be sure, the law of May 29, 1911, declared that allotment land could become private property if it were conjoined with purchased land at the time when its owner was leaving the commune. This was an important concession to bourgeois principles, but the development of capitalist relations was not the paramount goal

[23]*PSZ*, 3rd ser., no. 28547.
[24]*Sbornik rechei*, 73.

of the reform. Although it removed the most significant impediments on the road to modernization of the village economy, the state did not abandon its traditional desire to regulate socioeconomic processes in the countryside and to maintain them at a particular level of development.

One important objective of the reform was to fortify the old political regime by resting it upon a somewhat renovated foundation, with the future prospect of transforming it into a constitutional monarchy. On the whole, the reform, directed against the revolution, was put into effect only after the revolution was defeated, but its counterrevolutionary orientation was maintained, assuming, as it were, a preventive character. After the coup d'état of June 3, 1907, Stolypin, submitting the decree of November 9, 1906, to the Third Duma for its ratification, repeatedly underlined its political character: The establishment of "strong individual proprietors" in the village was necessary "for the reorganization of our tsardom on firm monarchical principles" and for erecting a barrier to the spread of the revolutionary movement.[25] The calculation to rely on strong conservative support in the form of prosperous peasant smallholders was also inspired in part by the continuing decline of gentry landownership (it decreased by another 20 percent between 1905 and 1914), which threatened to undermine the positions of tsarism. A new social force was to become an integral component of the authoritarian system of June 3.

Stolypin's cabinet also hoped for great economic benefits from the agrarian reform. Not only was the village expected to flourish, but there would be general economic growth of the country as a whole. "We are building our economic renaissance," declared Stolypin, "on the foundation of the purchasing power of a prosperous and strong class at the bottom of society." More than that, without the restructuring of agriculture, noted A. V. Krivoshein, the prime minister's ally and follower, "Russia will not be able to stand its ground in the great economic competition of the nations."[26]

Stolypin did not see his activity bear fruit, and not only because some of his plans were utopian. The law of May 29, 1911, was to enter into force on October 15, but on September 1 the prime minister was assassinated. By that time, the political atmosphere in the ruling circles had

[25]Ibid., 75.
[26]B. V. Anan'ich et al., *Krizis samoderzhaviia v Rossii, 1895–1917 gg.* (Leningrad, 1984), 350.

substantially changed in any case. The defeat of the revolution had strengthened the conservative forces, which then gradually mobilized to revoke the concessions made by the government. Stolypin was losing power and influence even before September 1. All of his legislative proposals aimed at augmenting and strengthening the agrarian reform and somewhat modernizing the political system (reorganization of local government, reform of zemstvo and village self-government and canton courts, introduction of universal primary education) were rejected. The implementation of the agrarian reform, continued by Krivoshein, who headed the Main Administration of Land Tenure and Agriculture, was by then also encountering resistance.

ACHIEVEMENTS AND FAILURES OF THE STOLYPIN POLICIES

What were the real results of the reform in statistical terms? Between 1907 and 1915, there was a total of 2.7 million petitions to individualize peasant holdings as personal property and 5.8 million petitions for land settlement and establishment of farmsteads (both khutora and otruba).[27] According to the most recent calculations of Soviet scholars, somewhat more than 3 million proprietors de facto left the commune, that is, about one-third of all commune members in 1905, or about one-quarter according to the data for 1916 (which take into account the further parcelization of allotment lands in the interval).[28] About 2.5 million of the proprietors formally left the commune and individualized their allotments on the basis of the decree of November 9, 1906, and the law of June 14, 1910. As a rule, in such cases the allotments remained within communal landholding, and the proprietors themselves retained a close link with the commune and continued to use its unenclosed commons. Most of these individuals had received deeds of landownership by 1910. The process of individualization was swiftest and most widespread in the southern and southeastern provinces, where the commune was generally weak because it arose late and where agriculture was characterized by market relations. The average allotment here was somewhat greater than 8.6 desiatiny. The process was also advanced in the provinces of the

[27]K. A. Krivoshein, *A. V. Krivoshein (1857–1921)* (Paris, 1973), 92.
[28]Viktor P. Danilov, "Ob istoricheskikh sud'bakh krest'ianskoi obshchiny v Rossii," in *Ezhegodnik po agrarnoi istorii* (Vologda, 1976), 6: 104–6; Anan'ich, *Krizis samoderzhaviia*, 359.

central agricultural region, where the vestiges of serfdom were strongest. There, the average size of allotment was 4.3 desiatiny, and the proportion of pauperized peasants hoping to migrate was high.[29]

Beginning in 1911, the rate of increase in the individualization of allotments was sharply reduced. Instead, there was an increase in the number of proprietors of consolidated holdings. Between 1907 and 1915, more than 1.3 million of such consolidated farmsteads were created on allotment land, with a total area of 12.8 million desiatiny, and the Peasant Land Bank sold 3.7 million desiatiny, divided into 270,000 parcels, to the peasantry. By 1916, there were more than 1.6 million individual farms of former communal peasants, occupying an area of some 16 million desiatiny: 300,000 farmsteads (khutora) and 1.3 million consolidated holdings (otruba), constituting 10 to 11 percent of all peasant households.[30] Almost two-thirds of these individual farms were created by land settlement of entire communities and about one-third by individual proprietors who left their commune. Consolidated holdings were most widespread in the northwestern, western, southern, and southeastern provinces, where farms were characterized by a relatively high degree of market relations and where agrarian capitalism was better developed. The average farm size was about 9 desiatiny in the southern provinces, about 11 in the west, and about 20 in the southeast.[31] Almost 90 percent of the petitions regarding individualization of allotments were effectuated, but that was true of less than one-third of the petitions requesting land settlement, because the process was interrupted by war. On May 29, 1915, the government proclaimed cessation of work on land settlement until the end of the war.

To what extent were the aims of the reform realized? The most important of these was the dual goal of destroying the commune and creating a large social category of petty landholders. As far as the commune was concerned, Stolypin frequently spoke in favor of gradualism and caution when taking steps to abolish it and of the need to take into account regional peculiarities and to follow the principle of voluntarism. Actually, however, the legislation provided not only for economic pressure on the commune to induce divisions within its ranks but also for direct administrative intervention. Almost three-quarters of those who

---

[29]*Izvestiia zemskogo otdela Ministerstva vnutrennikh del,* 1915, no. 12: 419.
[30]Ibid., no. 7: 242.
[31]*Otchetnye svedeniia o deiatel'nosti zemleustroitel'nykh komissii na 1 ianvaria 1915 g.* (Petrograd, 1915), 21–51.

left the commune did so without receiving the approval of the village assembly, and the intervention of local authorities was necessary to grant their requests.[32] Numerous circulars from the Ministry of Internal Affairs demanded increased effort to help peasants depart from the commune.

And yet the commune survived despite these pressures. Many peasants who submitted requests to leave the commune later retracted them. Of the 3.5 million proprietors in nonrepartitional communes who were declared individual owners of their allotments in accordance with the law, only 470,000 (13.4 percent) obtained deeds confirming their proprietorship. Most such communes continued to function. Repartitional communes, despite prohibitions by the authorities, continued to conduct both general and partial repartitions.[33] The preservation of the communal organization of the peasantry was the result, on the one hand, of powerful traditions, rooted in the relatively low level of socioeconomic development of the village, and, on the other, of the fact that the commune to a certain extent had managed to adjust to the new conditions and even to promote agricultural progress. In any case, in 1917 there were about 110,000 communes on the territory of the present-day Russian Republic.[34]

The outcome of the effort to create a large category of peasant smallholders was also not unequivocal, for the creation of individual farmsteads was accompanied by the pauperization of a considerable number of former communal peasants, which also presented a problem. In approaching the destruction of the commune, Stolypin counted first of all on "blowing it up" from within, taking into consideration the relatively advanced process of social stratification in the village. In reality, the social elements that left the commune were first and foremost those at its extremes: those few households that possessed additional lands and the numerically predominant poor peasants, who intended to sell their allotments.

The peasants sold a total of about 4.1 million desiatiny during the reform process, or about one-fourth of the land that had become individual property. The sellers amounted to 1.2 million proprietors, about

[32] Anan'ich, *Krizis samoderzhaviia,* 358.

[33] P. N. Zyrianov, "Zemel'no-rasporiaditel'naia deiatel'nost' obshchin v 1907–1914 gg.," *Istoricheskie zapiski* 116 (1988): 123.

[34] Viktor P. Danilov, *Sovetskaia dokolkhoznaia derevnia: Naselenie, zemlepol'zovanie, khoziaistvo* (Moscow, 1977), 97.

40 percent of all those who had left the commune. The motives and consequences of the sales greatly varied. A survey conducted by the Ministry of Internal Affairs in 1914 found that only one-quarter of the sellers sold allotment land in order to purchase other land for farm improvement. The rest sold their property because they were for all practical purposes no longer engaged in agriculture, or because they were unable by themselves to cultivate their allotment, or because they planned to emigrate to Siberia.[35]

The actions of the Peasant Land Bank intensified the process of income and social stratification in the village. Between 1907 and 1915, the peasants purchased from the bank or with its help 9.8 million desiatiny. The vast majority of the buyers were individual proprietors, who purchased more than 90 percent of the total.[36] The main goal of the bank was to help create model consolidated holdings, and these holdings, as already noted, numbered more than 270,000. But although it offered loans for as much as 95 percent of the purchase price, the bank priced the parcels it sold at more than one-third above their market value. As a result, bank debt was a heavy burden on its customers, making it more difficult for them to make improvements on their farms. Between 1906 and 1916, the bank repossessed more than 600,000 desiatiny from its debtors.

There was also a chronic shortage of agrarian credit. A special conference that discussed the problem of farm improvements in 1908 estimated required expenditures at half a billion rubles. The autocracy, however, busily preparing for war, refused to budget the requested sum and limited itself to relatively insignificant annual allocations.[37]

Thus, the reform noticeably intensified the process of mobilization of allotment lands and their concentration in the hands of the well-to-do peasantry. Migration was intended to serve as the instrument for removing the weak and impoverished elements from the village. The total number of peasants who migrated beyond the Urals from 1906 to 1916 was 3.1 million, which was more than double the figure for the preceding decade. Some of them managed to settle on the new lands and to establish their farms. Others scattered over the vast territories of Siberia

[35]Anan'ich, *Krizis samoderzhaviia*, 362–64.
[36]Sergei M. Dubrovskii, *Stolypinskaia zemel'naia reforma* (Moscow, 1963), 319–21.
[37]Anan'ich, *Krizis samoderzhaviia*, 355.

and never became independent farmers, and 546,000 of them, or 18 percent, returned to European Russia, adding to the pauperized social elements in the village.[38] Stolypin and Krivoshein soon realized the inefficiency and the political danger of the traditional policy that aimed at alleviating overpopulation in the village by the outmigration of landless peasants. Here, too, the wager was placed on the middle and well-to-do proprietors. In consequence, however, migration simply became one of the means for the opening up of new lands and the strengthening of the frontiers of the empire. After 1911, the numbers of migrants sharply decreased.

On the whole, rural migration did not play any noticeable role in the solution of the agrarian problem. Agrarian overpopulation, especially in the provinces of central Russia, became much worse. If at the beginning of the twentieth century there were 23 million "excess" workers in the countryside, by 1913 they numbered about 32 million. Rural migration absorbed 24.5 percent of the natural population increase from 1906 to 1910, but only 8.3 percent from 1911 to 1913. It was the cities that began playing an increasingly important role in absorbing village outmigration. Between 1906 and 1910, they absorbed 20.9 percent of the population increase (1.8 million people); between 1911 and 1913, the figure was 41.6 percent (2.3 million). Nevertheless, more than half of the natural population increase remained in the countryside, producing continued fragmentation of allotments and increasing the land hunger of the peasantry.[39]

As far as the new social layer of peasant proprietors created by the reform is concerned, one should note, first, that it was a relatively small group, and, second, that most of it consisted of small and petty proprietors. The average size of farmsteads and consolidated holdings was 9.8 desiatiny. This was larger than the average size of a communal peasant's farmland (7.1 desiatiny), but the average concealed great variations. In twenty-four provinces of central Russia, the average size of proprietary farms was less than 8 desiatiny (ranging from 3 to 7.6), which was less than the economic minimum.[40] A study conducted in 1913 of 22,400 consolidated households in twelve counties of various provinces in European Russia found that 33.7 percent had less than 5 desiatiny; 32.2

---

[38]*Statisticheskii ezhegodnik, 1916* (Petrograd, 1918), 100–101.
[39]Andrei M. Anfimov, *Krupnoe pomeshchich'e khoziaistvo Evropeiskoi Rossii (konets XIX–nachalo XX v.)* (Moscow, 1969), 370–71.
[40]*Otchetnye svedeniia*, 21–51.

percent had between 5 and 10; 17.7 percent, between 10 and 15; 10.4 percent, between 15 and 25; and 6 percent, more than 25.[41]

It is practically impossible to determine the economic consequences of the reform with any degree of exactitude. Russian agriculture in the early twentieth century and especially during the prewar years was undergoing profound changes that were connected with the generally favorable economic situation, structural changes in the nature of the economy, and the increasing modernization of the agrarian sector as a whole. Overall agricultural output grew markedly, as did its market value, and such other indices as crop yields and use of machinery and of fertilizers were also rising. Peasant savings in state savings institutions increased markedly, from 288.5 million rubles in 1905 to 505 million in 1914. Credit cooperatives, which numbered 1,700 institutions with 704,000 members in 1906, by 1915 had grown to 14,500 institutions and 9.5 million members. Between 1908 and 1913, they loaned a total of 2.6 billion rubles.[42]

It is also difficult to say what the contribution of consolidated holdings was to the progress of the agrarian economy. The 1913 study referred to above observed substantial positive results in their economy and in their business practices. For example, farm consolidation and closer homestead location significantly lowered production costs and allowed the introduction of new agricultural methods and crops. There was a considerable increase in the proportion of proprietors who were involved in credit operations (from one-half to two-thirds in southern counties), which allowed additional investment in the farm economy. The proportion of farmers using hired labor was greater by one-third. Crop yields were one-third to one-half again as large in comparison with households that remained in the commune. At the same time, owners had difficulties in keeping draft animals after leaving the commune, with the result that the number of cattle per capita decreased.

Undoubtedly, the reform contributed to the development of the internal market, in terms of both the consumers (the landless peasantry) and the producers (the proprietors of the khutora and otruba). Nevertheless, despite all the positive tendencies, the agrarian reform, from the economic point of view, did not on the whole succeed in justifying the

[41]*Obsledovanie zemleustroitel'nykh khoziaistv, provedennoe v 1913 g. v 12 uezdakh Evropeiskoi Rossii* (Petrograd, 1915).
[42]Korelin, *Sel'skokhoziaistvennyi kredit*, 135, 161, and 169.

hopes placed upon it. The rate of growth of agricultural production even decreased somewhat during the five years preceding the outbreak of World War I.

From the political point of view, the reform was an obvious failure. The monarchy was deposed in February 1917, and history did not allot Stolypin the twenty years of peace on which he had counted. But not only was the process of creating a mass of conservative peasant small-holders interrupted by the war. Even before that, the rates of implementation of the key aspects of reform had been on the decline: The number of requests to leave the commune had begun dropping after 1911, as did the number of rural migrants and the number of purchasers of land from the Peasant Land Bank, after 1912, and the number of requests for land settlements, after 1913.[43] This was an indication that the contingent of peasants who wanted to leave the commune in one way or another was being exhausted. The commune, having freed itself from both the proletarianized elements and the prosperous entrepreneurial peasant elements, became to a certain extent stabilized.

Furthermore, by intensifying the stratification of the peasantry, the reform sharpened social tension in the village. The members of the commune waged war on those who departed and strove to bring them back. The calculation that setting the peasants against each other would distract their attention from the gentry estates proved illusory. The idea of a general repartition was not abandoned by the peasantry, and it was the commune that realized it in 1917, swallowing up in the process not only gentry lands but also most of the farmsteads and consolidated holdings. Finally, forcible steps to implement the reform provoked dissatisfaction and increased conflict with the authorities. The number of peasant disturbances between 1907 and 1914 was apparently small, but they did not cease, and they were a constantly felt element of political instability.[44]

Thus, no goal of the agrarian reform was fully achieved. Time, resources, and political wisdom in the ruling circles were all lacking. From a theoretical economic perspective, Stolypin's plans were realistic and progressive. Their timely and reasonable implementation, without administrative pressure, might perhaps have averted the peasant revolution.

[43]Dubrovskii, *Stolypinskaia zemel'naia reforma*, 203, 241, and 390; *Otchet krest'ianskogo pozemel'nogo banka za 1906* (St. Petersburg, 1907); *Otchet krest'ianskogo pozemel'nogo banka za 1915* (Petrograd, 1916).
[44]Dubrovskii, *Stolypinskaia zemel'naia reforma*, 518, 520–21, 530, and 536.

But the evolutionary path of any country depends to a considerable extent not only on objective circumstances but also on a subjective predisposition in favor of reform within the ruling circles, their willingness to abandon the old and to embark on the path of transformation.

The ossification of the Russian autocracy and the social egotism and conservatism of the landed gentry represented powerful elements retarding the modernization of the country. In particular, the evolution of the village after 1861 was slowed down and deformed by the government's agrarian policy. Half a century was lost, a period of time long enough for Germany to reform its agrarian system and to give a capitalist impulse to the development of agriculture. The Russian experience of agrarian reform in 1861 and 1906–11 demonstrates that the autocracy, even in crisis situations, constantly delayed necessary transformations, and even after having decided to embark upon them could not avoid contradiction, inconsistency, and bureaucratic footdragging during their implementation. The autocracy yearned for the past, and it constantly looked backward rather than moving ahead. Virtually every reform step was involuntary, made under the pressure of extraordinary circumstances and having as its most important goal the stabilization of the political regime. And when the pressure of circumstances decreased, when the immediate threat of revolution receded, the ruling circles of Russia strove to derail the reform and to delay change once again.

Stolypin's attempt to formulate and implement a new course in the government's agrarian policy as an alternative to revolution collapsed. The old regime could not withstand the test of war, when all the contradictions in Russian society grew more acute. As Stolypin foresaw, the failure of his policy not only ended the government's vain attempts at reform, but it also presented the revolutionary forces, whose standing among the peasantry sharply rose, with their chance.

After the victory of the October Revolution, the Soviet government to a certain extent proved capable of taking into account both the sentiments of the peasant masses and the experience of the recent agrarian reform. The decree on land, adopted on October 26, 1917, by the Second All-Russian Congress of Soviets, reflecting the will of the majority of the peasantry, abolished private landed property and proclaimed land a national resource. The Russian republic's Agrarian Law Code of 1922 declared land to be state property but envisaged a variety of forms of land tenure, depending on local conditions: communal (including leveling repartitions), household (with the right of the household to cultivate land in open-field, farmstead, or consolidated-holding form), and co-operative (communes, cooperatives, or associations for joint land cultivation).[45] This path of development would involve the peaceful if competitive coexistence of these forms, intended to demonstrate which one was the most vital and effective, but it was forcibly cut off in the late 1920s. The administrative approach to a solution of the problems of the village prevailed once again. The lesson of the Stolypin reform, that forcible imposition of forms of property and economy upon the countryside by the bureaucracy brings seriously adverse consequences, was not heeded. This lesson presumably should be taken into account in our times, too.

[45]*Sbornik dokumentov po zemel'nomu zakonodatel'stvu SSSR i RSFSR, 1917–1954* (Moscow, 1954), 11–12 and 164.

7

Agricultural reform and political change: the case of Stolypin

DAVID A. J. MACEY

The "agrarian question" and agricultural productivity have been central to all periods of reform in Russian and Soviet history, from the Great Reforms of the 1860s to the Gorbachev era and its aftermath. In large part, this has been because each regime has seen a solution of its agrarian problem as the key to its political survival. But even beyond that, the solution has generally been viewed not only as a "quick fix" for what immediately ails the regime but as a panacea for all of its current problems. Moreover, the solution has always been introduced as part of a "revolution from above." Consequently, the short-term issues of preserving or restoring political order have tended to take precedence over strictly agricultural concerns, which are, by definition, usually long-term in nature. Focusing on one example of agrarian reform, this essay is intended to throw light on the problem of such reform in both Russian and Soviet history and on the linkages between economic and political reform in general.

The Stolypin agrarian reforms have long been identified as the key to understanding the fate of tsarism. At the time they were adopted, they were hailed by their creators and supporters as the culmination and final realization of the emancipation—as, indeed, a second emancipation. Yet this perception was inaccurate in certain respects, for it suggested a degree of continuity between the two sets of reform legislation that did not in fact exist. By contrast—and also, in part, inaccurately—the political opposition saw the Stolypin reforms as an ad hoc response to the threat of revolution, designed primarily to preserve the political dominance of the landowning nobility. The opposition acknowledged that if the reforms were successful, they would significantly change the political environment, although there was no agreement as to whether such an outcome was desirable. In the aftermath of tsarism's collapse, however, these concerns became largely irrelevant, and attention was focused on the reforms' relative or absolute failure as demonstrated by the agrarian revolution of 1917–18.

In retrospect, these interpretations seem narrow and partisan. On the one hand, they place far too much emphasis on the role of individual politicians and fail to see that reform is the product of a complex and protracted series of intellectual, social, and political processes. On the other hand, they demand a view of the reforms exclusively in terms of such political events as the collapse of the monarchy and the revolution, although these events were largely independent of whatever had happened in the countryside as a result of the Stolypin reforms. More important, such interpretations prevent one from seeing the reforms more broadly, and in their own right, as Stolypin and other ministers frequently asserted, as the "axis of our domestic policy"[1]—an assertion that suggested and was intended to suggest that the reforms were part of a larger social, political, and economic program designed to achieve a radical reform of the existing system and to preserve political continuity. Thus, just as the Great Reforms began with the emancipation, which made necessary a series of subsequent reforms, so in 1906 Stolypin adopted a new agrarian policy that also presumed and made necessary a whole series of further reforms. It is precisely such a long-term perspective, which deliberately highlights the similarities between the Stolypin reforms and both the Great Reforms and the Gorbachev policies, that I will adopt in this paper.[2]

THE PRECONDITIONS

I would distinguish four stages in the preparation of the Stolypin reforms that seem to apply equally well to any program of reform: (1) the identification of a problem, (2) a perceptual or ideological revolution that

[1]See, for example, the closing speech of A. I. Lykoshin to the Congress of Permanent Members of Provincial Boards on November 1, 1907, in *Trudy s"ezda nepremennykh chlenov gubernskikh prisutstvii 24/X–1/XI/1907 g.* (St. Petersburg, 1908), 7–9.

[2]For a more direct comparison, see David A. J. Macey, "Gorbachev and Stolypin: Soviet Agrarian Reform in Historical Perspective," in W. Moskoff, ed., *Perestroika in the Countryside: Agricultural Reform in the Gorbachev Era* (Armonk, N.Y.: M. E. Sharpe, 1990), 3–18.

permits both the abandonment of those attitudes and policies that helped produce the problem and the adoption of a radical new approach, (3) the organization of these ideas and their propagation to a broader forum within both government and society, and (4) the emergence of a political figure able to weld together the political support necessary to win approval for the reforms and, subsequently, to implement them.[3]

Identification of the problem. The structure of peasant life and agriculture in the second half of the nineteenth century had, of course, been determined by the statues emancipating the serfs in 1861.[4] Three features of that legislation proved central to all subsequent reform efforts, even though each had been adopted on the laissez-faire assumption that social, economic, and political developments would eventually make it obsolete. First, the peasants were denied equality of status with the other social classes and hence were isolated within their own social and legal system. Second, the traditional peasant commune was transformed into the lowest cell in the hierarchical system of bureaucratic administration and was subordinated to a new level of administration created at the canton level, including a separate court that operated on the basis of customary law.[5] Third, in order to strengthen the commune's authority and effectiveness and to prevent social differentiation and the emergence of landlessness and a rural proletariat, the legislation incorporated the traditions of mutual responsibility for the payment of taxes, periodic repartitions of arable land, and the existing forms of both family and communal ownership of property. In addition, restrictions were placed on the right of either individual peasants or villages to change their status. Unfortunately, as the emancipation's framers noted at the time, these measures, while guaranteeing [repayment of] the government's loan to the peasantry and preserving social, economic, and political stability, contradicted the equally important economic need to raise peasant

---

[3]For a detailed account of each of these stages, see David A. J. Macey, *Government and Peasant in Russia, 1861–1906: The Prehistory of the Stolypin Reforms* (De Kalb: Northern Illinois University Press, 1987).

[4]The best and most recent treatments of the emancipation and the era of the Great Reforms are Daniel Field, *The End of Serfdom: Nobility and Bureaucracy in Russia, 1855–1861* (Cambridge, Mass.: Harvard University Press, 1976); and W. Bruce Lincoln, *In the Vanguard of Reform: Russia's Enlightened Bureaucrats, 1825–1861* (De Kalb: Northern Illinois University Press, 1982), and *The Great Reforms* (De Kalb: Northern Illinois University Press, 1990).

[5]On the commune, see Dorothy Atkinson, *The End of the Russian Land Commune, 1905–1930* (Stanford, Calif.: Stanford University Press, 1983).

agricultural productivity, because they reinforced the communal form of land use, with its three-field system of cultivation and such associated problems as fragmentation, open fields subdivided into strips, common pasturing, and compulsory crop rotation. As a consequence, during the rest of the century, both individual peasants and whole villages would find it extremely difficult to introduce agricultural improvements.

While the emancipation was deemed by the government to have solved the "peasant problem," its critics within "civil society" began by the end of the 1860s to talk of the growth of peasant impoverishment and the emergence of a new "agrarian problem."[6] The explanation, according to both critics and peasants, was a land hunger that originated in the inadequacy of the initial allotment of land by the former noble owners. In the final analysis, as would become clear by the end of the century, land hunger was a product of an essentially finite quantity of land combined with a growing population. At the time, however, although the government acknowledged the existence of peasant impoverishment, it refused to accept the proposed explanation lest that imply acceptance of the proffered solution: additional allotments of land from the holdings of the nobility. Nonetheless, the government did accept responsibility for finding a solution.

During the rest of the nineteenth century, the government made two major attempts to deal with the growing agrarian problem.[7] The first of these came in the early 1880s, in the aftermath of Alexander II's assassination. It consisted of three components: tax concessions, government-regulated migration to the east, and the creation of the Peasant Land Bank to facilitate the peasants' acquisition of additional land. Together,

---

[6]The classic study of this period is Geroid T. Robinson, *Rural Russia under the Old Regime: A History of the Landlord-Peasant World and a Prologue to the Peasant Revolution of 1917* (New York: Longmans, Green, 1932; reprint, Berkeley: University of California Press, 1967). Some supposed features of the "agrarian problem" have been challenged in recent years, beginning with J. T. Simms, Jr., "The Crisis in Russian Agriculture at the End of the Nineteenth Century: A Different View," *Slavic Review*, 36 (1977): 377–98. Two recent volumes of articles dealing with aspects of this question are R. Bartlett, ed., *Land Commune and Peasant Community in Russia: Communal Forms in Imperial Russian and Early Soviet Society* (London: St. Martin's, 1990); and Esther Kingston-Mann and Timothy Mixter, eds., *Peasant Economy, Culture, and Politics of European Russia, 1880–1921* (Princeton: Princeton University Press, 1991).

[7]The principal studies of agrarian policy for that period are I. V. Chernyshev, *Agrarno-krest'ianskaia politika Rossii za 150 let* (Petrograd, 1918); and V. G. Chernukha, *Krest'ianskii vopros v pravitel'stvennoi politike Rossii (60–70 gody XIX v.)* (Leningrad, 1972), and *Vnutrenniaia politika tsarizma s serediny 50-kh do nachala 80-kh gg. XIX v.* (Leningrad, 1978).

these measures constituted the essence of the government's agrarian policy down to and even beyond the Stolypin reforms. In the later part of the 1880s, D. A. Tolstoi, as minister of internal affairs, sponsored a different explanation of the agrarian problem, which blamed the breakdown of local authority and the absence of an effective system of local administration.[8] His solution was the creation, in 1889, of the position of land captain, a strong local official whose functions were to protect peasant welfare, extend the rule of law to the countryside, and combat some of the negative aspects of the communal system of land use, thereby inhibiting any further social or economic changes in the countryside.

To the same ends, Tolstoi also sponsored legislation to restrict and in some cases prohibit both family partitions and communal repartitions of land as well as peasant rights to leave the commune with land. The government abandoned its earlier laissez-faire attitudes toward the peasantry and replaced them with a more paternalistic policy of bureaucratic tutelage (*opeka*). These reforms not only failed to stem the tide of rural change; they also reinforced the communal system of land use and the peasants' supposedly temporary legal exceptionalism. As a consequence, the peasant commune was effectively transformed into one of the two pillars of tsarist ideology and the tsarist political system, alongside the autocracy itself.

Thus, although the problem had now been identified and some reforms proposed, the results were negligible if not counterproductive. In the aftermath of the crop failure and partial famine of 1891–92, the agrarian problem returned to center stage. It has frequently been argued that reforms, when they finally came to Russia, did so as a response to some kind of "crisis" or "revolutionary situation."[9] However, we ought to be reasonably precise about the meaning of such terms. For my purposes, I will define "crisis" and "revolutionary situation" as a period in which the government loses its credibility and the political regime collapses from its own internal weaknesses. Such a situation is clearly revolutionary, in that revolution becomes possible though not inevitable.

---

[8]On Tolstoi and the era of the counterreforms, see Thomas S. Pearson, *Russian Officialdom in Crisis: Autocracy and Local Self-Government, 1861–1900* (Cambridge: Cambridge University Press, 1989).

[9]See, for example, A. Presniakov, "Samoderzhavie Aleksandra II," *Russkoe proshloe*, 1923, no. 4: 3–20, as well as Lenin's many writings on the subject of "revolutionary situations." On Lenin and the peasantry, see Esther Kingston-Mann, *Lenin and the Problem of Marxist Peasant Revolution* (Oxford: Oxford University Press, 1983).

February 1917 is a good example of a situation of that kind. But, we need to distinguish these from situations that fall short of complete collapse, in which political continuity is preserved but reform remains possible. I will call these "precrisis" situations. It is always possible for a precrisis situation to develop into a crisis or revolutionary situation; whether or not it does will depend in part on the success of the reforms that are introduced. To avoid the pitfalls of teleological thinking, however, it is necessary to make a distinction between the two stages.[10]

Thus, despite the famine of 1891–92 and the so-called agrarian crisis at the end of the nineteenth century, not to mention the "miniature revolution" in left-bank Ukraine in 1902 and the nationwide agrarian disorders of 1905–7, and contemporary rhetoric and the historiographical consensus notwithstanding, it seems clear that the period at the turn of the century was not a revolutionary situation but rather a precrisis situation as it has just been defined. For, as everyone would agree, the tsarist government did in fact succeed in preserving its legitimacy and continuity, restoring order, and introducing a program of reforms that promised to usher in a new stage of development.[11] But between the early 1890s and 1905, well before the precrisis situation matured, a perceptual or ideological revolution took place, leading both to a reconceptualization of the agrarian problem and to the development of innovative and radical solutions.

The perceptual revolution, or "new thinking." It is hard to say whether the perceptual revolution began in society or in government. After all, proposals to reform peasant agriculture had been floating about in Russia since the eighteenth century. It seems most accurate to say that the process was taking place simultaneously in government and society, and it was the complementarity of these changes that made it possible for the Stolypin reforms to be eventually adopted. A variety of social and intellectual influences were at work.[12] Perhaps the most important were those that helped bring government and society into closer contact. Among them was the so-called gentry reaction, which followed the

---

[10]Some of my thinking on this subject was stimulated by the comments on the background to the Gorbachev era of reform in Timothy J. Colton, *The Dilemma of Reform in the Soviet Union* (New York: Council on Foreign Relations, 1986), 57–67.

[11]The most recent and most comprehensive treatment of the agrarian background to the 1905–7 revolution is Teodor Shanin, *The Roots of Otherness: Russia's Turn of Century*, 2 vols. (London: Macmillan, 1985–86).

[12]Macey, *Government and Peasant*, 44–53.

emancipation and led some nobles to become more involved in agriculture, eventually producing a stratum of capitalist agriculturalists among the landowning nobility.[13] Another was the creation of the zemstvo in 1864, which encouraged a deeper involvement of the nobles in local affairs and gave rise to increased political activity on their part. These developments were paralleled by the growth and expansion of the bureaucracy, especially at the local level, which resulted in an increase in the number of those with direct knowledge and experience of peasant agriculture and local administration and in the diffusion of this knowledge and experience within the central bureaucracy. Equally important were a variety of informal contacts that brought government and society closer together, the most notable of which was the salon of K. F. Golovin, whose members were especially interested in rural affairs.[14]

A number of intellectual trends in the late nineteenth century also influenced educated society and government and helped shape the emerging perceptual revolution. In the realm of economics, the proponents of reform were able to combine earlier laissez-faire, liberal, and individualistic perspectives with a more materialistic approach borrowed from Marxism. In the realm of politics, the traditional commitment to autocracy was combined with a deep and profound respect for history and for gradual processes of change, which compelled a commitment to the rule of law and might ultimately have limited the autocracy. More specifically, there was a veritable explosion of information about peasant society, deriving from both government and nongovernment sources.

From the perspective of state policy, the most important consequences of these developments were the social and intellectual revolution they produced within the government and the emergence of a new generation of enlightened or liberal bureaucrats who were committed to a program of national economic growth and development. Born in the 1850s or 1860s, and thus thirty or forty years old by the turn of the century, these men were free of that mythical hold which "the Emancipation" had exercised over their predecessors. They were also too young to have played any significant role in previous attempts to reform peasant agriculture. The typical career path for this generation began with the study of law at either St. Petersburg or Moscow University or at the Imperial

---

[13]Roberta T. Manning, *The Crisis of the Old Order in Russia: Gentry and Government* (Princeton: Princeton University Press, 1982), 4–24.
[14]Macey, *Government and Peasant*, 48–49.

School of Jurisprudence, where they seem to have imbibed a great respect for history and the law. Subsequently, they would enter government service at the local level, as land captains or marshals of the nobility or in local offices of the ministries of internal affairs, agriculture, or justice. During these years, many served in the western borderlands and Poland or were involved in the resettlement of migrants in Siberia. In the process, they not only became familiar with the problems of peasant society and administration, but they were also exposed to the more individualistic and market-oriented forms of agriculture and social organization that existed in these regions. As a result of those experiences, they seem to have become convinced of the bankruptcy of the government's traditional agrarian policy and the complete failure of the administrative and regulatory approach to rural problems. In their view, it was not only futile to pass laws that did not conform to peasant needs and concerns; it was counterproductive, insofar as it destroyed the peasants' respect for both governmental authority and the law. Many of them set forth their novel ideas on the agrarian question either publicly, in print, or privately, within court or bureaucratic circles.

In the 1890s, this new generation of agrarian and legal experts began returning to St. Petersburg to take up positions in the central government. A key role in their recruitment was played by the ministries of agriculture, finance, and internal affairs, and by the respective ministers, A. S. Ermolov, S. Iu. Witte, and V. K. Plehve. Concentrated within a few specific departments and agencies, these new men were eventually responsible for drafting, enacting, and implementing the so-called Stolypin agrarian reforms. The best known were Vladimir I. Gurko and A. A. Rittikh. (Another was the Danish agronomist A. A. Kofod, though he was something of an outsider.) They were supported by a group of between twenty and forty others who shared their ideas. Indeed, virtually every young official who, prior to 1906, had criticized the government's traditional approach in favor of a policy of individualization and intensification seems to have ended up as part of the reform apparatus. Eventually, there were several thousand of these reformers, most of whom appear to have been convinced supporters of the reforms they were implementing.

The essence of this "new thinking" was not simply a rejection of traditional agrarian policies for having failed either to inhibit social and economic change or to inculcate a respect for law, let alone to resolve the agrarian problem.[15] Beyond that, it recognized that although the country might be in only a precrisis situation, the continuation of those policies would ultimately undermine the country's economic growth and political power and thus threaten the very existence of the state. Economic health—that is to say, economic growth—was thus identified as central to political health. As a result, the entire agrarian question was recast within an economic and materialistic framework that recognized the centrality of agriculture and the peasantry both to economic development, including the development of industry, and to political survival. However, at this precrisis stage, politics was of distinctly secondary concern, because it was widely assumed that successful economic reforms would eventually resolve Russia's political problems as well.

Within this general framework, the new generation of agrarian experts offered an interpretation of the agrarian problem that specifically rejected the approaches of the opposition and of the peasantry. As they saw it, the real problem was the low level of agricultural productivity and the inadequate development of a market or money economy, which together had produced a crisis in the government's tax collections. The culprit, in their view, was the peasant commune or, more accurately, the communal system of land use. In effect, they argued, the problem was one not of absolute land hunger but of relative land hunger. The solution, therefore, was not to grant additional allotments but to raise productivity by restructuring peasant agriculture and encouraging the development of a market economy. The resultant rise in peasant income would then solve the problem of both the peasants' and the government's poverty. To this end, it was recommended that peasants be granted the freedom to leave the commune and consolidate their strips into more compact units or individual farms (*otruba* and *khutora*). At the same time, in order to facilitate the development of a land market as well as the acquisition of capital to finance agronomical improvements, it was proposed that the head of each household be granted individual title to the land. The effects of these innovations would not be limited to agriculture, for implicit in the set of proposals was the elimination of the peasants' exclusionary status and legal isolation and their integration into civil society. And that, it was acknowledged, would en-

[15]Ibid., 56–68, 77–81, 83–98, 102.

tail reforms in local administration and self-government and, if not the creation of a constitutional monarchy, at least, presumably, the creation of a more law-governed state or the rule of law.

The emergence of this new thinking among isolated individuals, however, would not in itself have been sufficient to initiate the process of reform. Many of these ideas had been around for a long time, but they had not yet been systematized and transformed into a viable political program that could be propagated on a wide scale in order to develop the support necessary to enact it into law. The years 1902–5 were decisive in these respects.

Organization and support. A critical role in the development of these ideas into a comprehensive program of reform was played by two governmental bodies that were convened in 1902: the interdepartmental Special Conference on the Needs of Agriculture, which was chaired by Sergei Iu. Witte, though actually run by Rittikh, who was his special assistant; and the Ministry of Internal Affairs' Editorial Commission for the Review of Peasant Legislation, chaired by Gurko, head of the ministry's rural section, and under the rather loose supervision of Plehve.[16] Created independently and frequently seen as being deliberately at cross-purposes, the work of these two commissions was in fact completely complementary. Indeed, it is almost as if there was a purposeful division of labor between them. Thus, Gurko's commission initially developed the ideas of the perceptual revolution into preliminary legislative form, and the Special Conference took up many of the same ideas and developed them further. Gurko's commission also played the role of a propagandist for the new program, as it canvassed the local government bureaucracy for its input and opinion, and Witte's Special Conference played a similar role with respect to local "educated" society. The Special Conference then propagated its somewhat biased interpretation of the educated public's ideas more broadly within both government and society.

It was Gurko and Rittikh, together with their colleagues in these two organizations, who were primarily responsible for the development of a new agrarian policy. By 1903, they were in fundamental agreement not only as to what needed to be done but also on how to go about doing

---

[16]On these two bodies, see ibid., 54–56, 82–83.

it. The essence of their program involved the gradual individualization and intensification of peasant agriculture and its eventual transformation into a system of small-scale property ownership based on the family farm (khutor). They sought to demonstrate not only that the peasants themselves were aware of the problems with the existing system but also that they were already prepared for and in favor of the changes being proposed. In contrast to the most recent attempts at reform, though not unlike past and future proposals for radical reform, these ideas were seen both as a direct reflection of the peasants' needs and as being in complete correspondence with long-term trends in the development of the rural economy. But the reformers recognized that the needed transformation could not rely on peasant initiative alone. To achieve any degree of success, reform would have to be introduced "from above." However, although the program they developed called for direct government intervention to stimulate change, it was evolutionary, pragmatic, and experimental in nature, reflecting the actual processes of rural change as they understood them. Above all, both Gurko and Rittikh believed that this program of reform was essential to rebuilding the peasants' respect for law and for government authority and for developing a new relationship of trust between the government and the peasant that could serve as a basis for the further development of the economic and political system.

Meanwhile, despite the seemingly unprecedented nature of these proposals, the surveys that the two commissions conducted in provincial society, both official and unofficial, demonstrated a remarkably high level of support both for transferring the peasantry to individually owned farms and for ending their isolated legal status.[17] The publication and wide dissemination of the commissions' proceedings and other materials were designed to broaden that support even further. The victory of this perceptual revolution became manifest during the last three months of the Special Conference's existence—it was dissolved at the end of March 1905—and before the real significance of the revolutionary events of 1905 had become clear.[18] During its final discussions, the conference's thirty-one full members and eighteen advisory members, representing a cross section of senior members of the government who

[17]Ibid., 68–77, 98–102.
[18]Ibid., 103–18.

were either involved in or interested in the agrarian question, expressed virtually unanimous support for the program of individualization and intensification worked out by Rittikh and Gurko.

The revolution in policy. Significant portions of the central government bureaucracy, provincial officialdom, noble landowners, and liberal elements within the zemstvos apparently had, by late 1904 or early 1905, abandoned such shibboleths of government policy as the commune, peasant exceptionalism, and the fear of a landless proletariat and adopted such new ones as the farmstead (khutor) and a conviction that it represented both history's goal and the true peasant dream. But these developments were not sufficient to transform the new thinking into government policy. The final stage in this process involved the political task of welding together a coalition of reform-minded liberals and conservatives within the government and educated society and then winning the tsar over to this program.

However, as the scale of rural disorders grew during the summer and fall of 1905, many within the government began to suspect that a policy of expropriating private land on the peasants' behalf would be a politically more viable approach. As a consequence, toward the end of 1905, in part under Witte's leadership, the government considered a number of so-called projects for compulsory alienation.[19] Although expropriation was indeed one component of these projects, it was combined with and subordinated to the tasks of agricultural improvement, the elimination of both open fields and the communal system of land use, and, ultimately, the transformation of the entire system of peasant agriculture into one based on the principle of individually owned private property. Simultaneously, Witte launched an aggressive campaign to increase the sales of noble lands to the peasantry both directly and through the Peasant Land Bank. This combination of intensification and extensification was necessary if the government was to have any chance of reaching a modus vivendi with its moderate liberal opposition. Unfortunately for the cause of reform, negotiations to form a coalition cabinet with the liberals broke down. And that, in conjunction with the emergence of a number of more conservative groups such as the Octobrists and the United Nobility, who were dedicated defenders of gentry private property, brought to an end the government's dalliance with schemes of compulsory alien-

[19]Ibid., 121–50.

ation, though some high officials, including Witte, continued to believe that some form of expropriation was essential if the government were to preserve or win back the peasantry's support.

Notwithstanding the moderate, centrist nature of these initiatives, their endorsement of the principle of compulsory expropriation aroused widespread noble opposition. Furthermore, the atmosphere within the government changed as a result of both the success of its first punitive campaigns into the countryside and a vigorous propaganda campaign against any form of expropriation. The initial sallies were launched by members of the Golovin circle, long-time opponents of what they perceived as Witte's one-sided policies of industrialization. The principal spokesman for this point of view was none other than Gurko himself. This was followed by a veritable storm of criticism from within both the government and the landowning nobility. Meanwhile, from the beginning of 1906, a host of new proposals favoring the individualization and intensification of peasant agriculture and based on the principle of private-property landownership began to appear in the government's chancelleries and in the public arena, either in the daily press or in pamphlet or book form.

Subsequent efforts to respond to the widespread peasant discontent and to develop an agrarian program that would meet both peasant and national needs were hindered by the government's own internal divisions. In part, these were the result of conflict between those who supported extensification and some form of compulsory expropriation and those who supported intensification and individualization. But the government was also divided over whether it should act prior to the Duma's opening, wait and present its program to the Duma, or wait and see what program the Duma itself decided upon, even if, as some believed, that meant granting an additional allotment. The positions of specific individuals on these questions depended on whether they saw the government's future as resting upon the peasantry or upon the political parties and the level of their commitment to the rule of law.

Over the three months leading up to Witte's dismissal as chairman of the Council of Ministers and the opening of the First Duma at the end of April 1906, a number of commissions began working on a variety of projects for administrative, judicial, and agrarian reform.[20] Those who favored individualization and intensification and who believed in the

[20]Ibid., 150–73.

need to adopt preemptive measures prior to the opening of the Duma were successful in getting two of the projects enacted into law. The first, which was adopted on March 4, 1906, had been worked out by a commission headed by A. V. Krivoshein, the future minister of agriculture, and provided for the establishment of special land-organization commissions to administer just such a program. By the time the project was adopted and funded, however, the responsibilities of these commissions had been reduced from the initial and extremely modest one of helping peasants to improve their forms of land use by eliminating some of the most unproductive features of the open-field system to one of making it easier for the Peasant Land Bank to help needy peasants to acquire land, on the basis of the principles of individual ownership and use. The bill's sponsors vigorously opposed any concessions to the idea of increasing peasant landownership, no matter on what principles it was undertaken. Despite the changed emphasis in the commissions' responsibilities, the law of March 4, 1906, was significant because it marked both a major expansion of governmental authority and bureaucratic power at the local level and an explicit commitment to direct government intervention in the peasant economy with an eye to resolving the agrarian problem and improving peasant welfare. The new commissions also signaled the first stage of a bureaucratic attack on local society, designed to place agrarian reform firmly in the hands of government.

The second initiative was sponsored by those who favored political concessions and an expansion of peasant landownership as part of the solution, and it involved a series of minor revisions in the Peasant Land Bank statute that would enable it to take a more active role in purchasing land for resale to the peasantry. The government's internal disagreements were too great to permit any further initiatives prior to the Duma's opening. Thus, when in March 1906 the Council of Ministers, with the tsar's support, forwarded to the Council of State a project for agrarian individualization and intensification that had been worked out by a third commission, headed by Gurko, and that was based on Gurko's and Rittikh's pre-1905 proposals and contained the essence of the future Stolypin reforms, the Council's Combined Departments rejected it. Resubmitted in May 1906 to the Council of Ministers, it was turned down by it as well.

While this was taking place, the Council of Ministers changed its strategy and formed yet another commission, this one under the chairmanship of the new minister of agriculture, A. P. Nikol'skii. The mandate of this body was to coordinate the development of a comprehensive program of rural reform that, while conforming to the government's conception of its own and the national interest, would also provide a basis for cooperation with moderates of both left and right once the Duma convened. Basing itself on the work of the earlier commissions, the Nikol'skii commission directed the appropriate ministries either to draft legislation or to draw up a set of principles to guide its preparation in the areas of peasant administration, civil and personal rights, property rights, renting of land, land reorganization, education, rural credit, and improvement of local means of communication. Meanwhile, and again with the goal of achieving a compromise with the liberal opposition and the peasantry, yet another commission, headed by Rittikh, began drafting legislation to spell out specifically how peasant land hunger would be resolved through the sale of state and private land.

With the dismissal of Witte and his cabinet, and his replacement by I. L. Goremykin, nothing came of these initiatives until after the First Duma had been convoked and dismissed, and Stolypin had been appointed chairman of the Council of Ministers. The government had adopted a wait-and-see attitude, in the hope that some kind of compromise could be worked out with the Duma after it met and began defining its own political program. Such cooperation, however, proved impossible, for the government and the Duma quickly came into conflict over the issue of compulsory expropriation. From this point on, it became clear to all parties that the "peasant problem" had become *the* central political issue and the one upon whose resolution the very existence of the regime ultimately depended.

In retrospect, it appears that, although Witte and his government had developed a compromise policy of agrarian reform as part of a broader program of renovation and reform that was designed to appeal both to peasants and to the liberal opposition, this was not enough to win its adoption as the government's new agrarian policy. Witte's failure in this respect was a result of a combination of factors, the most important of which was undoubtedly his loss of credibility with the tsar. At the same time, however, it also appears that for any agrarian policy to have been adopted, it would have had to have the support of the landowning nobility. Witte was clearly not the person to win that support, given the long-standing noble opposition to his liberalism and his policies favoring industrialization and a market economy, not to mention his sponsorship of compulsory alienation.

The leading role in winning the support of the nobility was played by a newly formed organization known as the United Nobility.[21] The group's first congress, which met at the end of May 1906 in the apartments of the newly appointed minister of agriculture, A. S. Stishinskii, was a rather curious phenomenon. Although it was the product of several conservative strains, this congress, unlike the ones that followed, was dominated by nobles who were closely associated with the government and its bureaucracy. Some were capital-city dignitaries, others were bureaucrats, and still others were modernizing noble agriculturalists. Several of the participants were members of the Golovin salon, to which both Stishinskii and Gurko belonged. There was also an influential contingent from Saratov, where the future chairman of the Council of Ministers, Peter A. Stolypin, had been governor for the preceding several years.

One of the most important topics of discussion at the first congress was an agrarian platform that had been drawn up by, among others, S. S. Bekhteev, another member of the Golovin circle, and D. I. Pestrzhetskii, Gurko's co-worker in the rural section of the Ministry of Internal Affairs and himself an active publicist on behalf of individualization and intensification. Not surprisingly, this platform coincided very closely with what had already been worked out within the government under Gurko's and Rittikh's supervision. Moreover, during the discussion, the speakers repeated many of Gurko's arguments against expropriation and, like Gurko, frequently characterized the alternatives facing Russia in apocalyptic terms as a choice between private property and socialism, or between monarchy and socialism. While the congress never formally adopted this platform, it is clear from the discussions that it was supported by a majority. However, there was a significant minority that wanted to take a more conciliatory approach toward both the liberals and the peasantry by combining intensification and individualization with measures to eliminate land hunger with the aid of the Peasant Bank. In either case, it appears that the United Nobility had, in effect, been manipulated into adopting the bureaucracy's program. In any case, its support was important in bringing about that policy's eventual adoption.

The first sign that the government had finally decided to adopt this centrist and compromise program came at the beginning of June, when it submitted a series of projects to the First Duma that combined indi-

---

[21]Ibid., 174–95.

vidualization and intensification with measures to expand peasant land-ownership either from the sale of state land or with the help of the Peasant Bank.[22] They also included a proposal to abolish the office of land captain, long a bête noire of the left. Although they were designed to appeal to both the peasantry and the liberal opposition, the projects were less radical than those submitted to the Council of Ministers and the Council of State by Gurko's commission in March and May, in the hope of allaying conservative fears of any sudden changes in the peasant way of life. Thus, for example, the government's tutelage over the peasantry was preserved, in order to inhibit the development of a land market and the potential proletarianization of the peasantry. To this end, it was further proposed to establish limits on the quantity of allotment land that individual peasants could own and to prohibit sale of allotment land to nonpeasants. In conformity with the proposals made by Rittikh, the separation of peasants and their land from the commune was conceived as a gradual, two-stage process that would involve first a claim of title and then the consolidation of strips into a compact holding. On the other hand, the projects also included a provision for the automatic transfer to individual ownership of communities where there had been no repartition in the previous twenty-four years.

Clearly, the government's goal was to win support not only among the peasantry but also from the political center. Its program also represented a compromise between the various factions within the government—though Stolypin and others, including even the tsar, continued to see some form of compulsory expropriation as a probable political necessity. Despite all of these efforts, however, negotiations to form a coalition cabinet with the Constitutional Democrats (Cadets) and the Octobrists again broke down, and the Duma ended up expressing its support for compulsory expropriation. Interpreting this move as a commitment to socialism and as a direct threat to the government's survival, the tsar immediately prorogued the Duma. It was during the subsequent interregnum, prior to the convocation of the Second Duma, that the government finally introduced its program of radical agrarian reform, or rural perestroika.

The key figure in the final phase of the adoption of a government program was Stolypin himself.[23] Stolypin embodied all of the various

---

[22]Ibid., 196–210.
[23]Ibid., 213–24. See also Mary S. Conroy, *Peter Arkad'evich Stolypin: Practical Politics in*

forces that had come together to produce first the revolution in perceptions and then the revolution in policy. As a self-described social activist
who combined the roles of modernizing noble landowner, marshal of
the nobility, and government official, he symbolized the coming together
of government and society that had made possible the revolution in perceptions in the first place. In addition, his age, education, and service
profile were virtually identical to those of the new generation of bureaucrats, and, like them, he was both an opponent of the commune
and a supporter of individualization and intensification. Finally, he was
close to several of the more moderate and compromise-oriented founders
of the United Nobility. These characteristics, together with his well-
known calmness, strength, and self-confidence, seem to have been largely
responsible for his rapid promotion from provincial governor to chairman of the Council of Ministers. Most important, and unlike Witte,
Stolypin seems to have won the tsar's confidence, precisely because he
was the kind of person who was not only capable of establishing a
consensus within the government and between it and the Duma but who
could also take the initiative and preempt the Duma in the struggle over
a new agrarian policy.

Thus, when negotiations to form a coalition government collapsed
yet again, Stolypin immediately seized the initiative and began introducing the government's new agrarian policy, taking advantage of article
87 of the constitution.[24] It is important to point out that the content
neither of this policy nor of the larger government program of reform
had been worked out by Stolypin. Virtually all of the policies that Stolypin enacted or tried to enact were outgrowths of projects first discussed
prior to the outbreak of disorders in 1905 and then developed by various
commissions during Witte's premiership and subsequently passed on to
the Goremykin and Stolypin governments.

THE REFORMS AND THEIR GOALS

The program of reform associated with Stolypin's name was divided into
four parts and was adopted in four stages.[25] The initial measures were
part of the government's ongoing efforts to achieve a compromise with

---

Late Tsarist Russia (Boulder, Colo.: Westview, 1976), and George Tokmakoff, *P. A.
Stolypin and the Third Duma: An Appraisal of the Three Major Issues* (Washington,
D.C.: University Press of America, 1981).
[24]Macey, *Government and Peasant,* 224–38. [Article 87 allowed the emperor to legislate
by decree in certain cases when the Duma was not in session.—Ed.]
[25]Ibid.

the liberal opposition and involved a continuation of earlier initiatives to combat land hunger by expanding peasant landownership through land sales. Thus, in August and September 1906, laws were enacted providing for the sale to the peasantry of some nine million *desiatiny* of land belonging to the state, the tsar, and the royal family. This was supplemented by other measures that lowered interest payments on peasant loans and provided for the Peasant Land Bank to be reimbursed by the treasury for any losses incurred. To spur on his fellow nobles, Stolypin himself sold land to the Peasant Land Bank for resale to neighboring peasants.

September also saw the adoption of an "instruction" to the land-organization commissions that focused their initial activity on facilitating the sale of state and Peasant Land Bank land to the peasants. In pursuit of his broader political goal of building bridges to the various political parties, Stolypin also urged consideration of several additional measures designed to assist the land-hungry peasantry: an expansion of migration, the introduction of an American-style "homestead law," the grant of an additional allotment to those peasants (*darstvenniki*) who had received one-quarter allotments gratis at the time of the emancipation, the provision of additional pasture land, and the establishment of a state agricultural bank. However, nothing came of these proposals, because of opposition both from within the cabinet and from the United Nobility.

Then, in October, the government promulgated a law expanding peasant civil rights and moving a step further toward the peasants' integration into civil society on an equal basis with other social groups. This was followed by the well-known decree of November 9, 1906, which addressed questions of property rights and land organization and use and made it possible for individual peasants, groups of peasants, and whole villages to separate from the commune with their land. The final component of the reform program, and a logical consequence of the previously adopted measures, was the preparation of drafts for the reform of local administration and courts on an all-class basis. These were presented to the Second Duma in 1907, but they, too, failed to win approval, because of the opposition of the United Nobility.[26]

Finally, although Stolypin himself was in no way responsible for the

---

[26]The most complete and most recent study of the local reforms is Francis W. Wcislo, *Reforming Rural Russia: State, Local Society, and National Politics, 1855–1914* (Princeton: Princeton University Press, 1990), especially 243–304.

democratization of political life brought about by the establishment of the Duma, he was nonetheless committed to the development of a more democratic system of government, based on the rule of law—despite the June 3, 1907, coup d'état, the field courts-martial, and other breaches of the strict rule of law. Stolypin later developed these ideas further and began thinking about even more comprehensive reforms.[27] Unfortunately, his star was by then in decline and hence he was never able to act on them.

It is often asserted by Stolypin's admirers, when they look back on these efforts, that he had a comprehensive plan of reform, whereas his critics accuse him of seeking merely to restore the status quo ante and of simply responding in an ad hoc fashion to the various crises that faced the tsarist regime. Neither of these judgments is wholly accurate. On the one hand, it is fair to say that Stolypin did possess a patriotic and long-term vision of Russia's future that foresaw her development along more or less Western lines. What this seems to have meant, beyond the obvious preservation of Russia's great-power status, was economic and social modernization, including the development of an industrial economy and a more or less capitalist and certainly market-based agriculture, the equalization of all social classes on the basis of individual freedom and rights, and the rule of law.

Yet, on a practical level, the crucial factor shaping Stolypin's policy was the need to construct a working political alliance with the opposition in order to win the reform program's adoption, first within the government itself, and then by the Duma, but without antagonizing the peasantry, with its presumably conservative mentality. At the same time, these pressures made it impossible for the government to commit itself to the development of either a completely unregulated peasant individualism or a fully developed market economy in agriculture.[28] Thus, despite Stolypin's slogans of "get rich" and a "wager on the strong and sober," the new reforms preserved and in some cases extended certain aspects of the government's traditional system of bureaucratic tutelage, most notably by creating a huge apparatus to implement the reforms and by transforming the land captains into instruments of social engineering. Various constraints were eventually also placed on the devel-

---

[27]A. V. Zenkovsky, *Stolypin: Russia's Last Great Reformer* (Princeton: Princeton University Press, 1986).
[28]Macey, *Government and Peasant*, 239–48.

opment of a land market, by retaining limits on the disposability of peasant allotment land and by placing maximum and minimum norms on the amount of allotment land that could be owned. Hence, the newly created forms of peasant property were accurately described not as "private" but as "personal" property.

When it comes to the political structure, the picture becomes somewhat fuzzy. In the short term, it appears that there was an unquestioned commitment to the preservation of the autocracy. At the same time, there was an implicit willingness to work within such newly established political structures as the Duma and the Council of Ministers and to strengthen the links between government and society at all levels. From our perspective, such an attitude presupposes an end to autocracy and the establishment of a constitutional monarchy. Whether Stolypin—not to mention other members of his cabinet—was committed to or even foresaw such an eventuality is, however, less clear. So, for example, the proposals for local administrative reform combined provisions for integration and equality with an expansion in both the size of local officialdom and the authority of the central bureaucracy.

Ultimately, the key to Stolypin's program was the agrarian reform, not only because of the peasantry's demographic and political weight and the immediate threat that it posed to economic and political stability, but also because of the reformers' conviction that a healthy agriculture was critical to all further development, both economic and political. In turn, the essence of the agrarian reform was the attempt to find a long-term solution to the problem of raising agricultural productivity. But of course there is much that can intervene to create that familiar gap between theory and practice. Hence, a full understanding of the Stolypin reforms requires an examination of what happened once they were implemented, specifically of how the legislation was understood at the local level and how it was modified as a result of both political concerns and practical experience.[29]

[29]For more detailed treatments of the reforms' implementation, see George Yaney, *The Urge to Mobilize: Agrarian Reform in Russia, 1861–1930* (Urbana: University of Illinois Press, 1982); Judith Pallot, "Khutora and Otruba in Stolypin's Program of Farm Individualization," *Slavic Review* 42 (1984): 242–56; Judith Pallot, "Open Fields and Individual Farms: Land Reform in Pre-Revolutionary Russia," *Tijdschrift voor Economische en Sociale Geografie* 75 (1984): 46–60; Judith Pallot, "Peasant Responses to the Stolypin Reforms, 1906–1914" (paper delivered at the Annual Meeting of the American Historical Association, Washington, D.C., December 1987); J. Pallot and D. J. B. Shaw, *Landscape and Settlement in Romanov Russia, 1613–1917* (Oxford: Oxford University Press, 1990), 164–92; David A. J. Macey, "The Peasant Commune and the Stolypin Reforms: Peasant

THE SOCIAL, ECONOMIC, AND POLITICAL EFFECTS

The results of the Stolypin reforms have conventionally been measured by statistics concerning the number of farmsteads and consolidated holdings (khutora and otruba) formed.[30] However, the interpretation of these data varies. Liberal Western and émigré historians generally see the figures in a positive light, with the qualification that the reforms were not given sufficient time to have their full effect.[31] Soviet historians, on the other hand, looking at the same figures, tended to argue that the reforms were a failure.[32] Both Western and Soviet historians more recently began to focus attention on the government's supposed use of force during implementation and on peasant opposition, as shown primarily in complaints and other manifestations of the peasant movement in those years.[33]

Yet, as in the case of the analyses of the reforms' origin and nature, these evaluations of their results are too narrowly conceived, and they end up distorting the nature of both the government effort and the peasant response. To be sure, there were individual cases of force and the application of "administrative" methods, yet the government specifically eschewed force and made considerable efforts to discourage its use and to follow up on reported incidents and rectify them. In fact, a major component of government activity, with respect to both its own officials and the peasantry, was educational or propagandistic in nature. On the other hand, there is no question but that the government's intervention into rural life helped generate confrontation and conflict; this was inevitable, given that in practical terms the reforms amounted to a surveying operation that sought primarily to reorganize peasant landholdings and property rights—two of the most sensitive and contentious

Attitudes, 1906–14," in Bartlett, *Land Commune and Peasant Community*, 219–36; and David A. J. Macey, "Government Actions and Peasant Reactions during the Stolypin Reforms," in Robert B. McKean, ed., *New Perspectives in Modern Russian History* (London: Macmillan, 1992).

[30]See especially Dorothy Atkinson, "The Statistics on the Russian Land Commune, 1905–1917," *Slavic Review* 32 (1973): 773–87.

[31]Good examples are G. Pavlovskii, *Agricultural Russia on the Eve of Revolution* (London: Routledge, 1930; reprint, New York: Howard Fertig, 1968), and Andreas Moritsch, *Landwirtschaft und Agrarpolitik in Russland vor der Revolution* (Vienna: Bohlau, 1986).

[32]The most comprehensive Soviet study is S. M. Dubrovskii, *Stolypinskaia zemel'naia reforma: Iz istorii sel'skogo khoziaistva i krest'ianstva Rossii v nachale XX veka* (Moscow, 1963).

[33]See especially G. A. Gerasimenko, *Bor'ba krest'ian protiv stolypinskoi agrarnoi politiki* (Saratov, 1985), as well as the articles and the paper by Judith Pallot cited in n. 29.

issues in any rural society. However, the government had anticipated these consequences and tried to minimize them as far as possible by setting up the land-organization commissions as conflict-resolution mechanisms that used what amounted to collective-bargaining procedures to resolve disputes.

In this context, it is critical to remember that the reforms were conceived in gradual and evolutionary terms, in part because it had been feared that, although the peasants may ultimately have favored individual property, they would nonetheless resist change because of their preference for the routine and the traditional. The sole incentive offered to the peasant was the opportunity to become the "master" of his own land and to attain the eventual, though probably remote, possibility of "getting rich." Finally, given the reformers' belief that their program not only conformed to the peasant dream but also anticipated the actual path of historical development, as observed both in Western Europe and in the western regions of Russia, it was felt that the best approach was to imitate the process of change as it occurred in the countryside.

Thus, it had been decided not only to adopt Rittikh's gradualistic, two-stage process for the claiming of title and the separation of individual farms but also to focus initially on the formation of individual farmsteads that would serve as models and beacons to encourage the less adventurous to follow suit. The changes being introduced were not to be compulsory: Those peasants who wished to leave the commune could leave, while those who did not could remain. Furthermore, the government sought to provide legal procedures that would guarantee the ability of individual peasants to realize this freedom of choice in practice. Only in this way, it was felt, would the peasants be convinced of the government's sincerity and rest their trust in the law and in government authority. To this end, the commune was also given some power to protect its own interests.

When it came to implementation, however, the long-term economic goals of the reforms, which had in part inspired their voluntary, evolutionary, and noncoercive provisions, collided with two short-term goals that were primarily political and to some extent even at odds with each other: the expansion of private property and winning the peasants' trust and support. At first, much of the local reform officials' energy was directed toward encouraging peasants to claim title to their land, in the belief that this step was an end in and of itself. Actually, as we have seen, title claims had been intended as only the first stage in the formation of a farmstead. But the government discovered that a large number of peasants who claimed title viewed that stage as an end in itself, for they were seeking to sever their ties with agriculture. A later version of the law thus conflated the two-stage process as far as possible into a single one.

Considerable pressure was applied from above to form as many individual farmsteads as possible. As a result, the reform apparatus developed a campaign-style approach that produced a wave of what the government's critics and the press labeled "khutoromania" and that led to charges that the government was trying to impose its own "checkerboard fantasy" on the countryside.[34] Thus, we have the not unfamiliar problem of "tempo," as the reforms' local officials strove to create exemplars as rapidly as possible in order to create the impression of meaningful change and to encourage other peasants to follow. Most of these farms, however, seem to have been formed on Peasant Land Bank land rather than carved out of existing villages. On the other hand, there were also numerous cases of bribery and coercion and other illegal procedures, as local officials tried to respond to the government's pressure.

It soon became clear to the government that its initial measures were proving counterproductive. On the one hand, the pressure from above generated considerable opposition and conflict and thus undermined the government's other goal of winning the peasants' trust. On the other hand, the government realized that it was a more efficient expenditure of resources to transfer groups of peasants and whole villages to farmsteads in a single process. As a consequence, emphasis shifted away from claiming title and forming individual farms toward achieving agreement among the various parties involved. As the government became more aware of the obstacles that the peasants faced, it became increasingly willing to accept forms of agricultural organization that fell short of complete "individualization." Another factor underlying this newfound tolerance was the assumption that peasants would eventually see the advantages of creating a farm. Thus, as officials became educated to the process of reform, bureaucratic procedures were constantly refined and changes were made in the laws, in an effort to overcome problems in the reforms' initial design as well as practical obstacles to their implementation.

[34]B. D. Brutskus, in *Trudy Vol'nago ekonomicheskago obshchestva* 1–2 (1909): 50, and Yaney, *The Urge to Mobilize*, 380.

In retrospect, it seems that criticism of the reforms for their lack of coherence stemmed primarily from a tendency to consider any kind of reform short of a complete, revolutionary transformation of the existing system as having no real significance. Yet the great virtue of the Stolypin reforms was surely their gradualistic, evolutionary, pragmatic, and open-ended nature. For by constantly monitoring its activities in the countryside, the government was able to avoid the arrogance of urban intellectuals and theorists and learn from its mistakes.

Another criticism of the reforms and their supposed lack of coherence involved the ultimate economic goal of raising agricultural productivity and the government's failure to make any provisions for agronomical aid. In fact, the initial legislation had provided for some, admittedly moderate, financial assistance, in the form of both grants and loans. As the reform organization became more involved in land reorganization proper, the necessity of providing newly independent peasants with technical assistance became apparent. In the summer of 1909, Stolypin dispatched an emergency telegram urging the zemstvos to become directly involved in providing aid to peasants who had taken advantage of the reforms.[35] This was the first step along a path that led to a huge expansion in the government's involvement in providing agronomical aid over the next five years.

If we now shift our perspective and look at the reform process from the government's point of view, it is important to realize that when it embarked upon the reforms, the government had no idea how the peasantry was going to respond, though it had assumed that there would be considerable resistance. But the peasants responded with far greater alacrity than the government had expected, thereby placing a tremendous strain on its organization and particularly on its supply of surveyors, who were the key link in the reforms' implementation. From the very beginning, the reform movement in the countryside proceeded spontaneously and at a pace that often exceeded the government's capacity to keep up. Nonetheless, the government did what it could, and indeed it was remarkably successful. If one measures the reforms' results not by the number of farmsteads that were formed, nor by any rise in agricultural production, but rather by the number of peasants who sought government help, then one can appreciate the scale of the peasant response. By the beginning of 1916, when the reforms came to a halt as a result

[35]*Izvestiia Zemskago otdela* 10 (1909): 312–13.

of the war, about 50 percent of peasant households had requested some form of government assistance in reorganizing their holdings. This suggests not only that the government had begun to win the peasants' trust but also that new agricultural forms were becoming institutionalized and integrated into existing rural structures, thus becoming an accepted part of Russia's rural scene.

The conflict and even chaos that accompanied these changes were not, to be sure, desirable, but they seem to have been manageable. Moreover, there are some questions about who the reforms' beneficiaries were and even whether those moderate changes that had taken place were real or not. There are also questions about the actual level of chaos that existed in the Russian countryside. In any event, rather than viewing the conflict that did occur in a purely negative light, it seems more accurate to see it as a sign that the countryside was coming to life and beginning to show an unprecedented degree of individual and social initiative. On the other hand, it is also true that the reforms were being thwarted by a shortage of funds and the finance minister's lack of cooperation.[36] A major change in fiscal policy was being readied in 1914 that was designed to remedy these deficiencies, and had the war not intervened, it may well have provided the reforms with a stronger basis of fiscal support. One possible final indication of the reforms' increasing success is that, as the years passed, the "agrarian problem" began to disappear from the headlines and seemed to arouse less and less public concern and attention.

The Stolypin reforms sought to initiate a cultural revolution in the Russian countryside that would mobilize the population, transform its values and attitudes, stimulate individual and social initiative, and bring Russia closer to the Western model of social, economic, and political life. In these respects, they resemble the reforms that preceded and followed them. What distinguishes the Stolypin reforms from the others are their essentially democratic, voluntary, and legal methods. These methods were a direct result of the government's political centrism and its efforts to achieve a compromise between left and right alternatives as well as between individualism and collectivism, and between market and tutelage. In the last analysis, it seems that what is most important about

[36]David A. J. Macey, "Bureaucratic Solutions to the Peasant Problem: Before and After Stolypin," in R. C. Elwood, ed., *Russian and East European History: Selected Papers from the Second World Congress for Soviet and East European Studies* (Berkeley: University of California Press, 1984), 73–95.

these reforms—indeed, any reforms—is not the degree to which their results do or do not conform to some interpretation of their original goal, for most reforms are transformed by the process of implementation. Rather, what is most important is the process itself. And by that criterion, the Stolypin reforms deserve to be regarded as successful.

Yet in the larger, political perspective, Stolypin's reform program must be judged a failure, chiefly because the compromises he succeeded in building within the central government, between the government and the political parties in the Duma, and between the government and society proved evanescent. As soon as the reforms were adopted, the United Nobility defected; those of its members who were not part of the bureaucracy asserted their power and became more critical of the government's agrarian policy, especially its program of increasing the sales of land through the Peasant Land Bank.[37] They then went on to help defeat Stolypin's reform of local government and administration. Meanwhile, although Stolypin temporarily succeeded in working with the Duma, his basis of support there also collapsed, forcing the government to choose sides. Given the continued strong roles of the court and the conservative landowning nobility in the political system, the government's choice was inevitable. At that point, and especially with the onset of war, there was clearly little possibility for those within the government who still supported a moderate program of reform to revive Stolypin's efforts to build a new coalition with educated society in conjunction with the peasantry, even though the agrarian reforms had begun to create the necessary social basis.

[37]Manning, *Crisis of the Old Order*, 325–71; Wcislo, *Reforming Rural Russia*, 243–304.

8

United government and the crisis of autocracy,
1905–1914

DAVID M. McDONALD

THE REFORM OF THE COUNCIL OF MINISTERS

Two days after he promulgated the manifesto of October 17, 1905, Nicholas II issued a companion decree creating a reformed Council of Ministers.[1] The new council superseded and amalgamated the existing Council of Ministers and the Committee of Ministers. It was to serve as an instance for the "direction and unification of the chiefs of the departments, on subjects both of legislation and of higher state administration." No measure of "general significance" could be taken by any ministry or department without reference to the new council.[2]

The council was to be presided over by a chairman with broad authority to unify governmental activity. In addition to enjoying the right to report directly to the emperor, he was to be kept informed by his colleagues of ongoing developments in their departments. Any ministerial reports to the emperor touching on matters of "general significance" were also to be submitted to the chairman, who was to have an important voice in the determination of what such matters constituted. As was already widely known before the formal act of October 19, the council's first chairman was to be Sergei Iu. Witte, previously minister of finance and chairman of the now defunct Committee of Ministers.

[1] "O Sovete ministrov," *Svod uchrezhdenii gosudarstvennykh*, book 2 (St. Petersburg, 1906), pp. 1–5. The original act was an imperial decree to the Senate, "O merakh k ukrepleniiu edinstva v deiatel'nosti ministerstv i glavnykh upravlenii," Tsentral'nyi gosudarstvennyi istoricheskii arkhiv, St. Petersburg, *fond* 1276, *opis'* 1, *delo* 29, p. 1 (hereafter cited as TsGIA).
[2] "O Sovete ministrov."

Although it has been the subject of little scholarly attention,[3] the reform of the council is generally explained as springing from the desire in official circles for state authority to present a solid front to the new Duma, which was expected to be hostile and ready to exploit any disunity within government ranks. This was certainly the chief goal of the reform as set forth in the memorandum by the assistant minister of internal affairs, S. E. Kryzhanovskii, which served as the working paper for the discussions in the Special Conference, headed by D. M. Sol'skii.[4] Subsequent historical treatments have given the same explanation, which does fit into the larger perspective on the last years of the autocracy as a growing crisis occasioned by irreconcilable contradictions between state (*vlast'*) and society (*obshchestvennost'*).[5]

However, as the unification of the ministries was being discussed in the Sol'skii conference, it became evident that certain reformers, led by Witte, were equally interested in another purpose of the reform, which was also alluded to in the Kryzhanovskii memorandum—namely, to institutionalize and render exclusive the empowering link between the autocratic sovereign and his subjects through the intermediary of the chairman, to whom the council would be subordinated. In other words, the reform of the council was an attempt to limit the autocrat's exercise

[3]The most detailed treatments of this institution are by Soviet scholars: M. F. Florinskii, "Sovet ministrov Rossii v 1907–1914 gg." (candidate diss., Moscow State University, 1978); idem, "Sovet ministrov i ministerstvo inostrannykh del v 1907–1914 gg.," *Vestnik Leningradskogo gosudarstvennogo universiteta: Istoriia, iazyk, i literatura* 2 (1977); idem, "K istorii obrazovaniia i deiatel'nosti malogo Soveta ministrov: 1906–1914 gg.," ibid., 1; and N. G. Koroleva, "Sovet ministrov Rossii v 1907–1914 gg.," *Istoricheskie zapiski* 110 (Moscow, 1984): 114–53. A briefer discussion can be found in N. G. Koroleva, *Pervaia rossiiskaia revoliutsiia i tsarizm* (Moscow, 1982), 28–31. The best treatment of the reform of the council itself is B. V. Anan'ich et al., *Krizis samoderzhaviia v Rossii, 1895–1917* (Leningrad, 1984), part 2, chap. 3. See also G. A. Hosking, *The Russian Constitutional Experiment: Government and Duma, 1907–1914* (Cambridge: Cambridge University Press, 1973), 6–7, and Andrew Verner, *The Crisis of Russian Autocracy: Nicholas II and the 1905 Revolution* (Princeton: Princeton University Press, 1990), 218–25.

[4]This memorandum is in TsGIA, f. 1544, op. 1, d. 5, pp. 3–9. There is some controversy as to its authorship. Several Soviet historians follow E. D. Chermenskii, *Burzhuaziia i tsarizm v pervoi russkoi revoliutsii,* 2nd ed. (Moscow, 1970), in attributing it to A. V. Krivoshein, a claim seconded by Krivoshein's son in a biography of his father, citing Chermenskii as an authority: Anan'ich, *Krizis samoderzhaviia,* 217, n. 8; V. A. Krivoshein, *A. V. Krivoshein (1857–1921 gg.): Ego znachenie v istorii Rossii v nachale XX veka* (Paris, 1973), 23. Kryzhanovskii, however, is more probably the author, for he has written in his memoirs that he composed such a memorandum for his chief, the minister of internal affairs, A. G. Bulygin: S. E. Kryzhanovskii, *Vospominaniia* (Berlin, n.d.), 50–51.

[5]Two classic such studies are L. Martov, P. Maslov, and A. Potresov, eds., *Obshchestvennoe dvizhenie v Rossii v nachale XX-go veka,* 4 vols. (St. Petersburg, 1909), and V. A. Maklakov, *Vlast' i obshchestvennost' na zakate staroi Rossii* (Paris, 1930).

of his power, or at least to oblige the emperor by institutional means to limit himself.

From the very inception of the ministerial reform, its potential as a check on autocratic power was recognized by conservatives, who warned repeatedly in the Sol'skii conference that the unification of the council under an authoritative chairman would be tantamount to the creation of a "vizierate" (*vizirat*) limiting the power of the autocrat.[6] The image of the council's chairman as a vizier was a recurring motif in conservative criticisms of the government until 1914. Bernard Pares noted of the reform that "this was in principle one of the greatest of all the changes which took place [in 1905], and the one which the Emperor most resented."[7] V. I. Gurko likewise remarked on Nicholas's resentment of the council and of its chairmen, Witte and later (1906–11) Peter A. Stolypin, as encroachments on his authority, and he described the emperor's efforts to weaken the institution during the chairmanship of Vladimir N. Kokovtsev (1911–14), an account echoed in greater and pained detail by the latter in his own memoirs.[8] Indeed, this aspect of the council's reform and its subsequent history under Stolypin and Kokovtsev reveal an interesting and often neglected aspect of the general crisis confronting the autocratic order on the eve of its demise, and they also reflect the limits and paradoxes characterizing the worldview and identity of senior officials at the time.

The experiment in cabinet rule after 1905 saw such officials seeking to apply to their relationship with the sovereign emperor the same "legal consciousness" that they and their predecessors had applied to relations with society and the people since the Great Reforms. But they were unable to separate the person of the emperor from the power he embodied, which served as the irrefragable source of their own authority. Thus, if, as has been argued, the downfall of autocratic government is to be found in the personality of Nicholas II, who undermined the post-1905 regime in order to regain his lost power, it must be found equally in the failure of senior officials to impose their views of good government on Nicholas, leading in some cases to a mutual isolation, but more fate-

[6]See the minority opinion attached by A. S. Stishinskii and A. P. Ignat'ev to the final report of the Sol'skii conference, TsGIA, f. 1544, op. 1, d. 5, pp. 403–4.
[7]Bernard Pares, *The Fall of the Russian Monarchy: A Study of the Evidence* (New York: Knopf, 1939), 87.
[8]V. I. Gurko, *Features and Figures of the Past: Government and Opinion in the Reign of Nicholas II* (Stanford, Calif.: Stanford University Press, 1939), 516; V. N. Kokovtsev, *Iz moego proshlogo* (Paris, 1969).

fully to growing disarray at the top of the state structure well before the outbreak of the war that is often held to have brought the Russian Empire down.

THE PARADOX OF THE REFORM

Like much of the constitutional settlement of 1905–6, the reform of the council resulted from a variety of causes driven together by the events of 1905. The revolution and the forthcoming creation of the Duma were but the most immediate of these causes. Certainly, there had been a long tradition of attempts to rationalize or integrate policy making and a division of labor at the top of the imperial administration, from Peter I's reign, through Nikita Panin's proposals for an Imperial Council, to Alexander I's institutional reforms and the efforts to reinvigorate the Council of Ministers under Alexander II.[9] But, as Kryzhanovskii noted in his reform proposal, these efforts had foundered on fears of too highly centralized an executive authority, or the "establishment of a vizierate with a Grand Vizier at its head."[10] This latter apprehension emerged as a motif in criticisms of "united government" and identified succinctly the political problems arising from placing institutional trammels on the tsar's personally held sovereign power.

One very important impulse shaping the reform of the council concerned the expected role and authority of its chairman. Throughout the discussion in the Sol'skii conference, Witte, who was widely seen as the future chairman, had sought the greatest possible prerogatives for this office. The chairman, "also called the prime minister," would serve as the exclusive link between other ministers and the emperor.[11] This impulse was also evident in the responses to Witte's insistence on elimination of individual ministerial reports [traditionally presented to the

[9]See Peter I's "General'nyi reglament," *Polnoe sobranie zakonov,* no. 3532 (hereafter cited as *PSZ*); David Ransel, *Nikita Panin and the Politics of Catherinian Russia* (New Haven: Yale University Press, 1975), chap. 4. For Alexander I's ministerial and Senate reforms, see *PSZ,* no. 20405 ("O pravakh Senata," September 8, 1802); no. 20406 ("Ob uchrezhdenii ministerstv," September 8, 1802); no. 20064 ("Obrazovanie Gosudarstvennogo soveta," January 1, 1810); and no. 24686 ("Obshchee uchrezhdenie ministerstv," June 25, 1811). These reforms are discussed in Grand Duke Nikolai Mikhailovich, *Imperator Aleksandr I* (Petrograd, 1914); and M. V. Dovnar-Zapol'skii, "Zarozhdenie ministerstv v Rossii i ukaz o pravakh Senata 8-go sentiabria 1802 goda," in *Iz istorii obshchestvennykh techenii v Rossii* (St. Petersburg, 1905).
[10]TsGIA, f. 1544, op. 1, d. 5, p. 6.
[11]"Dnevnik Polovtseva," *Krasnyi arkhiv* 4: 65, entry for September 21, 1905 (hereafter cited as *KA*).

emperor by the minister in a private audience—ed.]. Witte demanded that they be mediated by the chairman.[12] Significantly, he was badly defeated by those who argued that a position empowered with the prerogatives that he envisioned would be tantamount to that of a "vizier, limiting autocracy."[13]

Witte's stress on the creation of a powerful "prime minister" was seen at the time as evidence of the same ambition that had led to his predominance in government before his dismissal as minister of finance in August 1903.[14] Undoubtedly, given the strength of his position after the Peace of Portsmouth and during the prelude to the October Manifesto, Witte was seeking a measure of dominance, not to say vengeance, within a reformed state structure. When seen against the background of the years immediately preceding the revolution, however, Witte's efforts show the degree to which the traditional attempts to impose cabinet rule had been transformed and sharpened by the rule of Nicholas II.

Witte and many other high state officials had been forced to confront the importance of the relationship between tsar and state late in 1902. In the eyes of many officials, Nicholas had begun to rule more "personally" and assertively at the expense of his official government, toward which he showed a signal lack of confidence.[15] The most obvious, and the most galling, symptom of his new attitude toward his role as autocrat was the rise of a veritable pleiad of nonofficial favorites—people such as A. M. Bezobrazov and his associates, Prince V. P. Meshcherskii, and "Monsieur Philippe" (the spiritualist Philippe Nizier-Vachot). Nicholas's hostility to his official advisers was increasingly perceived and deplored in ministerial circles.[16] The minister of justice, N. V. Murav'ev, complained

---

[12] Ibid., entry for September 28, 1905. See also TsGIA, f. 1544, op. 1, d. 5, pp. 270–71, which contain correspondence to and from Witte arising from his proposal to model the powers of the Council's chairman on the Prussian law of 1852, which gave the minister-president exclusive authority to mediate between the king and his ministers.

[13] "Dnevnik Polovtseva", *KA* 4: 73, entry for October 4, 1905, and 4: 76, entry for October 12, 1905, in which Polovtsev identifies the opponents as A. P. Ignat'ev and A. S. Stishinskii (see n. 6).

[14] See, for example, Aehrenthal to Goluchowski, Haus-, Hof- und Staatsarchiv, Vienna, Politisches Amt 10, 126/1, Bericht 59-B (hereafter cited as HHSA). Aehrenthal forwarded the misgivings of several members of the Sol'skii conference, where the ministerial reform was deliberated. Gurko, *Features and Figures of the Past,* 316, attributes Witte's aims to the inception of the idea of unifying government in the wake of the decree of December 12, 1904.

[15] See David M. McDonald, *United Government and Foreign Policy in Russia, 1900–1914* (Cambridge, Mass.: Harvard University Press, 1992), chaps. 1–3.

[16] See "Dnevnik Polovtseva," *KA* 3: 164–65, on the ceremonies surrounding the centenaries of the Senate, the Committee of Ministers, and the Corps of Pages, in which Nicholas

during this period "about the sovereign's mistrust of the ministers . . . the sovereign wants to know the truth, but he seeks it in hallways, in dark corners. . . . If he does not have confidence in one or another minister, then he must replace him—that is more correct."[17]

The political effects of Nicholas's new tack were manifest in a series of acts and policies with ludicrous or disastrous outcomes, ranging from the high-handed—and arguably illegal—canonization of Serafim of Sarov to engagement in a war with Japan that unleashed the forces of revolution. Witte had also been a victim of Nicholas's declining confidence in government when he was dismissed as minister of finance,[18] largely at the instigation of Bezobrazov but with the support of V. K. Plehve.

Nicholas's behavior during this period had forced state officials to reconsider their understanding of the nature and meaning of "autocracy," as it bore on their conception of their own roles and their legitimacy vis-à-vis the autocrat at a time of increasing social and political ferment. Products of a process of socialization and professionalization, whose progress through the nineteenth century has been well charted,[19] these officials were confronted with the inherent duality of the autocratic power which they had upheld so strongly against the claims of "society." As many of them lamented, since the reign of Alexander I emperors had

obviously favored the last of these over the other two. One cannot but be struck at how widespread were such reactions. In his diary, Kuropatkin made observations very similar to Polovtsev's: *Dnevnik A. N. Kuropatkina* (Nizhpoligraf, 1923), 15, entry for December 17, 1902. Gurko, *Features and Figures of the Past*, 33, drew similar conclusions in remembering these festivities. He felt that Nicholas's behavior revealed that veteran officials "were under suspicion." See also Murav'ev's remarks at this period in "Dnevnik Kuropatkina," *KA* 2: 11.

[17]"Dnevnik Kuropatkina," *KA* 2: 11.

[18]*Dnevnik A. N. Kuropatkina*, 56–57, entry for August 4, 1903. At an audience with Nicholas in early August, Kuropatkin declared to the emperor that "nobody knew whom to obey, where authority lay; that all of this had a pernicious effect on the legitimacy of power . . . the Sovereign's distrust of the ministers was becoming a well-known fact and was discussed by the public."

[19]Walter Pintner and Don Karl Rowney, eds., *Russian Officialdom: The Bureaucratization of Russian Society from the Seventeenth to the Twentieth Century* (Chapel Hill: University of North Carolina Press, 1980); George Yaney, *The Systematization of Russian Government: Social Evolution in the Domestic Administration of Imperial Russia, 1711–1905* (Champaign-Urbana: University of Illinois Press, 1973); P. A. Zaionchkovskii, *Pravitel'stvennyi apparat samoderzhavnoi Rossii v XIX v.* (Moscow, 1978); Francis W. Wcislo, *Reforming Rural Russia: State, Local Society, and National Politics, 1855–1914* (Princeton: Princeton University Press, 1990); Richard Wortman, *The Development of a Russian Legal Consciousness* (Chicago: University of Chicago Press, 1976); and Daniel Orlovsky, *The Limits of Reform: The Ministry of Internal Affairs in Imperial Russia, 1802–1881* (Cambridge, Mass.: Harvard University Press, 1981).

ruled through their officials, eschewing the more "personal" style associated with the arbitrariness of Paul I, for example.[20] Now they found themselves dealing with an emperor who, for reasons of his own, was again asserting "personal" authority, in terms implied by the writings of his mentor, C. P. Pobedonostsev.[21]

Witte's experience of Nicholas's declining confidence in the government ran counter to his own ideas about the nature of the links binding autocrat and state, most clearly stated in a letter he wrote to the minister of internal affairs, D. S. Sipiagin, in 1900:

> You say: the tsar is autocratic—he creates laws for his subjects, but not for himself. I—I am nothing—only a reporter, the tsar will decide, ergo no rules are needed; he who demands rules wishes to limit the tsar. [But in such a case] there would be no autocracy, but rather a chaotic administration. The tsar is autocratic because it depends upon him to impart action to the machine, but since the tsar is a man, he needs the machine for the administration of a country of 130 million subjects, since his human strength cannot replace the machine.[22]

This conceptualization of the relationship between the sovereign and his government was interesting and significant, for it conveyed both Witte's idealization of the structure of autocracy and the vision guiding his efforts to regularize the relations between autocrat and government after the disasters of 1904–5. At the same time, there is implicit in this formulation a paradox that bedeviled Witte in his tenure as the council's chairman and that shaped the developing "crisis of autocracy" during the subsequent career of united government. Even after having failed to put their conceptions into practice, both Witte and Stolypin were able only tenuously to grasp the essence of this paradox, which had undermined them. The emperor had a choice as sovereign as to whether or not to rule through his administration. If, as in the years before the war with Japan, he withdrew his "confidence," Witte and his colleagues had no means by which to effect a response. Their authority rested ultimately on the emperor's personal favor. Thus, in crucial fashion, the fate of what Witte called "the machine" depended absolutely on Nicholas's attitude toward it. Witte never fully resolved this problem.

The course of united government documents well the nature and effects of this paradox. Exposed to the pressures of "national" claims for self-determination, members of the cabinet were dependent on Nicholas

[20]"Dnevnik Polovtseva," *KA* 3: 99–100, entry for July 22, 1901.
[21]Verner, *The Crisis of Russian Autocracy,* chaps. 2 and 3.
[22]B. A. Romanov, ed., "Pis'ma S. Iu. Vitte k D. S. Sipiaginu," *KA* 18: 31–32.

for the authority to counter or deal with these pressures. Nicholas further complicated matters by giving mixed signals about his own attitude to the new regime, as can be seen in the careers of Witte, Goremykin, Stolypin, and Kokovtsev. As a result, the office of chairman became the point of intersection between the institutional and the personal elements that gave Russian autocracy its distinct cast: The council was effective as a cabinet only when its chairman enjoyed Nicholas's confidence. The solution devised by Witte, and strengthened by Stolypin, was a mix of the two elements, demonstrating the extent to which Russian officials could entertain simultaneously seemingly contradictory notions of power and authority.

In creating a "strong" office of council chairman, Witte seems to have been striving to render this office—and by extension, the government directed by the prime minister—the exclusive instance for the mediation of the sovereign power embodied in the emperor. Although he never disputed the fact that the emperor was the source of all power and authority in the state, a viewpoint he argued forcefully in his memorandum "Autocracy and the Zemstvo,"[23] he was equally emphatic that this power was subject to constraints. He sometimes made this argument allusively, as he had in 1900, and sometimes directly, as he did in the debates during the spring of 1906 on the revision of the Fundamental Laws. In the discussion of the clause defining the emperor's powers, he declared that, since the reign of Alexander I, there had been "a basic article stating that the Russian state is governed on the firm basis of laws. Once there is such an article, the interpretation of unlimited power of rule no longer arises, for in reality the supreme power submits itself to law and is regulated by it."[24]

Thus, in his effort to create a strong premiership, Witte was searching for an institutionalized means by which to harness the emperor's sovereign power to the "machine" of state. Having seen official government outflanked, to disastrous effect, by Nicholas's recourse to favorites, Witte now sought to establish hard and fast institutional channels through which the emperor would be required to act. The thrust of this effort was well understood by conservatives, who warned of the dangers of a "grand vizier." These defenders of autocracy invoked the entrenched

---

[23]Peter Struve, ed., *Samoderzhavie i zemstvo: Konfidentsial'naia zapiska Ministra finansov Stats-Sekretaria S. Iu. Vitte (1899 g.)* (Stuttgart: J.H.W. Dietz, 1903).

[24]"Tsarskosel'skie soveshchaniia," *Byloe*, 4 (26) (1917): 206. See also V. I. Gurko, *Tsar' i tsaritsa* (Paris: Vozrozhdenie, 1927), 30–39, in which the same argument is set forth.

view of the tsar's power as literally absolute. The virtue of his autocratic power lay precisely in the arbitrariness (*proizvol*) and exclusivity inherent in his personal exercise of power; he could rule through whom he chose, since his will was law. The creation of a permanent, institutionalized nexus between the autocrat and the rest of the world would amount to the usurpation of the tsar's power by such an interposed "vizier." Witte's efforts in this direction were also indicative of the conceptual cul-de-sac into which tsarist statesmen, even the most "bureaucratic," had been driven in their attempts to regularize the operations of the autocracy. Sovereignty still resided in the hands of a person with his own interests and perceptions.

Nicholas's attitude toward Witte and his cabinet raises yet another aspect of the crisis of autocracy as it unfolded after 1905. The atmosphere of urgency that had forced Nicholas to concede the October Manifesto, the council's reform, and the revised Fundamental Laws lent an air of provisionality to the entire set of accords. There is a tendency to depict state and society during those years in images connoting a mechanism—for example, referring to them as the "Third of June system."[25] In actuality, the entire postrevolutionary order was a jerry-built set of structures whose role and nature was the topic of debate throughout the duration of the "constitutional experiment." This provisionality was illustrated in a remark by A. A. Polovtsev, one of the participants in the ministerial reform, about the decision to make the Council of Ministers the sole organ for policy making. Despite the important changes in procedure, which he supported, he concluded with the observation that the emperor's will "after or without any conference" was still "holy."[26]

This sense of impermanence pervaded all levels of political activity at the time. Between government and Duma, there ensued a series of constitutional crises over issues such as the naval staffs bill, local administration, education, and the western zemstvo legislation, the last of which ultimately cost Stolypin Nicholas's confidence and his own career. These crises are often seen as confrontations over issues of power between the irreconcilable principles of state and society, but they can equally well

---

[25]This tendency is especially pronounced in certain Soviet sources—e.g., Koroleva, "Sovet ministrov Rossii v 1907–1914 gg.," and Florinskii, "Sovet ministrov Rossii v 1907–1914 gg." Some Western writers also tend to err on the side of exaggerating the durability of the reform structure, most notably Marc Szeftel, *The Russian Constitution of April 23, 1906: Political Institutions of the Duma Monarchy* (Brussels: Editions de la librairie encyclopédique, 1976).

[26]"Dnevnik Polovtseva," *KA* 4: 74, entry for October 4, 1905.

be understood as a series of attempts to settle conflicts over prerogative—between government and Duma, on the one hand, and officials and tsar, on the other—that were left unresolved in the fevered atmosphere that had produced the "granting" of the October Manifesto.

The ability of the state to pursue its goals in this troubled relationship with society was governed by the interaction of Nicholas and the chairmen of his council and by the extent to which the emperor was prepared to accept the imposition of a united government as a restraint upon himself. The reform of the council had taken place in the heat of revolutionary circumstances, with the result that, as soon as normality returned, or was imposed, questions that had been forced into abeyance reemerged to challenge the very notion of united government and the authority of the chairman. Nicholas was deeply ambivalent about virtually all aspects of the accommodation that had been forced upon him. He made his attitude very clear in a letter to his mother written on the day he had signed the legislation creating the Council of Ministers: "It makes me sick to read the news!" he wrote. "Nothing but new strikes in schools and factories, murdered policemen, Cossacks, and soldiers, disorder, mutinies. But the ministers, instead of acting with quick decision, only assemble in council like a lot of frightened hens and cackle about united ministerial action."[27]

By early 1906, Nicholas had begun to express misgivings about the amount of power that he had ceded in the previous fall. He said to his minister of finance, Kokovtsev, "It seems that . . . it is possible and even probable that I will be deprived of my power, because this is needed for the pacification of the country, but where is there a limit at which one may stop?"[28] These misgivings were also in evidence during the revision of the Fundamental Laws.

Witte was forced very quickly to confront the implications of Nicholas's ambivalence as it affected united government. The emperor seemed to ignore even the limited powers that Witte had secured for the office of the chairman. Despite Witte's complaints, the ruler dealt with ministers behind Witte's back and appointed ministers over Witte's objections, yet refused to grant the chairman's requests to relinquish his post.[29] At the end of January 1906, the emperor wrote to Witte that "in

[27]E. J. Bing, ed., *The Letters of Tsar Nicholas and Empress Marie* (London: I Nicholson and Watson, 1937), 186–87.
[28]V. N. Kokovtsev, *Iz moego proshlogo* (Paris, 1969), 1:132.
[29]TsGIA, f. 1662, op. 1, d. 107. Barely a month after the inauguration of united govern-

my opinion, the role of chairman of the Council of Ministers should be limited to the unification of the ministers' activity, while all executive work should remain the obligation of the appropriate ministers."[30] When Witte again asked to resign in April, citing disunity in his cabinet, among other complaints, Nicholas finally granted his request.

Nicholas seemed to indicate his general attitude toward the principle of cabinet rule in his choice of Ivan L. Goremykin to succeed Witte. The conservative Goremykin was little enamored of the idea of united government. He "took no pains to conceal the little respect he had not only for the Duma but even for the Council of Ministers, considering that institution as a useless innovation and [giving] his colleagues to understand that he called them together merely for the sake of form."[31]

THE APOGEE OF UNITED GOVERNMENT: STOLYPIN'S TENURE

The crisis attendant upon the dissolution of the First Duma, and the subsequent effort to form a ministry of "public confidence" in the summer of 1906, marked a turn in the fortunes of united government. Nicholas replaced Goremykin at the head of the Council of Ministers with Stolypin, who was then the minister of internal affairs. During Stolypin's tenure as chairman, he shaped that office into the seat of authority envisioned by Witte. His success was such that, when he was in turn succeeded by Kokovtsev, the latter treated the post as an office with certain legally prescribed prerogatives. The process by which he was able to do so reflected the dynamic of high politics during the postrevolutionary period.

Contributing to Stolypin's success was a variety of factors: his own

---

ment, Cecil Spring-Rice, the British chargé d'affaires in St. Petersburg, observed that "although [Witte] is nominally at the head of a 'homogeneous government' the former departmental independence still appears to prevail in almost undiminished vigour." Spring-Rice to Lansdowne, Despatch 710, December 2, 1905 NS, Public Record Office, Foreign Office 65/1704, p. 2 (hereafter cited as FO).

[30] S. Iu. Vitte [Witte], *Vospominaniia* (Moscow, 1960), 3: 334.

[31] A. P. Izwolsky [sic], *Recollections of a Foreign Minister* (New York: Doubleday, 1921), 180. He placed part of the blame for this situation on Nicholas (p. 82), a view partially corroborated by Spring-Rice. The British chargé, noting in mid-March the rumors of Witte's impending resignation, remarked that "the general belief in Court circles seems to be that with Count Witte's retirement the office of President of the Council will lose its importance and that the old system of independent ministries will again come into force." Despatch 21, March 28, 1906 NS, FO 418/31, p. 71.

abilities and vision; the political conjuncture within and outside the empire; and Nicholas's "retreat," as it might be called, from an active role in government. Ironically, though, Stolypin's very success in consolidating and institutionalizing the role of council chairman led to his own political demise and to the final phase of the crisis of autocracy.

Stolypin's ability to strengthen the prerogatives of the premiership depended both on his ability to impose solidarity on his colleagues and on the continuing confidence of Nicholas II. In the first of these, he was aided by several factors. As an "outsider," having arrived relatively recently in the St. Petersburg political milieu, Stolypin was unencumbered by the personal animosity that had been generated by Witte and his activities as a powerful minister of finance. His own moral authority had been markedly enhanced both by his energy in elaborating reforms for the empire and by the sangfroid that he had exhibited during the assassination attempt of August 1906.[32] Another favorable circumstance was the course of the revolution itself during the period between the dissolution of the First Duma and the coup of June 3, 1907. The constant pressure of dealing with revolutionary events and the drafting of reforms to counteract them imparted willy-nilly the habit of conciliar consultation to the members of Stolypin's cabinet.[33]

As important as the force of learned behavior for the effective unification of government was Stolypin's strong belief in its necessity. His image of unified ministerial rule was quite possibly rooted in his experience as provincial governor. While a member of Goremykin's caretaker government during the First Duma, Stolypin had deplored the chairman's apathy toward the new principle of ministerial rule: "He has a highly original way of thinking," he said of Goremykin. "He simply does not recognize any sort of unified government, and says that the whole government is the tsar alone, and that he will say what we will execute, but so long as there is no clear instruction from him, we must wait and be patient."[34] Before acceding to Nicholas's request to take over as the council's chairman in the summer of 1906, Stolypin insisted on the dismissal of two conservative members of the Goremykin cabinet; and later, during the imbroglio surrounding June 3, he in like manner secured the

[32]Kokovtsev, *Iz moego proshlogo,* 1: 231–32.
[33]Ibid., 1: 235–36; see also Izwolsky, *Recollections of a Foreign Minister,* 241–43.
[34]Conversation cited in Kokovtsev, *Iz moego proshlogo,* 1: 203.

dismissal of the conservative state comptroller, P. Kh. Shvanebakh, who had objected publicly and privately to Stolypin's cooperation with the Duma.[35]

After the coup of June 3, Stolypin was able to impose his vision of united government upon his cabinet colleagues. He brought foreign policy within the council's purview in the wake of Izvol'skii's debacle in the Bosnian crisis.[36] In the parliamentary crisis of the spring of 1909, he persuaded his cabinet to resign en masse if that proved necessary. Finally, he brought into the council ministers who were sympathetic to his views of policy and procedure. Most significant among such appointments was that of his brother-in-law, S. D. Sazonov, as minister of foreign affairs in 1910.

Central to all of these successes was the continued confidence of Nicholas II. The years from 1906 to 1911 were an interesting hiatus in the crisis of autocracy, so far as Nicholas's involvement in affairs of state is concerned. Nicholas seems to have withdrawn from power after his expression of dissatisfaction with affairs during the months after his grant of a constitution and his success in undermining Witte in the spring of 1906. There are many probable causes for such a withdrawal. He had witnessed the effects of direct rule in a series of disasters: the Russo-Japanese war, the revolution of 1905 and its consequences, and the abortive Russo-German agreement at Björkö during the summer of 1905, all of which can only have exacerbated his notorious ambivalence toward his position as ruler.[37]

Nicholas's moves against Witte were notable for the equal amounts of vindictiveness and diffidence that they evinced. Having accepted the accommodations of October 1905, he did not challenge them directly and confront the overweening Count Witte. Displaying a flair for intrigue that emerged on several other occasions during his reign, he ultimately managed to make the chairman's position impossible, prompting a request to resign that was quickly granted. However, after appointing Stolypin, Nicholas seems to have remained in the background, having an unusually steadfast confidence in his premier. This was most probably due partly to the strength of Stolypin's personality

[35]Berchtold to Aehrenthal, June 25/July 8, 1907, HHSA, Politisches Amt 10, 131, Bericht 29 A–B, pp. 142–46.
[36]See I. V. Bestuzhev, Bor'ba po voprosam vneshnei politiki Rossii, 1906–1910 (Moscow, 1964), and McDonald, United Government and Foreign Policy, chaps. 6 and 7.
[37]On Nicholas's attitude to his position, see Verner, Crisis of Russian Autocracy.

and partly to Stolypin's program for combating revolution, a program which achieved a great deal of initial success. Continually, and often surprisingly, especially to conservatives who abominated everything about the new constitutional order, Nicholas maintained his support for Stolypin as chairman even against such defenders of autocracy as Shvanebakh and despite occasional disagreements over issues such as that of the naval staffs crisis.[38]

Nicholas's increasing reliance on Stolypin created mixed results for Stolypin's career and for united government. Stolypin succeeded in fostering an atmosphere of normality in the political and institutional life of the empire, despite his own repeated warnings of the fragility of the nascent order. However, the very stabilization of the political situation after 1907, reflected in the development of state-Duma relations and in the détente following the Bosnian crisis, eliminated the reasons for Nicholas's support in the first place.

Indeed, the return of calm allowed many to begin to question anew the wisdom of having capitulated to the forces of revolution at the expense of autocracy in 1905–6. As Stolypin's colleague and successor, Kokovtsev, noted, "the experiences of the revolutionary times . . . were replaced by the following seven years of internal tranquillity, and made a place for ideas of the greatness of the Sovereign's personality and a faith in the unlimited devotion of the popular masses to him as God's Anointed."[39] For Stolypin, this new attitude was manifest in a recrudescence of the image of the council's chairman as grand vizier to the entrapped autocrat.[40]

In some circles, the stigma of usurper was attached not only to the person of Stolypin but also to the reformed council itself. An anonymous memorandum submitted to Nicholas as early as 1909 contained an extended critique of the new institution.[41] This document noted that "the authors of the new statute on the Council of Ministers and its relations to the Tsar [acted] not from frivolity but with the intention (*zamysel*) of

---

[38]See Nicholas's rescript to Stolypin, January 1, 1907, in *Predsedatel' Soveta Ministrov P. A. Stolypin (sostavleno E. V. po soobshcheniiam pressy za tri goda)* (St. Petersburg, 1909), 21–23. For an English translation, see Nicolson to Grey, January 15, 1907 NS, FO 418/38, Despatch 25, pp. 31–32, 37. See also Berchtold to Aehrenthal, June 25/July 8, 1907, HHSA, Politsches Amt 10, 131, Bericht 29 A–B, pp. 142–46. Here Berchtold registers a conservative's dismay at the outcome of the Shvanebakh incident and cites Stolypin's victory as an example of Nicholas's "unshaken faith" in the premier.
[39]Kokovtsev, *Iz moego proshlogo*, 2: 153.
[40]A. V. Bogdanovich, *Tri poslednikh samoderzhtsa* (Moscow and Leningrad, 1924), 480.
[41]Tsentral'nyi gosudarstvennyi arkhiv oktiabr'skoi revoliutsii, f. 543, op. 1, d. 528.

seizing the greatest possible power for the Chairman of the Council of
Ministers—not only are the Ministers brought down to the role of bureaucrats subordinated to him, but Your executive power has been more
restricted than the power of the German Emperor under the constitutional structure." Further, the note alluded to the widespread feeling
"that the power of the Sovereign had fallen under the control of the
Council of Ministers and its chairman, without which [power the Sov-
ereign] can neither name a Minister, nor give him orders." Indeed, Stolypin was reported to have said that "the Sovereign reigns (*tsarstvuet*),
but I rule (*upravliaiu*)." Interestingly, the memorandum blamed the entire situation on Witte. The only way to rectify matters would be to
abolish the post of chairman, whose role would be taken over by the
emperor himself.

As long as Stolypin enjoyed Nicholas's confidence, such criticisms presented little danger. However, Stolypin's success in amassing authority,
and in restoring order to the empire under "the Third of June system,"
also gave an increasingly palpable center around which opposition could
rally. This opposition—which included Witte's bête noire, P. N. Durnovo—found a compelling opportunity in the western zemstvo crisis that
reached a climax in the first week of March 1911.[42] In this incident,
Nicholas seemed actively to abet the efforts of those in the Council of
State who opposed the government's program and whom Stolypin
termed "reactionaries."

The result was to precipitate a critical audience between Nicholas and
Stolypin, which dealt directly with the relationship between the two.[43]
When Stolypin complained of the intrigues mounted by the opposition
in the Council of State, Nicholas distanced himself from his premier by
asking, "Against whom? You or me?" Stolypin tried to close this distance by stating that one could not divide "the steward (*prikazchik*) and
the master (*khoziain*)." This interview was in effect the death knell of
Stolypin's career as an authoritative premier,[44] but it was also an illus-
tration of the extremely tenuous nature of the ties that bound united

---

[42]See Hosking, *The Russian Constitutional Experiment*, chap. 5; V. S. Diakin, *Samoderzhavie, burzhuaziia, i dvorianstvo v 1907–1911 gg.* (Leningrad, 1978), chap. 10; Wcislo,
Reforming Rural Russia, 281–84.

[43]Stolypin's notes of this audience are in TsGIA, f. 1662, op. 1, d. 324, p. 1.

[44]When Stolypin asked to resign, Nicholas demurred for lack of a suitable replacement
(ibid.); see also Kokovtsev, *Iz moego proshlogo*, 1: 458.

government. Stolypin's juxtaposition of the twinned images of steward and master betrayed his basic agreement, in formal terms, with critics who charged him with having created a vizierate. These images revolved around a passive center of power—perhaps an absentee "landlord," such as Nicholas had been, on whose behalf authority would be exercised by an agent.

In the last analysis, Stolypin was caught in the same conceptual bind that had ensnared Witte. All of his authority depended upon and resided in Nicholas's confidence. Although he had succeeded in consolidating, and indeed in routinizing, the mechanisms of united government, Stolypin was defenseless when the emperor decided for reasons of his own to withdraw his support. Thus, as had been the case with Witte, Stolypin's system had foundered on the inherent blurring of office and person that dwelt at the very center of the autocracy.

THE PARADOX OF THE AUTOCRACY

The identity and experience of Stolypin's successors in the office of chairman demonstrate the mixed legacy bequeathed to the government by his efforts to make the most of the institutional structures left him by Witte. The choices of Kokovtsev and of Goremykin (the latter for the second time) to fill Stolypin's post were also an indication of Nicholas's increasing disaffection with united government. This disaffection noticeably increased during the tenure of Kokovtsev in particular, and it represented nothing less than a rebellion, in more muted terms than what had taken place before 1905, by Nicholas against one tendency in the evolution of imperial government. The consequences of Nicholas's wavering confidence in his government had ramifications both for the increasingly infirm relationship between state and society and for his own rule as a whole.

Kokovtsev's appointment was intended to represent a stark departure from Stolypin. Kokovtsev had been one of the strongest original opponents of Witte's call for a strong chairman. By the time he succeeded Stolypin, however, he had become a staunch advocate of united government and a defender of Stolypin's legacy as chairman. Empress Alexandra chided Kokovtsev for identifying with his predecessor, complaining that he "attribute[d] too much significance to [Stolypin's] activity and his personality."[45] Alexandra's rebuke was a harbinger of Nicholas's own shifting attitude toward his government.

With Stolypin's political and then physical departure, circumstances changed for the principle of united government. One jaundiced observer remarked of the Council of Ministers under Kokovtsev that "the idea of 'united government' remained only in his imagination, as well as in his endless explanations, intolerable in their length, to the Council of Ministers."[46] Kokovtsev's efforts to impose unity on the council reveal something of the worldview of the tsarist administrator, as well as—once more—the necessity of having Nicholas's confidence to make the system work.

The most vivid example of Kokovtsev's legalistic style in the defense of united government came when, shortly after his appointment to the chairmanship in the autumn of 1911, he sought Nicholas's approval for the formal integration of foreign-policy discussions under the auspices of the council.[47] This had been the prevailing practice under Stolypin since the Bosnian crisis of 1908–9, but Kokovtsev wanted to obtain formal recognition of this prerogative of the council, reflecting a desire for institutional and legal formalism, as evidenced in his arguments on behalf of the measure. His success in gaining acceptance of this measure was his only victory as a proponent of united government. In fact, for the rest of his tenure he presided over a body that became increasingly incoherent as an authoritative instance of government. His failures indicate in retrospective relief the sources of Stolypin's success.

Kokovtsev was saddled with a set of liabilities that were more mundane, but ultimately more debilitating, than those facing Stolypin in 1906. First among these was the fact that the Council of Ministers over which he presided was not "his"—the majority of his colleagues had served under the more assertive and charismatic Stolypin. Whereas Stolypin had been an outsider, Kokovtsev's professional life had been spent in the corridors of power in St. Petersburg. Moreover, virtually all of the ministers had had some occasion in previous years to resent Finance Minister Kokovtsev's tight-fisted economic and budgetary policies.[48]

[45]Kokovtsev, *Iz moego proshlogo*, 2: 7.
[46]Baron M. Taube, manuscript memoir, Bakhmeteff Archive of Russian and East European History and Culture, Columbia University, New York, 172.
[47]See TsGIA, f. 1276, op. 1, d. 29, pp. 261–64.
[48]Gurko, *Features and Figures of the Past*, 517; Vladimir A. Sukhomlinov, *Vospominaniia* (Berlin: Russkoe universal'noe izdatel'stvo, 1924), 217.

Kokovtsev's lack of moral authority within the cabinet was paralleled by a lack of support on the part of Nicholas. This became evident in Kokovtsev's repeated clashes with the minister of war, General V. A. Sukhomlinov, over issues ranging from the budget for the army to the conduct of Russian military operations at the height of the First Balkan War in 1912.[49] In all of these instances, Kokovtsev's entreaties and threats to resign were met with Nicholas's impassivity; the emperor would neither dismiss Kokovtsev nor discipline Sukhomlinov.

Nicholas showed a similar attitude in the matter of ministerial appointments. Where the emperor had given Stolypin his way, he ignored and even flouted the suggestions of Kokovtsev, particularly in the appointment of the reactionary N. A. Maklakov as minister of internal affairs, after dismissing from that post Kokovtsev's one appointee on the council, A. A. Makarov. Ironically, Nicholas seemed to give lip service to the principle of united government by offering to appoint Kokovtsev as ambassador to Germany after dismissing his appointee.[50]

By 1913, the council was losing any semblance of the unity that Kokovtsev had been able to persuade it to maintain. Ministers displeased with Kokovtsev's policies, particularly Sukhomlinov, sought redress with the emperor, who indulged them. Kokovtsev was forced to remind the council, in vain, that when a decision was taken, "it is a decision of the united government and of course not one of its members has the right to protest against it."[51]

Behind the advancing decay of united government was the figure of Nicholas II. In the years after 1911, the emperor voiced increasing dissatisfaction with the entire order that had been created in 1905–7, and this mood intensified following the celebration of the Romanov dynasty's tercentenary in the spring of 1913. Kokovtsev reflected in uncharacteristically precise terms on the political implications of the tercentenary's observance: "The Sovereign's tour was evidently given the meaning of a 'family' celebration of the House of Romanov, and the 'state' character was in no way accorded a fitting place . . . the view became apparent that the government formed some sort of 'barrier' be-

---

[49]See, e.g., Kokovtsev, *Iz moego proshlogo*, 2: 68–69; Sukhomlinov, *Vospominaniia*, 217, 220; A. A. Polivanov, *Iz dnevnikov i vospominanii po dolzhnosti voennogo ministra i pomoshchnika ego* (Moscow, 1924), 76. This conflict was also well known to foreign observers; see Buchanan to Grey, April 2, 1912 NS, FO 371/1468, p. 259.
[50]Kokovtsev, *Iz moego proshlogo*, 2: 84.
[51]Taube, MS memoir, 184.

tween [tsar and people], in some way impeding their mutual coming together."[52] Of course, this was a restatement in different terms of the moral cum political view behind the accusation that the council's chairmanship represented an attempt to create a vizierate limiting the autocrat. Prince Meshcherskii's paper, *The Citizen Grazhdanin* resurrected this very charge late in 1913.[53] Indeed, at the time of the tercentenary celebrations, Nicholas implicitly questioned the regime that he had acquiesced to in 1905, complaining that "I no longer have the right to do what I find useful, and I am becoming fed up with that."[54]

Nicholas's growing self-assertion and impatience with institutional limits on his power were reflected in a number of ways, all of which served to widen the rifts that had cleft the post-1905 order since the spring of 1911. Nicholas was truculent with the Third Duma in its last days. Then, late in 1913, supported by Maklakov, the ruler contemplated dissolving what promised to be a confrontational Fourth Duma and drastically altering legislative procedures by restoring to himself final decision on bills that failed to clear both houses.[55] Within the council, Nicholas's support of opposition to Kokovtsev led to the division of the ministers into two factions, which agreed only on their disdain for the chairman.[56] Several of the ministers mounted a bitter campaign over the Ministry of Finance's exploitation of the vodka monopoly to what they believed was the moral detriment of Russian peasants and workers.[57] They were aided by figures as disparate as Meshcherskii, with his allusions to the "vizierate," and Witte, an erstwhile beneficiary of the monopoly and now a councillor of state. Finally, at the end of January 1914, Kokovtsev was dismissed as premier and as minister of finance.

In addition to the personal factors that contributed to Kokovtsev's downfall and to his failure to uphold the unification of government (i.e., his lack of moral authority with his colleagues and Nicholas's desire to reassert his own power in ruling Russia), institutional factors were also at work. Kokovtsev's understanding of his role was rooted in the same approach to the legal instruments defining the functions of government and their relationship to the sovereign that had informed Witte's com-

[52]Kokovtsev, *Iz moego proshlogo*, 2: 155–56.
[53]Ibid., 130. [Prince Meshcherskii was a confidant of both Alexander III and Nicholas II; *The Citizen Grazhdanin* was a prominent right-wing paper.—Ed.]
[54]Ibid., 143.
[55]Hosking, *The Russian Constitutional Experiment*, 202.
[56]Krivoshein, *A. V. Krivoshein*, 170–74; Taube, MS memoir, 171ff.
[57]Hosking, *The Russian Constitutional Experiment*, 203.

ments in 1900 about the administrative "machine" and in 1906 during the conferences on the Fundamental Laws. Despite his initial opposition, Kokovtsev had accepted the idea of united government as a necessary regulator of the increasingly complex relationships binding—or failing to bind—emperor, state, society, and people under the new regime. Yet, like his more dynamic predecessors, he was unable to address the central issue: the indispensability of the emperor's confidence to the premier's ability to govern effectively.

In a different way, Nicholas also demonstrated his appreciation of the institutional factors affecting united government. This was particularly evident in his actions accompanying the dismissal of Kokovtsev. As he indicated to Kokovtsev, Nicholas had decided to end the practice of combining the post of council chairman with another portfolio.[58] The new chairman, Goremykin, was a double expression of Nicholas's attitude toward united government. He had served briefly and ineffectually as chairman between Witte and Stolypin in 1906, and he was also widely seen as either apathetic or hostile toward the idea of cabinet rule. The crowning irony came when Nicholas met with the Council of Ministers shortly after Kokovtsev's dismissal. Here, "he administered a little lecture to his ministers, impressing on them the necessity of working together as a united government" in their relations with the representative institutions.[59]

From his confrontation with Stolypin in 1911 until the appointment of Goremykin, Nicholas's behavior seems to have been a muted recapitulation of his conduct toward his government before 1905. Indeed, it is striking that in both periods he mounted a struggle against the means of his own rulership and, in so doing, attacked those institutions, practices, and prejudices that tacitly questioned his view of his own power and prerogatives, while also abetting "from above" the disintegration of the order that his officials upheld in his name.

By 1914, with the appointment of Goremykin, an impasse had emerged at the heights of the autocracy. One side sought, through the link between emperor and premier, to institutionalize "confidence" for the unification of government called for by the postrevolutionary order. On the other side were the ruler's personal views of his power as still

---

[58]Ibid., 204; Kokovtsev, *Iz moego proshlogo,* 2: 278–79.
[59]Attributed to Sazonov by Sir G. Buchanan, in Buchanan to Grey, March 3, 1914 NS, FO 371/2091, pp. 121–22.

absolute and exclusively his. The failure to reconcile these positions bore
ominous implications for the fortunes of autocracy.

The events of 1902–5 had led Witte, and later Stolypin, to confront
the problem of regulating the relationship between emperor and state.
Yet they had been unable to resolve the problem of "confidence" in a
meaningful way. They could "unify" government only if armed with the
emperor's support. Their inability to pursue the separation of the person
of the tsar from the sovereign emperor was the final testimony to a
paradox in the constitution of autocratic power that is perhaps clearer
in retrospect than it was at the time. In fact, it was only in the wake of
their failures as premier that either Witte or Stolypin addressed the problem of relations between ruler and state. Stolypin merely referred again
to the image of "landlord" and "steward." Witte, however, in contem-
plating the same problem, came to a much more radical and, for him,
a sadder conclusion.

In his memoirs, Witte acknowledged that Russia's well-being as an
autocracy depended on the qualities of the ruler. It was difficult to maintain autocracy when the autocrat himself took unwise actions and when
the future inspired no hope, especially given the rise of the "popular
masses," whose strength was growing with the encouragement of the
liberation movement. Thus, he concluded, while his heart still loved autocracy, his mind and experience argued for limitations on the ruler;
constitutions were a historical necessity.[60]

By the same token, Nicholas had weakened his government and its
authority by his disinclination to accept the settlement forced upon him
in 1905. This was a particularly dangerous position to take in the atmosphere of gathering crisis punctuated by the Lena massacre of 1912,
the ensuing growth of worker unrest, and the elections to the Fourth
Duma. Ironically, Nicholas's ambivalence toward his government mirrored that of his premiers to his sovereign power. He abided by the
formal principle of united government, but in so doing he identified the
principle with its exponents, particularly the successive chairmen. As he
became increasingly dissatisfied with the effects of the post-1905 settlement on his own power, which he and many others continued to see as
autocratic in the old sense, he sought to refashion united government to
suit his own ideas of the proper relationship between government and
sovereign. Thus, he replaced the powerful Stolypin, whose authority he

[60]S. Iu. Vitte [Witte], *Vospominaniia* (Leningrad, 1923), 1: 250–51.

had created, with the more tractable Kokovtsev. When the latter turned out to espouse his predecessor's views of united government, he was replaced in turn by Goremykin, whose ideas about cabinet rule were as formal and empty as Nicholas's own.

In his efforts to find a congenial government, Nicholas seriously eroded the unity that Kryzhanovskii and others had seen as necessary for dealing with the postrevolutionary order. This led to a deterioration in the relationship between Duma and government. The emperor's behavior also resurrected the endless intrigues and discord that had characterized the prerevolutionary order, as had been noted in Kryzhanovskii's 1905 memorandum.[61]

Finally, and perhaps most fatally, Nicholas had failed to heed one of Kryzhanovskii's admonitions. Kryzhanovskii had warned that "autocratic power must above all be equally raised above all parties and estates, over rulers and ruled."[62] The inviolability of supreme power depended on its not being drawn into partisan strife. Nicholas had violated this stricture in his intrigues first against Stolypin and then against Kokovtsev. The ultimate effect of this was to collapse the "distance" or majesty necessary for the maintenance of autocratic power.

The effects of Nicholas's entry into mundane politics were beginning to appear on the eve of the First World War. Witte's prophecy about the fate of autocracy was one official's response to this, and the mounting scandal surrounding Rasputin debased the emperor further in public opinion. In seeking a united government through which he could rule as he wished, Nicholas had weakened its ability to act as its creators had felt it must, and he had reduced his own legitimacy in the eyes of rulers and ruled. The effects of both processes became dramatically clear in the violent resolution of the "crisis of autocracy" in 1917.

[61]See n. 4.
[62]TsGIA, f. 1544, op. 1, d. 5, p. 5.

9

▰▰▰▰▰▰▰▰▰▰▰▰▰▰▰▰▰▰▰▰▰▰▰▰▰▰▰▰▰

Russia's parliament of public opinion: association, assembly, and the autocracy, 1906–1914

JOSEPH BRADLEY

After a year of agitation on the part of society for civil liberties and a constitution, in 1905 the imperial Russian government relented and promised fundamental changes in the sovereign powers of the autocrat. The manifesto of October 17 promised civil liberties and the participation of society in a legislative assembly, the Duma. It appeared that autocracy had finally legitimated a "public sphere," in which critical discussion of matters of general interest was institutionally guaranteed.[1] But the Fundamental Laws of 1906 restricted the powers of the Duma, and subsequent changes in the electoral laws limited the representation of the public sphere. In addition, by allowing a wide latitude for arbitrary application, regulations governing freedom of association and assembly restricted the legitimate public participation of society.

One way to study the participation of society in the public sphere after 1905 is to study the many congresses of national associations that convened between the revolution of 1905 and the outbreak of World War I. Government and society alike were well aware that these congresses demonstrated the ability of private persons to come together on their own initiative, set an agenda for their meeting, and, in effect, publicly monitor state authority through informed and critical discourse. In the absence of a more powerful and more representative parliament, the

---

[1] Jürgen Habermas, *The Structural Transformation of the Public Sphere: An Inquiry into a Category of Bourgeois Society,* trans. Thomas Burger and Frederick Lawrence (Cambridge, Mass.: MIT Press, 1989), xi, 25, 27, 83.

national congresses by 1914 had become a "parliament of public opinion" for voices that could not be heard in the Duma. They typically published a journal (*dnevnik*) during the congress itself and sometimes a record of the proceedings (*trudy*) afterward, although this often came several years later. Many of the congresses were covered in the newspapers and in the so-called thick journals. Besides their publications, the associations supported museums and exhibitions and promoted education and the rational use of leisure time.[2] An examination of these meetings reveals much about the public sphere in late imperial Russia, the confrontation between society and the autocracy and its bureaucracy, and the divisions within society itself.[3]

ASSOCIATION AND ASSEMBLY IN THE LAW

The Fundamental Laws of 1906 gave Russian subjects the right to organize peaceful meetings and to form societies and unions that were "not contrary to the law," and this became the legal basis for society's participation in the public sphere. The conditions for holding meetings and for forming societies were to be "determined by law."[4] However, no such "law" was ever written. Instead, the Temporary Regulations of March 4, 1906, governed association and assembly.[5]

[2]For an introduction to the sources available, see the studies of the Soviet historian A. D. Stepanskii: *Samoderzhavie i obshchestvennye organizatsii Rossii na rubezhe XIX–XX vv.* (Moscow, 1980); *Istoriia obshchestvennykh organizatsii dorevoliutsionnoi Rossii* (Moscow, 1979); and "Materialy legal'nykh obshchestvennykh organizatsii tsarskoi Rossii," *Arkheograficheskii ezhegodnik za 1978 g.* (Moscow, 1979), 69–80.

[3]For present purposes, a sample of these congresses was studied, the most important of which were the Tenth and Eleventh Congresses of the Pirogov Society of Russian Physicians in 1907 and 1910, the All-Russian Congresses of Cooperatives in 1908 and 1913, the Writers' Congresses of 1908 and 1910, the First Women's Congress of 1908, two Congresses of Factory Physicians and Representatives of Factory Industry in 1909 and 1911, the Congress on Alcoholism in 1909, the Congress on Prostitution in 1910, the Second Artisans' Congress in 1911, the Congress of Agronomists in 1911, the Congress of Retail Employees in 1913, the Agricultural Congress of 1913, and the All-Russian Teachers' Congress of 1913–14. The analysis of the role of Russia's associations and societies in the development of civil society is part of a long-term project; see Joseph Bradley, "Voluntary Associations and the Emergence of Civil Society," in Edith Clowes, Samuel Kassow, and James West, eds., *Between Tsar and People: Educated Society and the Quest for Public Identity in Late Imperial Russia* (Princeton: Princeton University Press, 1991). The present essay is based on the published record.

[4]The Fundamental Laws are in *Polnoe sobranie zakonov Rossiiskoi imperii*, 3rd ser., vol. 26, no. 27805 (hereafter cited as *PSZ*). On the many facets of the problem of civil rights in Russia, see Olga Crisp and Linda Edmondson, eds., *Civil Rights in Imperial Russia* (Oxford: Oxford University Press, 1989).

[5]"Vremennye pravila ob obshchestvakh i soiuzakh" and "Vremennye pravila o publi-

The Temporary Regulations made a crucial distinction between public and nonpublic meetings. The latter were defined as meetings attended only by members of a legal association and not by outsiders. Nonpublic meetings could be held without request to or prior authorization from the authorities (*iavochnym poriadkom*). Public assemblies, on the other hand, defined as meetings of an undetermined number of people not known personally by the organizers, required permission of the authorities and were subject to a variety of rules and regulations. Furthermore, meetings held at theaters, concert and exhibition halls, and other public places were considered public in any case. Thus, Russian subjects received the freedom of private assembly, but freedom of public assembly was still severely circumscribed. Organizers of a public meeting had to apply for permission from the local police in writing three days in advance of the meeting or three days prior to the first public announcement about the meeting. The application was to include the names and addresses of the organizers, the topic of the meeting, and the names and addresses of any persons presenting a paper or giving a speech.[6]

The Temporary Regulations gave few reasons for denying permission to hold a public assembly. One, however, was broad enough to fit any occasion: It was forbidden to hold public assemblies whose purpose or

chnykh sobraniiakh," *PSZ*, 3rd ser., vol. 26, nos. 27479 and 27480. These regulations were appended to articles 115 and 118 of the Statute on the Prevention and Deterrence of Crime in the 1906 and 1908 supplements to the Digest of Laws (*Svod zakonov Rossiiskoi imperii*, vol. 14, *Ustav o preduprezhdenii i presechenii prestuplenii*). Much of this statute had remained unchanged since 1782, when the Statute on Public Order (*Ustav blagochiniia*) had forbidden "all suspicious gatherings [*skhodbishche*]" and "all crowds and meetings for consultations or activities that are contrary to public peace and tranquillity." (*Svod zakonov*, vol. 14, chap. 5, arts. 157 and 159.) See also I. E. Andreevskii, *Politseiskoe pravo*, 2 vols. (St. Petersburg, 1871–73), 2: 228–29; K. Il'inskii, *Chastnye obshchestva: Sbornik zakonov, rasporiazhenii pravitel'stva, i reshenii Pravitel'stvuiushchego Senata* (Riga, 1913), 526; Stepanskii, "Materialy," 75; and Stepanskii, *Samoderzhavie*, 6. The question of enacting a permanent law on assembly was raised in the first Duma; see Gosudarstvennaia duma, 1-yi sozyv, 1-aia sess., *Stenograficheskii otchet* (St. Petersburg, 1906), 1400–1468 (hereafter cited as *GDSO*). See also V. G. Matveev, *Pravo publichnykh sobranii: Ocherk razvitiia i sovremennoi postanovki publichnykh sobranii vo Frantsii, Germanii, Anglii* (St. Petersburg, 1909), 383–93.
[6]"Vremennye pravila o publichnykh sobraniiakh," no. 27480, arts. 1–4, 8, 9, and 20. Prior permission of the authorities was necessary for the establishment of any society or association. Before the era of the Great Reforms, permission to form a society or association could be granted only by the Committee of Ministers. Beginning in 1862, societies whose applications conformed to specified standard or model charters could be authorized by the local authorities (governors, governors-general, and city prefects). However, authorization for holding public lectures, readings, exhibitions, and congresses remained a function of the department of police of the Ministry of Internal Affairs. K. G. Fon-Plato, *Polozhenie o chastnykh obshchestvakh, uchrezhdaemykh s razresheniiami ministerstv, gubernatorov, i gradonachal'nikov* (Riga, 1903), 1; Stepanskii, *Samoderzhavie*, 6.

subject violated the criminal laws or public morality, or that threatened public tranquillity and safety.[7] It was the government, rather than the public, which defined public morality and public safety. Given the vagueness of the procedures, local authorities had a wide latitude to restrict the public sphere on a case-by-case basis, and they were often more fearful of disorder than were the central authorities. As a result, despite the promise of freedom of assembly, the public could not tell in advance what was permissible and what was not.

During the meeting itself, its organizers were responsible for maintaining order and in particular "for eliminating all illegal manifestations." The government took no chances, however: The Temporary Regulations authorized the governor or the chief of police to send a representative to all public assemblies. The police were to warn the assembly if any "illegal manifestation" occurred. If order was not restored after two such warnings, the police could close the assembly if any of the following conditions was observed: deviation from the approved subject, expression of opinions that stirred up hostility against a particular group of the population, unauthorized collection of money, the presence of unauthorized persons at the assembly, demonstrations inciting insubordination to the authorities, or criminal acts whereby the assembly would present a threat to public tranquillity and security.[8] This constituted a serious restriction of another civil liberty promised by the October manifesto—freedom of speech. Such conditions left ample room for arbitrary application. To point to just one inconsistency, since the application to hold an assembly did not include a list of persons in attendance, in principle there could be no "unauthorized" persons present.

CONFLICTS OVER THE EXERCISE OF FREEDOM OF ASSEMBLY

The Temporary Regulations provided ample opportunity for the authorities to limit freedom of assembly—before, during, and after a meeting was held—and to control the public sphere. The government could, of course, refuse permission to hold a congress, or it could limit participation and restrict the agenda. The police sometimes interfered with the

---

[7]"Vremennye pravila o publichnykh sobraniiakh," no. 27480, arts. 6, 7, and 10.
[8]Ibid., arts. 13–18.

proceedings of a congress—their very presence created a chilling effect on its organizers—and they harassed participants even after the close of congresses. The First Women's Congress (1908), the Second Artisans' Congress (1911), the Congresses of Factory Physicians (1909 and 1911), the All-Russian Congresses of Cooperatives (1908 and 1913), the First Writers' Congresses (1908), and the Congress on Alcoholism (1909), among others, provide examples of the conflicts between government and society.

The Ministry of Internal Affairs insisted that only members of the St. Petersburg Women's Mutual Aid Society, the congress organizers, and representatives of other societies pursuing similar goals could attend the First Women's Congress. This had two effects. First, it made the congress less accessible than it otherwise might have been to women of modest means who could not afford the annual dues for one of these societies. Second, it established the principle that the delegates were assembled solely for the pursuit of charitable goals.[9]

One of the most meticulous attempts to restrict participation occurred in connection with the Second Artisans' Congress. The great majority of the more than three hundred delegates represented artisan proprietors, though there were thirty-three delegates representing trade unions and a smattering of delegates from societies such as the Free Economic Society and the Technical Society. Authorization to attend had been given only to artisan proprietors, their representatives, and the representatives of organizations with special expertise; thus, for example, laborers in artisanal establishments were not represented directly. In addition, the government considered the allegedly large number of delegates at the First Artisans' Congress in 1900 to have been "unnecessary and undesirable," and so the second congress was authorized only on the grounds that it

[9]Z. S. Mirovich, "Pervyi Vserossiiskii zhenskii s"ezd," *Vestnik Evropy* (January 1909): 411–15; A. Ermanskii, "Vserossiiskii zhenskii s"ezd," *Sovremennyi mir* (January 1909): 103–12; and O. N. Vol'kenstein, "Itogi pervogo vserossiiskogo zhenskogo s"ezda," *Russkaia mysl'* (February 1909): 146–53. The congress is given considerable attention in Linda Edmondson, *Feminism in Russia, 1900–1917* (Stanford, Calif.: Stanford University Press, 1984), 83–106. Other examples of government restrictions on authorized participants were the Eleventh Congress of the Pirogov Society of Russian Physicians and the Congress of Retail Employees. For example, Dmitry Zhbankov, a veteran of zemstvo medicine and a critic of famine relief and corporal punishment, was not permitted to attend the former. See Severianin, "Pirogovskii s"ezd 1910 g.," *Russkaia mysl'* (July 1910): 29–39; I. Zhilkin, "S"ezd torgovykh sluzhashchikh v Moskve," *Vestnik Evropy* (September 1913): 351–56; and Nancy M. Frieden, *Russian Physicians in an Era of Reform and Revolution, 1856–1905* (Princeton: Princeton University Press, 1981), 191–92, 194, 197.

be "businesslike" and not have a large number of participants. The government also limited the number of representatives from St. Petersburg and Moscow, because it considered big-city delegates to be unreliable and prone to discuss politics.[10]

Approval of participants by one office did not always mean approval by another, as the Second Congress of Factory Physicians and Representatives of Factory Industry illustrates. The Ministry of Internal Affairs initially refused to approve a charter that invited trade-union representatives, in the belief that Social Democratic union representatives would use the congress for political agitation and fearing that such a congress could lead to an "all-empire" (*vserossiiskii*) meeting of illegal and underground organizations.[11] The ministry relented, however, and permitted a few union representatives to attend. But the Moscow city prefect was not willing to take any chances. He refused to allow the participation of certain union delegates—tailors, bakers, cooks, and hairdressers—on the ground that they were not engaged in factory industry, and the Moscow police arrested twenty of twenty-seven labor delegates before they even got to the congress.[12]

The government also tried to keep "inappropriate" subjects off the agenda. For example, the 1908 Cooperatives' Congress was not allowed to discuss amalgamation of cooperatives. Other subjects, even if approved by the Ministry of Internal Affairs, could be addressed only in certain ways; thus, speeches at the general meeting on the relations between cooperatives and trade unions and on the position of paid employees in the cooperatives, as well as speeches "tending to impart a spirit of class struggle," were forbidden by the governor-general of Moscow.[13] Yet such topics were often of central concern to the groups involved.

Because memory of the turbulent aborted writers' congress of 1905 was still fresh, the First Writers' Congress of 1908 was instructed by government authorities to avoid politics. Indeed, the major political issue, freedom of the press, was ordered stricken from the agenda.

[10]Severianin, "Vtoroi Vserossiiskii s"ezd po remeslennoi promyshlennosti," *Russkaia Mysl'* (March 1911): 10–11.

[11]N. I. Letunovskii, *Leninskaia taktika ispol'zovaniia legal'nykh vserossiiskikh s"ezdov v bor'be za massy v 1908–1911 gg.* (Moscow, 1971), 55–56. Letunovskii candidly documents the Social Democrats' use of national congresses for political agitation.

[12]"Moskovskii s"ezd fabrichnykh vrachei," *Vestnik Evropy* (May 1911): 373–74.

[13]S. Prokopovich, "Itogi kooperativnogo s"ezda," *Vestnik Evropy* (September 1913): 341; Letunovskii, *Leninskaia taktika*, 14–19. For some of the opinions of the delegates themselves regarding the problems of cooperatives in the villages, see Tan, "Na kooperativnom s"ezde," *Russkoe bogatstvo* (May 1908): 30–50.

Whether or not there should even be a second writers' congress was a much-discussed issue among writers and journalists in 1910, when the authorities for the second time removed from the program the subject of the legal status of the press.[14] Despite professions by the organizing committee that the 1909 Congress on Alcoholism would be truly apart from "politics and party," the city prefect of St. Petersburg, working closely with the organizing committee, prohibited "inappropriate" papers, speeches, and resolutions on two subjects that would seem to have been at the heart of the congress: the state liquor monopoly and the social and economic causes of alcoholism.[15]

Because the government had authorized the Women's Congress only for the pursuit of charitable goals, the draft program of the congress included no sessions on such issues as child labor, women factory inspectors, or women's participation in zemstvo and municipal government. However, even this self-censorship did not satisfy the authorities: The Ministry of Internal Affairs deleted from the program an entire section entitled "On the Struggle at Home and Abroad for the Political and Civil Rights of Women and on the Necessity of Equality and Accessibility of All Occupations and Government Administration for Women." All references to talks about the political movement in the West had to be deleted, and a paper on the women's movement in England was canceled on the eve of the first session. After recounting other examples of government meddling in the program, Zinaida Mirovich concluded, "Here, in the twentieth century, we again feel the patriarchal spirit of a pre-Petrine age when the doors to the West were securely closed and all westerly winds were pronounced pernicious and fatal."[16]

Government attempts to control the work of the congresses continued after they opened. The most blatant form of control over the public sphere was the requirement of the Temporary Regulations that a police representative with broad powers be in attendance at all times to ensure strict adherence to the authorized program. One or two police officers

---

[14]V. Miakotin, "Nabroski sovremennosti: O pisatel'skom s"ezde," *Russkoe bogatstvo* (August 1908): 109–10; "Obshchestvennaia khronika," *Vestnik Evropy* (August 1908): 822–24.

[15]John Hutchinson, "Science, Politics and the Alcohol Problem in Post-1905 Russia," *Slavonic and East European Review* 2 (1980): 247–54.

[16]Mirovich, "Pervyi Vserossiiskii zhenskii s"ezd." See also Ermanskii, "Vserossiiskii zhenskii s"ezd"; *Sovremennyi mir* (January 1909): 103–12; Vol'kenstein, "Itogi pervogo vserossiiskogo zhenskogo s"ezda"; *Russkaia mysl'* (February 1909): 146–53; and the account of the conference in *Russkie vedomosti*, December 16, 1908.

sat in on every session of the Women's Congress. Every time a speaker strayed from her topic, even with innocent remarks, the police interrupted. At one session, a speaker was stopped when she made a negative reference to the attitude of the Octobrist Party toward the women's question, on the ground that one cannot criticize a party in the Duma. (Whether criticism of an opposition party would be forbidden was not made clear.) Another speaker was stopped upon alluding to the extremely hostile attitude of a local priest toward the primary school. Police presence was even more marked at the well-attended meetings of the combined sections of the congress. According to one participant, "An innocent stranger would not have known what to make of the entrance to the meeting halls: The long column of city police headed by the district chief most likely would have suggested that she was lost and had wound up in the penal battalion, and not at a meeting of women discussing their own interests and needs."[17] Humiliating treatment on the part of the authorities was a common experience of many other congress participants.

One of the most closely policed meetings was the 1913 Cooperatives' Congress. At the sessions on producers' cooperatives, the police representative repeatedly indicated to the chair that the discussion was heading in an undesirable direction and insisted that speakers stick to the topic. This interference—censorship might be a better word—abated only after careful explanation from the chair that the speaker was not overstepping the boundaries of the program. On the second day of the congress, a worker arose and started eulogizing August Bebel. The police interrupted and demanded that the chair declare the speaker out of order, and when the chair obliged, a hubbub ensued. Only a sharp "On your feet!" command from the police, followed by an official warning, quieted the session—exactly as the Temporary Regulations envisioned.[18]

The government's clumsiness and extreme sensitivity to certain national issues, such as the death penalty, frequently gave political overtones to what would otherwise have been routine matters. One of the

[17]Mirovich, "Pervyi Vserossiiskii zhenskii s"ezd," 413.

[18]I. Zhilkin, "Provintsial'noe obozrenie," *Vestnik Evropy* (September 1913): 354; Prokopovich, "Itogi kooperativnogo s"ezda," 339–40. The official publications of the conference contain none of the contentiousness suggested by the journal reports. However, the official publications were delayed by two years, and according to the organizing committee, this was the result of delays and infelicities in the stenographic record. See *Vserossiiskii s"ezd po kooperatsii: Trudy* (Kiev, 1913), 1–3; and *Vserossiiskii s"ezd po kooperatsii: Doklady* (Kiev, 1913).

items on the agenda of the First Writers' Congress was a seemingly straightforward professional issue: the way in which writers should pay tribute to a fellow writer, Leo Tolstoy, on his eightieth birthday. But Tolstoy was not just any writer in the eyes of the government, and at the first session, "no sooner did one of the speakers in the most objective manner mention in passing, along with Tolstoy's name, the commandment, 'Thou shalt not kill,' and say the fateful words, 'the death penalty,' than the official dispatched by the city prefect stopped the speaker. The fate of the congress hung barely by a thread."[19]

The government did not always heed the distinction between open and closed sessions. According to the charter of the 1913 Cooperatives' Congress, only public sessions were subject to the law of assembly, requiring police attendance. Closed sessions fell under the procedures governing associations, which did not require police attendance. This was a neat trick—until the government caught on. A section on consumers' cooperatives declared its sessions closed. The next day, when members of a commission to study the situation of cooperative employees began their meeting, they were surprised to see the deputy chief of police stride into the hall and announce that the meeting could not proceed without police attendance. When the commission's chair refused, on the ground that this would violate the congress's authorized charter, the police left for consultations with the governor of Kiev. An hour later, the deputy chief of police returned to declare that a closed session of the commission would be permitted only if there were fewer people and if members of the commission were selected at public meetings. While this was more an irritant than a real impediment, the resulting need to reorganize the commission took two days, leaving only three days for the commission to conduct its business.[20]

The sharpest conflicts between government and society took place over the drafting of resolutions. All congresses drafted resolutions. Individual speakers proposed them at the various sessions, frequently as part of their papers. Delegates discussed and often amended the proposals. Many congresses had a committee responsible for drafting the final versions of resolutions, which were customarily read aloud and voted on at the final session. The proceedings of the congresses offer examples of resolutions proposed by delegates but not approved by the

[19]"Obshchestvennaia khronika," *Vestnik Evropy* (August 1908): 824.
[20]Prokopovich, "Itogi kooperativnogo s"ezda," 340.

resolutions committee, allegedly diluted, approved but not read, read but not voted on, voted on but not read, and read and voted on but not published.

The resolutions were a process by which congress activists could address two audiences. First, many resolutions were directed at the government, not only expressing society's grievances against the government but also looking to the government to solve social problems. Of course, the resolutions were not submitted through official channels; the government was not obliged to respond, and indeed, it routinely did not respond, as we will see below. Yet, no matter how futile these resolutions were, they frequently angered the government more than any other aspect of the congresses. Second, as will be examined in the following section, the resolutions were a way for congress activists, and advocates of diverse interest groups, to speak to their own constituents, to legitimate their public agenda, and to try to mobilize public opinion.

The Cooperatives' Congress of 1908, greatly relieved that the congress was able to close on schedule, could not present publicly the proposals drafted in the various sections and commissions; its resolutions had to be approved without being read aloud at the final meeting.[21] At one of the sections of the Women's Congress, E. D. Kuskova read a resolution attributing the oppressed condition of peasant women to low agricultural productivity, the low cultural level in the countryside, and the absence of civil liberties, whereupon the police interrupted and issued a warning. Kuskova refused to continue and stepped down from the rostrum, but another resolution brought up the idea of equal rights for peasants, provoking a second warning. When a third "inappropriate" resolution was presented, the meeting was closed down.[22]

Similarly, at the Congress on Prostitution in 1910, a resolution stating that the eradication of prostitution "could be realized only with complete freedom of assembly, speech, and association" was pronounced to be of a "political nature" by the representative of the police. Moments later, the police closed the morning session when the chair, A. V. Tyrkova, refused to halt a second attempt to introduce the issue of civil liberties into a resolution.[23] A final example comes from the 1911 Con-

---

[21]Tan, "Na kooperativnom s"ezde," 31; Prokopovich, "Itogi kooperativnogo s"ezda," 353; Letunovskii, *Leninskaia taktika*, 14–19.

[22]*Russkie vedomosti*, December 16, 1908.

[23]*Trudy Pervogo Vserossiiskogo s"ezda po bor'be s torgom zhenshchinami i ego prichinami*, 2 vols. (St. Petersburg, 1911–12), 1: 179–81. The unsuccessful resolution was in-

gress on the Family. A resolution had been drawn up to the effect that equality was subordinate to the interests of state security and that it meant only equality before the police, with no concept of rights or freedoms, and that children suffered from this. At the words "in the name of so-called state security," the police stopped the speaker.[24]

Government harassment continued even when the congresses were over. Following the 1909 Congress of Factory Physicians, union and Social Democratic delegates tried to take advantage of other meetings to call attention to their speeches and particularly to their victory on a resolution on the election of factory inspectors. The government, perhaps regretting that it had provided a convenient forum for union representatives, forbade the unions in St. Petersburg from holding meetings to discuss the congress, thereby making the congress itself a political subject. Delegates from the Moscow unions moved quickly to attend a meeting of the union members of the Society of Retail Employees, but at the last minute, the Moscow city prefect forbade reporting on the Congress of Factory Physicians and detained all those assembled at the meeting. Finally, however, the work of the congress became public knowledge in the world of labor when a meeting of the printers' union heard a report on the forbidden subject.[25]

In other instances, the police took more drastic action. They arrested almost all the forty-three union delegates to the Congress on Alcoholism, on the not entirely erroneous ground that they were Social Democratic activists who had tried to turn the congress into an antigovernment campaign. Twice during the next three years, the government refused to authorize a second Congress on Alcoholism, and in 1912 it disbanded the committee that had been charged by the first congress with the task of organizing the second one. In 1912, the government and the church managed to organize a less contentious congress, but by that time the likelihood of cooperation between government and society on the question had greatly diminished.[26] Finally, the Kievan authorities provide the

troduced by Zinaida M. Ivanova, a representative of the Moscow Union of Tailors, Seamstresses, and Furriers. When she later attempted again to make recommendations to combat prostitution, phrases pertaining to limitations on the exercise of civil rights and on the realization of the human dignity of women were deleted at the insistence of the police (ibid., 219).

[24] *Vserossiiskii s "ezd po semeinomu vospitaniiu: Trudy*, 2 vols. (St. Petersburg, 1914), 2: 703.

[25] Letunovskii, *Leninskaia taktika*, 34. See also G. R. Swain, *Russian Social Democracy and the Legal Labour Movement, 1906–1914* (London: Macmillan, 1983), 67–72.

[26] Hutchinson, "Science, Politics, and the Alcohol Problem," 250–51; Letunovskii, *Lenin-*

most amusing example of postcongress harassment: A pleasure cruise along the Dnieper River one day after the 1913 Congress of Cooperatives had ended was marred by the presence of "too many police darting about among the participants and interfering with the singing." It was rumored that thirty police were hiding in the hold.[27]

Three points should be made regarding the intricate game of cat and mouse between government and society for control of the public sphere. First, the congresses did not always produce confrontations. Although the contentious ones got more coverage in the liberal and radical press, there were many cases of cooperation and avoidance of delicate issues.[28] Second, it could be argued that the government's ideas about congress participation and agendas were not always irrational or reactionary. A case could be made for achieving regional balance at an artisans' congress by limiting delegates from Moscow and St. Petersburg, or for limiting a congress of factory physicians and representatives of factory industry to delegates representing factory work settings. However, by reserving to itself the right to make these decisions, by telling the public what was "appropriate," the government prevented society from acting on its own behalf and refused to share the public sphere. Third, while it is obvious that the government did not trust its subjects to behave properly, it is equally apparent from the reliance on the police that the government did not trust its own ability to control the congresses by limiting participation and restricting the agenda. In one congress after another, the police overkill and the refusal to let society act on its own

---

skaia taktika, 12; Swain, *Russian Social Democracy,* 89–91. The arrest of labor delegates was even discussed in the Duma on January 22, 1910, and an inquiry regarding the matter was submitted to the Ministry of Internal Affairs. *GDSO,* 3-ii sozyv, 3-iaia sess. (St. Petersburg, 1910), part 2, 81–94.

[27]Prokopovich, "Itogi kooperativnogo s"ezda," 341. Because the local governor did not allow nonresident Jews to remain an extra day in Kiev, these delegates were not able to go on the cruise. This resulted in a boycott of the cruise by worker delegates. *Vserossiiskii s"ezd po kooperatsii: Trudy,* 8.

[28]For example, the request for authorization to hold the Congress on Alcoholism emphasized that it would stand apart from politics or party. This strategy worked, and not only did Stolypin and Kokovtsev grant permission to hold the congress, but the government granted it a 10,000-ruble subsidy. One congress that turned away from its former "days of freedom" and was thoroughly businesslike was the Eleventh Congress of the Pirogov Society. The general impression was one of "grayness," and no particular "mood" dominated the meeting. The nearly two thousand physicians who attended found an overload of papers and material: "Since Russians cannot be brief and since they don't want to follow the example of the West and summarize their papers, many talks went on for three hours." Hutchinson, "Science, Politics, and the Alcohol Problem," 247; Severianin, "Pirogovskii s"ezd 1910 g.," 30–31.

behalf ensured that the very thing the government wanted most to keep out—politics—intruded into the congresses.

POLITICIZATION OF THE CONGRESSES

Despite government efforts to control agenda and attendance—to police the podium—politics came up. The striking characteristic of congresses of this period is not the suppression of politics but its persistent manifestation. The Congress of Representatives of Municipal Government, the Second Artisans' Congress, and the Congress on Alcoholism give examples of the politicization of congresses and the turn from moderate views to antigovernment positions.

The Congress of Representatives of Municipal Government, held in Kiev in 1913, provides an example of politicization brought about by government clumsiness. Consisting largely of mayors and city government officials, the participants were hardly a radical lot. The congress's first act showed that it was well disposed toward the government: It sent greetings to the chairman of the Council of Ministers, the Minister of Internal Affairs, and the chairman of the Council of State. But the government did not reciprocate this sentiment, perhaps because this congress came soon after a contentious congress on agriculture. The police enforced strict censorship, forbade criticism of any governments, even local ones, and prohibited discussion of improvements in the municipal statute or extension of the franchise. The conference leaders, who were summoned by the vice-governor whenever the latter did not like a speech, tried to "protect the congress" and not let politics come up. Yet this squelching of politics almost guaranteed an outburst, and it came in the closing session. Over the objections of the chair, A. I. Guchkov managed to read a resolution proclaiming that "further delays in enacting necessary reforms and the deviation from the principles of the October Manifesto threaten the nation with serious ruptures and mortal consequences." The audience greeted these words with tremendous applause, and when the chair refused to call a vote on Guchkov's resolution, voices in the hall shouted, "It's already passed!"[29]

At several congresses, "progressive" opinion grew in force over the course of the congress, despite the fact that most of the resolutions, or

[29]A. Petrischev, "Rechi, s"ezdy, rezoliutsii," *Russkoe bogatstvo* (November 1913): 339–40.

at least the early ones, reflected the predominance of established interests. For example, a speech early in the artisans' congress favoring corporal punishment met mounting criticism. Although at first the majority of the delegates did not want even to discuss the question of factory inspection, it became an unavoidable subject in later sessions. Although most resolutions reflected employer interests, at the end a majority approved extension of government factory inspection to artisan industry, with both proprietors and workers having a voice in the selection of inspectors.[30]

The Congress on Alcoholism provides perhaps the best example of the politicization of a congress. The attempts of the government and the congress's organizers to censor the discussions backfired, and the mood of the congress became markedly antigovernment.[31] The change in mood can be seen in the resolutions of the congress and in the "politics" of the composition of these resolutions. The first resolution certainly pleased the forces of tradition. By a vote of ninety-five to forty-three, the congress affirmed the fundamental principle of abstinence in the effort to combat alcoholism. From that point on, the resolutions touched more and more on issues beyond the narrow bounds of alcoholism. The congress unanimously passed a resolution that amounted to a disapproval of the government's contradictory policy of leading the temperance campaign while simultaneously extracting revenue from alcohol sales, and it recommended a gradual elimination of the state liquor monopoly. But the resolution did not stop there; it went on to recommend changing the entire government fiscal policy and implementing social and economic measures to improve the welfare of the population. The congress then adopted, by a vote of eighty-three to sixty-three, a resolution that had not been accepted by the commission that drew up the resolutions; it condemned the opportunities created by the liquor monopoly for private brewers to make enormous profits.[32]

A resolution on religious education as a means of combating alcoholism caused further consternation among the congress's leaders. By a vote of fifty-seven to forty, the congress deleted a passage recommending

[30]Severianin, "Vtoroi Vserossiiskii s"ezd po remeslennoi promyshlennosti," 13–15; A. Malin, "Vtoroi Vserossiiskii remeslennyi s"ezd," *Vestnik Evropy* (March 1911): 287.

[31]M. Lukomskii, "Trezvyi s"ezd (protivoalkogol'nyi s"ezd)," *Sovremennyi mir* 2 (1910): 59, 65, 68.

[32]*Vserossiiskii s"ezd po bor'be s p'ianstvom: Trudy*, 3 vols. (St. Petersburg, 1910), 1: 147; "Pervyi Vserossiiskii s"ezd po bor'be s p'ianstvom i otnoshenie k nemu ofitsial'noi pechati," *Vestnik Evropy* (February 1910): 338; Lukomskii, "Trezvyi s"ezd," 68–69.

greater religious and moral foundations in education. At this point, all but a few of the clergy walked out of the congress. It then passed the amended resolution, which recommended removing restrictions on public libraries, reading rooms, and public lectures; permitting the organization of temperance societies among students; and removing all obstacles to public education. This prompted the chair to appeal to the image the congress might project to the authorities: "Look what you're doing, gentlemen! How will they regard our congress now? What value will our petitions have in the eyes of the authorities?" Dr. N. I. Grigor'ev, editor of the journal *Vestnik trezvosti* (*Herald of Sobriety*) and one of the meeting's organizers, was even more forceful: "I propose declaring in the minutes that the resolution is invalid because representatives of worker organizations were among those voting against the religious and moral principles!"[33] But even more antigovernment resolutions were to come.

A resolution on temperance societies, supported by D. N. Borodin, one of the congress's organizers, was actually defeated and replaced by one more critical of the official temperance societies. The substitution stated that the transfer of temperance societies to the jurisdiction of local governments could have meaning only if the latter were democratized. It also called on city governments to set up employment bureaus. In a similar vein, a resolution recommending complete freedom for worker organizations in order to combat more effectively alcoholism among workers passed by a vote of eighty-eight to twenty-five.[34] Another resolution demanded universal primary education, autonomy for institutions of higher education, improvements in the economic and legal status of teachers, and a sweeping curricular reform "on the basis of the natural, free development of the personality of the child and adolescent, and on the basis of the full, free growth of their independent activity and creativity." Another resolution linked the antialcohol movement with civil rights for women:

Whereas the reduction of drunkenness is intimately connected with raising the economic and spiritual level of the people, and whereas an improvement in the living conditions of the masses depends directly on an improvement in the material and legal situation of women, the congress acknowledges that the struggle

---

[33] *Vserossiiskii s"ezd po bor'be s p'ianstvom: Trudy,* 1: 90–91, 172; Lukomskii, "Trezvyi s"ezd," 66–68; "Pervyi Vserossiiskii s"ezd po bor'be s p'ianstvom," 340.
[34] *Vserossiiskii s"ezd po bor'be s p'ianstvom: Trudy,* 1: 93–95, 176; Lukomskii, "Trezvyi s"ezd," 68.

with the use of strong drink will fully succeed only if women can enter it as citizens with equal rights.

Finally, the congress also approved a resolution to improve the economic, social, and legal status of minorities and to grant them autonomy in local affairs.[35]

Although secondary accounts are sketchy, the submission and adoption of many of these resolutions prompted conflict between the congress's organizers and the delegates, amid charges that the organizing committee initially refused to read resolutions submitted by the congress as a whole and not by the resolution commission, changed the wording of several resolutions, and in general made decisions reflecting the views of a conservative minority, not those of the entire congress.[36]

Three observations may be made regarding the politicization of the congresses. First, it is quite likely, though difficult as yet to demonstrate, that a few activist left and liberal delegates—politicized well before the congress opened—were disproportionately influential. Second, a variety of interest groups represented at a congress—such as women, teachers, and labor—were sometimes able to link the grievances of their constituents to the "official" subject of the congress. Many resolutions display a skillful piggybacking of elements; for example, no success can be expected in curbing public drunkenness until x is changed in national life, where x could be guaranteeing civil liberties, democratizing local government, establishing child-centered pedagogy, or improving the condition of rural women. Third, such politicization became part of an emerging "collective memory" of congresses. Supporters of a second writers' congress tried to convince skeptics that a congress could still be useful even if the authorities banned touchy topics. The issue of freedom of the press, they said, would come up even if it were officially off limits, in the same way that congresses of doctors "went astray in politics" or that "the congress on alcoholism turned to forbidden political themes every day despite the efforts of organizers."[37]

POLITICAL, CLASS, REGIONAL, PROFESSIONAL, AND GENDER DIFFERENCES

Our picture of the confrontation between society and autocracy over the issue of freedom of association and assembly would be incomplete if it

---

[35] *Vserossiiskii s"ezd po bor'be s p'ianstvom: Trudy,* 1: 90–91, 93–94.
[36] Ibid., 1: 96, 147, 170; Lukomskii, "Trezvyi s"ezd," 69.
[37] "Byt' ili ne byt' vtoromu s"ezdu pisatelei," *Vestnik Evropy* (March 1910): 446.

did not take account of confrontations within society itself. At the same time that society and government were vying for control of the public sphere, various interest groups within society were vying with each other for a voice within that sphere. The national congresses again provide a window into these divisions within society.

The Artisans' Congress of 1911 illustrates the complexities of class divisions in the post-1905 period. The larger proprietors set the overall tone of the congress, but, according to two reports, this tone differed significantly from that of the first congress in 1900. "Our artisans are surely not like that anymore! The last ten years have taught them and advanced them a lot," said one observer. To another, the congress reflected the "rise of initiative and independence among the people." "Europeanism" had penetrated deeply into the previously inert small producers; they defended their interests with consistency and logic. If at the first congress the proprietors praised "the fist and the birch rod," at the second they rejected corporal punishment on the job without debate and recommended general, free, and compulsory education in the native language.[38] But "Europeanism" hardly signified harmony, and the congress reflected class divisions on a wide range of issues, such as apprenticeship, factory inspection, labor contracts, education, and corporate organization. On every issue, the interests of employers clashed with those of laborers, journeymen, and apprentices. Whereas workers wanted to replace apprenticeship with vocational training at special workshops at state expense, the owners wanted to retain the existing system and rejected proposals for allowing apprentices to attend school during the day and for setting a minimum working age of sixteen. Owners also insisted on written agreements between proprietor and apprentice, over the objections of labor that this reinforced the system of indenture.[39]

Although "Europeanism" implies that employers were capable of a more modern and sophisticated defense of class interests, they nevertheless frequently resorted to traditional categories to defend privilege. For example, owners who had long conceived of a homogeneous artisan industry deserving of special consideration from the government could not accept division within the industry or the argument of labor that

---

[38]Severianin, "Vtoroi Vserossiiskii s"ezd po remeslennoi promyshlennosti," 13–14; Malin, "Vtoroi Vserossiiskii remeslennyi s"ezd," 287.
[39]Ibid.

there was no such thing as a special artisan industry, only large- and small-scale production. Nor were the rights of association and assembly, and the exercise of these rights by society vis-à-vis the state, a burning issue to the employers. The closest the congress came to this issue was the debate on which organization should represent the interests of wage laborers in artisan establishments. Employers wanted the old guilds and artisan boards to represent wage laborers, but the latter, most of whom were not members of the artisan estate, favored their own organizations to represent them.[40]

Several congresses displayed professional differences. Both the Congress of Agronomists in 1911 and the Agricultural Congress in Kiev two years later illustrated divisions among professionals over government policy common during this period. For example, for several years, agronomists had been divided between those who wanted to continue to work within the framework of the zemstvos and those who wanted to work with the small independent peasant agricultural societies, in which peasants, or at least the better-off peasants, had been recently displaying public initiative.[41] The Second Congress of Physicians' Assistants (feldshers) in Kiev, which met from June 10 to June 17, 1909, showed that there were also status differences within a profession. "Complaints from the feldshers about their unjust and inhuman treatment at the hands of the physicians resounded at the congress." The feldshers pointed out that the organizing committee of the Eleventh Pirogov Congress had refused to accept feldsher delegates, although feldshers had been allowed to participate in the Tenth Pirogov Congress.[42]

At the Agronomists' Congress, it was not professional disagreements among agronomists or disputes between the zemstvo and the government that provoked the sharpest antagonism, but rather the differences between men and women. A woman agronomist told the congress of the difficult situation facing women agronomists, similar to that faced by women physicians two generations earlier. Women had to put up

[40]Malin, "Vtoroi Vserossiiskii remeslennyi s"ezd," 288, 291. Traditional and modern values among one group of artisans are explored in Mark D. Steinberg, "Culture and Class in a Russian Industry: The Printers of St. Petersburg, 1860–1905," *Journal of Social History* 3 (1990): 513–33.

[41]I. Zhilkin, "Agronomicheskii s"ezd," *Vestnik Evropy* (April 1911): 365.

[42]G. P. Zadera, "O Vserossiiskom fel'dsherskom s"ezde," *Russkoe bogatstvo* (February 1910): 30. For more on the feldshers, see Samuel C. Ramer, "The Transformation of the Russian Feldsher," in Ezra Mendelsohn and Marshall Shatz, eds., *Imperial Russia, 1700–1917: State, Society, Opposition* (De Kalb: Northern Illinois University Press, 1988), 136–60.

with the disrespect not only of the zemstvo boards but also of male agronomists. The speech expressed hope that as their numbers increased, women agronomists would experience less and less prejudice from their male colleagues. The notion that women could work alongside men or that there might be prejudice apparently was an eye-opener for the delegates to the congress, and they passed a resolution recommending that the zemstvos offer more jobs to women at all levels.[43] Thus, at a congress not devoted to gender issues, the public forum provided an opportunity for the grievances of women professionals to be heard.

Regional divisions emerged at the First Writers' Congress. The provincial press expressed resentment against the liberal Moscow and St. Petersburg press. Several provincial journalists wanted to discuss professional issues but were allegedly thwarted because the "literary generals from St. Petersburg are totally ignorant of the reality of newspaper life in the provinces."[44] The Second Congress of Cooperatives and the Agricultural Congress also displayed regional divisions. At the former, the Moscow proponents of a centralized amalgamation of cooperatives disagreed with the Kiev proponents of a more decentralized federation. There was a similar division at the Agricultural Congress between the more centralizing, communal-property "northerners" and the more federative, private-property "southerners." When the link between economic freedom and political freedom came up, as it did again and again, the northerners argued that only a free Russia could be rich, and the southerners countered that only a rich Russia could attain political freedom.[45]

Just as autocracy had proprietary claims over the public sphere vis-à-vis the congresses, congress leaders often claimed control over a congress vis-à-vis dissenting voices from within. Illustrations can be found in the congresses on alcoholism, prostitution, and cooperatives. Al-

---

[43]Zhilkin, "Agronomicheskii s"ezd," 365. Zhilkin went on to recall that, during one of his frequent visits to Novgorod province, he had heard of a very successful short course in dairy farming taught by a woman agronomist. The peasant women responded well and were much more enthusiastic than during similar courses taught by men. In particular, the woman agronomist widened the peasant women's world, and many of the women were asking the village elders to let them study farming more seriously. But peasant men seemed more conservative than peasant women, and while they were amused at the fervor of their daughters, they were unwilling to let them study agricultural science.

[44]V. Miakotin, "Nabroski sovremennosti," 109–10; "Obshchestvennaia khronika," 822.

[45]*Vserossiiskii s"ezd po kooperatsii: Trudy,* 1–9; Prokopovich, "Itogi kooperativnogo s"ezda," 339–56; I. Zhilkin, "Sel'sko-khoziaistvennyi vserossiiskii s"ezd v Kieve," *Vestnik Evropy* (October 1913): 360.

though the Congress on Alcoholism brought together representatives of the church, the Guardianship of Public Sobriety, and many societies dedicated to temperance and moral improvement, the overall tone of the congress was set by representatives of the medical and scientific community, local government, and the cooperative movement, and was secular and progressive.[46] The organizing committee, out of a desire to ensure that the congress would do productive work, kept close tabs on the proceedings, distributed the papers, and led the discussions. After one rather stormy session, at which the liquor monopoly was criticized, the organizing committee interrupted the speaker with shouts of "Don't interfere with our productive work!" At another session, a worker delegate, A. I. Iatsynevich, tried to read a report on the efforts of unions and cooperatives to combat alcoholism. He was frequently interrupted by the chair, D. N. Borodin, a lawyer and editor of the journal *Trezvost' i berezhlivost'* (*Sobriety and Thrift*), as in the following exchange:

Iatsynevich: "The capitalist system . . ."
Borodin: "That is irrelevant!"
Iatsynevich: "The workers' move[ment] . . ."
Borodin: "The workers' movement has nothing to do with alcoholism!"

In the end, the attempts of the government and the congress's organizers to censor the congress backfired, and the mood of the congress, as we have seen above, became markedly antigovernment.[47]

The Congress on Prostitution witnessed a similar conflict between the conference establishment and the labor delegates. The secretary of the Moscow Printers' Union, P. S. Pavlov, introduced a four-point resolution, which included the statement that unions needed freedom to agitate and to amalgamate into regional and national organizations. After a warning by the police that the latter point deviated from the program and could not be discussed, the chair of the session, A. K. Von-Anrep, a physician and Duma representative, requested that Pavlov "cease this

---

[46]Hutchinson, "Science, Politics, and the Alcohol Problem," 247, 253–54.
[47]Lukomskii, "Trezvyi s"ezd," 59, 65, 68. Borodin's outbursts were deleted from the official proceedings of the congress. Yet the proceedings reveal that the police frequently interrupted worker delegates speaking about the reasons for alcoholism among workers and that reports entitled "The Interrelationship between Poverty and Alcoholism" and "The Popular Religious Struggle against Alcoholism" were denied a reading by the city prefect. *Vserossiiskii s"ezd po bor'be s p'ianstvom: Trudy*, 1: 177, 191. Iatsynevich, who was listed as a delegate from the St. Petersburg Sampson Education Society, delivered a talk entitled "Trade Unions, Cooperatives, and Other Worker Organizations in the Struggle against Alcoholism." Another worker delegate was Semen Kanatchikov, whose talk was entitled "Workers and the Temperance Societies." Ibid., 1: 36.

excursion into extraneous matters and yield the floor. . . . The [paragraph] is political in nature and therefore cannot be put to a vote."

Pavlov: "I protest against . . ."
Von-Anrep: "I permit no protests against my orders."

Later, Von-Anrep refused to bring to a vote another resolution introduced by Pavlov regarding working hours and freedom for worker organizations, on the (not entirely erroneous) ground that the resolution was unrelated to the subject of the congress. Responding that "we cannot work with such constraints on freedom of speech," Pavlov announced that the workers' delegation was leaving the congress.[48]

Harassment from the leadership in the person of the chair was also apparent when it came time to read resolutions at the Congress of Cooperatives. One hour before the end of the congress, the chair, Count D. F. Geiden, refused to let a speaker from the cultural and educational commission read a resolution recommending greater public activity. A resolution about political liberties (from the Agricultural Section, no less) was also denied a reading. When a speech was then delivered about resolutions that could not be read, it brought a thunder of applause from the thousand delegates in the hall and was said to be the most moving moment of the entire congress.[49]

THE CONGRESSES AS A PARLIAMENT OF PUBLIC OPINION

The confrontation between society and government, the increasing politicization of society, and the division of society itself into quarreling interest groups all took place in the forums of national congresses in the post-1905 period. These congresses reflected the tensions of Russian politics and society, and therein lies perhaps their greatest significance: Under autocracy, they acted as a surrogate national parliament. Because normal channels for the free exchange of ideas in representative institutions were still circumscribed, politics appeared elsewhere. The congresses debated a wide range of issues and made what amounted to policy recommendations, provided voice and representation to a number

---

[48]*Trudy Pervogo Vserossiiskogo s"ezda po bor'be s torgom zhenshchinami i ego prichinami,* 2: 578–80, 590–91.

[49]*Vserossiiskii s"ezd po kooperatsii: Trudy,* 39–50, 213–14. However, a resolution was read that called for extending the zemstvos to nonzemstvo provinces (ibid., 43). See also Prokopovich, "Itogi kooperativnogo s"ezda," 342, and Zhilkin, "Provintsial'noe obozrenie," 355.

of groups, and fostered the revival of public life that was so noteworthy in the two to three years before the outbreak of World War I.

The Congress on Alcoholism, for example, took place at a time when the topics of alcoholism, public drunkenness and disorder, and the state liquor monopoly were before the Duma. The solutions advocated by the Duma emphasized restrictions on sales and punishment of individuals; the Octobrist delegates opposed discussion of social and economic reform. Hence, it was left to the First All-Russian Congress on Alcoholism to debate all the other issues—agriculture, industry, family education, public health, crime, prostitution, and the national budget. Various interest groups aired their resentments and expressed their recommendations in unexpected ways, and agendas only indirectly related to alcoholism acquired a brief, if furtive, exposure. The reaction of the official and right-wing press was predictable. The newspaper *Rossiia* (*Russia*) denounced the alleged falsehood of Russian progressivism: "While not in any way trying to prevent the initiative of society, the government naturally cannot permit a school of revolutionary agitation to be founded under the flag of public opinion." In the same vein, *Novoe vremia* (*New Times*) opposed not the convening of the congress but its oppositional nature: "Our liberal government poorly serves the state principle by allowing political congresses without good reasons; the government gains nothing from a political congress and only loses authority."[50]

As at a genuine national parliament, the congresses heard voices from many parts of the country. The Congress of Retail Employees showed that questions of governance had become part of public discourse in the provinces. Such an event could not have transpired ten years earlier, when, as one observer said,

There was no way out, when society had no strength, but only a depressing lack of coordination, unpreparedness, an ignorance of elementary things, and was too timid to take the initiative. . . . But congresses like that of the retail employees and of the cooperatives indicate the tremendous regeneration of Russian life, which no force can stop. A growing public will is ever more authoritatively demanding a restructuring of life (and in part has already restructured it), and sooner or later it will be necessary to bow down before this will.[51]

[50]Quoted in "Pervyi Vserossiiskii s"ezd po bor'be s p'ianstvom," 339. A more extensive selection of press reports may be found in *Vserossiiskii s"ezd po bor'be s p'ianstvom: Trudy,* 1: 287–364.
[51]Zhilkin, "S"ezd torgovykh sluzhashchikh v Moskve," 352, and Zhilkin, "Provintsial'noe obozrenie," 358.

The businesslike sense of purpose and open discussion at the Teachers' Congress (1913) was described as "an unexpected and inspiring sight. . . . The living provinces have surged into the capital . . . and have agitated and shaken up St. Petersburg. . . . A thousand silent, seemingly apathetic, forgotten, and truly enigmatic provincial localities have spoken."[52]

That the same subjects came up again and again in resolutions is further indication that the congresses functioned as a surrogate national parliament. The Librarians' Congress (1911) passed a resolution calling for the democratization of local government. The Congress on Livestock Insurance (1913) supported complete freedom of association for cooperatives. The Congress on Fire Insurance (1913) resolved not only that public insurance should replace private but also that the power of the police needed to be curtailed, that local government needed to be democratized, and that a lower-level zemstvo organ needed to be created.[53] According to one observer, the congresses were displaying more and more unity between "left" and "right" and among the "reasonable people" who thought that things would be better for them after the October Manifesto:

There are many of these congresses and meetings these days. Their plenitude is a sign of the times, an indication that both sides really need a "compact" "to put their heads together." . . . Everyone knows that in the present situation, the morals of the police won't change, that there will never be a local zemstvo organ, that municipal government won't be democratized, that formalism and indifference won't disappear, that there will be no freedom of association for cooperatives. . . . Nothing will improve without a fundamental change—the realization of the principles of the October Manifesto.[54]

The frequency of resolutions calling for the realization of the freedoms promised in the October Manifesto suggests that these parliaments of public opinion were trying to complete work that had been begun a decade earlier. At the Agricultural Congress, the first resolution, introduced by the section on public agronomy, stated: "Having entered into a discussion of the working conditions of local agronomists, the congress

---

[52]I. Zhilkin, "Vserossiiskii s"ezd narodnykh uchitelei," *Vestnik Evropy* (February 1914): 383. For a report on a related congress, on public education, see A. K. Ianson, "Pervyi Vserossiiskii s"ezd po narodnomu obrazovaniiu," *Russkaia mysl'* (February 1914): 148–52.

[53]*Vserossiiskii s"ezd po bibliotechnomu delu: Trudy* (St. Petersburg, 1912), 199; A. Petrishchev, "Rechi, s"ezdy, rezoliutsii," 341–42.

[54]Petrishchev, "Rechi, s"ezdy, rezoliutsii," 342.

recognizes that the enormous responsibility of reviving our agronomy, which the government, the Zemstvo, and the nation have entrusted to the agronomists, can be carried out most fully by the steadfast realization of the principles of the October Manifesto."[55] Indeed, the mood at several pre-1914 congresses was reminiscent of that prevailing on the eve of the 1905 revolution. Reports on the 1913 Agricultural Congress resembled those in *Osvobozhdenie* (*Liberation*) about the Agricultural Congress of 1901 and the handicrafts (*Kustar'*) congress of 1902. The 1913 congress discussed the same themes—reform of the zemstvo electoral law, equalizing the peasantry with the other estates, an all-estate canton assembly—and expressed the same desire to emancipate the village from the tutelage of the bureaucracy.[56]

The role of the congresses as a parliament of public opinion was explicitly recognized by several observers, pointing out that this was a role not being played by the Fourth Duma. In publicly proclaiming that Russia needed to return to the principles of the October Manifesto, wrote the correspondent for *Russkoe slovo* (*The Russian Word*) about the Agricultural Congress, "members of the congress are quite pleased that they have performed their civic duty."[57] Of the same congress, a commentator for *Vestnik Evropy* (*Herald of Europe*) wrote, "As you read the newspaper reports of the congress, you came to the realization that members of the congress were enthusiastically undertaking parliamentary work."[58] And this congress was only one of a great many that were held in the summer of 1913 (twelve of them in Kiev alone, in a kind of "Kiev summer"), leading the *Vestnik Evropy* commentator to write:

The congresses of the past summer have seemed like a parliament of public opinion [*obshchestvennyi parlament mnenii*]. . . . In any event, this is a striking sign that after a long deadening silence and alongside an ineffectual Duma, the new public voices of the multitude are resounding at congresses. The tremendous public work that has already been done, and which has been such a healthy surprise for many, has been paraded in full review at these congresses. In a thousand organized voices, public opinion started right away to talk about the

[55]Kievskoe obshchestvo sel'skogo khoziaistva i sel'sko-khoziaistvennoi promyshlennosti, *Trudy Pervogo Vserossiiskogo sel'sko-khoziaistvennogo s"ezda* (Kiev, 1913), 1: 3.
[56]Ibid., 1: 3–45; V. Kuz'min-Karavaev, "Kievskie s"ezdy," *Vestnik Evropy* (October 1913): 429. On congresses during the 1905 revolution, see the comprehensive study by Jonathan Sanders, "The Union of Unions: Political, Economic, Civil, and Human Rights Organizations in the 1905 Russian Revolution" (Ph.D. diss., Columbia University, 1985).
[57]Quoted in Zhilkin, "Sel'sko-khoziaistvennyi vserossiiskii s"ezd v Kieve," 358–59.
[58]Ibid., 363.

practical and political needs of the nation. The crystallization of opinion from the depths of the populace, expressed by a thousand public representatives at congresses, will inevitably fortify the nation's public will.[59]

This "parliament of public opinion," of course, was not a true parliament, because it had no political power. Nevertheless, in the years before the outbreak of World War I, as in 1905, the many national congresses played a crucial role in the process of consciousness-raising and in the coalescence and mobilization of special-interest constituencies. The presence of like-minded people at national meetings broke down the sense of isolation. The publicity attached to the meetings served as propaganda for a multitude of causes. Overcoming the fear of the authorities, private individuals came together at their own initiative and formed a public. The congresses made policy recommendations on a wide range of national issues, policy recommendations that were directed simultaneously at the government and at the participants themselves. The congresses made an important contribution to the process by which Russian subjects were becoming citizens. The repeated thwarting of such attempts at reform from below, coupled with the serious divisions within society that were also reflected at the congresses, set the stage for the political and social revolutions soon to follow.

[59] I. Zhilkin, "Znachenie s"ezdov nyneshnego leta," *Vestnik Evropy* (October 1913): 364.

10

The reforming tradition in Russian and Soviet
history: commentary

ALFRED J. RIEBER

I have been asked to comment on the Stolypin reforms and the essays
that deal with them, but my comments will extend beyond those specific
reforms to address what I call the pattern of reform in imperial and
Soviet Russia, a tradition that stretches from Peter the Great to the present day. The Stolypin reforms are simply one episode in this tradition.
Reform should be viewed as more than a matter of continuity and
change. It seems to me that we must recognize that different reform
episodes took place within the context of a changing social order. Thus,
it is somewhat misleading simply to enumerate similarities in the reforming process over time without bearing in mind the changes in society
that occur as a result both of previous reforms and of the reaction
against them, the counterreforms. The Stolypin reforms, for example,
are a phase of the reforming process that took place in a richer and more
complex social order than had previously existed in the imperial period.
This notion of a changing social order should be kept in mind as I
discuss the eight key elements that I believe characterize the reforming
tradition from Peter I to the present.

The first element is that the initiative for reform always comes from
above and comes in response to what I call a systemic crisis. Since the
seventeenth century, three crises were imposed on Russia from the outside world in connection with Western European or global events: the
gunpowder and military revolutions of the seventeenth century, the
steam and mechanical revolutions of the late eighteenth and early nineteenth centuries, and the scientific-technological revolution of the mid-
twentieth century. Each of these transformations posed a chal-

237

lenge to the government in maintaining Russia's position as a great
power—and the perceived need to maintain that position guided the
reforming impetus throughout the imperial period. Zakharova ably demonstrated the role of the Crimean War in stimulating the Great Reforms,
and Korelin's citation of Krivoshein's statement that without reform
Russia would not be able to stand its ground in the great economic
competition of the nations revealed the same motives at work in the last
decade of the tsarist regime. In the 1890s and afterward, the momentum
of the steam and mechanical revolutions delivered a series of seismic
shocks to the Russian system. The failure to keep up technologically with
the West had serious effects on agriculture and military preparedness:
the famine of 1891–92, certain developments in military hardware and
the impact of the railroad on the disposition of military forces, the agrarian crisis of 1902 (which to a large extent resulted from the inability of
the fragile, unresponsive agricultural base to meet the need for massive
exports), and finally, the Russo-Japanese War. These shocks to the system reflected an intertwining of imperialist expansion and domestic stagnation. They also forced the government to reconsider the one-sidedness
of the Witte reforms and to pay attention to the agrarian sector.

The second element in the reforming tradition is the need for a pre-
paratory period preceding the major legislative acts. The required preparation is both short-term and long-term in nature. The insights of
Zakharova, Korelin, and Macey enable us to discern this phenomenon
of prereform preparation. The immediate preliminary to the Stolypin
reforms, for instance, was the Special Conference on the Needs of Agriculture; the long-term preparation can be traced back to the emancipation of the serfs in 1861. Macey points out that the Nikol'skii
commission envisaged many of the institutional reforms that later become law. I think that, by the time of the Stolypin reforms, we can see
that reform is a continuous stream; sometimes it flows along the surface
of society, sometimes it moves underground, but its traces can always
be detected by the zealous researcher. On the one hand, there are pockets
of reformers in bureaucratic institutions, the universities, and the research institutes of the Academy of Sciences; on the other hand, there is
the rise of professional and other private organizations, discussed by
Bradley, that crowd the years before 1905. A few of these, such as the
Russian Technological Society or the Society for the Encouragement of
Russian Industry and Trade, have their roots in the 1860s. There is an
exponential increase of them as the end of the century nears. They considerably broaden the social base of the reforming cadres.

The third element in the reforming tradition is the lack of an integrated or comprehensive plan for reform. The uneven and ad hoc way in which the reforms are implemented leads to confusion and hesitation among the reformers and, in the final analysis, weakens the reforming impulse. A paradoxical situation develops. A small number of reformers do know precisely what they want, and they make concrete, rational, and systematic proposals for reform. But they fall victim to the institutional and social fragmentation of Russian society. There is no unified government or solid class foundation on which to build. They envision reform as carried out through one or another agency of the government bureaucracy, be it the Ministry of Finance or the Ministry of Internal Affairs, or, less frequently, through the agency of a quasi-governmental institution like the Russian Geographic Society. But they lack a broader view. This tunnel vision is characteristic not only of the bureaucrats but of private individuals in the society as well. Thus, legislative programs become bogged down in the cumbersome machinery of the state. Macey calls attention to the plethora of unsuccessful committees that marked the prehistory of the Stolypin reforms, and Korelin repeatedly demonstrates how political trade-offs led to temporary or provisional concessions made with no understanding of their relation to the main aims of the reform.

The fourth element is the intense bureaucratic infighting that develops once the reforms are begun. This struggle cannot be understood in traditional political terms by using the simple duality of left and right: reformers against counterreformers, liberals against conservatives, feudal landowning aristocrats against the (objective or subjective) bourgeoisie. The struggle is far more complicated than that. So-called liberals like the Miliutin brothers later become radical chauvinists and imperialists, opponents of local autonomy in the Baltics and in Poland and expansionists in the Caucasus and Central Asia. Dmitry Miliutin believed that a constitution in Russia in the 1860s would weaken the force of autocratic reform. A constitutional regime might well mean domination of the government by reactionary landed gentry who would oppose reform. Is he to be perceived as liberal? Are the people who wanted constitutional reform, who sought some kind of representative government and consultation—the Shuvalovs and Valuevs—liberals? Both Korelin and Macey describe the struggle over the agrarian reform that illuminates this problem. There were disputes over how to define the problem and how to approach its resolution. The materials of the Special Conference amply demonstrated that representatives of the zemstvo "third element" and liberal gentry (who later become either Cadets or left-wing Octobrists) had very different views on what constituted the proper approach to reform, yet both groups were reformers. This struggle has to be understood in terms of disagreements about the nature and pace of reform and about the intended beneficiaries of reform. The struggle broke out anew, of course, in the 1920s, and again in the 1980s.

A fifth element enters when the intragovernmental struggle spills over into the public arena, as it soon does, involving the press and private or voluntary organizations. As the press expands its influence, as the voluntary organizations become more numerous, as a Duma is created, the struggle becomes wider until, ultimately, most of literate society is involved. The bureaucrats, players in the intragovernmental part of the struggle, seek allies in society. Beginning as early as the 1860s, leaks to the press become a part of the process. Certain organs of the press play an active role in presenting reform ideas; among them at that time were *Vestnik promyshlennosti* (*Herald of Industry*), *Moskovskie vedomosti* (*Moscow News*), and, later, *Golos* (*The Voice*). Public debate becomes part of an educational process; communication networks are established that are never destroyed, not even at the height of the counterreform in the 1880s. Of course, censorship is applied, but the mass press and public organizations are never abolished; they continue and the exchange of information continues, even during the worst years of the counterreform era.

The sixth element is the debate that emerges over the idea that Russia's economic development in the nineteenth and twentieth centuries represented a special path—a *Sonderweg,* as the Germans say (the Russian terms were *osobyi put'* or *osobaia doroga*). This debate has had two dimensions. On one level, it raged among the contemporaries and involved the bureaucracy, liberal opinion, the populists, and the Marxists. On another level, it has continued to preoccupy scholars of economic development. These debates are well known in the literature. But from our perspective, they lead to an obvious question: What country does not follow a Sonderweg? Marx said the future of every country was written in the past of Great Britain. No country, however, followed the British path to industrialization—not France, or Italy, or Russia; nor did any of these countries imitate the economic development of some other country. Zakharova points out that the Russians borrowed models of development from both the French and the Prussians. To be sure, the tsarist statesmen wanted to avoid a repetition of 1789 and 1848 in Russia, and they wanted to prevent the proletarianization of the peasantry, but we must remember that their eyes were fixed not only on Europe but on the Ottoman Empire as well. If they did not want what happened in France in 1848, neither did they want what happened to Ottoman Turkey: the decline of a powerful empire and the growth of economic dependence upon other nations. Yet the Sonderweg idea has its uses in comparative history. It is particularly applicable to the role of the state in the development of capitalism in both Germany and Russia. Similarities of this kind must, of course, be balanced against important differences in the agrarian systems of the two countries.

Another aspect of Russia's special path has to do with what one might label "the way of dual power" (*dvoevlastie*)—or, more specifically, the different and even contradictory patterns of economic development in the center and on the periphery of the empire. The state's attempt to resolve that contradiction is a very special Russian problem, which has its closest parallel in the history of the Ottoman Empire. While for a time more successful than the Ottomans in pushing through socioeconomic reforms, the Russian and Soviet governments eventually failed in this endeavor.

The seventh element is that the reforms are always incomplete, especially if one evaluates them according to the standards of the reformers. They remain incomplete because the reformers inevitably become involved in a political struggle. Here we must ask ourselves a fundamental question: Is reform a discrete or a continuous process? Was the New Deal "complete"? Were the reforms of the British liberals in 1911–12 complete? The process of reform really should be regarded as a continuous one, because as certain institutions are changed, other institutions must also be changed. Korelin remarks that it is dangerous to talk about optimists and pessimists with respect to reform, for different kinds of evidence can be found to support either side. In fact, as McDonald points out, the failure to institutionalize a united government blunted the edge of Stolypin's socioeconomic reforms. If the Great Reforms of the 1860s were incomplete even in the eyes of some of the leading reformers, as Zakharova argues, it was due largely to the absence of a unified political will. The autocratic tradition was opposed to a cabinet system, but by midcentury, the government had become too complex to be run by a single man. Alexander II tried to solve this dilemma by becoming a "managerial tsar." He himself did not draft a reform program, but he managed it by playing the reformers against the counterreformers in order to bring about changes with which he was comfortable without jeopardizing his monopoly of power. This meant that the only way the reformers could push through their programs was to try to secure control over as many of the ministries as possible, to "colonize" the bureaucracy. Reutern tried it as a reformer; Shuvalov tried it as a counterreformer. Witte perhaps came close to bringing it off, but he never controlled the Ministry of Internal Affairs. Stolypin succeeded, but that was highly unusual. Perhaps even more unusual was Nicholas II's reaction after he abandoned Stolypin. As Richard Wortman has noted, Nicholas reverted not to the tradition of the managerial emperor but to that of the seventeenth-century tsar.

The eighth and final element in the reforming tradition is the social response "from below." As Jeffrey Brooks and Ben Eklof observe in another context, the Russian peasant marches to a different drummer. The peasantry was not a monolithic estate or class; different groups and individuals within it reacted differently to the Stolypin reforms. As indicated by Korelin, some peasants became individual farmers while others remained within the commune. Peasant Russia has also meant enormous regional differences in terms of institutions and culture: the cooperative movement, patterns of landholding, village architecture, customary law. One must take into account the great heterogeneity of the Russian peasantry when evaluating the effects of reform.

These elements of the reforming tradition in Russian history are also applicable to the Soviet period, but it remains to be seen how the 1920s and Stalin fit within this overall framework. Three facts could be cited in support of the contention that the 1920s were also an era of reform. First, although the Soviet system of the 1920s was a one-party state, the Bolshevik Party was not monolithic. Despite the Tenth Congress's prohibition on factions, the Party was riven with them. And even though Stalin managed, by a rhetorical trick, to identify everybody else as being a member of the opposition, he himself was also part of the opposition. Where did all the Left Socialist Revolutionaries, anarchists, maximalists, and other people go after 1921 or 1922? They went into the Bolshevik Party, and they did not convert quickly or easily. Second, intellectual life in the 1920s may or may not have been as free as in the prerevolutionary period, but it was certainly pluralistic to some degree. Third, there was some reconstruction of the economy not only in the countryside but in all the legislation of the New Economic Policy. I think that if one looks at the last days of Lenin, as does Moshe Lewin, then one sees the outlines of a reform program: reinvigoration of the soviets, reconstitution of a genuine federation, and a reduction of the centralizing tendencies of the bureaucracy. In my mind, therefore, reform was alive and well in the 1920s.

By contrast, Stalinism was an interruption of the reforming process. The Stalin era was not a revolution from below, or a reform from above, or stagnation—the three basic elements that I identify in Russian political culture—but rather, a *revolution from above* that incorporated perhaps the most destructive and brutal elements of any political regime. It smashed the institutions of reform, which had been built up over several centuries; it devastated the social cadres of reform, which had been in formation since the time of Alexander I, if not earlier; and it created a massive social dislocation among the working class, the peasantry, the intelligentsia, and all the other social strata, a dislocation that has severely hampered social evolution in Russia and the Soviet Union over the last forty years. Whereas the reforming tradition continued in the 1920s, Stalin represented a pathological deviation from the normal processes of Russian history.

Part III

The uncertain interlude

11

The evolution of Bolshevik cultural policies during the first years of Soviet power

PETER KENEZ

The concept of reform is notoriously slippery. According to the dictionary, "to reform" means "to improve, to remove faults, to eliminate errors." In the terminology of politics, we usually contrast reform with revolution: Reform "improves" the existing system, but revolution transforms it. We tend, however, to take a normative view and consider as reforms only those changes that make a regime more liberal and open. It is difficult to justify such an approach. After all, what is improvement for one person is not necessarily improvement for another. From the point of view of the leaders of a regime, any change that increases their chances of remaining in power is an improvement. But the motives for making changes, whether liberal or conservative, centralizing or decentralizing, are generally the same: a recognition by people in authority that the present system is not working as they would like it to work.

Many observers have described the Soviet system as rigid and resistant to change. Actually, the opposite has been true; the reforming urge has been constant from the time of the revolution. The new order was built on a utopian scheme, one that by its very nature could not possibly be realized. Therefore, there has always been a gap between overt goals and performance, between what the world should have been according to theory and what the world really was. The leaders have frequently attempted to narrow this gap by trying new approaches when they found the old ones to be unsatisfactory. The Bolsheviks have been possessed with a veritable mania for reorganization. Constant intervention in all aspects of the life of the polity and society fitted their authoritarian-

247

totalitarian style; after all, what was the point of having unlimited power if it was not exercised?

The first years following the revolution were a period of particularly intense change. The introduction of War Communism in 1918, and of the New Economic Policy (NEP) three years later, implied a rethinking of the fundamental features of the emerging Soviet order. In 1918, the system was in the process of being created, and utopian enthusiasm was at its highest. The revolutionaries had defeated their enemies, the bureaucrats and liberal politicians; the old order had crumbled, and now nothing seemed beyond the realm of the possible. Lenin and his comrades improvised the system of War Communism but soon came to think of it as the only system consistent with Marxist theory. A short time later, when they abandoned that system and allowed a partial restoration of the market, they came to believe with just as much conviction that the NEP was a necessary first step toward the creation of a socialist society.

The question emerges of how different aspects of the new Soviet system—political, economic, social, and cultural—fit together. We tend to assume that profound changes in one sphere necessitate adjustments in all others. A goal of this present study is to examine the evolution of Bolshevik cultural policies during a time of rapid change in the first years of Soviet power.

Paradoxically, it was their ideology that allowed the Bolsheviks to change their convictions often but remain utterly sincere about every change. Marxism-Leninism encouraged them to believe that they knew the direction of progress, the shape of future society, and that they were controlling social processes. The genuine Marxist-Leninist faith of the early Bolsheviks stands in great contrast to the outlook of the architects of perestroika. Gorbachev and his comrades in the 1980s could not even delude themselves into believing that the process of change was predictable and controllable. Ideology had outlived its usefulness.

THE INTELLECTUAL BACKGROUND

During the formative period of the Soviet system, the leaders improvised as they responded to an ever-changing environment. They had no clear ideas about the system that they were creating and no blueprint or model to follow. They came to power in circumstances that they had not foreseen and faced problems that they had not anticipated—problems that political elites in other countries had not faced either. The Bolsheviks improvised solutions to some of these problems, but the fact that they were great improvisers did not mean that ideology did not matter. On the contrary: Ideology determined what the Bolsheviks considered significant and insignificant, it set broad limits to their actions, and it predisposed them to look on one solution to their problems more favorably than on another. Also, ideology gave them confidence: Although they were improvising and faced an uncertain future, their firm belief in Marxism enabled them to act decisively and to make compromises. Their picture of the immediate future might have been cloudy, but their image of a distant, just, and socialist society was clear.

The Bolsheviks' attitudes to freedom of thought and speech, and their willingness to tolerate a degree at least of cultural autonomy, were important and were closely connected to their views of politics. Allowing a variety of views to be expressed, even if only in the realm of the arts and sciences, implied a certain degree of pluralism and thus of intellectual freedom.

In order to understand the cultural policies of the Bolsheviks and to make sense of the seeming contradictions in them, we must first examine the intellectual baggage that they had brought with them. Whether they admitted it or not, they were descendants of the nineteenth-century Russian intelligentsia, sharing more attitudes and assumptions with them than perhaps they themselves realized. Members of that intelligentsia had taken it for granted that ideas mattered greatly, for only that assumption allowed them to think of themselves as making a contribution to society and gave purpose to their lives. Because of this deep conviction, they held their ideologies with passion, and from passion there often followed intolerance toward the views of others.

Bolshevik leaders always had an ambivalent attitude toward the intelligentsia. On the one hand, they admired cultural attainment and shared tastes and interests with other intellectuals; but on the other hand, they were consciously rebelling against at least some of the traditions of the intelligentsia. They had contempt for the intellectuals' scruples, hesitations, and habit of endless discussions. They knew their fellow intellectuals to be hopelessly impractical. Trotsky expressed great hostility toward both the Russian and the Western intelligentsia in two essays, "The Intelligentsia and Socialism" (1910) and "On the Intelligentsia" (1912). In these, he accused the intellectuals of a variety of sins, such as looking down on the people, not being able to integrate themselves into the socialist movement, and being unable to move from theory to practice or to rise above their inherent individualism. Trotsky thought that the intellectuals had deluded themselves. Even though they liked to think of themselves as representing the people, in fact the bourgeoisie had bought them with the promise of a good and comfortable life. The hostility that was so clearly expressed by the future people's commissar of defense, and that was, not so incidentally, shared by Lenin and other prominent leaders, soon would have practical consequences.[1]

The Bolsheviks' faith in the power of ideas was reinforced by their reading of Marx. This might seem contradictory: Marx was, of course, proudly materialist and claimed to regard ideas and culture as parts of the "superstructure," a mere reflection of the material world, of the development of the means of production and social relations. However, Marxism was a doctrine developed by intellectuals and with a special appeal to intellectuals. It was an intellectually complex structure, and for the proper understanding of it a considerable educational background was necessary. As Marxists saw it, social relations had to be understood before they could be changed. Thus, it was impossible to believe in the importance of Marxism without also believing in the power of ideas.

Because of this belief, the Bolsheviks vigorously propagated their own ideas after their victory in the revolution. But because they recognized the subversive power of their own message, they attributed similar power to the ideas of their numerous enemies. The only way they could deal with them was to suppress them.

Russian Marxists, more than Marxists elsewhere, regarded their ideology as a science, the only science that allowed a correct interpretation of historical phenomena. When they carried out propaganda, they believed they were not misleading or lying but on the contrary, helping people to understand their true conditions and therefore their tasks. They were convinced that, unlike the bourgeois propagandists, they were bringing enlightenment. It was this conviction that they and they alone were in possession of the truth that allowed them later to repress others, for, as they saw it, that repression was an attack not on truth but only on falsehood.

According to the Russian Marxists, Russia was not different from

---

[1] For a discussion of these two essays, see Baruch Knei-paz, *The Social and Political Thought of Leon Trotsky* (Oxford: Oxford University Press, 1978), 215–24.

other societies, with a special genius, distinctive achievements, and a unique future; it was simply backward. In the near future, it would follow the path that had already been traveled by others. From their point of view, Russia lacked not merely western European capitalist development but also European culture. This consciousness of backwardness was a main motivating force of Bolshevik policies after the revolution. Leaders who had spent years in foreign exile may have overtly disdained the comfortable, nonrevolutionary ways of Western workers and intellectuals, yet they could not help but admire their culture.

The Marxists believed that the workers could not carry out their revolution without the aid of the intellectuals. The primary task of the revolutionary intellectuals was to bring their Marxist knowledge and their understanding of the work of history to the proletariat. Only in this way could the proletariat acquire class consciousness and accomplish its assigned historical task. Lenin developed this line of reasoning, which was already widespread among Russian Marxists, in his well-known work, *What Is to Be Done?* What is often regarded as the heart of Leninism, the need for a revolutionary party, grew out of Lenin's assumption that the workers would never advance further on their own than a struggle for immediate economic benefits. But if the workers' struggle was hopeless without the revolutionary intelligentsia, so also was the position of the revolutionaries without the workers. The crucial link in making the revolution was the transmission of ideas: the creation of class consciousness among the workers.

The Leninists brought an intolerance to their reading of Marx. Any other interpretation of the theory or the political circumstances was not a mere intellectual error, but one that threatened the primary task, the development of proper revolutionary consciousness among the workers. Therefore, it was the internecine warfare among the socialists themselves that was most passionate. Errors in interpreting Marx or in evaluating the concrete historical circumstances were matters of the greatest political significance. Lenin expressed this intolerance in one of the most famous passages in *What Is to Be Done?*:

Since there can be no talk of an independent ideology formulated by the working masses themselves in the process of their movement, the *only* choice is—either bourgeois or socialist ideology. There is no middle course (for mankind has not created a "third" ideology, and, moreover, in a society torn by class antagonisms, there can never be a non-class or an above-class ideology); hence, to belittle socialist ideology *in any way, to turn aside from it in the slightest degree,* means to strengthen bourgeois ideology. There is much talk of spontaneity, but the spontaneous development of the working-class movement leads to its subordination to bourgeois ideology.

He went on, a few paragraphs later:

But why, the reader will ask, does the spontaneous movement, along the line of least resistance, lead to the dominance of bourgeois ideology? For the simple reason that bourgeois ideology, being far older in origin than socialist ideology, is more fully developed and has at its disposal *immeasurably more means of dissemination.*[2]

These paragraphs are most revealing. Lenin, of course, never was and never pretended to be a liberal. He certainly did not believe that ideas should be combated with ideas and ideas only. These sentences also show him as an opponent of compromise, a man convinced that there were no shadings, no gray area between right and wrong. Those who were not supporting him were his enemies. But between the lines one also senses a lack of self-confidence. It is odd that Lenin would regard socialist ideology as less "fully developed" than bourgeois ideology, and that he would see the superiority of bourgeois ideology in the fact that it was older. In Lenin's view, the revolutionary always had to be on guard. Believers in bourgeois ideas, with their superior means, were always ready to take advantage of those not properly alert and vigilant.

THE CIVIL WAR

The Bolshevik Revolution, like all great revolutions, was fought in the name of liberty. Soon after their victory, however, the Bolsheviks decided to sacrifice an essential aspect of freedom in order to increase their chances of staying in power. The issue of freedom of expression almost immediately caused a split among the revolutionaries. On November 4, 1917 (old style), the Central Executive Committee of Soviets debated whether the ban on publication of the "bourgeois" newspapers, introduced as a temporary measure at the time of the takeover, should be continued. Would the newly established socialist government curtail freedom of expression more severely than the previous "bourgeois" regime? The debate in the Executive Committee, which was dominated by

[2]V. I. Lenin, *Polnoe sobranie sochinenii,* 5th ed. (Moscow, 1958–65), 6: 39–40 (hereafter cited as *PSS*); emphasis in the original.

the Bolsheviks but included other socialists, was extraordinarily interesting, for it posed sharply and for the first time the issue of what kind
of regime the Bolsheviks would introduce.[3]

The arguments of the two sides were expressed passionately and ar-
ticulately. The Socialist Revolutionaries (SRs), some ex-Mensheviks, and
many Bolsheviks argued that revolutionaries should trust the power of
their ideas and the intelligence of the people and ought not fear the
falsehoods of the bourgeois press. They also contended that morality
transcended politics, and because the Bolsheviks in the past had demanded freedom of expression, they were now obliged to act on the
basis of that principle. They said that a socialist society could not be
established by the force of arms alone, and even if it could be, such a
society was not worth struggling for. The issue was considered so important that when their motion failed, several Bolshevik commissars,
including V. P. Nogin, A. I. Rykov, V. P. Miliutin, and I. A. Teodorovich, resigned from the government.

Lenin, Trotsky, and their followers, by contrast, argued that the suppression of the opposition press was a legitimate act of war. In their
view, the young and insecure regime could not afford to show tolerance—to, as Lenin put it, "add the bombs of falsehood to the bombs of
Kaledin."[4] But in addition to the concern for security, the Leninists
brought forth a point of principle. They rejected the "bourgeois" notion
that allowing the rich "to buy quantities of newsprint and hire a mass
of scribblers" was genuine freedom. Trotsky responded to his opponents
in these words: "You say that [before the revolution] we demanded the
freedom of the press on behalf of *Pravda*. But then we were living under
conditions which were apposite to our program-minimum; now we are
putting forward the demands in our program-maximum." Nonetheless,
Trotsky intimated that the repression of the free press was a temporary
phenomenon and that restrictions would be lifted at the end of the Civil
War.

It took some time before the Bolsheviks had enough strength to act
on the principles expressed in the decision of the Executive Committee

[3]John Keep, ed. and trans., *The Debate on Soviet Power: Minutes of the All-Russian
Central Executive Committee of Soviets* (Oxford: Oxford University Press, 1979), 68–89.
[For a more extensive discussion of this debate, see Peter Kenez, *The Birth of the Prop-
aganda State: Soviet Methods of Mass Mobilization, 1917–1920* (Cambridge: Cambridge
University Press, 1985), 38–40.—Ed.]

[4][A. M. Kaledin was an ataman of the Don Cossacks and one of the leaders of the Whites
at the beginning of the Civil War.—Ed.]

to continue the ban on publication of the "bourgeois" newspapers. The abortive rising of the Left SRs eliminated all possibility of cooperation with non-Bolshevik parties, and the Leninists used the opportunity to suppress all dissenting voices. By the end of the summer of 1918, only Bolshevik newspapers were allowed to be published in territories controlled by the Reds. The Bolsheviks thus acquired a monopoly over the interpretation of political events, which meant that discussion of politics was removed from the public realm. The fundamental issues facing Soviet society were not openly discussed again in public forums until the era of Gorbachev.

It was one of the important insights of Lenin that a newspaper could be used not only for carrying out propaganda but also as an organizational tool.[5] Acting on this insight, the Bolsheviks suspended freedom of organization simultaneously with the suppression of their opponents' newspapers. They not only disbanded opposition parties but also made impossible the functioning of all autonomous organizations. They either took over these institutions, like the trade unions, or they closed them down, even if they were no more dangerous than the Boy Scouts.

The victorious revolutionaries saw no contradiction between their determination to suppress heterodox thought on the one hand and their desire to advance "culture" on the other. The Bolsheviks had breathtakingly ambitious plans, and the issue of cultural backwardness had political meaning for Lenin and his comrades. The Mensheviks had attacked them by arguing that Russia was not yet ripe for socialist revolution. This was a stinging attack, for the Bolsheviks themselves had doubts on this score; they were painfully aware of the backwardness of their country. However, they could not afford to admit that Russia was not ready for the historical transformation, for that would have undermined the legitimacy of their revolution.

The conclusion was inescapable. In order to build a socialist society, the cultural level of the Russian people had to be brought up at least to that of Western Europeans. Lenin believed that the socialist revolution in Russia had preceded the attainment of a certain necessary level of culture. However, the fact that the proletariat was now in power made it possible to achieve a great deal within a short time. Russians would not only catch up quickly but would soon overtake Westerners.[6] But it

---

[5] V. I. Lenin, "Kak nachat'?" (1901), *PSS*, 5: 11.
[6] These thoughts were expressed in Lenin's short but important articles, "O kooperatsii" (1923) and "O nashei revoliutsii" (1923), *PSS*, 45: 378–82.

is one of the ironies of history that the Bolsheviks, the most extreme Westernizing group,[7] made up of people who saw nothing admirable in traditional Russian ways, ended up by widening the gap between their country and the rest of Europe. Instead of catching up with Europe, instead of serving as an example for others to follow, they set their country on an altogether separate path.

The Bolsheviks were convinced that the work of "catching up" with Western culture had to begin immediately, even while the regime was engaged in a life-and-death struggle. For the Bolsheviks, as for the Russian intelligentsia in general, "culture" primarily meant material civilization. Electrification, an efficient postal service, good roads, and personal hygiene were essential aspects of "culture." Lenin conceded that, without these preconditions, it was impossible to even talk about socialism.[8] Culture also meant the internalization of discipline, which the Leninists rightly considered to be one of the necessary components of an industrial civilization. By contrast, spontaneity, so much distrusted by Lenin, was a characteristic of backwardness.

But the Bolshevik concept of culture also included high culture, the greatest human achievements in the arts and sciences. The Bolsheviks were convinced that the values inherent in science and the arts were congenial to the principles of socialism. Culture in this sense was to be a helpmate in the building of socialism. The Bolsheviks assumed that, unless there were particular reasons to distrust some artists or scientists, these people were working for the same goal that they were: bringing about enlightenment and through it a better future for mankind. They did not yet understand that some values inherent in the arts might be contrary to what they wanted to accomplish.

There was not much that the Bolsheviks could do for the time being to advance material civilization. As long as the Civil War continued, as long as the new rulers could not even protect their people from cold and famine, plans for the electrification of the countryside, for example, were just empty talk. Dreaming about a better future may have helped the revolutionaries through those difficult times, but it had little practical significance.

On the other hand, there was an immediate question as to what steps

---

[7][Emmons demurred, contending that the history of Russian Marxism was to a large extent the history of the adaptation of Marxism to the specificities of Russian culture, society, and politics, with the Bolsheviks being the group that went furthest in "Russifying" Marxism.—Ed.]

[8]*PSS*, 36: 272–73.

the Bolsheviks could take to raise the cultural level of the people and, correspondingly, how they should treat the "workers of culture," the members of the scientific and cultural intelligentsia. By and large, the intelligentsia, especially the scientists and professors, were hostile to the new regime. Most of them were supporters of the parties that had participated in the Provisional Government, and they did not believe that what seemed to them to be the outlandish ideas of the Bolsheviks could possibly serve as the foundation of a new society. The revolutionary principles of the Bolsheviks, their radical egalitarian slogans, their illiberalism, and the terror which they almost immediately began applying to their enemies were bound to alienate the scientists.

In the face of this hostility, which they encountered from the very beginning, the Bolsheviks showed remarkable tolerance. By and large, they treated scientists better than they treated artists, because they respected them more. Science impressed them. In their eyes, science was a component of modernity, and they were passionate partisans of modernity. Also, they regarded scientists almost as comrades; scientists were establishing the laws of nature, just as Marxists were uncovering the laws governing social change. In a more practical vein, the Bolsheviks took it for granted that scientists would be needed in the rebuilding of the economy. Scientists were experts, and the new rulers admired expertise in all fields.[9]

In their treatment of scholars, the Bolsheviks made distinctions. The schoolteachers' organization, dominated by the SRs, was perceived as an enemy and was dealt with as such. On the other hand, the Leninists understood that ill treatment of famous scientists would bring international opprobrium; the more famous a scientist was, the better he was treated by them. The universities and especially the Academy of Sciences were able to retain a degree of autonomy. S. F. Oldenburg, who had served as minister of education in Kerensky's government, headed the academy all through the NEP period. He was the only member of that government who continued to play a significant role in the vastly changed political environment. He and other individual scientists were won over by the commitment of the new authorities to intellectual en-

[9]Adam Ulam, *The Bolsheviks* (New York: Collier, 1965), describes Lenin as a man deeply hostile to the intelligentsia. Kendall Bailes, *Technology and Society under Lenin and Stalin* (Princeton: Princeton University Press, 1978), considers Lenin to be an admirer at least of scientists and engineers. I believe that Bailes has the better part of this argument.

deavor. (Oldenburg compared Lenin favorably with Nicholas II.) The majority of professors and scientists, however, were less sympathetic.[10]

In any case, there were bound to be conflicts between the new authorities and the scientists. At a time of extreme privations and scarcity, the Bolsheviks could hardly afford to give much material support to scientists. Besides, the revolutionaries wanted to make the universities accessible to the lower classes, and this effort was contrary to the notions of good scholarship held by the professors. In the provinces, less enlightened Bolsheviks often regarded intellectuals simply as members of the hated bourgeoisie and treated them as such. However, the revolutionaries did not make any attempt to interfere in the scientific enterprise itself; it had not yet occurred to them to rule topics out of bounds for ideological reasons.

The Party's relationship with artists was even more complicated. The ideological commitments of artists varied a great deal. Most of them were hostile to the revolution; many of the most famous ones left the country even before the outcome of the Civil War was certain. The film industry, for example, was devastated. Prominent film directors and actors first went to the south, which was controlled by the Whites, and then moved to European capitals, primarily Paris and Berlin. Only a minority of well-known artists greeted the revolution enthusiastically, and even they were not actually Bolsheviks. Rather, they were attracted to the apocalyptic vision of the revolutionaries and to their announced desire to destroy the old order. But their enthusiasm for the revolution was based on a misunderstanding. The artists loathed the previous social order because it seemed to them "petty bourgeois." They deplored the taste of the common people and wanted to demolish the old cultural norms. Somewhat naively, they believed that the Bolsheviks' goals were similar to their own; they saw themselves as the equivalents of the Bolsheviks in their own fields. Many of them claimed to speak for the "proletariat," even though their artistic methods and concerns held no interest whatsoever for real-life workers. Like the Bolsheviks, they created in their own mind an ideal "proletariat," one which never existed and could not possibly exist.

[10]On the treatment of the universities and the Academy of Sciences, see James McClelland, "The Professoriate in the Russian Civil War," and Kendall Bailes, "Natural Scientists and the Soviet System," both in Diane Koenker, William Rosenberg, and Ronald Suny, eds., *Party, State, and Society in the Russian Civil War: Explorations in Social History* (Bloomington: Indiana University Press, 1989).

The Bolsheviks recognized that in spreading their ideological message, the services of writers, musicians, and painters could be useful. However, they did not extend the same degree of respect and admiration to artists as they had to scientists. Although it seemed sufficient simply to leave the scientists alone, giving them as much support as was possible under the prevailing circumstances, the Bolsheviks could not avoid taking an active role in the arts and in the effort to raise the cultural level of the masses.

There was general agreement that the single most important task was to end illiteracy, that sad heritage of the tsarist era. In this area, the Bolsheviks expended considerable energies. They had political reasons to be so concerned, for it was assumed that the literate person could be reached more easily with the Bolshevik message. The Party organized a national campaign, set up schools for instructors, and even passed a law requiring the literate to teach their less fortunate comrades. The fact that little was accomplished was not the Bolsheviks' fault; circumstances were too difficult.

Nevertheless, there were accomplishments. In 1920, the Commissariat of Enlightenment (Narkompros) established the All-Russian Extraordinary Committee for the Liquidation of Illiteracy—abbreviated, in Russian, VChK/lb. The similarity in name with the dreaded political police, the Cheka (ChK), was deliberate. It was intended to signal to the population that the Bolsheviks took this agency seriously. The agency received a budget that was large enough to enable it to order the printing of textbooks, and it even imported paper and pencils from abroad.[11] With the aid of mass organizations such as the Komsomol and Zhenotdel (the Party's youth and women's groups) and the trade unions, VChK/lb organized a network of literacy schools. These were reasonably successful in reaching the organized part of the population, primarily the soldiers and to a lesser extent the workers. But reaching the peasants on a large scale—and the peasants were the majority of the population—proved to be as yet impossible. A. V. Lunacharsky, the commissar of enlightenment, at first declared that three million people had learned to read and write during the Civil War, but he later admitted that this estimate was grossly inflated.[12] Exact numbers aside, from the Bolshevik

[11] Peter Kenez, "Liquidating Illiteracy in Revolutionary Russia," *Russian History* 9 (1982): 173–87.
[12] Kenez, *Birth of the Propaganda State*, 82.

perspective the literacy drive was a success. It created a framework that could be further developed in a more settled time, and most important, the drive itself was used as an instrument of propaganda, or what the Bolsheviks called "political education."

Lenin's government also supported the publishing industry. During the months following the revolution, the government, for all practical purposes, exercised no censorship; the presses, like the rest of industry, remained in private hands, and the publishers continued to print what they believed would make money. Most of the books published at the time were romances and adventure stories, but books on religious subjects, idealist philosophy, and other subjects equally undesirable from the Bolshevik point of view were also printed. The problem for the publishers was not government censorship but the collapse of the economy. It was the lack of raw material and the disintegration of the distribution system that closed down the private publishing houses, rather than governmental intervention.

In May 1919, the government organized the State Publishing House, Gosizdat, in order to centralize publishing. Although some feared that this move would result in increased government control, the main impetus for this move came from economic difficulties.[13] The country was suffering from an extreme shortage of paper, and in order to deal with the problem, the government established a paper monopoly. All supplies of paper not issued by the government became subject to confiscation. This regulation, however, like so many others at the time, remained unenforced. Private publishing houses evaded it by hiding their supplies and therefore managed to remain in existence until the very end of War Communism. Gosizdat had a dual relationship with these firms: It competed with them, and it had censorship powers over them. The announced policy of Gosizdat was to encourage the publication of works that it considered useful, to remain neutral toward those that had no political significance, and to oppose the publication of those that were deemed to be anti-Marxist. The censors were liberal, and in practice they rarely exercised their powers. Moreover, publishers were able to take advantage of the confusion that prevailed at the time and publish anti-Marxist works in the provinces.[14]

---

[13]A. Nazarov, *Oktiabr' i kniga* (Moscow, 1968), 139–40.
[14]These issues are discussed in greater detail in Kenez, *Birth of the Propaganda State*, 100–3.

The Bolsheviks were willing to make sacrifices in order to provide readers with books; as already noted, the state used some of its precious foreign currency to buy paper abroad. In an unusual move, through the intercession of Maxim Gorky, the government set up a cooperative venture with a German publishing firm, Grzhebin. The plan was for this firm to produce Russian books, mostly nineteenth-century classics, for sale both in Soviet Russia and abroad. However, the cooperation soon broke down over questions of precisely what should be published.[15]

In an effort to deal with the difficulties of the publishing industry, the Moscow soviet, in October 1918, ordered the book trade to be taken over by the municipal government, and the soviets in other major cities later followed suit, but that only led to further disintegration.[16] The nadir was reached in April 1920, when the government outlawed the buying and selling of books and nationalized book supplies. Books were to be distributed free. It is hard to evaluate the consequences of this extraordinary and utterly utopian move. By that time, the chaos was so great that governmental decisions had little practical impact. Hunger, devastation, and cold were not favorable conditions for the spread of enlightenment.

THE NEP PERIOD

The introduction of the New Economic Policy transformed the life of the country and made reconstruction possible. It also had far-reaching ideological implications; the revolutionaries now accepted that socialism would be built gradually. But there were few changes in the realm of intellectual freedom. Economic liberalization was not accompanied by political reforms or by greater openness in discussing social and political problems. The principles that governed Bolshevik policies at the time of the Civil War remained in force.

The Bolsheviks made economic concessions because they believed that they had to. Restrictions on peasants' marketing of their produce had to be loosened in order to feed the population. There was no comparable pressure for political reforms or for extending intellectual freedom. Unlike the case later at the time of collectivization, a reorganization of the economy, as far as the Bolsheviks were concerned, did not call for a new

[15]Ibid., 103.
[16]Ibid.

vision of politics. The end of the Civil War did not allay the fears of the new rulers. The Bolsheviks did not believe that the time was propitious for broadening the public sphere. On the contrary: The beginning of NEP seemed to the Bolsheviks to be an especially dangerous moment. On the one hand, they had to watch their enemies grow stronger; on the other, they had to deal with the disappointment of their activists. Many devoted Communists, especially among the young, who had taken the Party's previous slogans seriously, felt abandoned and betrayed.

To make matters worse, in order to revive the economy the Bolsheviks had to restore certain practices of financial orthodoxy. Expenditures had to be cut, and consequently subsidies for cultural work and for propaganda and indoctrination were seriously curtailed. In the new economic environment, there could be no free distribution of books and newspapers. The government that had contributed so much to the literacy drive in the past now attempted to make society assume the burden. Hundreds of literacy schools had to be closed down.

There was no question of allowing non-Bolsheviks to publish newspapers. In fact, measures against the remnants of SR and Menshevik organizations became more severe than ever. There was to be no competition with the Bolsheviks in the interpretation of the news. Newspapers were now expected to be self-financing, but their character did not change. They reflected only indirectly the bitter struggle that was taking place among the leaders; the major issues were not discussed openly but were resolved with secrecy in a narrowly restricted political arena.

The principles of NEP were introduced into publishing, but with some delay. The leaders understood that this industry was not exactly like others and that it required careful oversight; they were determined to protect themselves from ideological and political damage. Only in August 1921 did the Moscow city soviet rescind its municipalization order. Once again, private publishing houses could be licensed. At the same time, however, the Politburo ordered agencies of state control to follow carefully what was being printed and distributed.[17] The Bolsheviks wanted to prevent the spread of religious literature, pornography, and "counterrevolutionary works." In the political climate of 1921, they considered the writing of the SRs to present the greatest political danger, and so it was their fellow socialists who suffered most from the effects of censorship.

[17]Nazarov, *Oktiabr' i kniga*, 234–35.

During NEP, private publishing houses printed only a small and declining share of the total output. Yet they made a considerable contribution to the variety available for the Soviet reader. They brought out a large share of the books on philosophy and psychology and of translations and belles lettres. Gosizdat continued to exercise "supervisory authority"—that is to say, censorship—over the publishers. However, during Lunacharsky's tenure as commissar of enlightenment (Gosizdat was a part of Narkompros), few manuscripts were refused publication. In Petrograd, for example, private publishers submitted 190 manuscripts in the course of the first three months of 1922, of which only 10 were rejected. In Moscow, Gosizdat disallowed 31 out of 813 manuscripts.[18]

This small number of rejections may give a misleading impression of the effects of censorship, for there is no way of determining the number of authors who decided not to submit their works because they considered publication unlikely. Yet in the early stages of NEP, authors such as D. S. Merezhkovskii, N. A. Berdyaev, S. L. Frank, and N. O. Losskii were published in Soviet Russia. In retrospect, it is clear, however, that this tolerance was born out of weakness and an inability to control rather than being based on a respect for freedom of speech. As time went on and Bolshevik rule became more secure, censorship grew not more lax but stricter.

The Bolsheviks were primarily interested in preventing the spread of "harmful literature" among the "simple people," and so they did not particularly mind if some esoteric, long, and scholarly books contained veiled anti-Marxist references. In this respect, they followed the example of their tsarist predecessors. Narkompros periodically issued circulars about purging village libraries and the book collections of the cultural departments of trade unions. These lists were remarkably comprehensive. They included adventure stories, the lives of saints, the works of Plato and Kant, and even some writings of Lenin that had appeared under a pseudonym, as well as "outdated" agitational pamphlets, that is, writings that did not reflect the current political line.[19] The authorities followed similar policies toward the cinema. They assumed that city dwellers were more politically "mature" and therefore could be allowed a wider choice of films than the peasants. The most interesting and com-

---

[18]N. L. Meshcheriakov, "O rabote chastnykh izdatel'stv," *Pechat' i revoliutsiia*, 1922, no. 1: 128–34.

[19]Kenez, *Birth of the Propaganda State*, 248–49.

mercially successful films of the decade, such as *The Bear's Wedding*, *Aelita*, and *Three Meshchanskaia Street*, were considered far too risky for peasant audiences. Filmmakers occasionally prepared bowdlerized versions of such films to be shown in the villages.[20]

Justifying the continuation of censorship after the Civil War had ended was a serious problem for the Bolshevik leaders. There were considerable differences among them; some were more comfortable with the existing situation than others were. Lenin and his ideological comrades unabashedly proclaimed that censorship was a legitimate weapon in the class struggle. Trotsky's position was close to Lenin's. Having supported censorship in 1918 as a temporary necessity, he now advanced new arguments. In 1922, in reply to Kautsky's criticism of Red terror and suppression of newspapers, he maintained that it was wrong to equate bourgeois and Communist suppression of the press, for the bourgeoisie was a dying class and was merely attempting to retard history, whereas Bolshevik suppression simply accelerated the historical process.[21] Three years later, he expressed himself somewhat less polemically:

If the revolution has the right to destroy bridges and art monuments whenever necessary, it will stop still less from laying its hand on any tendency in art that, no matter how great its achievement in form, threatens to disintegrate the revolutionary environment or to arouse the internal forces of the revolution, that is the proletariat, the peasantry, and the intelligentsia, to a hostile opposition to one another. Our standard is, clearly, political, imperative and intolerant. But for this very reason it must define the limits of its activity clearly. For a more precise expression of my meaning, I will say: We ought to have a watchful revolutionary censorship, and a broad and flexible policy in the field of art, free from petty partisan maliciousness.[22]

By contrast, others evidently felt uncomfortable in the new and unaccustomed role of censor. Commissar of Enlightenment Lunacharsky wrote in 1921:

The person who tells us that censorship is necessary, even when it prevents the publication of great works of art when these hide obvious counterrevolution, is correct. So is the one who says that we must choose, and we must give only

---

[20]See Peter Kenez, "Peasants and Movies," in Sheila Fitzpatrick, Alexander Rabinowitch, and Richard Stites, eds., *Russia in the Era of NEP: Explorations in Soviet Society and Culture* (Bloomington: Indiana University Press, 1991).

[21]Irving Howe, ed., *The Basic Writings of Trotsky* (New York: Random House, 1963), 152.

[22]Leon Trotsky, *Literature and Revolution* (Ann Arbor: University of Michigan Press, 1960), 220–21.

third, or fourth, priority to undoubtedly necessary works in comparison with books for which we have the greatest need. But the person who says: "Down with all those prejudices about the freedom of expression. State leadership in literature corresponds to our new, communist order. Censorship is not a terrible component of our time of transition, but a regular part of socialist life," the person who draws the conclusion that criticism should be turned into some kind of denunciation and that artistic work should be turned into primitive, revolutionary slogans—he only shows that under the communist exterior, if you scratch him a bit, will find in reality, Derzhimorda.[23]

Lunacharsky's words came as close to a defense of the freedom of expression as any Bolshevik leader was to come in the early 1920s.

During the first years of the Soviet era, a considerable degree of intellectual freedom and therefore of cultural pluralism existed. This situation was partly the consequence of the fact that the Bolsheviks did not consider such pluralism dangerous. On the contrary: They believed that allowing scientists and artists to do their work would benefit the cause of socialism. Their policies discriminated against the less educated, because they implicitly assumed that an uneducated person was particularly vulnerable to "harmful" heterodox ideas. But intellectual freedom was also a consequence of Bolshevik weakness; at a time of confusion, the new rulers were not in a position to control everything. It would happen in the early 1920s, for example, that the authorities forbade the showing of a film in one city, and the distributor simply took it to another.[24]

From this review of the status of intellectual freedom during the Civil War and at the beginning of NEP, it is evident that we may not simply assume that there is a necessary connection between economic reform and increased freedom of expression. At least at that time, the realms of economics and of culture followed different dynamics.

[23]A. Lunacharsky, "Svoboda knigi i revoliutsiia," *Pechat' i revoliutsiia,* 1921, no. 1: 8. [Derzhimorda ("Grabface" or "Seize-him-by-the-snout") is a minor character in Gogol's play *The Inspector General;* he has become a stock figure of a brutal, rude, and stupid policeman in Russian culture.—Ed.]

[24]A. Gak, "K istorii sozdaniia Sovkino," *Iz istorii kino* 5 (1962): 133.

12

Local power in the 1920s: police and administrative reform

NEIL B. WEISSMAN

The search for historical precedents for the extraordinary events that were taking place during the 1980s in what was then the Soviet Union heightened interest in the era of the New Economic Policy (NEP), and appropriately so. NEP ushered in Soviet Russia's first great effort at reform. After the upheavals of October and the Civil War, the Communist government set out, temporarily at least, to achieve its revolutionary ends through evolutionary means. Given the breadth of the communist vision of societal transformation, reform under NEP was an unusually complex undertaking, with crucial political, economic, social, and cultural dimensions. This essay focuses on a single aspect of the overall reform process, the attempt to create an effective regular police force.[1]

THE POLICE IN THE TSARIST ERA

On the surface, the question of police reform, particularly as applied to the regular police, the militia (*militsiia*), rather than to their political counterparts, seems an unlikely candidate for extended investigation. The militia as an institution did not have high priority for Soviet rulers during the 1920s. There were no thunderous debates over alternative approaches to policing comparable to those surrounding such matters as Party organization or industrialization. Although in this sense histor-

[1]Research for this essay was supported by the American Council of Learned Societies, the Kennan Institute for Advanced Russian Studies, and the National Endowment for the Humanities.

ically unobtrusive, the issue of police reform offers substantial insight into the broader processes of change under NEP.

The militia was a key part of the Soviet administrative apparatus in the early years of NEP, when the local agencies of the other branches of government were weakly developed. Indeed, the police had more extensive and diverse interaction with the populace than did virtually any other state agency; militia officials calculated that in 1927 the force had direct contact with one of every seven adult males. As a result, the regular police were not only essential to the regime in routine maintenance of order; they also implemented administrative measures in a variety of fields beyond law enforcement. For many citizens, they were the chief representatives of the new Soviet state. Examination of government policy on policing, therefore, reveals the basic concepts that Soviet leaders sought to apply in their effort to restructure the state administration during NEP and suggests fundamental obstacles to the achievement of this (or any other) reform. The militia stood squarely in the space in which the abstract reform programs of the government leaders encountered social reality.

According to David Bayley, a leading student of modern law enforcement, "Policing in the world today is dominated by agencies that are public, specialized, and professional."[2] By these standards, the nineteenth-century tsarist police force had not advanced far into modernity.[3] Police, in the sense of career public employees, were few in number and were largely restricted to urban centers. In the countryside especially, routine security was maintained by estate functionaries—village elders and peasant watchmen—rather than by the state police. Even when, toward the end of the century, the government became convinced of the inadequacy of village institutions of order, the authorities resorted to establishment of a quasi-estate office, the gentry land captain, to improve matters.

As to specialization, little had been done to narrow police duties. The police function was defined in tsarist law and practice broadly, in effect as coterminous with administration as a whole. In part, this reflected the

[2]David Bayley, *Patterns of Policing* (New Brunswick, N.J.: Rutgers University Press, 1985), 23.
[3]On the nineteenth-century tsarist police, see Robert Abbott, "Police Reform in Russia, 1858–1878" (Ph.D. diss., Princeton University, 1971); idem, "Police Reform in the Russian Province of Iaroslavl, 1865–1876," *Slavic Review* 32 (1973): 292–302; and Neil Weissman, "Regular Police in Tsarist Russia, 1900–1914," *Russian Review* 44 (1985): 45–68.

persistence of the continental European understanding in which policing meant all executive functions that were not ecclesiastical. Yet the lack of police specialization in nineteenth-century Russia was also a function of limited administrative resources and political choice. Few other branches of the central government had the wherewithal to develop effective local agencies to implement policy. At the same time, fear of weakening autocracy prevented tsarist authorities from allowing the institutions of self-government, the zemstvos and municipal councils, to establish their own executive forces. In many functional areas, therefore, the police served as the local foundation for the edifice of government by sheer default.

Yet despite the obvious importance of the police force to state administration, the tsarist government did little to assure its effectiveness. Because service was simultaneously demanding and poorly rewarded, police chiefs found it difficult to require much in the way of qualifications from potential recruits. Once enrolled, the average patrolman received relatively little training or material support, though his power over the populace was largely unrestrained. As a result, the force was notorious for graft, incompetence, and caprice, its dominant operational mode summed up by the term "the law of the fist" (*kulachnoe pravo*).

Scholars have had difficulty identifying the precise causes of modern police reform.[4] In the Russian case, political violence undoubtedly was the motor force for change. In particular, the revolutions of 1905 and 1917 ended the relative complacency that had characterized nineteenth-century thinking about the police, jolting the traditional foundations of order and generating alternative models for peacekeeping. Two of these—the tsarist and the Bolshevik—are of particular importance in understanding the NEP experience in police reform. Though polar opposites in intent (to preserve a social order or to destroy it) and in form (a professional or citizen police), both models were antithetical to Russia's traditional modes of policing.

Although the 1905 revolution failed to overthrow the imperial government, it did shake up the tsarist system thoroughly. Awareness of the need for change extended even to the previously neglected area of policing.[5] The central authorities established in 1906 a commission, chaired

---

[4]See, for example, the discussions in Bayley, *Patterns of Policing*, chap. 2, and Eric Monkkonen, *Police in Urban America, 1860–1920* (Cambridge: Cambridge University Press, 1981), chap. 1.

[5]On tsarist reform efforts after 1905, see Neil Weissman, *Reform in Tsarist Russia* (New

by A. A. Makarov, to reorganize the police force, and they dispatched experts to study Western forms of law enforcement. In concert with the Department of Police, reformers launched a periodical, *Vestnik politsii* (*Police Herald*), to spread information and to press for change. As one might expect in the wake of revolutionary upheaval, virtually all tsarist officials called for a larger police force with more punitive authority. Yet reformers within the government also articulated a new vision of the tsarist police, centering on the concept of professionalism. Their definition of a "professional" police had several basic elements.

First, the reformers insisted upon specialization, a narrowing of police functions. Essentially, this meant abandoning administrative service duties, such as tax collection and supervision of sanitation measures, in order to concentrate on crime control. As one government law-enforcement specialist, V. E. Frish, argued in 1905, in rejecting the traditional understanding of police as general administrators: "Acting on everything and for everyone, they are unable to perform their central function—defending public security and tranquillity. Here is the primary reason why the police in Russia do not possess the respect and popularity present in other Western European states."[6]

The logical corollary to specialization was training. Freedom from the distractions of general administration would, the tsarist reformers believed, allow the policeman to learn. In part, this was a matter of basic education. The Makarov commissioners, for example, proposed that literacy be made a requirement for recruits. (Frish's recommendation of stiffer educational standards was regretfully rejected as unrealistic.) Between 1905 and 1911, provincial authorities established fourteen schools for police sergeants (*uriadniki*); reading, writing, history, and geography occupied prominent places in the curriculum.

Even more important to the reformers than general education, though, was expertise in crime fighting. Government leaders hoped that the entire police force could be schooled in the most up-to-date techniques of criminal investigation, but they focused their attention on the detective (*sysknye*) departments. Held in popular contempt as corrupt and repressive, the detective units seemed an unlikely vehicle for pro-

---

Brunswick, N.J.: Rutgers University Press, 1981), 202–20. Abbott, "Police Reform in Russia" and "Police Reform in the Russian Province of Iaroslavl," examines earlier attempts at reform based on the concept of professionalism.

[6]V. E. Frish, *Proekt uchrezhdeniia gosudarstvennoi strazhi v Rossii* (St. Petersburg, 1908), 22–23.

gress. Nevertheless, in 1908 the government expanded the detective network from a handful of cities to eighty-nine urban centers. Reformers within the Department of Police cheered the measure as a means of importing modern, Western methods of controlling deviance. Interestingly, they defended this effort to enhance "police science" by pointing to the growing expertise, or professionalism, of the "criminal class."[7]

Finally, beyond specialization and expertise, the tsarist police reformers called for a changed attitude toward the law. Where the traditional patrolman was notorious for arbitrary behavior and caprice, the new police professional would scrupulously adhere to legal procedures. Indeed, the reformers believed that an impersonal, restrained style based on strict conformity to written codes was the key to winning popular respect for both the police and the regime they served. "The constant resistance that police encounter at every turn from simple people on up to members of the intelligentsia," the *Police Herald*'s columnist L. Kosunovich wrote in 1909, resulted from a failure to persuade the citizenry that "police action is not wild and capricious but rational."[8] "Rational," for Kosunovich and his colleagues, meant, above all, legal.

This emphasis on law and popular approval was prompted in part by the constitutional measures that the revolutionary movement had forced on the regime in 1905. Yet tsarist police reformers did not view legality—or any other aspect of their program—as a concession to the liberal opposition. Rather, specialized training and strict adherence to legal norms were, for them, a means of instilling discipline among police, guaranteeing their reliability. With command over the police still fully in the hands of the imperial government's local agents (governors and police chiefs), reform would make the force more rather than less responsive to central direction.

The ideal of professionalism spread rapidly among police forces everywhere in the nineteenth and early twentieth centuries, touching nations as different as Victorian England and Meiji Japan. Its attractiveness to reformers, as Bayley has noted, lay more in its promise of managerial efficiency than in any connection with democratic political reform.[9] In the United States, for example, progressives championed professionalism as a means of improving the police by insulating them from the cor-

[7]See, for example, the discussion in *Vestnik politsii*, 1909, no. 2: 1–3.
[8]Ibid., no. 20: 407.
[9]Bayley, *Patterns of Policing*, 51.

rupting influence of local political machines.[10] In Russia, tsarist officials seized upon the potential of professionalism for separating the "expert" policeman from the local citizenry even more enthusiastically. For them, police reform could help protect the force not merely from venality or party politics but also from any significant community control.

REFORM EFFORTS AFTER THE OCTOBER REVOLUTION

If the failed revolution of 1905 produced a model of police reform aimed at preventing more radical change, the successful revolution of October 1917 brought the introduction of a Bolshevik model of policing so transformative that the term "reform" hardly applies.[11] As it turned out, this initial Bolshevik model for peacekeeping was applied only briefly. Yet its significance was substantial, for it drew on basic elements of Party ideology that continued to operate powerfully under NEP.

The approach to policing articulated by Lenin and his colleagues in 1917 was the polar opposite of that developed by tsarist reformers. Whereas the imperial officials embraced the dominant trend toward professionalism, the Bolsheviks rejected the very concept of a standing police force. Instead, they called for peacekeeping by the masses through an ultrademocratic proletarian militia. Ultimately, this militia would embrace all adults of both sexes; every citizen would serve briefly on a rotational basis. Such a scheme obviously excluded all the hallmarks of professionalism—specialization, extensive training, and career dedication. This set the nascent Bolshevik state apart from virtually every other modern government.

This strikingly bold policy was in part dictated by practical politics. The standing police force had been a major pillar of the tsarist regime, and such a force might have served this function again for the Provisional Government. Yet beyond tactics, the Bolshevik determination to destroy the police as an institution was also fueled by deeper convictions about the nature of postrevolutionary society. Lenin expressed these con-

---

[10]See, for example, Gene Carte and Elaine Carte, *Police Reform in the United States: The Era of August Vollmer, 1905–1932* (Berkeley: University of California Press, 1975).

[11]The revolution of February 1917 created still another model of policing, though it will not be discussed here. See the insightful comments in Daniel Orlovsky, "Reform during the Revolution: Governing the Provinces in 1917," in Robert Crummey, ed., *Reform in Russia and the U.S.S.R.* (Urbana: University of Illinois Press, 1989), 100–125.

victions most explicitly in *Can the Bolsheviks Retain State Power?*, written in September 1917.[12]

Endeavoring to persuade fellow socialists of the feasibility of an immediate seizure of power, the Bolshevik leader argued that a revolutionary government could "lay hold of" and employ existing capitalist institutions, including the banks, the post office, and syndicates. But such pragmatism, for Lenin, was predicated upon a radical transformation of the police, the army, and other elements of the civil service. Only broad participation by the masses in key administrative functions, including the defense of order through policing, could make the policy of cooptation—and, indeed, the very idea of creating a proletarian state—possible. In Bolshevik thinking at the time, citizen policing was a necessary instrument of democratization. Not surprisingly, therefore, within three days of the October Revolution, the new People's Commissariat of Internal Affairs (NKVD) issued a circular directing worker and soldier soviets to organize proletarian militias as a first step toward peacekeeping by the entire populace.[13]

Neither the tsarist nor the Bolshevik program for restructuring the police was implemented in a sustained way. Each was overwhelmed by the very currents of political change that created it. In the tsarist case, the outbreak of war in 1914 slowed an already halting reform process. Three years later, the regime's collapse shifted responsibility for policing into new hands. The Bolshevik experiment with citizen enforcement was even more short-lived. By the spring of 1918, the Soviet government decided to drop popular peacekeeping in favor of a new standing police force, the Worker-Peasant Militia. Subsequently, under the pressure of the Civil War, the authorities purged anti-Communists and militarized the force. It became, in essence, a poor man's version (or, as militia officials preferred to put it, the "younger sister") of the Red Army.[14]

---

[12]V. I. Lenin, *Collected Works* (Moscow, 1964), 26: 108–13. For a detailed discussion of Lenin's writings in this area, see Neil Harding, *Lenin's Political Thought* (New York: St. Martin's, 1981), 2: 120–22.

[13]Some scholars have questioned the degree to which the circular actually embodied the new government's thinking on policing; see E. N. Gorodetskii, *Rozhdenie sovetskogo gosudarstva, 1917–1918 gg.* (Moscow, 1965), 306–7, and V. N. Prokopenko and V. M. Romanov, *Sovetskaia militsiia (1917–1920 gg.)* (Moscow, 1965), 17. Subsequent statements by the authorities, however, confirm their intention of transforming peacekeeping; see, for example, *Vestnik otdela mestnago upravleniia komissariata vnutrennikh del*, 1918, no. 2: 6.

[14]For the early history of the Worker-Peasant Militia, see S. V. Bilenko, *Sovetskaia militsiia Rossii* (Moscow, 1976).

Despite these unhappy histories, both the tsarist and the Bolshevik models of policing remained as potential programs for NEP reform, together offering strikingly different alternatives for restructuring the militia.

In choosing policies for police reform, NEP leaders were obviously constrained by external circumstances. For example, the parlous state of the Soviet economy after the Civil War placed severe limits on resources. Seeking to balance the overstrained state budget, the central authorities in 1922 transferred financial responsibility for a number of administrative agencies, including the police, to the local soviets. Desperately short of funds themselves, executives in the provinces had no choice but to prune back the bureaucratic apparatus drastically. In the militia's case, this contributed to a stark reduction of the force from more than 300,000 in the fall of 1921 to less than 70,000 two years later.[15]

In addition to such constraints, the direction of NEP police reform was also determined by conscious choice, by goals set by Soviet leaders working through the NKVD and its militia administration. Unfortunately, we lack extensive records of government policy discussions on this issue. Still, in a number of statements published in 1922–23, NKVD officials clearly outlined the regime's intentions in rebuilding the militia.

All Soviet leaders started their comments on policing by stressing the need to break with the prerevolutionary past. As Russian militia chief T. Khvesin declared in November 1922, "The militia is the antipode of the police."[16] This did not, however, mean a return to the early Bolshevik model of policing by the people. The approach that had been adopted in the first months after October was, if mentioned at all, dismissed as a perhaps admirable but impractical transitional policy. Khvesin, for instance, made no reference to it, arguing only that militiamen differed in antipodean fashion from their tsarist predecessors simply by virtue of the fact that they served a proletarian state. The Soviet leaders in 1922 left no doubt that the appropriate mechanism for law enforcement under NEP was a standing police force. Indeed, they insisted that such a force be characterized above all by its professionalism.

The hallmarks of professionalism outlined by the militia chiefs were familiar. First, policing was to be viewed as a career, with recruits committed to long-term service within a hierarchically structured apparatus.

[15] *Vlast' sovetov*, 1922, no. 1–2: 50–51; 1923, no. 4: 89; and 1923, no. 11–12: 127; and I. I. Kizilov, *NKVD RSFSR (1917–1930 gg.)* (Moscow, 1969), 114–15.
[16] *Raboche-krest'ianskaia militsiia*, 1922, no. 1: 6 (hereafter cited as *RKM*).

In fact, militia commanders urged the NKVD to retain the quasi-military organization adopted during the Civil War.[17] Second, the police were to be regarded as specialists in crime control. The militia, Commissar of Internal Affairs A. G. Beloborodov maintained in 1922, would be characterized by "a careful division of labor and specialization by each worker in his area."[18] The epitome of this policy was the network of criminal investigation (*ugrozysk*) units to be established to replace the prerevolutionary detective divisions. Third, the Soviet police were to be intensely schooled, from the standpoint of both general education and professional technique. NKVD officials were wont to describe the model policeman as a kind of walking encyclopedia, conversant with both the details of Soviet law and the broad principles of communism. "The more advanced the intellectual development of our militiaman," declared the head of state, M. I. Kalinin, "the better he will champion the ideas of Soviet Power."[19]

Finally, NKVD leaders added respect for the law to their definition of police professionalism. As an integral part of the transformation of state policy from War Communism to NEP, the Soviet government had committed itself to the concept of "revolutionary legality." For the militia, this meant rejection of the wartime tactics of arbitrary command in favor of restraint and conformity to legal norms. Indeed, Soviet authorities were convinced that such an operational style could be a powerful instrument for winning the citizenry over to the regime. "Nothing better inculcates among the populace . . . respect for the law," wrote A. Prigradov-Kudrin in the official militia journal, "than adherence to the laws by the organs of authority themselves."[20]

As in the prerevolutionary era, concern for legality, and professionalism in general, went hand in hand with a commitment to centralization. Soviet leaders, especially from outside the NKVD, did emphasize citizens' rights under NEP, including those of newly legitimized capitalists. And the Communist rulers allowed local authorities, through the soviet executive committees, to have some say in police affairs. Yet, as the retention of a quasi-military organization indicates, the militia re-

---

[17]See the resolutions of the First All-Russian Congress of Militia Workers in *Vlast' sovetov*, 1922, no. 3: 67.
[18]*Pravda*, 1922, no. 256.
[19]Quoted in *RKM*, 1922, no. 1: 3. See also Izgoi, "Metody raboty admpolitorganov i politprosvetraboty v militsii," ibid., 23.
[20]A. Prigradov-Kudrin, "Revoliutsionnaia zakonnost' i militsiia," *RKM*, 1922, no. 1: 36.

mained a hierarchical institution, with ultimate control (on paper, at least) in the hands of the NKVD. Professionalism, defined, as it was before 1917, in terms of discipline and obedience to abstract norms, was deemed entirely consistent with this approach.

It is tempting, then, to characterize the model of policing outlined by Soviet authorities early in the NEP period as a revival of the tsarist reform program. NKVD officials were familiar with their predecessors' plans; they referred at times quite explicitly to the Makarov commission's work.[21] Yet there are good reasons to resist making a direct connection between the tsarist and NEP reformers. The militia was among the Soviet institutions with the least personnel carryover from the prerevolutionary era. At the same time, the police had one of the strongest ideological-historical rationales for rejecting the past. It is more plausible that the Soviet police leaders, like their tsarist counterparts, succumbed to the mystique of the professional that was so widespread abroad. And like reformers in prerevolutionary Russia and elsewhere, militia authorities believed that professionalism could be turned to their own particular ends. For the Communists, this meant a politically reliable police responsive to central direction.

Some measure of the success in building a new, professional militia during NEP can be obtained by examining (if only briefly) three topics: specialization, training, and distribution of police authority.

Reform efforts to the contrary notwithstanding, the tsarist government had to the end viewed the police as general administrators responsible for carrying out a variety of executive tasks. NKVD authorities vigorously rejected this traditional approach. Outlining the commissariat's view later in the decade, for example, I. Liubimas drew a sharp distinction between the police and other civil servants. Where the latter performed constructive, ameliorative functions, he argued, the police were concerned primarily with interdiction. "The militiaman can be a good defender of public order," Liubimas insisted, "but a bad treasury agent, a poor executor for the courts, and so on. The heart of the matter is *specialization* in a given type of work."[22]

The Soviet government did make some progress in implementing this view during NEP. Most notably, the almost tripling of the number of

---

[21]See, for example, the comments on rural police in E. Shavrov, "Volostnaia militsiia," *Administrativnyi vestnik,* 1925, no. 5: 37 (hereafter cited as *AV*).
[22]I. Liubimas, "Bol'noi vopros," *AV*, 1928, no. 3: 25; emphasis in the original.

tax inspectors (from 1,117 before the war to 3,113 in 1925) and the hiring of a whole new contingent of finance agents (2,718 by 1925) allowed the Commissariat of Finance to relieve the police of primary responsibility for revenue collection.[23] Yet in other areas, ranging from delivery of court documents to enforcement of sanitation measures, progress was minimal. The uneven development of the state apparatus in the provinces left the militia heavily saddled with service tasks. Indeed, the campaigns for bureaucratic economy launched periodically by the Communist party throughout the decade worsened matters, as administrative agencies sought to achieve staff reductions by shifting executive tasks to the militia. In 1928, Liubimas estimated that up to half of police activity was devoted to service functions.[24]

No less important than specialization in the NKVD's policy of professionalism was training. Extensive schooling was critical to the reformed militiaman in his various roles as expert in crime control, enforcer of revolutionary legality, and propagandist for new Soviet values. In order to transform a Civil War militia that was ill-trained and largely illiterate or semiliterate, the NKVD in 1922 initiated a major educational effort. The commissariat combined a campaign against illiteracy with ambitious plans for establishing a three-tiered network of militia schools.[25] Although the inadequacy of resources soon forced a shift in emphasis away from police academies toward short-term training courses, militia leaders still hoped to achieve substantial levels of expertise among the police. In 1925, RSFSR Deputy Militia Chief P. Zaitsev estimated that within twelve years the entire complement of middle-rank commanders could be put through NKVD training institutes.[26]

As with specialization, the NEP era did see advances in police education. At the most rudimentary level, militia authorities were able to make considerable gains in literacy. By the decade's end, 80 percent of all patrolmen claimed some attendance at primary schools, and 20 percent of the command corps reported secondary-school experience.[27] Yet in terms of professional education, the accomplishment was quite limited. Zaitsev's projections for middle-rank commanders, for instance,

---

[23]V. Grossman, "O nalogovom apparate," *Vestnik finansov*, 1926, no. 3: 86–87.

[24]Liubimas, "Bol'noi vopros," 23.

[25]P. Astakhov, "Shkol'naia podgotovka militsii," *RKM*, 1922, no. 1: 27–28, and the commentary in *RKM*, 1923, no. 2–3: 5–16.

[26]P. Zaitsev, "Derevne nuzhen kul'turnyi militsioner," *AV*, 1925, no. 4: 4.

[27]Ia. Bineman and S. Kheinman, *Kadry gosudarstvennogo i kooperativnogo apparata SSSR* (Moscow, 1930), 56.

proved wildly optimistic. At the start of 1928, fewer than 2 percent of all commanders had attended NKVD institutes for middle-level officers. Only a fifth of the police command corps had had any professional training at all. Among the militia rank and file, the comparable figure was 10 percent.[28]

The reasons for the NKVD's relative failure in raising the level of professional education among the police are worth reviewing. Limited funding put restraints on the establishment and support of a network of academies. Moreover, the drastic reduction in the militia's size at the Civil War's close, a cutback that in many locales left police complements smaller than in the prerevolutionary era, made it difficult for commanders to spare personnel for training. Demands on staff were particularly pressing as a result of the NKVD's continuing inability to free the police from the burden of various service tasks. In this sense, the campaigns for specialization and for training were closely interdependent.

Militia authorities did try to work around the limitations. For example, many local commanders, with NKVD encouragement, set up intensive after-hours instruction for patrolmen. Even when well attended, though, such sessions could not surmount one more obstacle to police training: the very high rate of turnover in militia ranks. Of all the complaints voiced by police chiefs during the NEP years, concern over fluctuations in personnel was the most pronounced.

Throughout the 1920s, militiamen remained among the worst-paid civil servants; the only occupations with lower pay were prison guards and child-care workers. In the broader labor market, wages were higher not only for skilled but even for unskilled industrial workers. Indeed, in the middle of the decade, city militiamen were earning only fractionally more than female unskilled workers.[29] At the same time, working conditions for the police could be very taxing. Exempt from the Labor Code's provision for an eight-hour day, militiamen typically served long shifts, in which petty aggravation and tedium alternated with dan-

[28]*AV*, 1929, no.2: 6.
[29]K., "Zarabotnaia plata sluzhashchikh uchrezhdenii i torgovykh predpriiatii v gubernskikh (oblastnykh) gorodakh RSFSR v 1924–25 g.," *Statistika truda*, 1926, no. 1: 11–15; M. Katel', "Zarabotnaia plata sluzhashchikh uchrezhdenii . . . v 1-om polugodii 1925/6 g.," ibid., 1928, no. 7–8: 1–14; "Differentsiatsiia zarabotnoi platy sluzhashchikh v marte 1926 goda," ibid., 1926, no. 11–12: 1–9; and A. Rashin, "Zarabotnaia plata rabotnits v 1924–1926 gg.," *Statisticheskoe obozrenie*, 1927, no. 2: 73–78.

ger.[30] As a result of the great contrast between the rewards and the burdens of service in the militia, recruits rarely chose to stay long in the ranks, viewing the militia as a temporary haven. Some saw enlistment, which conferred the union card required to apply for more attractive positions in other state institutions, as a means of upward mobility. For peasants, service provided a useful source of supplemental earnings in slack agricultural seasons. For city dwellers, police duty could be a cushion against unemployment, until a better opportunity came along.

The precise dimensions of turnover in militia ranks are difficult to determine. Rates varied by time and place, and police record keeping was frequently spotty. A rough estimate is that up to half the posts in the Soviet militia changed hands annually during the first half of the decade. Deputy Commissar M. Boldyrev reported that, as of the last quarter of 1924, only 45.7 percent of the force had served more than a year; I. Kiselev, head of the RSFSR militia, placed the turnover rate for patrolmen in 1927 near 54 percent.[31] Whatever the precise figures, service patterns were erratic enough to weaken the NKVD training program and undermine the policy of professionalism in general. "Everyone knows that the general and legal literacy of militiamen and detectives is very low and must be liquidated soon," Boldyrev admitted in 1925. "But is this possible, given the turnover that's draining staff?"[32]

Even more basic to a program of professionalism than specialization or training is the concentration of police authority in the hands of specially employed functionaries for whom policing is a career. As noted, much of tsarist peacekeeping failed to conform to this principle. In cities, the government's patrolmen shared responsibility for order with porters (*dvorniki*) and privately funded factory guards. More important, rural policing remained largely in the hands of estate officers, ranging from gentry land captains to menial peasant watchmen (*desiatskie* and *sotskie*).[33] Only in 1903 did the tsarist government launch a major effort

---

[30]The militia were brought under the Labor Code in 1925, but with important loopholes that left local administrators with considerable freedom of action. See the NKVD commentary in *AV*, 1926, no. 2: 31–33, and no. 3: 41–42.

[31]M. Boldyrev, "Kak dolzhny rabotat' v derevne admorgany," *AV*, 1925, no. 9–10: 7–9; *AV*, 1928, no. 11: 3.

[32]Boldyrev, "Kak dolzhny," 8.

[33]*Desiatskie* and *sotskie* were lower-level police officials, originally elected by, respectively, ten and one hundred peasant households. For further information, see Weissman, *Reform in Rural Russia*, 14.

to extend the regular police into the countryside by replacing the sotskie with state troopers (*strazhniki*). Even then, the troopers were stationed in towns and large settlements, leaving the often ineffective desiatskie to provide nominal daily policing in most villages.

The revolutions of 1917 and the ensuing Civil War ostensibly created optimal conditions for more thorough professionalization of law enforcement. Estate institutions were swept away, and by 1918 the Soviet government had committed itself to the establishment of a standing police force. Indeed, the new government's struggle for survival prompted the Communists to view popular participation in policing, especially in villages, as dangerous. In this sense, power considerations reinforced the impulse to professionalism by underlining the role of a politically reliable militia. Yet throughout the 1920s, the NKVD found it difficult to shake tradition and concentrate policing in militia hands.

Before 1917, the Bolsheviks had tended to view apartment-house caretakers, or porters, as suspect, because of their association with bourgeois landlords and the police. But Civil War violence forced militia chiefs to follow prerevolutionary practice and use the porters as law-enforcement auxiliaries. The NEP cutback in the militia's size, coupled with revival of the tsarist practice of deploying urban police at stationary posts, guaranteed continuation of this policy through the 1920s.[34] Equally important, the insecurity accompanying the revolution had prompted many offices and enterprises to hire their own guards. War Communism's widespread nationalizations then gave these watchmen quasi-official status. During the first years of NEP, both the State Political Directorate (GPU) and the NKVD sought to gain control over these security agents, but with mixed success. In 1924, the NKVD was authorized to enter into agreements with other institutions to turn the guards into more professional "agency [*vedomstvennye*] militiamen."[35] But the agreements were voluntary (key bodies, including the Supreme Council of the National Economy, or Vesenkha, resisted) and gave militia chiefs only limited control over the guards.

Porters and militiamen functioned largely in cities. In the countryside, the government was compelled to make an even more substantial concession in distributing police authority. Early NEP staff cuts applied to

---

[34]The government's 1925 regulations on porters are in *NKVD Biulleten'*, 1925, no. 15: 131–33.
[35]*RKM*, 1924, no. 11: 32–33.

all police forces, but rural units were most dramatically reduced. Although four-fifths of the Soviet population lived outside cities, only one-quarter of the militia was stationed there. This urban orientation in policing persisted throughout NEP, unchanged even by the regime's "Face to the Countryside" campaign.[36] In fact, according to one official estimate, the rural militia had fallen by 1925 to 60 percent of the tsarist complement.[37] In the context of vast territorial expanses, poor communications, and an inadequate supply of horses for the police, this level of staffing ruled out an effective militia presence in the countryside.[38]

Soviet authorities admitted as much in 1924 by re-creating the post of peasant watchman—or, as it was now to be called, "village deputy" (*sel'skii ispolnitel'*).[39] Hoping to break with tsarist practice, the government radically democratized the position. Virtually all adults, including women, were to serve in two-month shifts. Indeed, the authorities expected that popular rotation would not only make policing more effective but also turn the post into a vehicle for schooling villagers in Soviet values. In actuality, peasants responded to the new office in traditional fashion, avoiding enrollment as an onerous burden. If anything, the two-month rotation undermined service, by making it impossible to provide even rudimentary training.[40] As in the prerevolutionary era, professional policing beyond town borders was largely a matter of sporadic intervention.

ACHIEVEMENTS AND FAILURES IN POLICE REFORM

Given the limitations on police specialization, training, and presence, should the NKVD's effort to develop a professionalized militia during NEP be judged a failure? Evaluation of this reform, like any other, depends in large part on the standard against which progress is measured. Certainly, as compared with the prerevolutionary Ministry of Internal Affairs, the NKVD made significant strides in the 1920s. Some gains,

[36]*Gosudarstvennyi apparat SSSR* (Moscow, 1929), 29–30.
[37]Boldyrev, "Kak dolzhny," 11.
[38]The problems of rural law enforcement are discussed in detail in Neil Weissman, "Policing the NEP Countryside," in Sheila Fitzpatrick, Alexander Rabinowitch, and Richard Stites, eds., *Russia in the Era of NEP: Explorations in Soviet Society and Culture* (Bloomington: Indiana University Press, 1991), 174–91.
[39]*NKVD Biulleten'*, 1924, no. 12: 52. For the rationale behind the measure, see V. Pomerantsev, "Volostnoi militsioner i sel'skii ispolnitel'," *RKM*, 1924, no. 1: 5–7.
[40]For a useful analysis of the relevant problems, see I. Zaitsev, "O sel'skikh ispolniteliakh," *AV*, 1926, no. 2: 17–20.

such as improved literacy or partial lifting of the burden of tax collection, have already been noted. And there were others. For example, militia detective divisions expanded rapidly, by 1927 producing a network of 358 registration bureaus with 400,000 files, as opposed to tsarist totals of 89 and 60,000.[41]

By the late 1920s, however, most Soviet authorities, including NKVD leaders, were deprecating supposed advances and favorable comparisons with the past. Instead, they characterized policing in terms of abject failure. Participants in the Second All-Russian Congress of Administrative Workers in 1928, for example, spent much of their time in mutual recrimination. Local representatives' criticism of the NKVD ("the fish stinks from the head") was answered by central officials' complaints about failings in the provinces ("The tree withers from the roots"). Referring to the soviet executives and police chiefs gathered at the congress, Commissar of Internal Affairs V. Tolmachev concluded that "if not all, then the overwhelming majority, find the present situation . . . unsatisfactory."[42]

Pessimism in militia ranks had two sources. Tsarist authorities had viewed the police force essentially as a passive instrument for defending the status quo. Its most sustained effort (in concert with the military) had been repression of the revolution of 1905. Soviet leaders understood policing differently. Ideologically committed to the transformation of Russian society even under NEP, the Communists saw in the militia a tool for eradicating social ills and inculcating new values. Specialization might narrow the range of police operations but was not intended to diminish their intensity. On the contrary, Soviet leaders believed a more focused militia could be far more active. They signaled their enthusiasm for putting the police to use from the very start of NEP.

The Soviet militia emerged from the Civil War undoubtedly in need of rest and reorganization. In October 1922, the central authorities began to shift financial responsibility for the force to the local soviets. A month later, they initiated a major purge of militia personnel. Despite these dislocations, the government simultaneously committed the police to combating one of the most entrenched popular practices, home brew-

[41]N. A. Nikolaevskii, "K desiatiletiiu organizatsii i deiatel'nosti organov ugolovnogo rozyska," *AV*, 1927, no. 10–11: 36–37.
[42]NKVD, *Vtoroi Vserossiiskii s"ezd administrativnykh rabotnikov 23–30 aprelia 1928 goda* (Moscow, 1929), 64–65.

ing.[43] The Communists had inherited a prohibition on the sale of liquor from the tsarist government.[44] Although they approved of the policy, the Civil War had prevented them from making any sustained enforcement effort. In the winter of 1922, however, they launched a major assault on home brew. Egged on by bounties and a shrill press campaign, militiamen carried out hundreds of thousands of raids, often with scant regard for legal niceties. Jails filled with home brewers, many drawn from groups supposedly favored by the regime, such as unemployed female workers and poor peasants. In 1922 alone, the NKVD reported 538,502 cases.[45] Excesses in repression eventually prompted changes in tactics. Moreover, in 1925 the regime reintroduced the sale of full-strength vodka as a state monopoly. Still, operations against illicit distilling continued in varying form throughout the decade, joined after 1925 by repression of private speculation in vodka.

The campaign against home brew had been prompted in part by special circumstances, including fear for the nation's grain supply. Yet the effort also reflected a general belief in an activist militia. As pressure eased on the antialcohol front in 1925, therefore, the government engaged the militia in an operation against another perceived social ill. During the prewar years, there had been growing concern in tsarist society over the spread of petty deviance or, as it was loosely termed, "hooliganism."[46] Under NEP, this concern was revived. Responding to a perceived wave of antisocial acts ranging from vandalism to gang rape, the government in 1925 directed judicial and police agencies to attack hooliganism.[47] The result was another sharp increase in police raids, court convictions, and administrative sanctions. Only in 1927 did the campaign slacken.

[43]Neil Weissman, "Prohibition and Alcohol Control in the USSR: The 1920s Campaign against Illegal Spirits," *Soviet Studies* 38 (1986): 349–68.

[44][In August 1914, the tsarist government decreed a prohibition on the sale of liquor for the duration of the war. As in the United States, this prohibition was marked by lax enforcement and massive violations. See Michael T. Florinsky, *Russia: A History and an Interpretation* (New York: Macmillan, 1953), 2: 1359.—Ed.]

[45]*Vlast' sovetov*, 1925, no. 31: 26–27.

[46]See Joan Neuberger, "Crime and Culture: Hooliganism in St. Petersburg, 1900–1914" (Ph.D. diss., Stanford University, 1985), and Neil Weissman, "Rural Crime in Tsarist Russia: The Question of Hooliganism, 1905–1914," *Slavic Review* 37 (1978): 228–40.

[47]For a sample of the substantial literature on this subject, see Gosudarstvennyi institut po izucheniiu prestupnosti i prestupnika, *Khuliganstvo i khuligany* (Moscow, 1929). On the NKVD campaign, see V. Vlasov, "Itogi bor'by s khuliganstvom," *AV*, 1927, no. 9: 11–23.

The prohibition and antihooliganism campaigns amply demonstrated that the pressure on the NKVD to reform had to keep pace with steadily accelerating demands on the militia, despite limited resources. The operations also exposed internal contradictions in the Soviet approach to law enforcement under NEP. In several basic respects, the government's campaign methods ran counter to the NKVD's program to professionalize the police.

For one thing, the campaigns were often conducted with considerable disregard for the law. Militia raids on home brewers, for example, frequently involved confiscation not only of stills but also of household goods. In drafting local ordinances against hooliganism, local officials showed a similar inclination to excess; in some places, for example, all evening entertainment and singing were banned. Both campaigns caused a drastic increase in the imposition of administrative fines, regardless of the class background of offenders or legal limits on sanctions. In part, such tactics were a legacy of the Civil War, a melding of Bolshevik ideological drive and military mentality. But they also reflected ambiguity in the NEP concept of revolutionary legality itself. Put most simply, "legality" meant strict adherence to codified procedural norms. However, the adjective "revolutionary" implied a goal of rapid change, overriding any impediments imposed by legal technicalities. Selected to articulate the new approach to the militia in 1922, A. Prigradoc-Kudrin insisted that revolutionary legality was not the same as legality in general. It involved not formal obedience to codes but "their implementation on the basis of revolutionary consciousness of the interests of the laboring masses."[48] Thus, respect for law coexisted uneasily with an impulse to expediency.

Campaign tactics demonstrated another, equally powerful countercurrent to the goals of professionalism and legality. In 1917, the Bolsheviks had emphatically endorsed policing by the citizenry as a means of transforming the bourgeois state into a revolutionary one. Although this policy was soon superseded by the commitment to a standing police force, the desire to mobilize the populace for law enforcement persisted. In the campaigns against both home brewing and hooliganism, the central government called upon local soviets, unions, Party bodies (including the Komsomol), and individual citizens for active support. Indeed,

[48]Prigradov-Kudrin, "Revoliutsionnaia zakonnost' i militsiia," 35.

the authorities encouraged the creation of new avenues for participation, such as a national temperance society. In part, popular mobilization focused on "cultural-educational" programs to prevent deviance and violations of the reform programs. But the citizenry was also expected to play a punitive role, patrolling factories and villages and informing on lawbreakers.

Mass mobilization for peacekeeping was more than a campaign expedient. Throughout NEP, Soviet leaders were sensitive to criticism that, in rebuilding and extending the machinery of government, they were creating a new exploitative apparatus. The militia, as a coercive institution inheriting a tradition of arbitrary behavior, was especially vulnerable to such accusations. The authorities, therefore, looked to popular participation as an antidote to potential "bureaucratic degeneration" of the regime and its police. The fundamental principle distinguishing the communist from bourgeois states, wrote militia spokesman V. Vlasov, was "the inseparable link between the Soviet apparatus and the populace."[49] NKVD leaders sought to cement this tie by assuring citizen access to the police. For example, they established a bureau within the commissariat to receive citizens' complaints against administrators, and they pressed militia chiefs to make frequent reports to mass gatherings. Most important, the government in 1927 directed local soviets to establish special sections or commissions of activists to supervise and take part in militia affairs.[50]

Judging from the available evidence, the policy of popular mobilization had only a modest impact on police operations. Data on the prohibition campaign, for instance, indicates that few arrests resulted from citizen initiative.[51] Similarly, police chiefs reported in 1927 that popular activity against hooliganism had been very disappointing, and the NKVD concluded that that campaign had run "primarily, if not exclusively, along administrative-judicial lines."[52] Except for successes in Leningrad and a few other places, efforts to establish a vital network of public-order sections and commissions under local soviets also made lit-

---

[49]V. Vlasov, "Formy i vidy sviazi administrativnykh organov s naseleniem," *AV*, 1927, no. 12: 12.

[50]For a review of these and other steps, see ibid.

[51]The NKVD reported that, of a quarter of a million searches for home brew conducted during the first half of 1923, fewer than twenty thousand had been prompted by citizens. *Vlast' sovetov*, 1923, no. 11–12: 127.

[52]Vlasov, "Itogi bor'by s khuliganstvom," 21.

tle headway. Even Vlasov, enthusiastically in favor of these bodies, described the sections as being "in the vast majority of cases passive," with most members regarding service as an onerous obligation.[53]

The primary significance of popular policing under NEP was not the concept's reality but rather its utility as an alternative policy for critics of the NKVD's program of reform through professionalism. When the Communist party launched a particularly violent assault on "bureaucratism" toward the end of the decade, the militia was an obvious target. In 1928, the Workers' and Peasants' Inspectorate (*Rabkrin*) and the Party Central Control Commission investigated the police force and found fundamental flaws.[54] Many of the reported shortcomings—poor training, lack of discipline, and especially abuse of authority—might well have been characterized as a lack of professionalism. But critics of the militia argued in a very different direction. The police force suffered, in their view, from estrangement from the masses. Hence, detective divisions were attacked for reliance on secret informants rather than on open operations with mass support. The entire militia was denounced (somewhat inaccurately, it might be noted) for harboring "alien" elements, including former tsarist policemen and gendarmes. Most broadly, the police were criticized for a "militia deviation," an operational style in which coercion replaced legality and comradely suasion. As a corrective, critics endorsed establishment of a true "militia system" (*militsionnaia sistema*), in which workers and peasants would serve in the police on a rotational basis. In this scheme, the professional militia might ultimately be reduced to a small core of trainers and supervisors who would facilitate peacekeeping by citizen patrolmen.[55]

This antibureaucratic campaign threw the militia leadership into confusion and self-doubt. Commissar Tolmachev admitted to NKVD staffers attending the 1928 administrative congress that the commissariat's organs "have lost authority not only in the eyes of the Soviet public . . . but also in their own."[56] Some police officials, including Tolmachev, swam with the tide and endorsed the "militia system" in self-confessional terms. "The crudity, red tape, and frequent bureaucratism

[53]Vlasov, "Formy i vidy sviazi," 15.
[54]The investigation's results are summarized in S. N. Ikonnikov, *Sozdanie i deiatel'nost' ob"edinennykh organov TsKK-RKI v 1923–1934 gg.* (Moscow, 1971), 275–77, and *Izvestiia*, May 3, 1928.
[55]For the critique and the NKVD administrators' responses, see NKVD, *Vtoroi s"ezd*, 5–72.
[56]Ibid., 13.

more common in the militia than in any other Soviet agency," declared the commissar, would disappear if alongside the militiaman "sat a factory worker . . . a unique public commissar."[57] Other administrators resisted, some of them arguing for the very different course of militarizing the police, on the model of the Red Army or the Unified State Political Directorate (OGPU). All continued to support key elements of the program of professionalism, including more training and specialization, but with a fatalistic awareness that, in the existing atmosphere, resources needed for such a policy would not be forthcoming. In sum, the militia leadership faced the onset of the Stalin era in a state of disarray.

In review, it is clear that some aspects of the militia's lot in the 1920s were unique to the institution. This is true, for example, of the important issue of bureaucratic sponsorship. Shorn of control over the political police and closely associated with Trotsky in the Communist party, the NKVD was poorly placed to defend police interests. At the opposite extreme, there are aspects of the militia's experience during NEP that have been shared by all modern police forces. Everywhere, for instance, respect for law contends with a desire for efficiency, and investment in professional improvement is restrained by finite resources. Finally, between the particular and the universal, there are dimensions of the militia's early history peculiar to the NEP era but shared by other Soviet administrative institutions. Thus, the NKVD's attempt to remold the militia reveals salient features of the broader Soviet effort at governmental reform in the era between the Civil War and Stalinism.

Scholars have already noted the willingness of Lenin and his colleagues to employ the expertise of professionals in building their new state.[58] The Soviets created a Commissariat of Health, for instance, with precisely this in mind.[59] The commissariat's physician directors focused policy almost entirely on the role of highly trained specialists like themselves, at the expense of paramedics, nurses, midwives, and others. To cite another example, the Communists eagerly enlisted trained engineers

[57]Ibid., 19.
[58]See, for example, Kendall Bailes, *Technology and Society under Lenin and Stalin* (Princeton: Princeton University Press, 1978), chap. 2.
[59]See Neil Weissman, "Origins of Soviet Health Administration," in Susan Gross Solomon and John Hutchinson, eds., *Social Medicine in Revolutionary Russia* (Bloomington: Indiana University Press, 1990), 97–120, and Don Rowney, *Transition to Technocracy: The Structural Origins of the Soviet Administrative State* (Ithaca, N.Y.: Cornell University Press, 1989), chap. 4. Rowney explicitly places the experience of the Commissariat of Health within the context of that of the state apparatus as a whole.

when they established the State Planning Commission in 1921. Such enthusiasm was not surprising in medicine, economic planning, and other very technical fields prone by their nature to domination by specialists. But policing, as an administrative branch in which generalists were only beginning to give way to experts, was different. Indeed, the willingness of the militia leaders, men who, like Beloborodov, were often drawn from the working class, to embrace professionalism was quite striking. Their endorsement of the policy of reforming the militia demonstrates powerfully the pervasiveness of the ideal of the expert among NEP chief administrators.

Conversely, the militia's turn to professionalism helps explain the attractiveness of the concept to the Soviet rulers. For the Communists, professionalism had two-pronged utility. As in the West, the policy promised efficiency, heightened managerial effectiveness through training, and rational organization. Yet at the same time, professionalism differed from many other Western concepts in that it was readily adaptable to a variety of political contexts, including the authoritarian. Tsarist police reformers had believed that this approach was amenable to autocracy. In the Soviet case, professionalism went hand in hand with the creation of a centralized and politically reliable standing police force. So, for instance, the purge of the militia at the beginning of NEP simultaneously targeted those poorly qualified for service and those sympathetic to opposition political views.

The NKVD's struggle to rebuild the militia on a more professional basis also exposed the enormous obstacles to this type of reform in NEP Russia. Most immediately, the effort confronted painful limitations of human and material resources. Funds were short for wages, training, and even uniforms and arms. Low levels of popular education meant that recruits with more than rudimentary literacy, if that, could not always be found. Moreover, as personnel turnover vividly demonstrated, the revolution had introduced an element of flux into social relations that subverted the stability needed for an effective program of professionalization. The human resources needed to achieve the effectiveness promised by professionalism were not only scarce but also difficult to retain.

It is worth noting that the problem of resources also thwarted the attainment of the political, as well as managerial, goal of professional police reform. The transfer of financial responsibility for the militia to the local soviets in 1922 inevitably meant some devolution of power as well. For example, the NKVD jealously reserved final say in the appointment of police chiefs, yet throughout the 1920s, the commissariat was unable to stop local soviets from shuffling chiefs about and assigning them to additional administrative posts as a means of economizing.

The NEP militia was, as noted, poorly positioned in the struggle among Soviet institutions for resources. But more favored agencies suffered the same difficulties in supporting comparable programs of professionalization. The Commissariat of Finance, for example, found it difficult to implement revenue policy efficiently when almost two-thirds of its tax employees in central Russia had only elementary education and an even greater proportion had less than two years' experience at their posts. Furthermore, the ephemeral and speculative nature of NEP private businesses made it difficult to determine who should be taxed, while personnel turnover interfered with the development of a stable body of tax collectors.[60] The Commissariat of Health similarly found stable staffing of facilities, especially in rural areas, difficult to achieve; and like the NKVD after 1922, it encountered substantial resistance from financially strapped local soviets in implementing key policies of sanitation and social prophylaxis.[61]

The limited resources available to the militia and other Soviet administrative bodies under NEP dictated a gradualist approach to reform. In fact, viewed from this perspective, the police and other agencies made considerable progress in the 1920s. But gradualism, even in the NEP era, fit badly with the Communist regime's aspiration for social transformation. While administrative capabilities increased arithmetically, expectations grew geometrically. The government's willingness to commit the militia to ambitious campaigns against deviance demonstrated the conflict between means and ends in that institution, but the same was true elsewhere. The Soviet tax apparatus tripled over tsarist levels but still failed to keep pace with the growing demands of the regime's revenue policy. Health officials, even with expanded funding and an independent commissariat, were unable to make good on the regime's promise of free, professional care for all citizens.

Impatience with the incremental progress of reform during NEP was

---

[60]Grossman, "O nalogovom apparate," 86–89.
[61]See Weissman, "Origins of Soviet Health Administration."

strongly reinforced by communist populism. The Soviet government's commitment to professionalism was deeply ambivalent. At the same time that the authorities supported modernization through expertise, they also endorsed egalitarianism through social leveling. These two faces were clearly revealed in the policies on law enforcement, the radicalism of 1917 providing a sharp counterpoint to the measured professionalism of 1922. Through much of NEP, the regime sought to balance and even combine the two approaches. In the militia's case, this took the form of campaigns directed by the police but implemented (in theory, at least) with substantial popular involvement. For health officials, it meant mass mobilization in support of sanitation. By decade's end, the populist current in communist ideology overtook the efforts to contain it. Antibureaucratic campaigns shook the state apparatus with explosive force. Just as the police force was challenged by the militia system, the judicial administration was shaken by a campaign for more "revolutionary" forms of law.[62] This exacerbation of the basic contradiction in Soviet policy on administration finally defeated the NEP program of gradual, professionalizing reform.

Today, issues of government and administration continue to be debated as part of the broader effort to reform Russian society, but the comparisons with the NEP era are becoming increasingly remote. The context of the late 1980s, and especially the contemporary situation, differs fundamentally from that of the 1920s, in ways ranging from the levels of urbanization to the position of communist ideology. Because of the changed contexts, the basic ideas applied in the 1920s take on new and different meanings. The malleability of professionalism in settings as varied as tsarist Russia and the contemporary United States has already been noted. Centralization of policing, too, has quite different significance in, say, the Stalinist Soviet Union and in modern France. Still, the NEP experience does suggest likely lines of tension in the process of change. Contemporary reformers will need to be more sensitive than their predecessors to the potential conflict between aspirations for efficiency and expertise, on the one hand, and for equality and democracy, on the other. And, as the fragility of NEP's "revolutionary legality"

---

[62]Robert Sharlet, "Pashukanis and the Withering Away of Law in the USSR," in Sheila Fitzpatrick, ed., *Cultural Revolution in Russia, 1928–1931* (Bloomington: Indiana University Press, 1978), 169–88.

in the hands of an unreformed militia pressed to achieve results suggests, they must be more adroit in harmonizing the interlocking processes of defining goals and adopting ways of reaching them. As before, administration will be a key arena in which reformers confront the problem of ends and means.

13

The antibureaucratic campaigns of the 1920s

DANIEL T. ORLOVSKY

One disposition that Lenin, Trotsky, Bukharin, Stalin, and many of their followers had in common during the 1920s was that all of them spoke the language of antibureaucracy. No theme, it seems, was so well used in the political vocabulary and the political discourse of Russia during the period of the New Economic Policy (NEP). Indeed, Stalin would use it to mobilize both Party cadres and society at the end of the 1920s and through much of the next decade as well. Antibureaucracy as a mode of reform as well as revolution raises some major questions about Soviet history, the sources for its study, and the possibilities of alternative courses of reform during NEP.

The 1920s witnessed a series of antibureaucratic campaigns that began with Lenin's admonitions against bureaucracy in 1921 and helped define the political struggles that were taking place against the backdrop of NEP. Lenin's last writings set the tone by defining the bureaucratic problem in a rather peculiar way and placing it at the center of socialist construction. There followed a campaign for "rationalization" under the auspices of the Scientific Organization of Labor (Nauchnaya organizatsiia truda, or NOT) movement and the People's Commissariat of Workers' and Peasants' Inspectorate/Central Control Commission (Rabkrin/TsKK); a campaign to reenergize the soviets in 1925–26; a campaign for the "regime of economy" in 1926–28; and finally a campaign of self-criticism, accompanied by purges of the state, soviet, and Party apparatuses, conducted in 1928–29. All of these campaigns were portrayed as reforms and were designed to deal with real problems in the workings of governmental and administrative institutions. Several of them overlapped and had common elements. Each one seemed not to bring the desired results, thus necessitating a new campaign—one more attempt to overcome bureaucracy as a burden of the past and a product of the socialist future.

My goals here are to set out some details about these campaigns and the problems that they were meant to address, and to consider the function of the antibureaucracy campaigns in the emerging Soviet polity. It is important to understand how contemporaries interpreted the campaigns and how they received the campaigns' messages. It is also important to understand the campaigns from the point of view of those in power. Are we to take their protestations about bureaucracy—this "discourse of antibureaucracy"—at face value, or was something else going on? My research on white-collar workers (*sluzhashchie*) in the 1920s suggests that the idea of "bureaucracy" or the "bureaucrat" represented a negatively coded segment of political discourse, the counterparts of the positively weighted terms "proletarian" and "worker." In both cases, the terminology masked a more ambiguous social reality than official ideology would accept as legitimate. The language of antibureaucracy defined "otherness," those outside the proletarian commonweal (*obshchestvennost'*), and it served, like the language of "proletarian revolution," to mask certain important social and political realities of the emerging Soviet state and society (particularly the phenomenon of "layering"). An understanding of how this worked and the nature of the masked social reality of the 1920s can help us come to terms with the image and reality of NEP as an era of reform and possibility. These issues also shed light on Stalin's "revolution from above" at the end of the 1920s and the role of the theme of antibureaucracy in the politics and purges of the 1930s.

J. Arch Getty, for one, places antibureaucracy at the center of his interpretation of the 1930s.[1] In his view, there were genuine bureaucratic problems of center-periphery relations and sloppy management and personnel policy within the Party. Central authority—including Stalin, but not limited to the "dictator"—sincerely attempted to deal with these issues by means of the purge campaigns that had been tried during the 1920s. According to Getty, such purges had nothing to do with the Great Terror, the Ezhovshchina, until these were specifically and consciously linked in February 1937. What had been portrayed as a popular

---

[1] J. Arch Getty, *Origins of the Great Purges: The Soviet Communist Party Reconsidered, 1933–1938* (Cambridge: Cambridge University Press, 1985).

and legitimate mode of reform and mobilization of public opinion against the "bureaucratic enemy" merged with the violent excesses of a particular clique of officials to produce the unforeseen and unexpected consequences of mass terror. Leaving aside the issue of Getty's artificial separation of antibureaucracy and terror, we must ask whether the antibureaucratic mobilization campaigns of 1932–35 were as innocent as they seem and whether they might have had, at the time of their origin in the 1920s, a purpose or purposes less visible but more far-reaching than the goal of creating a more efficient apparatus.

Scholars outside the revisionist camp have reinforced Getty's observations about the antibureaucratic dimension of Stalinism. Beissinger, for example, entitles one of his chapters, "Stalinism as Antibureaucracy."[2] He argues that the industrial drive that began during NEP in 1926 ran up against the entire range of bureaucratic dysfunctions spawned by the Party-state since the October Revolution. When it appeared that industrialization and collectivization might not work, the appropriate guilty parties (class enemies) were found—kulaks, wreckers, and bureaucrats. Stalinism was "in many ways a deeply antibureaucratic movement that drew much of its strength from incessant attacks upon the *chinovnik* [civil servant—ed.] whose ubiquitous presence and vulnerability made him an inviting target for political rabble rousing." In Beissinger's view, "Trotsky's interpretation of Stalinism as the victory of the clerk was mistaken, for although Stalinism, like Leninism, was bureaucratic in form, it was essentially antibureaucratic in content." Much of Stalin's broad appeal in the late 1920s, Beissinger says, "lay in its frontal assault on bureaucratic stagnation in Soviet economic and political life and its harnessing of the social and ideological tensions that large-scale bureaucratic organization had fostered." If Lenin had authorized and legitimized the discourse of antibureaucracy, Stalin turned it into a "coordinated, sustained disciplinary strategy."[3] Here we have a question of historical interpretation. Did Stalin speak for or against the bureaucracy? Did he come to power representing bureaucratic interests or was he a populist? As we shall see, these are not exclusive categories.

[2]Marc R. Beissinger, *Scientific Management, Socialist Discipline, and Soviet Power* (Cambridge, Mass.: Harvard University Press, 1988), 91–126.

[3]Ibid., 93. While this approach parallels analyses of the Chinese cultural revolution decades later, the question remains of whether Stalin's assault on bureaucratism was popular and appealing, and if so, to whom.

Finally, the subject of antibureaucracy is relevant to the issue of reform in Russian and Soviet history. The government-generated reforms in tsarist Russia were relatively predictable and orderly (leaving aside the questions of implementation and success); the government-sponsored reforms in the 1920s were very different. Though we can speak of domestic policies and attempts of this or that institution to come to terms with the specific problems in its jurisdiction, it is much harder to unravel the mysteries and sources of central governmental or Party policy initiatives. The cumbersome yet wonderfully well-documented legislative process of the tsarist autocracy seems to have been replaced, even during the ostensibly benign NEP, by a series of campaigns and battles on not very well-defined fields, ending with victors and vanquished—and casualties strewn all about.

THE PROBLEM OF BUREAUCRATISM

Any discussion of antibureaucracy in the 1920s must begin with Lenin's writings, especially those of the summer and autumn of 1917.[4] They are important not so much as prescriptions of what needed to be done, much less of what in fact was done, but as early formulations of the acceptable language and themes of antibureaucracy. (Lenin's exhortations about the menace of bureaucracy at the Eleventh Party Congress in 1922 were an obligatory frontispiece for all official statements of the Union of Soviet and Commercial Employees during the antibureaucratic campaigns of the 1920s.) Even a cursory reading of Lenin's writings of 1917 and 1918 reveals a curious combination of obsession with the building of the state and the forms of state power and innocence, or possibly repression, of the cultural and social dimensions of the problem. His dreamy writings about the "commune state" in *State and Revolution* quickly gave way to more practical ruminations about the seizure of power in September and October 1917. In the latter, he emphasized the potential of the soviets as state organs, the creative energy of the "masses," who would flood the soviet vessels with creative revolutionary energy, and the almost miraculous power of "control" to eliminate the well-known and long-lamented abuses and dysfunctions of the old regime and of capitalist bureaucracy.

---

[4]All quotations and references to Lenin's writings are drawn from Robert C. Tucker, ed., *The Lenin Anthology* (New York: W. W. Norton, 1975). Emphases are in the original.

Control and mass participation came to dominate Lenin's thinking after October and the establishment of the Soviet state. In two of his major writings of those early days, he described the organization of an administration as the central task and postulated a system of national accounting and control from below to keep the holdover "bourgeois specialists" and the larger bureaucracy itself in line.[5] Lenin's formulation, which became embedded in the antibureaucracy discourse, ran as follows:

The fight against the bureaucratic distortion of the Soviet form of organization is assured by the firmness of the connection between the Soviets and the "people," meaning by that the working and exploited people, and by the flexibility and elasticity of this connection. . . . It is the closeness of the soviets to the "people," to the working people, that creates the special forms of recall and other means of control from below, which must be most zealously developed now.[6]

Much in Lenin's last writings also concerned bureaucracy, and there the contradictions were even more pronounced. As in his final writings on other themes, he seemed at last to recognize the cultural and social dimensions of the problem, in this case acknowledging that the new Soviet officialdom was behaving worse than its tsarist predecessor. In a letter to M. F. Sokolov in 1921, he rejected the young apparatchik's idea that bureaucracy could and must be swept immediately "from the face of the earth." He wrote:

That is wrong. The Tsar can be sent packing, the landed proprietors sent packing, the capitalists sent packing. That we did. But bureaucratism cannot be "sent packing" from a peasant country, cannot be "swept away from the face of the earth." One can only reduce it by slow, stubborn effort. . . . A boil of that kind cannot be "thrown off." It can only be cured. In *this* matter surgery is an impossibility; only *slow cure*—all else is charlatanism or naiveté.[7]

Lenin expressed the control side of his concerns a few months later in a letter to A. D. Tsiurupa: "The center of gravity of your work must be just this remaking of our repulsive-bureaucratic mode of work, the fight against bureaucratism and red tape, *check up on fulfillment*."[8]

The major works of Lenin on this subject concerned the need to create a suprabureaucratic control agency, which would overcome bureaucracy

---

[5] Lenin, "Can the Bolsheviks Retain State Power?" 440–41, and "The Immediate Tasks of Soviet Government," 446–47.
[6] Lenin, "The Immediate Tasks of Soviet Government," 458–59.
[7] Lenin, letter of May 16, 1921, to M. F. Sokolov, 716–17.
[8] Lenin, letter of January 24, 1922, to A. D. Tsiurupa, 718.

with bureaucracy.[9] Lenin railed against the "present utterly impossible, indecently pre-revolutionary form" of the Soviet bureaucracy. The cure was Rabkrin and the Central Control Commission, agencies that would carry out inspection and control with an eye toward the improved quality of cadres, reductions in staff, rationalization, and, of course, the involvement of the masses. Lenin attacked Communist boastfulness and lack of knowledge. In these last writings, bureaucracy had become his final obsession, replacing the hated "bourgeoisie" of the prerevolutionary period. Campaigns or "doing things in a rush, by assault, by vim or vigor" were not the answer. His admonitions against storming and against forcing the pace were provoked by the difficult problem of transforming the human material that filled the new governing apparatus. Lenin went on to sketch his solution: a new Rabkrin/Central Control Commission staffed by hand-picked. "workers" who would spearhead cultural change in the bureaucracy.

The problem with Lenin's naive vision of bureaucratic reform through control and of overcoming bureaucracy with bureaucracy was spotted immediately by his old colleague Leonid B. Krasin (though it had been seen earlier as well, in 1919–20, by the Workers' Opposition and especially by the Democratic Centralists).[10] An engineer and economic manager, familiar with the problems of factory production and construction in the nationalized economy of the Civil War years and the early 1920s, Krasin attacked Lenin's plan to transform Rabkrin into a control agency standing atop the entire Soviet state apparatus. Responding to Lenin's "Better Fewer, but Better," he agreed that the control function was both legitimate and necessary, and he claimed that he was in favor of developing control institutions, but he argued against the hypertrophy of control and the overvaluation of its potential and its purpose. Why, Krasin asked, should there be a dichotomy between production and control? Wasn't the latter simply the natural helpmate of production? Had Lenin created an artificial opposition?[11]

[9]Lenin, "How We Should Reorganize the Workers' and Peasants' Inspection: Recommendation to the Twelfth Party Congress," 729–33, and "Better Fewer, But Better," 734–46. The first of these was written on January 23, 1923, and printed in *Pravda* on January 25, after much conspiratorial struggle. The second, Lenin's last article, was dictated in February 1923.
[10]See especially the debates at the Eighth and Ninth Party congresses.
[11]Leonid B. Krasin, "Kontrol' ili proizvodstvo," *Pravda*, March 24, 1923. The article was recently republished in the Soviet Union with a commentary by Gavriil Popov in *Ogonek*, 1989, no. 24: 10–13. The dispute has also been discussed in Beissinger, *Scientific Management*, 44–50, and in E. A. Rees, *State Control in Soviet Russia: The Rise and Fall of*

The dichotomy, said Krasin, was manifested in the Soviet state and its production processes. The proponents of control had expressed a utopian belief in its power to cure any and all administrative dysfunctions. This faith, according to Krasin, was apparent as early as the Workers' Control movement of 1917, which became part of the method of the seizure of state power by the working class. Even then, productionists had had to adjust to control efforts and accept their influence on the organization of the production process. Krasin argued that it was wrong to divert so many factory workers and production specialists from production to control, especially at a time when economic growth, defined as rising productivity, was crucial to the Soviet experiment. "Our basic task, I repeat, is production, and our basic misfortune is that we can't, we don't know how to organize production."[12] And this was not a question of having adequate control organs. For Krasin, it related more to the essence of humankind as a productive species. Control should be seen only as a helpmate in the organization of production; indeed, the ideal would be the withering away of control as the institutions of production became totally efficient. Accordingly, the goal should be "maximum production—minimum control," not the creation of a supercommissariat with unlimited power, something unknown in any industrial country. In his view, "scholastic-clerkish prejudice" was the source of the belief in the necessity of control to organize production. Production people were needed to organize the economy, not officials (chinovniks). Moreover, Leninist, or bureaucratic, control ran counter to the concept of humankind as a species defined by its labor.

To Krasin, there was something obscene about the socialist state turning good workers and specialists into bureaucrats. Without realizing the irony, Krasin argued that once removed from production and placed in an office setting, the specialist would inevitably turn into a bureaucrat who would "wreck" industry. "Vladimir Ilyich had not taken into account the monstrosity that was our prerevolutionary State Control." Krasin believed that the desire for control had spread throughout the state institutions and had itself led to the growing bureaucratic threat, "our dangerous predilection for this type of state activity." One needed

the Workers' and Peasants' Inspectorate, 1920–1934 (New York: St. Martin's, 1987), 47–57.
[12]Krasin, "Kontrol' ili proizvodstvo."

to apply the principles of production to the bureaucracy, in order to rid the state institutions of all the forms of bureaucratic excess that had inspired Lenin in the first place. One could not overcome the bureaucracy through the bureaucracy of control and repression. Patient cultural and psychological work was necessary, including proper organization and material support, more intelligent selection of cadres, and an atmosphere of trust.

Krasin's call for what amounted to a social and cultural revolution in the bureaucratic workplace of course went unheeded, and the antibureaucratic discourse continued to develop with the patina of Leninist respectability. The soon-to-be-sanctified leader had enshrined the idea of antibureaucracy in the form of control, which we may see as another way of putting consciousness above spontaneity, or as a true expression of what was the essence of the Bolshevik mode of building a state and a party. Neither patience nor trust was notable in the antibureaucratic project and its campaign mode of operation.

The antibureaucratic campaigns of the 1920s took off from Lenin's conceptualization of the problem. By the end of the 1920s, the Party's industrialization and collectivization policies, which had to be implemented by bureaucracies, forced various leaders and officials to make further attempts to transform recalcitrant institutions and officials. Self-criticism and purging were placed on the agenda. Even the political struggles between the Stalin group and its oppositions were in part cast in terms of the bureaucratic problem. Resolutions at the Fifteenth Party Congress in 1927 lamely tried to distinguish the bad oppositional antibureaucratism from the good Party variety:

The opposition in the question of bureaucratism denies the proletarian nature of our state, the Leninist formulation of the problem of our apparatus, its illnesses and the means to cure it. The opposition's fundamental mistake is its lack of understanding that our state apparatus, despite its inadequacies and bureaucratic deformities, despite its current extraordinary cost, is still the highest form of administration in comparison with bourgeois democracy, a governing apparatus of a new ruling class, the working class that has actualized its power in alliance with the peasantry. The opposition in this question as in others fails to see the difference between our situation and that of the bourgeoisie. They don't see that bureaucratism in bourgeois society is an expression of class rule of capitalists that may only be liquidated by destroying the bourgeois state apparatus, whereas in our state, bureaucratism in part has arisen *despite* the class nature of the Soviet state as a result of economic and cultural backwardness that can be liquidated only by strengthening our state and raising it to a higher cultural level.[13]

To the student of Russian bureaucracy, the early attempts to combat bureaucratism seem highly reminiscent of the futile tsarist attempts to deal with similar problems in the nineteenth century. Efficiency, motivation, and fixing, redefining, and above all cutting the tables of organization—all of these were common to instances of bureaucratic reform before the revolution.

The story of the white-collar workers in the 1920s offers particular insight into the nature of the antibureaucratic campaigns and the social and cultural framework of the bureaucracy problem in early Soviet history. The white-collar workers were in fact the mass of the human material that inhabited the variety of structures described in the antibureaucratic discourse. I refer here not to the bourgeois specialists or ITR (engineering and technical personnel), who were easily identifiable and were identified during the 1920s as a real or potential class enemy and as misbehaving bureaucrats,[14] or to the mistrusted managers and bosses (*khoziaistvenniki*) in the economy, or to the other specialists or professionals, such as teachers, doctors and lower-status medical personnel, lawyers, agronomists, statisticians, middle-level managers, and economists. In general, members of these occupational groups had obtained secondary or specialized secondary education, if not higher education, and benefited from high salaries as well as various perquisites. The white-collar workers, on the other hand, were a low-status group, poorly paid and poorly educated. They were clerks, office workers, and minor functionaries in the vast state and Party bureaucracy, as well as employees in shops and commercial and financial institutions. As I have claimed elsewhere, the white-collar workers were a "hidden class" in the social fabric and the political language of the emerging socialist commonweal (*obshchestvennost'*) of the "proletarian" state.[15]

One is tempted to argue that in the period between 1918 and 1929, the greater was the influence of nonproletarian elements in the process of revolutionary state-building, the more vociferous were the claims for

---

[13]*Piatnadtsatyi s"ezd VKP(b), dekabr' 1927 goda: Stenograficheskii otchet* (Moscow, 1962), 2: 1438.

[14]On the ITR, see especially Nicholas Lampert, *The Technical Intelligentsia and the Soviet State* (New York: Holmes and Meier, 1979).

[15]Daniel Orlovsky, "The Hidden Class: White-Collar Workers in the Soviet 1920s," in Lewis Siegelbaum and Ronald G. Suny, eds., *Making Workers Soviet* (Ithaca: Cornell University Press, 1994).

the proletarian nature of the enterprise and the greater was the tendency of the Soviet state to act out its proletarian fantasies. The white-collar workers were hidden from view in the political language of the period. Because the white-collar workers had played such a large, though quiet, role in the revolution and in the establishment and building of Soviet power and the Bolshevik Party during the years from 1917 to 1921, and because they were part of the very fabric of the bureaucratic Party-state and society that had emerged from the revolutionary crucible, they were not regarded as a class enemy or as a social formation hostile to prole-tarian interests. For the white-collar workers, whose principal organi-zation was the Union of Soviet and Commercial Employees,[16] the task at the advent of NEP was to fit into the proletarian state as well as possible, to make the wheels of the state, Party, and commercial (gov-ernmental and cooperative) institutions work as smoothly as possible, so as not to call attention to the evident fact that this enormous group was different in cultural levels, values, and interests from the factory blue-collar proletariat in whose name the revolution functioned.

Yet this social formation was also hidden from view in the language of antibureaucracy. Indeed, unlike the bourgeois specialists, the white-collar workers had a sort of provisional status as fellow travelers of the proletariat and peasantry. In fact, they were much more important than any provisional label might indicate, because they were easily as nu-merous as factory workers; they had far more direct contact than did workers with the general population in their roles as mediators in the administrative and commercial structures; and during the 1920s, they were the principal group into which were drawn upwardly mobile peas-ants, via such institutions as the village and canton soviets and the co-operatives.

THE RATIONALIZATION CAMPAIGN

The first major antibureaucratic campaign of the 1920s centered around the idea of rationalization and the emergence of Rabkrin and the NOT

---

[16]The Union of Soviet and Commercial Employees was the largest of the fourteen combined production unions formed by the Bolsheviks at the end of the Civil War. By the late 1920s, the union had almost 1.3 million members. Other production unions (e.g., met-alworking, transport, medicine and public health, and education) also had significant numbers of white-collar employees as members. See D. Antoshkin, *Professional'noe dvi-zhenie sluzhashchikh 1917–1924 gg.* (Moscow, 1927).

movement (1923–29).[17] NOT was directed against bureaucratism and the dysfunctional side of administration, but it affected white-collar workers in numerous ways. NOT cells and operatives cropped up in the bureaucratic and trade institutions, and the union and national press organs carried on massive exhortation campaigns to publicize the triumphs of NOT and of rationalization in office and commercial settings. These campaigns were utopian attempts to infuse the production process with the ideology and practice of the assembly line. Because the white-collar workers, too, belonged to a "production" union, and because their work was so essential, this type of rationalization had to be brought to office work as well. Thus, we read of schemes for the proper organization of the office, from lighting and the design of typing tables and chairs to the revolutionary step of introducing a Western-style filing system in place of the traditional stacks of neatly tied folders (*papki*) that tended to hide needed information rather than make it more readily available.[18]

These schemes seem harmless enough, and indeed there were some positive results, but the utopian nature of the enterprise was to be found in the ideology that underlay the reforms. Mechanization and routinization of office work were meant not so much to improve efficiency as to make possible the inclusion of significant numbers of new peasants and workers in an expanding bureaucracy. To paraphrase one of Rabkrin's leading theoreticians, E. Rozmirovich, the goal of the Party and the revolution was to bring the masses into the state administration. This meant workers and peasants, but the peasants especially were culturally unfit and unsuited for office work. However, one should not try to alter their culture; rather, by means of mechanization and routinization the role of human will in administrative work would be eliminated. Then peasant culture would not stand in the way, would not matter any more.[19] This issue of different cultures, and Rozmirovich's failure to address either the problem of white-collar workers as a distinct social group or the full ramifications of affirmative action (*vydvizhenie*), was indicative of the limits of rationalization. In the bureaucratic setting at least, as distinct from factory production, the campaign for rationali-

[17]This is covered extremely well in Beissinger, *Scientific Management*, chaps. 1–3, and in Rees, *State Control in Soviet Russia.*

[18]One may read at great length of these innovations and their fate in the rationalization columns of the white-collar union's daily newspaper, *Nasha gazeta*, and its predecessor, the journal *Golos rabotnika*. See also *Tekhnika upravleniia*, the specialized journal of Rabkrin/TsKK devoted to such matters.

[19]See the article by Rozmirovich in the first number of *Tekhnika upravleniia*, 1925.

zation would fizzle out and be merged later in the decade with other kinds of campaigns.

THE REGIME OF ECONOMY CAMPAIGN

Once the regime had decided in 1926 to embark upon a drive to increase the tempo of industrialization, it needed to find new sources of capital without overtly pressuring either the factory workers or the peasantry. The Left Opposition stood for even faster tempos and the extraction of capital from precisely those groups, but Stalin and Bukharin settled upon a general program of cost cutting in economic enterprises and in the bureaucracy generally. Thus, the antibureaucracy theme was linked to industrialization, a link that would be even more securely forged during the first Five-Year Plan. This new campaign, the Regime of Economy (*Rezhim ekonomii*), was already beset with problems by the summer of 1926, but it persisted into 1927, when it was placed under Rabkrin and its new head, G. K. Ordzhonikidze, and it lasted until it overlapped with the 1929 purges. In April 1929, the Sixteenth Party Congress declared the campaign a success and cited savings of some 300,000,000 rubles and cuts in the apparatus of up to 100,000 officials.[20]

In 1926, a series of decrees, accompanied by strident denunciations of bureaucratism, mandated 10 percent cuts in operating budgets and reductions in personnel.[21] In October of that year, the Fifteenth Party Conference declared that bureaucratism was "a great evil throughout the whole period of the existence of the Soviet Government" and that it "was becoming even more dangerous at the present time."[22] On November 15, 1926, the Central Committee issued instructions to Party organs and especially to Rabkrin and the control commissions to eradicate bureaucratism and introduce strict economy measures.[23]

Ordzhonikidze spelled out clearly the nature of the campaign and its problems in a speech at the Seventh Trade Union Congress in December 1926.[24] He described how some comrades implemented the Regime of

---

[20]Rees, *State Control in Soviet Russia*, 145–48.
[21]Edward H. Carr, *Foundations of a Planned Economy, 1926–1929* (New York: Macmillan, 1971), 2: 293.
[22]*KPSS v rezoliutsiiakh* (Moscow, 1954), 2: 297–98, as cited in Carr, *Foundations of a Planned Economy*, 2: 292.
[23]Carr, *Foundations of a Planned Economy*, 2: 294.
[24]*Sed'moi s"ezd professional'nykh soiuzov SSSR (6–18 dekabria 1926 g.), Plenum i sektsii: Polnyi stenograficheskii otchet* (Moscow, 1927), 447–62.

Economy by removing one electric light bulb or by eliminating a single courier or watchman. And there were even worse distortions, in that some economic managers and administrators sought to economize at the expense of the legitimate needs and interests of workers. Ordzhonikidze said that the campaign had to become a long-term struggle to divert real savings into the industrialization effort. He used the example of white-collar employees in the Moscow banks to show that, during the Regime of Economy, the numbers of white-collar workers had increased significantly.[25] Were there really people sitting in responsible positions, he asked, who acted consciously against the government's will? Of course there were some, he argued, but the more important reasons lay elsewhere, in "the very system, the very organization, and the very work that we conduct in our institutions."[26] As a solution to the problem, Ordzhonikidze proposed a system of reporting (*otchetnost'*) that was bound to produce a flood of paperwork and a constantly growing army of functionaries. He invoked Lenin and his by-now sacred writings on bureaucracy, especially the notion that the essence of bureaucratism was its distance from the masses, its inclination to stand above the people rather than to govern through them. He gave example after example of useless, formal, and extremely expensive reports: thirteen volumes from a single agency, Mossukno, involved in the manufacture of cloth, eighteen thousand pages dealing with the twenty-seven railroads under the People's Commissariat of Transportation, etc. In fact, the railroad reports had been done according to formulas developed in the 1880s by the tsarist official Kandaurov, and Ordzhonikidze sarcastically noted that "the revolution had destroyed the tsar, the gentry, and all other swine [*svolochi*], but this Kandaurov was still with us." Although unemployment was certainly a problem, any staff cuts would be more than offset by increased production, by the creation of more Dneprostrois and Volga canal projects. Ordzhonikidze singled out the massive economic bureaucracies spawned by NEP, the trusts, and the credit and commercial institutions. He closed with Lenin's 1922 letter to the Fifth Trade Union Congress, in which streamlining the bureaucracy was held to be a primary Communist task.

The delegates responded skeptically to this campaign call. The Union of Soviet and Commercial Employees was already on record as sup-

[25]Ibid., 448.
[26]Ibid., 450.

porting cuts, but only if they were not "mechanical."[27] A representative of the Ukrainian branch of the union, one Makarevich, spoke of the early enthusiasm among white-collar workers for the campaigns against bureaucratism and the Regime of Economy. Indeed, the union rank and file had been brought into the fray and with positive results. The problem, however, was, in his estimation, again the attempt to overcome bureaucracy by bureaucratic means. In the Ukraine, the required 10 percent cuts had been made in a formalist manner, with no attention to real needs. The data were gathered through bureaucratic channels without mass participation. Moreover, the fresh blood in the apparatus, workers and peasants, were the first to be dismissed, largely for lack of knowledge and experience. Only the "bureaucrat" remained, and this only perpetuated the system. As to bureaucratism in the commercial apparatus, Makarevich argued that this was a psychological and social problem that was purely a result of state control of the economy and the transformation of the role of shop personnel under the NEP economy of scarcity. Because there was so little to buy, salesclerks, instead of being helpful personnel who mediated the purchase decisions of consumers in the shop setting, knowing that their help could shape those decisions and that lack of proper service might result in loss of sales, were reduced to turning away angry consumers with impersonal, if not hostile, responses to their questions. They had to spend all of their time dealing with the complaints of shoppers forced to wait in lines. "The salesclerk [*prikazchik*] has been transformed from a store employee into a functionary [*chinovnik*] of the distribution apparatus in the full sense of that term."[28] One of the older salesclerks had recently complained to Makarevich, "A century we've worked, thirty years in the shop, and now our work has been reduced to giving the answers 'we have it,' 'no,' 'here, take it,' 'you don't want it, get out'—the customers stand in line and we have become bureaucrats."[29]

Koshkarev of the central committee of the Union of Mineworkers blamed the problem on the "system of work," the "huge amount of

---

[27]Speech of Figatner at the Fifteenth Party Conference, October 26—November 3, 1926. Figatner, representing the union's central committee, was responding to a speech by Rykov calling for the Regime of Economy. In his view, the economic managers could not be trusted. They would make up for lost personnel by forcing others to work overtime (thus negating savings as well), and they already had a sorry record of firing or otherwise penalizing employees who proposed rationalization measures.

[28]*Sed'moi s"ezd professional'nykh soiuzov*, 464.

[29]Ibid., 464.

parallel and unnecessary work," the fact that "nobody was responsible." Accordingly, he argued, unless this culture of administration were altered, budget or personnel cuts could have no meaning whatsoever.[30] The reporting system described by Ordzhonikidze simply reflected this culture. The Supreme Council of the National Economy (Vesenkha), for example, demanded voluminous documentation in *anticipation* of hypothetical needs. Begin the campaign with the *glavki* ("main committees," branch industrial management units created during War Communism), he urged, because they were the source of much of the problem. Similarly, delegate Ugarov from Leningrad said that the Regime of Economy campaign had to a large degree been subverted by the economic managers, who were using it to deny workers their rightfully earned wages or bonuses, goods, and services in order to meet budget cuts. In fact, the workers had a slogan for the campaign: "The Regime of Economy is oppression by the economy" (*Rezhim ekonomii—prizhim ekonomii*). Delegate Podosenov from Moscow claimed that this same kind of subversion was happening right under the Kremlin's nose, and that many managers and their assistants still had not internalized the decisions of the Fourteenth Party Congress and the edicts of Rabkrin and the Central Control Commission.

Other speakers told of bosses who met their prescribed budget cuts by eliminating heating and lighting, and in one case by replacing one or two watchmen with a dog. Still others complained of lack of clarity in the campaign agenda and instructions. For too long, rationalization and other suggestions from below had been buried in the paper channels. Too many functionaries viewed the campaign as "seasonal," a passing fashion, much like the seizure of surpluses. "A little time will pass, we shall be a bit richer—and then the whole thing will be off."[31] Campaigning was not the answer, they insisted; the fight against bureaucratism must be a continual, integral task in the building of socialism. Seniushin of the Union of Medical and Public Health Workers pointed out the absurdity of accusing the already impoverished public-health sector of lack of discipline (*raskhliabannost'*), when millions of workdays were being lost because of epidemics, social diseases, and alcoholism.[32] He,

---

[30]Ibid., 465.
[31]Ibid., 480.
[32]Ibid., 482–83.

too, blamed the "economic organs" for administrative failures and outrageous paperwork requirements.

In general, the trade-union delegates lamented the fact that the building of state and society during NEP had resulted in an enormous growth of bureaucracy and bureaucratism. They placed much of the blame on "the center." In his closing speech, Ordzhonikidze spoke of the need to use production conferences to "construct a public opinion," to rouse working-class anger against bureaucratic and managerial excesses, excessive spending, and the like.[33] Despite its obvious faults, it was wrong to blame the center, he protested. Local activism was the answer: vigilance at the grass-roots organizational level, factory committees and Party cells that would unmask the culprits and bring them, as Lenin had suggested, to public trial. It was necessary to organize show trials (*pokazatel'nye protsessy*) and mobilize public—that is, worker—opinion around such trials. Of course, he continued, bureaucratism was not the expression of the evil will of this or that individual; it was the result of backwardness and lack of culture. But, he said, this was no justification, for what was excusable or tolerable in 1919 or 1920 was no longer acceptable in 1926, after the cultural and educational achievements wrought by socialism. This call for a public campaign of pressure built on the notion of shame would come to fruition in the self-criticism and purge campaigns of 1929.

Ordzhonikidze followed up his arguments in a report to the plenum of the Central Control Commission of the Communist Party.[34] The message was similar: "Industrialization requires a fit apparatus and we don't have it." In words that could have been scripted for today, he proclaimed that "it means that we not only should but must accomplish the restructuring [*perestroika*] of the apparatus. We must not continue to govern by the old administrative methods, because that would only slow down the tempo of the transformation of our industry, it would interfere with that transformation."[35] Again, Ordzhonikidze bowed to Lenin and his belief that bureaucratism was "the worst evil for Soviet Russia":

[33]Ibid., 493–94. An excellent discussion of the production conferences is in William J. Chase, *Workers, Society, and the Soviet State: Labor and Life in Moscow, 1918–1929* (Urbana: University of Illinois Press, 1987), 256–92.
[34]"Iz doklada tov. Ordzhonikidze plenumu TsKK VKP(b)," *Sovetskoe stroitel'stvo*, 1927, no. 2–3: 68–83.
[35]Ibid., 68.

That bureaucratism has not decreased in recent years. Our apparatus is not suited to serve the growing activeness of workers and peasants, it has closed in on itself, and it still has a powerful tendency to manage the nation and populace not through them, but by commanding them, a tendency that of necessity emerged during wartime. There is a rift between the Soviet apparatus and the population; instead of living human links, there is command through paper.[36]

Ordzhonikidze went on to describe the goals of Rabkrin in dealing with bureaucratism, and he singled out as problems key groups of white-collar workers in the state commercial, financial, and cooperative sectors. The problem called for new methods, and Ordzhonikidze spoke of what would become the watchword of Stalinist antibureaucracy—"maximum initiative in the localities": local initiative, mass participation, and "revolutionary zeal" (*revoliutsionnost'*). Tellingly, Ordzhonikidze warned that the recent battle against bureaucratism had produced a new type of "bureaucratic deformity," in that now the bureaucrats themselves screamed loudest of all against bureaucratism. This was deception, and it was the sacred duty of Rabkrin and the larger commonweal not to be fooled by it.[37]

THE SELF-CRITICISM CAMPAIGN AND THE PURGES

On June 22, 1929, M. I. Kalinin gave one of the major speeches at the Eighth All-Union Congress of the Union of Soviet and Commercial Employees.[38] Kalinin at that time was in charge of the soviet apparatus, and one of his major themes was the ongoing purge of soviet and Party employees that was already in full swing. With these purges, the antibureaucratic campaigns had reached a new peak. All of the previous campaigns were now drawn together in an attempt to solicit mass support for industrialization and collectivization and once again to overcome bureaucracy through bureaucracy. These purges were of course deeply threatening to white-collar workers, because they—especially they—could so easily be labeled "bureaucrats" and be pushed outside the bounds of socialist society. Stalin's reheated class war was already producing major casualties, even as it paved the way for a tremendous

---

[36]Ibid., 69.
[37]Ibid., 73.
[38]This and all subsequent material on the congress are taken from the full stenographic report in Tsentral'nyi gosudarstvennyi arkhiv oktiabr'skoi revoliutsii, *fond* 5468, and *Nasha gazeta*, June 22, 1929.

expansion in the number of both white-collar and blue-collar workers. The tone had been set earlier that year in the theses approved at the Sixteenth Party Conference and published in *Pravda*.[39] At that time, Ia. Iakovlev had reviewed the previous campaigns and noted that, with the increased tempo of industrialization, victory against bureaucratism was never more necessary. Now he declared bureaucratism as a form of class struggle practiced against the working class by the kulaks, the "urban bourgeoisie," and the "bourgeois intelligentsia." Industrialization, collectivization, and perestroika were impossible without a better state apparatus. Purges should be directed at those officials linked to bourgeois and kulak elements, and affirmative action should be applied to bring the masses into administrative work.

For the members of the Union of Soviet and Commercial Employees, purges were already taking place. Kalinin, however, severely criticized the campaign mode of reforming or transforming the bureaucracy. It was too destructive, he claimed, and moreover, it usually got rid of the wrong people. Purging, he argued, should not be carried out on the basis of social origin (he understood well the masked quality of Soviet society and the lack of correspondence between social origins and political consciousness). Rather, it should be based on performance and competence, and Kalinin appealed to the provincial union functionaries to purge only the "responsible" types. In Riazan, for example, fifteen hundred employees had been dismissed, but not the real troublemakers. He cited Stalin's dictum to go after the "big bureaucrat."

Participation in the purge mechanisms was not an honor or a mark of new acceptability or status, as some seemed to think. Kalinin argued that "we need quality purges, purges that are permanent, so that 75% of the banned functionaries do not reappear in other Soviet positions."[40] Purges required foresight and planning. In Tomsk, according to Kalinin, one thousand purged employees were replaced by blue-collar workers who had no qualifications to be office workers, bookkeepers, typists, or higher-level specialists and managers. This was a bad tendency, "mechanical affirmative action," and there were far too many reports of unhappy workers in new white-collar posts. Kalinin pointed out that the Central Executive Committee had taken in only five workers, and then

---

[39]"Itogi i blizhaishie zadachi bor'by s biurokratizmom," *Pravda*, April 12, 1929.

[40]It was easy for purged employees and officials to find other jobs in the late 1920s. Even the vast majority of those purged from the Party at that time were readmitted after cursory review procedures. See Getty, *Origins of the Great Purges*, 38–48.

only if they could be given full support and a trial period to see how
they liked their new occupations. It was dangerous, he warned, to remove valuable production workers from the factories to give them less
meaningful white-collar jobs. "Think of the factory and its leadership
and only remove blue-collar workers very, very carefully. A valued person makes good money in the factory, so don't promote a metal worker
into a typist, don't make them into bureaucratic paper pushers." So,
Kalinin told the union activists, if you are promoting hundreds of
thousands of blue-collar workers, you don't understand the issues.
Working in a campaign mode would destroy thousands of lives, and
nine hundred and ninety out of a thousand will be disillusioned.

Kalinin's preferred solution to the call for affirmative action was to
promote white-collar workers themselves within the soviet and commercial apparatus. Why, he wondered, was there no commentary in the
media about this kind of promotion?[41] Why was the press so negative
toward the soviet apparatus? The people in his audience, he said, de-
served better:

In twelve years, you, the white-collar workers, have fulfilled enormous state
tasks and created a huge cadre of selfless, wholehearted functionaries. You, the
functionaries, men, women, Red Army veterans, etc., should defend yourselves
as a corporate body, as a profession. Everyone looks at the Soviet apparatus.
We don't have former officials—in fact that is more true of the factories. We
must end the tyranny and arbitrariness of the managers and raise our self-
consciousness and professionalism.

Kalinin argued for a new corporate sense of group rights and status, as
white-collar workers helped lead the way forward in the construction of
the new socialist economy and state. The army of soviet and commercial
employees, he argued, was a "proletarian" army, proletarian in the "material and popular sense," though not sociologically speaking, because
so many employees came from the "petty-bourgeois ranks" and were
raised on petty-bourgeois values. The union and the Party together must
instruct the white-collar army in proletarian interests, ethics, and way
of life. Not only was this possible, but the immersion of white-collar

---

[41]The unspoken answer was that it was not appropriate in the contemporary political
    discourse to give status recognition to white-collar workers, who thus remained "hid-
    den." For a full discussion of the role of white-collar workers in the 1920s, their cor-
    porate sensibilities, and the idea that they comprised a "hidden class," see Orlovsky,
    "The Hidden Class."

workers in proletarian society would strengthen the soviet apparatus and ensure unity workers and peasants and the building of socialism.

Some bureaucrats were indeed removed as a result of the purge campaign, but many remained in their positions, as did the structures and the vast army of white-collar workers represented at the congress. Although their union leaders were purged, along with M. P. Tomskii and other central trade-union figures identified with the Right Opposition, the rank and file could look forward to their own legitimate place in the proletarian society. It is these social dynamics that are obscured in the language and campaigns of antibureaucracy, and they must be brought to light in order to assess the claim that Stalinism was a popular antibureaucratic movement.

THE MEANING OF THE DISCOURSE OF ANTIBUREAUCRACY

For both defenders and opponents of the regime, the language of antibureaucracy and the attacks on actual bureaucrats were useful. Unlike the regime's other enemies, the kulaks or the bourgeois (either the symbolic version or the more concrete NEP-men and-women), bureaucracy really existed as a gigantic force in the bloated structures of the post–Civil War state, Party, and trade unions. The bureaucracy served as a substitute for the old class enemy, though that label could also be applied to the perpetrators of bureaucratic misdemeanors. During the 1920s, "bureaucracy" acquired a newly charged meaning. On the one hand, it encompassed the hated tsarist inheritance of dysfunctional, antidemocratic organizational behavior; on the other, it represented the injustices and irrationalities of the plebeian, antimarket drive to construct socialism out of the chaos of the revolution. Bureaucracy, as a polemical tool, could refer to the prerevolutionary past or the postrevolutionary future and thus had a rich resonance in the minds of ordinary Soviet citizens and political activists alike. The opposition groups had accused Stalin of fostering bureaucracy, and so it made excellent political sense for the regime to outdo them on this issue. It did not hurt, either, that Bukharin and the Right in fact looked to managers and specialists (against whom there was considerable antagonism among white-collar and trade-union employees) as allies in the late 1920s. The emerging Stalin power bloc appropriated the discourse of antibureaucracy and used it even while relying on the bureaucracy and the army of white-collar workers as a prime body of social support, fulfilling their aspirations and meeting their needs with a program of full employment and higher wages and benefits and guaranteeing their inclusion in both the "proletarian state" and the socialist commonweal. As had been the case with the original language of "proletarian revolution" in the years from 1917 to 1921, the discourse of antibureaucracy served to mask the social reality of the emerging Soviet polity. By 1931, there would be a reprieve even for the abused bourgeois specialists, whom Stalin would welcome back into the fold.

The discourse of antibureaucracy contained a subtle message for the factory workers as well—to wit, that they should remain fragmented and subordinate to the bureaucracy in its reified and legitimate forms, the Soviet state and the Communist party. While it was proper to un-mask the bureaucratic enemy (an enemy that could easily remain hidden, much like the mystifying powers of capital to mask its own workings), it was not proper to question the bureaucratic organization of state power itself. One criticized not the bureaucratic-technocratic state, but only those who hindered its operations. Attacks on bureaucracy simul-taneously defined both the socialist commonweal and its opposite, the outsiders, the disenfranchised, those not entitled to the benefits of mem-bership in the new proletarian order. In this way, the discourse of an-tibureaucracy resonated to the experience of ordinary people in their daily lives. Bureaucracy was tangible, a fact of life faced by all. It could not help but promote social solidarity, like the reaction of workers and peasants to famine or pestilence. But this mobilizational tool had a built-in safety valve. Whereas the bourgeois, or the landlord, or especially the kulak, as a social category or type might be marked for extinction or elimination, that could never be the case with the bureaucrat, because so much of plebeian society and the emerging middle strata of Soviet society were themselves part of the bureaucratic structure. After a certain point, however, to attack the bureaucracy meant that society was at-tacking itself—and this was, indeed, one powerful force at work in the terror of the late 1930s.

14

◖━◗◖━◗◖━◗◖━◗◖━◗◖━◗◖━◗◖━◗◖━◗◖━◗◖━◗◖━◗◖━◗◖━◗◖━◗◖━◗◖━◗◖━◗◖━◗

The inconsistency of NEP: commentary

BEN EKLOF

Although I am sympathetic to much of what was being done under the New Economic Policy (NEP), as a professional historian I feel that we must be skeptical about the evidence and logic presented in defense of its viability. We need to distinguish between NEP's moral appeal and its concrete historical potential. Viktor Danilov has contended that, as far as the peasants were concerned, NEP really existed for only two years, from approximately 1925 to 1927. Moreover, NEP was structurally disaggregated; not all elements of the new Soviet reality necessarily fitted together or functioned in complementary fashion; so it is difficult to draw conclusions about the era by studying one of its aspects in isolation. NEP was inconsistent, to the point where one might question whether it was a single period of reform at all. Whether we examine cultural politics, the reform of the police and methods of local control, the rhetoric of antibureaucracy and the evolution of the white-collar employees as a social class, or education policy, the era of the 1920s was characterized by much improvisation and by oscillations between gradualist and campaign methods.[1]

---

[1][The meaning of the period of the 1920s provoked considerable debate at the conference. Several participants viewed it as a prelude to Stalinism. In contrast, Emmons saw it as a working out of the new socialist order established in 1917, but without necessarily leading to Stalinism, despite the presence of a revolutionary mindset, because elaboration of the system allowed for alternatives. Orlovsky observed that the very concept of reform was discredited in the heady aftermath of 1917 and that the term itself was not used in the 1920s. Weissman, however, noted that the impetus for change and the policy initiatives of the 1920s, while characterized by a revolutionary impulse, often did not come from above and frequently reflected the ideas and interests of midlevel individuals and organizations of the emerging Soviet society, perhaps still echoing the heritage of the late imperial period. This, of course, stands in marked contrast to the 1930s.—Ed.]

In broader historical perspective, I would even argue that NEP was the final phase of the Russian state's retreat from activist social policy dating back to the 1860s. William Rosenberg has claimed that, whereas the Great Reforms of the 1860s were state-driven reforms instituted for state-directed purposes, the period between the Great Reforms and 1929 saw Russian society and spontaneous processes of social and economic development take precedence over the state. The Russian state, in his view, became reactive rather than proactive during this latter period, responding to change rather than imposing it. This concept of a reactive state has direct relevance to the NEP period. As the materials in this volume make clear, the NEP era was essentially residual, and it can be interpreted as a partial withdrawal of the state—for example, from control of the economy or control over intellectuals. Seen within the larger framework of late imperial history, this partial withdrawal can be attributed to lack of funding, lack of initiative, or both. The 1920s can be seen as an aftermath of the era of the Great Reforms that was followed by renewed state initiative in 1929. Perhaps the most striking contrast between the late imperial and NEP periods is that intermediary organizations were far more active in the former, both in setting national agendas and in creating coherent, unified professional organizations to implement these agendas. One senses that this dynamic was changing in the 1920s, that these independent professional organizations were either missing, suppressed, or fatally compromised.

Despite the excellent chapters on the NEP in this volume, it seems to me that several issues of major importance have not been addressed. One of these is that of the environmental concerns and the models of nature in the 1920s, a subject on which Douglas Weiner has recently written an interesting study.[2] Given the catastrophic ecological situation of the former Soviet Union today,[3] this is an especially important topic, but the environmental issue is significant for earlier reform periods as well. The study of early environmental movements is analytically suggestive and may indicate whether we can view these movements as reflecting the emergence of a middle-class, or civic, consciousness in Russia.

---

[2]Douglas R. Weiner, *Models of Nature: Ecology, Conservation, and Cultural Revolution in Soviet Russia* (Bloomington: Indiana University Press, 1988).
[3]See Murray Feshbach and Alfred J. Friendly, *Ecocide in the USSR* (New York: Basic Books, 1992).

A second issue that deserves serious attention is the international context of the Soviet regime at the time. To Theodore von Laue, Russia's dependent status in the world was crucial to an understanding of the historical significance of Lenin and Stalin.[4] Most historians would agree that foreign relations and outside pressures have been a significant impetus to reform in Russian history and that Western models were often used as guidelines for reform.[5] Thus, if we are to pursue a rigorous, comparative analysis of reform models in different periods of Russian and Soviet history, we need to take into account the international context of each of these periods. We need to be very specific in our understanding of the changing dynamics of interstate relations and how Russia's relations with the outside world affected the reform eras, an issue that has been brought up elsewhere in this volume.

Thirdly, it would be very fruitful to look more closely at the Soviet penal system and, more broadly, at Soviet attempts to deal with deviance as a whole in the 1920s. Alexander Dallin, Boris Nicolaevsky, and, more recently, Peter Solomon[6] have argued that basically the Ministry of Justice administered the penal system during NEP. In those years, the penal system accounted for 150,000 prisoners, whereas the concentration camps run by the secret police accounted for only 30,000 prisoners. Solomon notes that the principle of "cost-accounting" (*khozraschet*) introduced during NEP, together with growing unemployment, undermined the sincere and heroic efforts of the Ministry of Justice to institute progressive and nonpunitive systems of rehabilitation. A general study of deviance in the 1920s and a comparison of Soviet government policies of that era with the policies of the era of perestroika, especially regarding the treatment of alcoholism and the perception and treatment of crime, would also be useful. Such a comparison would have to consider the measurement of crime and deviance, the perceptions of crime and deviance (and the treatment programs derived from these perceptions), and the shock value of glasnost, which, in both the twenties and the thirties, created almost a social psychosis about crime. Both then and

[4]Theodore von Laue, *Why Lenin? Why Stalin?: A Reappraisal of the Russian Revolution, 1900–1930* (Philadelphia: J. B. Lippincott, 1964).
[5]Dietrich Geyer, *Russian Imperialism: The Interaction of Domestic and Foreign Policy, 1860–1914* (New Haven: Yale University Press, 1987).
[6]Peter H. Solomon, "Soviet Penal Policy, 1917–1934: A Reinterpretation," *Slavic Review* 2 (1980): 195–217.

recently, the extent of criminality, or its supposed rate of increase, may well have been reported inaccurately, but the reports were universally accepted as true in discussions of the degradation of society. Why has there been this recurring gap between the perception and the reality of crime?

Although I am inclined to consider NEP as less than a coherent period, I concur with Kenez's contention that the reforming urge is a constant in Soviet history. But we must contrast this tendency with the reality of underinstitutionalization. These two elements of the political culture provide a significant continuity from the tsarist period through the NEP years and render moot, in my opinion, many of the intellectual debates over the meaning and direction of the 1920s as a particular era of Soviet history. It is well known that in comparison with Western governments, the tsarist Russian government was distinguished by the small percentage of money that it allocated to local affairs and local government. This sort of underinstitutionalization is a theme reiterated by historians, although we must recognize, as Bradley notes in his contribution, that intermediary organizations were indeed emerging in late imperial Russia. The Civil War, the October Revolution, and early Soviet policies eliminated but could not replace these intermediary organizations; we know that the commune existed in relative freedom in the 1920s for exactly this reason, certainly not because of a belief in the intrinsic virtue of the institution.

Finally, I believe we must recognize the impact of cost-accounting on the local institutional structure of Russia during the NEP years. Educational policies, police policies, penal policies—all measures, whether of the control or of the positive reformist type—were absolutely devastated by this approach. To cite only one example, the schools involved in the literacy campaign were left without any funding whatsoever after cost-accounting was introduced.[7] It appears that the same situation occurred in all other areas of local government and within the intermediary organizations as a whole during the 1920s. In fact, the overall impact of cost-accounting on society and the economy can be considered one of the most significant aspects of the NEP. There was a significant gap between the reform goals articulated in government policies and the

---

[7]Ben Eklof, "Russian Literacy Campaigns, 1861–1939: Historical and Comparative Perspectives," in Robert J. Arnove and Harvey J. Graff, eds., *National Literacy Campaigns: Historical and Comparative Perspectives* (New York: Plenum, 1987), 133.

means available to the regime for implementing them on the local level. Here we detect another continuity between the late tsarist period and the NEP, a continuity that once again argues for considering the 1920s as a final phase of the late imperial era.

Part IV

The challenge of pluralism from
Khrushchev to Gorbachev

15

Khrushchev and the crisis of the regime of the Marxian prince

CARL A. LINDEN

LEADERSHIP AND ORIGINS

The late Edward Crankshaw, an astute observer of Soviet politics, liked to raise a key question about political leadership: "Can a leader escape his origins?" In other words, can a leader free himself from the ruling orders and methods out of which he grew and create new orders and methods of rule? The question is peculiarly apt for the leader-reformer. Nikita Khrushchev and Mikhail Gorbachev represent two dramatic examples in Soviet history, and their political fates were joined. First one, then the other sought against odds to lift the yoke of the dictatorial rule under which both had risen to power. That yoke sapped the energy and initiative of the ruled to a point where the long-term vitality and survival of the Soviet regime were at stake. Khrushchev saw the danger coming, whereas Gorbachev arrived when the regime was already well on its way toward decline into stasis.

Khrushchev failed in his bold attempt to end dictatorship with an attack on Stalin's rule and a revival of the Marxian end goal of a society free of domination. The unintended result of his action was the shaking of the foundations of the Communist system itself. The core of that system had always been the rule of a Marxian "dictator-prince" who presided over an ideology-based principality.[1] This was the regime that

[1]The terms "prince" and "principality," though perhaps somewhat archaic, are revived here in the generic sense in which Machiavelli employed them. "Prince," in its primary sense, designates a class of leaders who seek, above all and often at any cost, to be the "first" (*princeps, primus,* or the "number one") in ruling power. It also bears a secondary meaning, referring to an office of supreme executive power and its apparatus. A "prin-

Lenin founded in fact, if not in theory, and that Stalin amplified into totalitarianism. Khrushchev's attempt to move away from the dictatorship led in time to his overthrow by the Communist party aristocracy, led by Leonid Brezhnev. With some reason, the latter feared that Khrushchev's actions were subverting the regime.

After the restorationist prince, Brezhnev, spent nearly a score of years in a losing battle to buttress the regime, Gorbachev rose to power and renewed the attempt at reform and reformation. This latest Marxian prince began with limited reforms but was driven to a drastic attempt to transform himself and his rule from prince of the Communist party to president of a nascent democratic republic. His attempt to change the regime brought on the crisis that undermined the Soviet empire itself.

In contrast to the founder of a new order of rule, Khrushchev and Gorbachev were encumbered with daunting burdens of the past. Their task was to remedy a flawed system of power without bringing about its overthrow. But Khrushchev's attack on Stalin planted the seed of the crisis of the Marxian ideocratic principality, founded by Lenin and perfected by Stalin, that ultimately bore its fruit during Gorbachev's reign.

The leader-reformer sees himself as correcting defects in rule that arose either at the very founding of the system or in subsequent years. Khrushchev and Gorbachev, initially at least, traced the defects to Stalin rather than to Lenin. Khrushchev believed that de-Stalinization—that is, an end to one-man dictatorship—and a turn to the path of achieving communism in the Soviet Union were all that was needed. But the rev-

---

cipality," then, is the executive rule of a state "from above," as distinguished from a "republic," a law-regulated rule resting on authority "from below," derived from the "people." Lenin was a prince in both senses. He not only assumed first place in the revolutionary coup of 1917 but he also was the creator of the Party apparatus as his instrument. He liked to boast that executive and legislative power were joined in his "proletarian dictatorship." In essence, his regime was a principality resting its authority on ideology.

Stalin fixed the office of the Marxian prince in the Party's general secretary. The holder of that office ever since could quite reasonably be called the "prince" of the Party. The term is more accurate than "leader" and "dictator." Not all princes are dictators, but all dictators are princes. The princely office of general secretary, as Gorbachev himself observed, was before his incumbency "an entirely unrestricted dictatorship" (*Pravda,* April 12, 1990).

Though Machiavelli lent the term "prince" a certain notoriety, it was in common use in its generic meaning in political discourse until recent times and is so used by some political scientists today; see, for example, Harvey C. Mansfield, *The Taming of the Prince: The Ambivalence of the Modern Executive Power* (New York: Free Press/Macmillan, 1989).

olution of 1989 in Eastern Europe and the demise of the Soviet Union revealed that the defects of the system were rooted in its very origins.

Like Khrushchev, Gorbachev began by asserting his fidelity to Lenin's conception, but his reforms increasingly undercut it. When Gorbachev created the Congress of People's Deputies in 1989, based mainly on popular election and standing outside the Party's direct control, he took a crucial step away from Leninism. The new congress, a body with original constitutional powers, was something of a return to the popularly elected Constituent Assembly of 1917.

Lenin's dissolution of that Constituent Assembly in favor of the Party's monopoly of power was the key act in the founding of his ideocratic autocracy. Conversely, the key act of Gorbachev's rule was his renunciation of the Party's monopoly of power—his acceptance of the principles of political pluralism and of popular representation. His risky move toward a representative civil state distinguished his strategy from Khrushchev's. Khrushchev had attempted to reach the regime's ideologically defined goal of achieving a communist society free of all dominion or rule, whether democratic or otherwise. What the two leaders had in common was that both of them sought to find an escape route from an unlimited despotism.

Despite his struggle to do so, Khrushchev was unable to make a complete break with his Stalinist origins. In his taped soliloquies, he himself honestly admitted that this was the case. His self-metamorphosis from Stalinist to anti-Stalinist was contradictory. On some occasions, his behavior showed the imprint of his training in the Stalinist school, yet on others, he broke loose, revealing a new persona who engaged in an attack on Stalinist methods of rule with passionate intensity. He was aware of the two sides of himself, and in his memoirs he noted how the Stalinist side of his psychology would "belch forth" while he was the leader.[2]

The question of origins, then, is a question about political character and personal identity. Can a leader change his identity after he has reached the pinnacle of power? Khrushchev rose within the circle of

---

[2]See Strobe Talbott, ed. and trans., *Khrushchev Remembers: The Last Testament* (Boston: Little, Brown, 1974), 67, where Khrushchev recalls denying the renowned nuclear scientist Peter Kapitsa permission to go abroad, in reprisal for the latter's refusal to work on nuclear weaponry. Khrushchev said the reason "was possibly that Stalin was still belching inside me. Keep in mind, I'd worked under Stalin for years and years, and you don't free yourself from [Stalinist] habits so easily. It takes time to become conscious of your shortcomings and free yourself from them."

Stalin's henchmen. Once in power, he strove to break out of that circle and reshape the party-state. He had used Stalinist organizational tactics in building his power in the Party secretariat, and he had used a Stalinist line to defeat Malenkov's attempt at reform through the state apparatus before unveiling his own reform strategy. With a shrewd, if not sophisticated, prescience he saw that the regime was headed for trouble if it did not change its ways.

The questions of origins and identity also hung in the balance for Gorbachev. He entered the circle of Brezhnev's neo-Stalinist Politburo, which had sacked Khrushchev as a failed leader but now was in its own troubled end-time. He was its singularly junior and evidently trusted protégé. But once in power, and after a brief interval of following the line of his predecessor from the old regime, Iurii Andropov, he took up where Khrushchev had left off. In that process, he brought to a head the very crisis of regime that his predecessor had feared was coming. The Gorbachev leadership, in fact, openly located its historical starting point in the Twentieth Party Congress of 1956, at which Khrushchev had delivered a dramatic indictment of Stalin's tyranny in the famous "secret speech."[3] But Gorbachev's attempt at combining Soviet socialism and Western-style pluralism went well beyond anything Khrushchev had conceived of. While Khrushchev tried to stay broadly within the ideological frame of the old regime, Gorbachev stepped out of it, introducing principles of rule from the representative civil state.

Nonetheless, it was Khrushchev who took the truly daring first step toward a major change of the political order: He attacked Stalin. His action was rash and risky in the extreme and cannot be reduced to a mere ploy in his drive for power. It was more than that. It was an act arising as much out of indignant passion as out of rational premeditation. He put his power as leader at great risk, and the backlash within the ruling group came within a whisker of bringing him down in the aftermath of the Hungarian revolt. He denounced Stalin before an assembly whose membership consisted of Stalin's creatures. His fellow leaders on the Politburo were, like himself, Stalin's heirs. None were disposed to launch such a powerful denunciation, which put the legitimacy of the Party regime itself into question. The only exception was Khrushchev's close ally, A. I. Mikoyan, who initiated direct but guarded

---

[3]See the interview with Ivan Frolov, *La Repubblica* (Rome), April 16–17, 1989, p. 13. Frolov was a close aide of Gorbachev's and the editor of *Pravda*.

criticism of Stalinist doctrines at an open session of the Twentieth Congress, thus paving the way for Khrushchev's onslaught on Stalin himself.[4]

Khrushchev's own later public explanation of his daring was that he was impelled to tell the truth in order to ensure victory for the communist cause. He said:

> I am often asked how I dared to deliver that report at the Twentieth Party Congress. We trusted that man for so many years! We raised him up. We created the cult. And then to take that risk. . . . But since I was elected First Secretary, I had to tell the truth, it was my duty. To tell the truth about the past, whatever it cost me and whatever risk it entailed for me. It was Lenin who taught us that a party that is not afraid to tell the truth will never perish. We learned the lessons of the past and we wanted the other fraternal parties to learn those lessons too, and then our common victory would be ensured.[5]

While that falls short of a full explanation, the motive of achieving the cause with which his life was identified was undoubtedly part of it. Moreover, his assertion that "we" trusted, raised, and adulated Stalin is at odds with the position he took in the secret speech—namely, that Stalin, not his followers, was to blame for his oppressive rule.

Khrushchev's attack on Stalin, so soon after the latter's passing, had a deeper significance. It was the crux of his attempt to escape his origins and also—though perhaps not wholly wittingly—to escape the form of rule in which he had been reared and over which he came to preside. His assault on Stalin proved to be the first deadly thrust at Communist rule in Eastern Europe and the Soviet Union, which expired in the last two decades of this century.

Why did the crisis begin with Khrushchev? Would it have begun to unfold when and how it did if another leader—Malenkov, or even Molotov, rather than Khrushchev—had risen to the top? Why did the Soviet regime experience the beginning of its "systemic" crisis so soon after Stalin's death, and was it "destined" to experience such a crisis at all?

It may be in the nature of human affairs that no complete answer to such questions is accessible to us. A key element in any answer resides in the complexities and puzzles of human personality. What has been often overlooked in Soviet and Communist history is the crucial impact of the leader's personality. The crisis of the ideocratic principality in

[4]*Pravda*, February 18, 1956, pp. 4–6.
[5]As quoted in Fedor Burlatsky, "Khrushchev: zametki k politicheskomu portretu," *Literaturnaia gazeta* (Moscow), February 24, 1988, p. 14.

general and Stalinism specifically is to be sought in the first place in the mind of Khrushchev, the dictator's successor as prince of the Party.

The monumental evil that Stalin perpetrated and into which Khrushchev was drawn rankled in his conscience in a way that it did not in the conscience of others around Stalin. While others shied away from the issue of Stalin's personality, Khrushchev was tireless in pursuing it, not only while in power but also when reminiscing in retirement. An unsophisticated man "from below," he saw Stalin's rule originally as an opening to a new day. But he soon found himself in a long night of terror-ridden despotism, in which he had the choice of being accomplice or victim.[6] The Twentieth Party Congress platform gave him the first opportunity not only to gain an upper hand in the power struggle with his rivals but also to be able to take vengeance on his tormentor and to restore the compromised Marxian expectation.

Khrushchev sensed that the regime's plan for reaching communism by force, indoctrination, and consumer deprivation was headed for a failure of performance and a loss of legitimacy in the eyes of the people subjected to its ruthless means. He saw the danger more clearly than the other heirs of Stalin and sought to reshape the ideology and the regime's behavior into something more acceptable and justifiable in the eyes of the ruled. Even Stalin's victory in World War II over the Nazis was a victory of the Russian nation, he insisted, not of the ideocratic power. The luster of victory, however, disguised but did not change or remove the question of the legitimacy of the ruling power. At the very core of Khrushchev's foundation-shaking secret speech was nothing more or less than elemental outrage at gross injustice and humiliation at having been both a tool and a silent sufferer of Stalin's enormities. Khrushchev's speech dealt a blow to the ideocratic principality that set it on its course toward revolutionary upheavals. Gorbachev, the last prince of the Party, was left to struggle to salvage something of the Soviet order out of its wreckage.

What these momentous events reveal is that the destiny of the modern Marxian principality is intimately tied to the character and fate of its princes. Unlike representative civil states, which are sometimes shaken

---

[6]Khrushchev spoke at various times of the fear that gripped the members of Stalin's circle. In the secret speech, he said that they could not enter Stalin's presence without wondering if they themselves were to be his next victims. He offered no defense of his collaboration with Stalin in repression, but what was implicit was that failure to cooperate meant death.

from below by broad conflict within the body politic, the ideocratic principality's unraveling began "from above" and in the prince himself.

Perhaps the most common blind spot in the study of the Soviet and Communist regimes lies in seeing their "systems" as standing on their own, apart from the form of their ruling power. Each of these systems, from its inception and ever since, has been nothing more than the "methods and orders" of rule of a dictator-prince who rested his power on an ideology-based, hierarchic party. The Communist system is what a reborn Machiavelli would have perceived as another form of princely rule. The Marxian prince's right to rule is based not in tradition or in personal prowess but in ideology and in his command "from above." That command is exercised first of all through the hierarchic apparatus of the Party and then through the other hierarchies of the party-state. Indeed, in surveying the history of communism, it is its ruling personalities that first come to mind: Mao, Tito, Kim Il Sung, Ceausescu, Castro, Pol Pot. Despite the Marxian ideology's denial of hero-leaders as movers in history, the personal rule of such figures has had a manifest and deep effect on the shaping of the politics of the twentieth century.

KHRUSHCHEV AS REFORMER

In a real sense, however, Khrushchev stands alone in this pantheon of hero-leaders and world movers. He was an unanticipated irruption of a singular personality into Communist politics. Unlike any other of the contemporary Communist princes, he dared to demolish the mythos of the succession of the true defenders of the Marxian ideological faith since Lenin. He plunged across his Rubicon, but unlike Caesar, his aim was to destroy not a republic but a principality. In doing so, he triggered the unraveling of the regime of the Marxian prince.

The ancient Greek proverb that "a man's character is his fate" applies with dramatic force to Khrushchev. None of his fellows among Stalin's heirs resembled him. None showed his recurring and passionate concern with good and evil, justice and injustice, around the question of Stalin.[7]

---

[7] Alexander Solzhenitsyn has said that Khrushchev unconsciously mirrored a Christian view of the human condition, sharply at odds with the Promethean view of man and his powers expressed in Marxist-Leninist ideology: *The Oak and the Calf* (New York: Harper & Row, 1975), 42. Here again, paradox is found in Khrushchev's personality. It will be recalled that he was fond of using Biblical examples and proverbs to give force to his

Indeed, it is unlikely that Malenkov, and most improbable that Molotov, if either of them had succeeded Stalin, would have administered the shock to the Soviet system that was contained in Khrushchev's surprise thrust at his master. Malenkov was a more cautious reformer, whose short-lived "New Course" sought an easing of East-West tensions and economic improvement at home without open challenge to the Stalinist system of coercion and command. Molotov made no bones of his intent to keep the "screws" tight. Although the ingredients of eventual crisis were present, Soviet history very likely would have taken different shape under their respective leaderships. In either case, a future Gorbachev would not have had Khrushchev's attack on Stalin to use as his cue for radical reform.

It is the grand irony of the history of the Marxian ideocratic principality that its founder, Lenin, denied the importance of hero-leaders in history. Though he himself fell into that class, he was dedicated to an ideology promising to end all forms of principality and personal domination. Here was the heroic antihero seeking to perform the ultimate feat. Nonetheless, Lenin was a founding prince, and the hierarchic party he invented established the orders and methods of rule for realizing the Marxian objectives. Stalin then went on to perfect the new principality as a system of totalitarian power and transformation. He fixed the prince's office in the post of general secretary of the Party. His command passed through the Party apparatus and thence into the other chains of command of the party-state. Lenin was also an ideologue-prince who formed a Marxian aristocracy, the Bolsheviks, around him to assist in attaining his goal. Centered in the Politburo of the Bolshevik Party, this new ruling elite was an early stage of the *nomenklatura*.

Lenin apparently saw himself not as the founder of a new principality but rather as the pilot of the Marxian dictatorship, guiding the class struggle toward a communist society free of principalities and dominions. Lenin's Marxism led him to minimize the importance of the first of the three perennial categories of human politics, the class of the Number One. Instead, he focused his attention on the Few and the Many—in his terms, the capitalists and the proletariat. In his well-known precept of "who gets whom" (*kto kogo*), he had in mind a struggle of these classes, not a struggle between individual personalities for supreme

arguments, yet he was ruthless and unrelenting in his persecution of Christians during his rule.

power. His lateness in raising the issue of the succession to himself is striking. Only on the eve of his death, in his testament, did he sound the alarm over Stalin's amassing of power. Trotsky, who was Lenin's partner in the Bolshevik Revolution, had once been more clear-sighted on this issue, for in 1903 he predicted that Lenin's idea of a centralized revolutionary party would in practice lead to a dictatorship.[8] Subsequently, he appears to have forgotten his prophecy, and he, too, was far too late in organizing opposition to Stalin. In any event, it took the supremely self-aware Stalin to perfect the new principality and locate the dictatorial power in the office of the general secretary. Gorbachev later declared that that post was "an entirely unrestricted dictatorship," although he added, self-servingly, that this was true only up to 1985, when he assumed power.[9]

It is indeed a paradox that a system of unlimited personal power rose to dominate more than a third of the world on the wings of ideas about human liberation and egalitarian fraternity. It came in the guise of a dictatorship to end dictatorship. Once established, it failed to wither away or realize the end of political rule, as promised in its ideology, but instead imposed a relentless repression upon its subjects. In 1924, Trotsky approvingly characterized Lenin's rule as the "iron clutch of a dictatorship unparalleled in history."[10] What he had in mind was the Marxian notion of a transitional class dictatorship—a dictatorship without a dictator. He had yet to meet his fate in mortal encounter with Stalin, the aptly self-named man of steel.

At all events, after Stalin's death Nikita Khrushchev at first followed in his master's footsteps in seeking the succession. He displayed his mastery as a trained tactician of the Stalin school of power struggle and emerged as the winner in the contest for first place. His Politburo colleagues underrated him and evidently saw no danger in turning over to him the post of general secretary. Like Stalin, Khrushchev used the office as a powerful organizational instrument for gaining primacy within the

---

[8]See Robert V. Daniels, ed., *A Documentary History of Communism* (New York: Random House, 1960), 1: 31.
[9]*Pravda*, April 12, 1990. Gorbachev made the remark in answer to a questioner at a Komsomol Congress who asked if his election to the new executive presidency was a halfway house to dictatorship. He distinguished the new presidential office from the dictatorship of the general secretary, seeing the former as a move toward "a rule-of-law state."
[10]Leon Trotsky, *Literature and Revolution* (Ann Arbor: University of Michigan Press, 1960; originally published in 1924), 185.

Politburo.[11] Following his mentor's path, he became the new prince of
the Party. Once well entrenched, however, he shed the Stalinist image
and advanced himself as both a counter-Stalin and a leader-reformer.
He not only attacked Stalin the man but also sought to put an end to
his legacy of terror-based despotism. In time, it also became clear that
Khrushchev was looking for ways to bring to an end, in the name of
Marxism, the regime of the dictator-prince itself. He may not have been
fully aware that, in principle, he was proposing to put his office and
himself out of business.

Khrushchev strove with great daring to disconnect the rule of the
Communist prince from the communist idea. His secret speech was
aimed at breaking the link between the two, a linkage embedded in the
psyche of the Party apparatus by long indoctrination and a habit of
obedience. As a substitute, he came up with his grand scheme, ratified
at the Twenty-second Party Congress in 1961, to fulfill the Marxian
expectation through a new Party program for reaching communist society in the Soviet Union. In a sense, Khrushchev was attempting to
resolve the paradox, found in Marxism itself, of how to end dictatorship
with dictatorship.

Whether the grand design for communism had been long present in
his mind or unfolded only in the wake of his attack on Stalin, Khrushchev had already begun to undermine the foundations of the ideocratic
principality in both theory and practice in an open session of the Twentieth Congress, before the secret speech. He used the congress as a platform for launching revisions of key doctrines that had long propped up
the principality's harsh rule. He concentrated on its ideology-based jus-
tifications for that rule, which portrayed it as a protracted emergency
regime for coping with the dangers of a global class war between two
hostile camps.

He first indicated that both war and violent socialist revolutions were
avoidable. He announced that war was no longer "fatalistically" inevitable and that "peaceful" transitions from capitalism to socialism had
now become possible. Later, at the Twenty-second Congress, he broadened the new doctrine into the categorical declaration that the danger
of war itself would dissipate entirely within the life of the present gen-

[11]For an original account of Khrushchev's resort to classic Stalinist tactics in struggle, see
Myron Rush, *The Rise of Khrushchev* (Washington, D.C.: Public Affairs Press, 1958).

eration. What was most striking about these pronouncements was that they overturned key doctrines not just of Stalin but also of Lenin. Stalin, after all, had merely elaborated upon Lenin with his formulations of hostile capitalist encirclement and two-camp class war. Khrushchev discarded Stalin's doctrine of capitalist encirclement at the specially called Twenty-first Congress in 1959.

This was the necessary groundwork for attacking Stalin's justification of a police state (which the Yugoslavs had ridiculed as "the state that does not wither.") At the Twenty-first Congress, Khrushchev disclosed that a new Party program, looking to an imminent coming of communism and the withering away of the state, was in preparation for the Twenty-second Congress regularly scheduled for 1961. The new program would replace the existing one, which had been produced under Lenin's aegis in 1919.

In keeping with his new doctrines on the reduced danger of war, Khrushchev further declared at the Twenty-first Congress that the victory of socialism in the Soviet Union was complete and final. This declaration was complemented by formulations about the waning of class struggle inside the Soviet Union and the ending of the need for "political arrests." These formulations undercut the Stalinist justification for maintaining an armed camp and police regime—to resist an increasingly dangerous and insidious class enemy alarmed by the successful advance of socialism.

Khrushchev's formulations were supposed to prepare the ground for what he intended to be a climactic Twenty-second Congress, which would both ratify this new program and provide him with an opportunity for another excoriation of Stalin and his works, this time a public one. His revisions of ideological doctrines, though seemingly a scholastic exercise, were of the essence in seeking change in the ideocratic regime. They opened the way for the revelation at the 1961 congress that the "dictatorship of the proletariat" instituted by Lenin and magnified by Stalin was at an end and that a new party and state "of the whole people" had emerged to replace it.[12] This meant, according to Khru-

---

[12]The announcement of the end of the dictatorship of the proletariat deeply offended the ideologically orthodox. Burlatsky, a long-time insider in Party circles, recalls that O. V. Kuusinen, then a member of the Party secretariat who supported Khrushchev on this issue, had sent out a memorandum to Party leaders explaining the forthcoming announcement. This memo, he says, caused "a real storm among many leaders." He re-

shchev's new program, that the Soviet state was "withering away," as foreseen by Marxism, and that its coercive agencies were losing their reason for being, as the classless society and communist self-rule approached.

Khrushchev promoted various measures to lend substance to these claims. For example, local volunteer militias and "comrades' courts" were formed through the allegedly spontaneous initiatives of workers and youth, as evidence of the development of popular self-governance. Under the new program, "public" organizations such as the trade unions and the Young Communist League, or Komsomol, were slated to take over gradually the functions of governance from the devolving state apparatus.

Khrushchev also combined the transition to communism with his much-heralded goal of producing an abundance of food and consumer goods. His drive to overtake the United States in per capita production of meat, milk, and butter was central to this objective, though it was to prove wholly unattainable. He made attempts to boost agricultural output and to raise the rural standard of living. He revived his old plan for agro-cities (*agrogoroda*), which he had boldly but fruitlessly urged on Stalin shortly before the latter's death. Khrushchev's optimism about improving living conditions rested on the brief spell of success that his agricultural program enjoyed in the second half of the 1950s. After Khrushchev's fall, Suslov made clear his detestation of such consumer or "goulash" communism.

Even before the new Party program was unveiled and the declaration made that the Soviet state was in the process of "withering away," Khrushchev had already begun major practical efforts to effect a devolution of the centralized state. In 1957, he introduced two sweeping reforms: a decentralization of industrial management through regional councils of national economy (*sovnarkhozy*) and the abolition of the system of machine-tractor stations (MTS) in the countryside. The Politburo majority that nearly ousted him in June 1957, failing only when Marshal Zhukov took his side, saw the reforms as impermissibly heterodox. With his chief opponents out of the way, Khrushchev implemented both re-

counts being present in Kuusinen's office when the latter received a call from another top Party leader (left unnamed), who "shouted at him over the telephone: 'How could you encroach on the holy of holies of Leninism—the dictatorship of the proletariat?' " Burlatsky, "Khrushchev."

forms. However, the central bureaucracy in time blunted their thrust and promoted various forms of de facto recentralization.

After the Twenty-second Congress, Khrushchev pursued a new line of attack. This time he struck without warning at the traditional command apparatus of the Party itself, which was the real stumbling block to his grand design for reform. In late 1962, he divided the Party hierarchy into a dual system of industrial and agricultural committees, replacing the "territorial" with a "production" principle of organization. His goal was to shift the Party's traditional concentration from political and ideological matters to economic matters—in effect, to convert regional and local Party secretaries from little Stalins to economic executives. The 1957 industrial reform and the 1962 Party reform were among Khrushchev's most notable attempts to undercut the overall structure of command "from above."

Khrushchev was striving to find, within the Marxian ideology and through the Party institutions, a way out of the centralized despotism of the Soviet regime. He saw no real alternative in strategy and perhaps could not conceive of any. He was by all indications genuinely under the spell of the Marxian utopian vision; indeed, he even proclaimed that the first higher stage of communism would arrive in the USSR by 1980.

Needless to say, his millennial expectations were not shared by his colleagues in the Politburo. The undertow of resistance in the Party elite to his program was also strong, and it ultimately prevailed. After deposing Khrushchev in 1964, the new prince of the Party, Brezhnev, and his allies in the Politburo repealed the reforms in short order. The gap between the image of the brave new world of communism just ahead and the harsh Soviet reality was too great. In the last analysis, this ruthless and hardheaded Communist ruler was the victim of an illusion.

Khrushchev's grandson, the historian Nikita Adzhubei, has observed that his grandfather "sincerely wanted to bring the cause to a logical conclusion" through his "concept of a dash forward to communism."[13] However, according to Adzhubei, Khrushchev came to realize toward the end of his rule that his concept was "incorrect." Adzhubei adds: "He began to depart from it and turn to new quests that were cut short by his downfall."[14]

---

[13]Interview on the Moscow television program "Vremia," August 2, 1989, in Foreign Broadcast Information Service (FBIS), *Daily Report: USSR*, August 4, 1989, p. 87.
[14]Ibid.

In the end, Khrushchev was brought down by the aristocrats of the ideocratic principality trained by Stalin. The nomenklatura's understanding of the necessities of power in sustaining such a regime collided with Khrushchev's utopianism. They saw his ideas as not only wishful thinking but a mortal danger to the regime's perpetuation.

That Khrushchev had in mind a transformed order of rule as part and parcel of his design for the transition to communist society was revealed in another of his radical proposals at the Twenty-second Party Congress. This was his plan for the periodic replacement of members of the leading group. A provision for the rotation of leadership was to serve as a barrier to the concentration and abuse of power. This notion that leaders were to be limited to fixed terms struck a highly sensitive nerve inside the Party apparatus. It stirred such opposition in the ruling elite that, by the time its final version had been incorporated into the new Party statutes, it had been greatly watered down. To have carried the plan out in its original form would have entailed a major change in the Party statutes and would have been a blow to its autocratic structure. This concept of rotation revealed Khrushchev's recognition of the need for a regularized process of selecting and retiring leaders, and it would have been a step in the direction of duly instituted rather than arbitrary rule.[15]

Khrushchev did not have a clear idea of what a legal regime and a legitimate rulership required, but over time he had come to see that something was missing in the Soviet order. There were, for example, several curious digressions in which he dwelt on the responsibility and accountability of leaders, including himself, to the people at large, for example, in a speech reported in *Pravda* (July 20, 1963). He concluded that ultimately leaders come under the judgment of the people.

Khrushchev also insisted that rulers were subject to the principles of ethics. He went beyond the Marxist-Leninist view that "History" penalizes "political mistakes" only in a technical sense. On the contrary, Khrushchev declared that history judged the good and the evil that leaders do. Even in power, he spoke of Stalin's deeds not simply as excesses committed in the name of revolution (as Molotov had asserted) but as works of evil—"black deeds" that could not be washed "white" by any

---

[15]According to Burlatsky, "Khrushchev," Khrushchev saw the rotation plan as a guarantee against the concentration of power in a single person and against leaders' "outstaying their time." Burlatsky also says that the proposal stirred up more dispute within the leadership than anything else on the eve of the Twenty-second Party Congress.

manner or means.[16] His strictures about the judgments made of rulers were aimed at the attitudes and practices of the Stalinist generation, of which he was a part. Though it was a case of the sinner calling sinners to repentance, his words were a prescient warning to that generation to mend its ways or face harsh judgment from those they ruled.

Khrushchev thus presented himself as a leader who sought both the Party's and the people's assent to his reforms. He introduced the innovation of convening frequent and enlarged Central Committee meetings. Detailed stenographic accounts of the previously secret proceedings were now published—a first step toward glasnost. He also began the practice of submitting his major reform projects to nationwide "discussion." Though they were rather contrived affairs, these publicity procedures were an ambitious attempt to form a popular consensus in support of his projects.

KHRUSHCHEV'S FAILURE

All of Khrushchev's attempts to regularize and legitimize leadership behavior suffered from a fatal flaw. There was no way of separating them from the constant struggle to secure his power over and against his colleagues in the leadership. This struggle nullified all efforts to institutionalize his reforms. Further, there was no way that the public opinion he sought to win over to his side could be brought to bear in overcoming opposition to his program.

Khrushchev was aware of the absence of any office within the structure of the Party in which the prince of the Party could enjoy secure and clearly defined executive authority. Stalin had insulated his arbitrary power from challenge through his personal apparatus of terror. Khrushchev did not resort to such means of securing his power but sought vainly to regularize his position of executive power. In time, it became evident that he was not content with the title of first secretary (which had replaced the title of general secretary), with its formal implication that the occupant of the post was beholden to the Presidium (as the Politburo was now called). He began a search for a way of instituting a formal executive position somewhere else in the structure of the regime. In the year before his downfall, he was on one occasion characterized

---

[16]See, for example, the full version of Khrushchev's speech of July 19, 1963, in FBIS, *Daily Report: USSR*, July 20, 1963.

as the "head" of the Party Presidium in a Central Committee decree, but no formal office placing him over the Politburo was ever established.[17] He had earlier created a Party bureau for the Russian republic (RSFSR), with himself as "chairman," laying the ground for justifying a similar post in the Presidium. But that plan never materialized, and the new bureau with its chairmanship did not survive its creator's fall.

Khrushchev also had himself made chairman of the Council of Ministers and thus the head of government, but he evidently saw no potential in converting the chairmanship of the Supreme Soviet—a purely ceremonial position at the time—into a legitimized supreme executive.[18] Khrushchev admired and perhaps envied his youthful opposite, John F. Kennedy, who enjoyed the stable authority of the U.S. presidency.

Khrushchev's efforts to legitimate a position of executive authority similar to that found in a representative civil state were doomed from the start. Neither Party tradition nor the consent of a legitimizing constituency existed to provide the foundation for such an office. He was hobbled both by the autocratic structure of power in which he rose and by his own inability to discern a path out of it. He also faced a dilemma. He was partly a victim of his own actions, for his attack on Stalin's tyranny, and his unwillingness and perhaps inability to resort to Stalinist terror in a power struggle, rendered him incapable of achieving the personal dominance so necessary to a prince of the Party.[19]

Nonetheless, he did seek, as other Communist princes had sought, to concentrate power in his hands in order to achieve his goals and defend himself against rivals. Even an incipient "cult of personality" was manufactured around him, but the image of hero-leader hardly fit his personality and produced little real effect.[20] Indeed, his program was itself

---

[17]*Pravda*, June 22, 1963. See Carl A. Linden, *Khrushchev and the Soviet Leadership: With an Epilogue on Gorbachev* (Baltimore: Johns Hopkins University Press, 1990), 179.

[18]Burlatsky has said that he once suggested to Khrushchev the creation of an executive presidency but that he was not responsive to the idea. Gorbachev did create such a position and so established a new base of power outside the Party.

[19]In an interview after his ouster, Khrushchev indicated that his position had been strong from the time he routed his opponents in June 1957 to the time of the U-2 incident in 1960 but that subsequently he "was no longer in full control." A. McGehee Harvey, "A 1969 Conversation with Khrushchev: The Beginning of His Fall from Power," *Life*, December 18, 1979. See also Linden, *Khrushchev and the Soviet Leadership*, 224.

[20]On May Day in 1959, *Pravda* contrived to apply the special Russian term *vozhd'*, or supreme leader—an epithet associated with Stalin—to Khrushchev, in connection with his receipt of the Lenin Peace Prize. The paper's editors rendered the common English word "leader," which had been used in a speech in English given by an Indian peace

a design for the devolution of power from the autocratic center. Yet he never found himself in a position in which he could let power go without danger to himself. For his pains in trying to pressure his colleagues into supporting his plans, they accused him of "commandism" and "hare-brained schemes" in their public criticism of his leadership after removing him from power. Ironically, Khrushchev's last act in office was his decision not to fight his challengers but to surrender his power to them.

In the last analysis, the defenders of the ideocratic principality rejected Khrushchev's vision of a devolution of power as called for by the ideology's ultimate goals. A restorationist prince then arose to lead the self-protective nomenklatura, in the figure of the uninspired and uninspiring Leonid Brezhnev. This prince of the last Stalin generation, with the aid of the Party's high priest, Mikhail Suslov, worked to salvage the ideocratic autocracy. The two rejected Khrushchev's "subjective" communist utopianism and replaced it with their soberly "objective" doctrines of "developed socialism" and "scientific communism."[21] The first of these negated Khrushchev's vision of imminent communism, asserting that the socialist stage was a lengthy historical process before the stage of communism was reached. The second restored the portrayal of a protracted struggle between the capitalist and socialist worlds. Discarded was Khrushchev's vision of a relatively safe and peaceful transition to world socialism. Khrushchev's notion of the "state-of-the-whole-people," though retained, was severed from any "withering away" of the state. Under Brezhnev, statist doctrines were reinforced and were codified in the constitution of 1977. Suslov also held that in its external relations the Soviet Union served as the vanguard of the "dictatorship of the proletariat" in the world struggle against capitalism.

Khrushchev's rotation-of-leaders statute also did not survive his downfall. Brezhnev and his colleagues reasserted the principle of the cooptation of all functionaries from the top down, and they even restored the traditional terms of Politburo and general secretary. The changes signified a return to the original forms of the ideocratic autoc-

---

activist praising Khrushchev's work for peace, as *vozhd'*. The application of this term to Khrushchev, however, was not repeated.

[21] An official textbook entitled *Nauchnyi kommunizm* (Moscow, 1983) elaborated this neo-Stalinist doctrine. The English edition, *Scientific Communism*, incongruously appeared in 1986, during Gorbachev's first year in power. Gorbachev soon disposed of this Suslov-inspired doctrine.

racy. Brezhnev as general secretary gradually built his dominance within the leading group, but he did so in the manner of an oligarch-in-chief. It would be another two decades before a new leader-reformer arose to make a perilous attempt to cross the bridge from prince of the Party to presidency of a nascent representative civil state.

Fortunately for his country and the world, Khrushchev was not like Stalin; he is said to have once quipped, regarding the Politburo of his time, that "if you laid fifteen of us end to end we wouldn't equal one Stalin."[22] His rise and fall illuminate the dilemma of the leader-reformer both in Russian and in Soviet history. Trying to escape from the bane of despotic power by means of that power is a "mission impossible" for any such leader. The need for reform in both eras grew out of the central defect of despotism: its tendency to drain away the spontaneous vitality of the peoples under its sway. That tendency was captured in the succinct sentence of the great Russian historian Vasily Kliuchevsky: "The state swells and the people shrink." Under the tsar, rule "from above" was justified by divine right; under the Marxian prince, by ideology.

THE ORIGINS OF THE IDEOCRATIC PRINCIPALITY

If Khrushchev was a victim of his origins, the larger question concerning the genesis of the ideocratic principality itself still remains. Although it found hospitable soil in the heartland of the Russian empire shaken by revolution in 1917, it cannot be attributed merely to continuity from tsarism and the autocratic element in Russian political culture. That something more was at work has become manifest in the fact that the Marxist ideocratic principality was implanted in many countries of widely different political cultures ranging from West to East, from Cuba to China. The Russian autocracy, for all its imperial ambitions, was traditional and nation-based; the ideocratic principality has been revolutionary and transnational in aspiration.[23]

---

[22][This remark has often been attributed to Khrushchev and has the ring of authenticity, but it lacks clear documentation—Ed.]

[23]In Carl A. Linden, *The Soviet Party-State: The Politics of Ideocratic Despotism* (New York: Praeger, 1983), the Soviet regime is classified as an "ideocratic party-state," which is presented as a counterpoint to the modern representative civil state. The party-state had its origin in a new kind of prince, and, as Gorbachev's attempt to reform the power structure of the party-state showed, it has depended fundamentally on its prince to maintain itself in power. In the chart on pages 92–93 of my book, Gorbachev's rule would be placed on the left side of the circle, below Khrushchev's concept of regime. Gorbachev moved downward toward the civil state and away from the ideocratic party-

The seed of the ideocratic principality came from the West. Combining ideology and power, it expressed something present not just in Russian but also in Western political culture. In fact, we must look back to the French Revolution, the precursor of the Russian Revolution, for illumination. The first modern ideocratic prince was Napoleon. His claim to dominion rested not on hereditary succession, as did that of the tsar and all traditional monarchs, but on a revolutionary idea. He was a new prince "from below" who rose to rule "from above." He was a self-appointed autocrat, in the literal sense of the term—a "self-power." Most fitting is the famous portrayal of Napoleon by Jacques-Louis David, showing him crowning himself. Napoleon took the ideas of the French Revolution and translated them into a new discourse of rule, a discourse that today is commonly called *ideology*. His famed remark, "I am the end and culmination of the Revolution," was prototypical of the standpoint of the new prince.

Napoleon was fascinated with Destutt de Tracy's formulation of the concept of *idéologie*. Destutt de Tracy was a member of the Revolutionary Convention's Institute of France, dedicated to spreading the ideas of the Enlightenment and the Revolution. His doctrine of ideology was designed to provide a scientific, nonreligious, and nonmetaphysical foundation for modern society.[24] Only later did the emperor turn to using established religion to legitimate his power and begin reviling the "ideologues" as subversives.

Lenin must be deemed the twentieth-century successor of Napoleon, an ideocratic prince par excellence. He also drew on the revolutionary idea and on the ideology of Marxism, which traced its origins to the French Revolution as well. Lenin's refurbished Marxism broadly conformed to the basic concept of ideology set forth by Destutt de Tracy. Lenin's great innovation was his concept of the party, which in his view was the ideology organized. In *What Is to Be Done?* he contended that without "revolutionary theory" there could be no movement or vanguard party; what he produced was nothing less than "ideocratic power" or "ideocracy."[25] Where Napoleon transformed the French army into

state, even though he was being subjected to pressure to halt the disintegration of the Soviet order.

[24] Antoine Louis Claude Destutt de Tracy coined the term and elaborated it into a doctrine in his five-volume work, *Les éléments d'idéologie* (1801–15). "Ideology" was to be a new science of ideas, on which all other sciences would rest, and a new basis for society, replacing religion and tradition.

[25] For a relevant passage, see Daniels, *A Documentary History of Communism*, 1: 11. The

an organ for the projection of idea-based power, Lenin created the party militant. Napoleon's army bore ideas as well as arms, but his imperium remained a kind of praetorian regime, in the tradition of Caesar. He lacked the conception of the ideocratic party that Lenin developed out of his reading of Marx. Lenin, it appears, was not fully aware of what he had wrought. He saw his "proletarian dictatorship" not as the new principality that it was but as a transitional regime to a classless society, a society without rulers and ruled.

Lenin believed his own fiction. This is a fault in a prince who, if he is to maintain his power, must stand above the ideology he propounds. While he must not act so as to reveal this truth about himself, he cannot afford to be a "true believer," in any simple sense of the term; if he were, he would be in danger of losing his grip on the realities of power that sustain his princely office. Khrushchev, like Lenin, also failed to understand this basic truth. He labored under the impression that he had merely restored the Party to its proper role as the agency of communist transformation, overlooking the fact that it was the executive apparatus of a principality. However, he did not have the protection of the prestige of the victorious founder that Lenin enjoyed and was brought down by a pretender from that apparatus.

Stalin, on the other hand, did understand this aspect of ideocratic autocracy very well. He was the ideologue-prince who brought the new office of general secretary to its full and self-conscious consummation and developed the totalitarian potential in Leninism. He used first the Party, then the organization of terror begun by Lenin, and finally the Party-controlled army to expand his ideocratic imperium at home and abroad. At all times, he understood that his princely power must stand supreme over and above its instruments, including the Party itself.

Khrushchev's attack on Stalin at the Twentieth Party Congress in effect removed the head from the body of the modern ideocratic leviathan. He believed, to his own cost, that the body could prosper without its

---

Russian philosopher Nicolas Berdyaev used the term "ideocracy" to characterize the Soviet regime in his book, *The Origin of Russian Communism* (Ann Arbor: University of Michigan Press, 1960; originally published in Russian in 1937). "Ideocracy" is a parallel term with "theocracy," but it is secular and combines dogma with power. John Adams, who reviled Destutt de Tracy's idea of ideology and detested notions of government resting on contrived abstract concepts, may have been the first person to use the term. He suggested that the emperor Napoleon "coin another word in his new mint, in conformity or analogy with Ideology, and call every government in France from 1789 to 1799, an IDEOCRACY." *The Works of John Adams* (Boston, 1850–56), 6: 402–3.

head. The Party and its ideology had been overridden but not fatally corrupted by the great dictator. Khrushchev did not fully realize that his design for reform was profoundly at odds with the kind of regime he led. What he later described as his contribution to a new "style of leadership" was precisely what paved the way to his overthrow in October 1964. He said:

I am old and tired. Let them cope by themselves. I've done the main thing. Relations among us, the style of leadership, has changed drastically. Could anyone have dreamed of telling Stalin that he didn't suit us any more, and suggesting that he retire? Not even a wet spot would have remained where we had been standing. Now everything is different. The fear's gone and we can talk as equals. That's my contribution. I won't put up a fight.[26]

Khrushchev's undermining of the position of the prince may have led to Brezhnev's coup d'état, but it also initiated the crisis of the regime, not only in the Soviet Union but throughout the Communist world.

Gorbachev saw the flaw in Khrushchev's design: The crisis of the ideocratic principality could be overcome not through its own doctrines but only through new doctrines and a new form of ruling power. Thus, in 1989 he abandoned the Party as his instrument of ruling power and attempted to shift his position as "Number One" to the apex of a newly created parliamentary government. Whether he could succeed in this bold venture, in the midst of the revolutionary upheaval that this very venture precipitated, was always very much in doubt. However, Gorbachev also looked westward for his pattern of reform, the pattern of the modern idea-based democratic republic of the American and French revolutions.

There is a strong impression that events have come full circle both in the history of Russia and in the history of the West. The circle began, it has been suggested, when Napoleon exploited the republican ideology of the French Revolution to form a new kind of modern principality. More than a century and a half passed during which the new principality and unstable French republics came and went. Finally, an innovative French prince, Charles de Gaulle, came upon the scene and gave to the French republic the stability that its democratic politics required, through the institution of an executive presidency. He also relinquished his princely powers for the sake of the republic. This was the constitu-

[26]William Taubman, ed., *Khrushchev on Khrushchev: An Inside Account of the Man and His Era by His Son, Sergei Khrushchev* (Boston: Little, Brown, 1990), 154.

tional innovation that supplied the missing link in French republicanism. That missing link goes back to the Revolution's killing of the monarch and thus the destruction of the principle of unity and legitimacy that the hereditary crown provided. De Gaulle's resolution of the antinomy between principality and republic, which disrupted France's politics for so long, rested, however, on the idea of a democratic republic as proclaimed by the French Revolution. The Napoleonic prince was domesticated in a strong but constitutionally limited presidency of the republic.

By contrast, the Marxian ideocratic principality founded by Lenin in this century had its roots in Marx's fateful rejection of democratic republicanism. Marx began as a radical democrat but was disillusioned by the compromises with the traditional order that the nineteenth-century republicans made in their rise to power. In anger, he turned to the idea of a universal class struggle leading to a revolutionary dictatorship and a communist society. Marx's theory provided the *sufficient* conditions for the emergence of the modern Marxian principality. Lenin, with his creation of the militant party of central command, provided the *necessary* conditions. Stalin perfected its totalitarian form and, along with Lenin, became the exemplar of the legion of Marxian princes of our century.

Khrushchev boldly ventured onto the path of reform to find an escape route from the form of rule that had carried him to power as a Marxian prince. His mission was prefigured in his attack on Stalin, was implied in his reforms, and was made explicit in his program for a shortcut to communism, his vision of a society free of domination "from above." In his quest, he tried to erase the traces of his Stalinist past and sever the Marxian ideology from its tie with the rule of the dictator-prince. In the end, this "counterprince" of the Party was unable to break free from his origins. The Stalin-trained party oligarchs around him turned against him in alarm over the direction he was taking. His successor, Brezhnev, worked to repair the internal injury done to the regime by Khrushchev's destruction of the Stalin myth and his unintended exposure of the utopian character of the communist goal. The regime's claim to legitimacy was compromised, however. Brezhnev rebuilt the ideocratic principality after a fashion, but it proved to be a transitory restoration. Under his policy of immobilism, the Soviet command system lost momentum and sank into inertia and corruption. He presided over a Politburo gerontocracy that slowly faded from the scene upon his own lingering demise and the fleeting incumbencies of the ailing figures of Iurii Andropov and Konstantin Chernenko.

Gorbachev took the stage with the aim of rescuing the Soviet regime in some recognizable if altered form. However, his bold but improvisational forays into radical reformation only brought the underlying crisis into the open. In his search for a way out, he executed a dramatic but perilous leap from the post of prince of the Party to that of president of a new republic. He looked to the representative civil states of the West for a cure for the malady of ideocratic despotism. But with the old regime in dissolution and the new in precarious genesis, the Soviet Union itself disintegrated into its constituent nations. Once again, the lands of the former Soviet Union face the choice between democratic and national revolution and the tragic return of despotism.

16

Khrushchev's reforms in the light of perestroika

VITALII S. LEL'CHUK

THE REEVALUATION OF KHRUSHCHEV

Nikita S. Khrushchev was first secretary of the Central Committee of the Communist Party of the Soviet Union between 1953 and 1964 and chairman of the Council of Ministers from 1958 to 1964. But scholarly analysis of the changes he instituted in Soviet society has only recently begun in Russia. Some attempts were made in the Soviet Union in the late 1950s and early 1960s, but those works were openly laudatory. Just about every action undertaken by Khrushchev was portrayed as a major accomplishment of the Party and government, designed to strengthen the cause of world peace and socialist forces and to increase the economic and political might of the Soviet Union as well as both the cultural growth and the prosperity of its people. Such publications reached their peak when Khrushchev's seventieth birthday was celebrated in April 1964.

These works are now viewed through the prism of the decades that followed; yet taken as a whole, they permit us to recognize what was radically new in Soviet life at that time, what the limits of innovation were, and what remained of the former way of life: of the psychology, habits, and stereotypes that arose and were perpetuated during Stalin's regime.

The events of October 1964 demonstrated the correlation of the old and the new. The elite, who until then had been pulling along with Khrushchev in the same harness, stripped the leader of all his posts and sharply broke with him, accusing him of "subjectivism" and "voluntarism." It became obvious that the system that had been formed chiefly during the 1930s and 1940s, now often referred to as the "administrative-command" system, remained viable and rested on a broad base of support.

Only in the late 1980s, from the perspective of perestroika, could Soviet society soberly evaluate both the first post-Stalin decade and the character of the retreat from the decisions of the Twentieth through the Twenty-second Party congresses, which have by now become firmly linked with Khrushchev's "thaw." The problem of Khrushchev's reforms and their fate was especially urgent and relevant in light of the growing resistance encountered by Gorbachev. To reduce the question to "inconsistencies" in the Khrushchevian reforms would be to minimize the complexity and significance of the fundamental change that had occurred. An objective approach is necessary not only to explain the meaning of this first stage in overcoming Stalinism but also to help us better understand and resolve the crisis situation that followed.

One additional aspect of the problem should be noted. The leadership that deposed Khrushchev did not dare publicly to question the principles that were embodied in the decisions of the Twentieth and Twenty-second Party congresses. It did, however, begin immediately to change the previous policies and to cast the very name of the former leader into oblivion. Was this just a question of personal hostility, or did Brezhnev and his collaborators really view Khrushchev as an accidental and historically insignificant reformer?

Khrushchev's enemies were no fools. They well knew his leadership qualities: a thirst for action, extraordinary organizational skills, and immense drive, informed by extensive political experience. Many instinctively and some consciously were fearful and worried, not so much about the future evolution of society as about their personal careers and privileges. These were provided by the system whose very existence was now becoming, or could become, questionable. These men were taught early on that the key question of revolution is the question of power. As soon as they were threatened with the possibility of losing power, they united against the individual who embodied the threat most clearly.

The slogan of the victors was a return to "stability." The second half of the 1960s and the early 1970s were filled with all sorts of discussions and promises, primarily of economic reform. The promise of reform permeated the work of the plenums of the Central Committee of March and September 1965 and of subsequent Party congresses. Reforms were to embrace agriculture, industry, transport, construction—the entire economy. By now, we know what this led to.

For many years after the October 1964 plenum of the Central Committee, Party documents, textbooks on the history of the Party and the Soviet Union, and hundreds of books, articles, and dissertations uniformly referred to the historical role of that meeting. In these interpretations, the plenum struck a crushing blow against voluntarism and subjectivism and set a course toward stabilization, a course that produced positive results and permitted the adoption of more thoughtfully considered decisions. Such evaluations persisted for a long time, and their echoes can be found even in Mikhail Gorbachev's book, *Perestroika and New Thinking,* published in late 1987. Similar formulas could be found in the new Party program, also adopted in 1987.

After October 1964, Khrushchev's name, as a rule, was absent from scholarly works and official documents, or it appeared only to accuse him of error or miscalculation. His photographs and portraits also disappeared, and cuts were even made in documentary films that had showed him meeting with the cosmonauts and the heads of foreign governments and attending various conferences. One may well ask where the millions of secondary-school and college students, graduating into the labor force in the 1970s and 1980s, could get any idea whatsoever about the real life and activity of Khrushchev, who was fated to begin the process of the de-Stalinization of Soviet society. As always happens in such cases, society would pay dearly for elisions of historical memory among the broad masses of the population.

Perestroika made it crucially important not only to remove the so-called white spots from our history but also to rethink the conceptualization of the basic stages in the evolution of Soviet society. The urgent need to escape Stalinist fetters and the whole system of rule by administrative command resurrected the figure of Khrushchev from oblivion. The breakthrough took place in 1988, when articles about him and his reforms began appearing in newspapers and in historical, literary, and public-affairs periodicals. Well-known commentators and literary critics, such as Fedor Burlatsky and Anatolii Strelianyi, took up their pens, as did representatives of the younger generation of Soviet historians—E. Zubkova, V. Glotov, L. Openkin, N. Razuvaeva, and others.[1] The pub-

---

[1] Fedor Burlatsky, "Posle Stalina: Zametki o politicheskoi ottepeli," *Novyi mir,* 1988, no. 10; Anatolii Strelianyi, "Poslednii romantik," *Druzhba narodov,* 1988, no. 11; E. Zubkova, "Opyt i uroki nezavershennykh povorotov 1956 i 1965 godov," *Voprosy istorii KPSS,* 1988, no. 4; V. Glotov, "O nekotorykh urokakh istoricheskogo opyta deiatel'nosti KPSS vo vtoroi polovine 50-kh—pervoi polovine 80-kh godov," ibid.; L. Openkin, "Byli

lication of excerpts from Khrushchev's reminiscences and of the memoirs of his son-in-law, A. Adzhubei, were important events.[2] A clear indication of public interest in Khrushchev's personality can be seen in the volumes of reprinted newspaper and journal articles and recollections of Khrushchev's life and activity, pertaining mostly to the 1950s and 1960s.[3]

It was still too early then to make a well-rounded judgment. Some writers knew their "hero" personally and had worked under him. For them, he remained a living individual, capable of making major decisions affecting the country as a whole and at the same time a generous host, a jokester, a feisty conversationalist unafraid of vulgarities, and a passionate aficionado of stories about the past. In this approach to illuminating the past, personal feelings often submerge objective evaluation. Such works, therefore, should be treated not so much as scholarly studies, even if the authors intended them as such, but rather as historical sources requiring analysis. The works of historians, meanwhile, still lacked the necessary body of factual data. This circumstance inhibited reaching sound conclusions and sometimes inspired overly generalized, abstract judgments about possible options in the struggle for power after Stalin's death, about alternatives that were not realized, about turns in policy that were not implemented. Moreover, works by Russian historians have largely been written without reference to foreign scholarship, whose findings could and should be taken into account. Nevertheless, these were promising beginnings.

New materials that appeared in 1988 and 1989, especially the publications of N. Barsukov and Khrushchev's son, Sergei,[4] and *Ogonek*'s interview with Vladimir Semichastnyi,[5] who headed the KGB in the early 1960s, gave a clear picture of what was involved in deposing

li povoroty v razvitii sovetskogo obshchestva v 50-e i v 60-e gody?" ibid., no. 8; N. Razuvaeva, "Ekonomicheskaia politika KPSS v 60-e—pervoi polovine 80-kh godov: protivorechiia i trudnost' razvitiia," ibid., no. 9.

[2] Nikita S. Khrushchev, "Vospominaniia," *Ogonek*, 1989, nos. 27, 28, 30, 31, and 33–37, and 1990, nos. 1–8; "Memuary Nikity Sergeevicha Khrushcheva," *Voprosy istorii*, 1990, nos. 1–5; A. Adzhubei, *Te desiat' let* (Moscow, 1989).

[3] Nikita S. Khrushchev, *Materialy k biografii* (Moscow, 1989); *Svet i teni "velikogo desiatiletiia": N. Khrushchev i ego vremia* (Leningrad, 1989). The latter work is a collection that includes articles and essays by, among others, V. Tendriakov, L. Kolodnyi, M. Romm, and M. Gefter.

[4] N. Barsukov, "Proval antipartiinoi gruppy," *Kommunist*, 1990, no. 8; idem, "Kak smeshchali Khrushcheva," *Obshchestvennye nauki*, 1989, no. 6; Sergei N. Khrushchev, "Pensioner soiuznogo znacheniia," *Ogonek*, 1988, nos. 40–43.

[5] V. Semichastnyi, "Ia by spravilsia s liuboi rabotoi," *Ogonek*, 1989, no. 24.

the head of the Party and of the motives behind it. It had been a real conspiracy that united quite disparate forces. The victors were members of the elite ranks of the Party-state apparatus, who soon began a campaign to rehabilitate Stalin and the methods of government characteristic of his regime. The previous forms of centralized administration were revived, and no desire was shown to change the existing state of affairs. Now that we are aware of the consequences of this policy for Soviet society, we must reevaluate the decisions of the October 1964 plenum, and we must reconsider Khrushchev's reforms. As part of this effort, it is worthwhile to acquaint ourselves with Khrushchev's own testimony, given when he was in retirement.

THE STRUGGLE FOR POWER

Khrushchev was once asked what future generations would perceive as his greatest service to posterity. He, in turn, asked the opinion of his questioner, who said that Khrushchev would be known in history primarily as an enemy of Stalin's cult of personality. Khrushchev demurred, insisting that any leader of the Party and the country would have had to do the same, as there were no alternatives. He then gave his own answer: "I see my chief merit to have been the liquidation of Beria and of his system. People may also give me credit for housing construction, for [my] concern for the people. Indeed, I expended much effort and health on that business. Perhaps descendants will think of adding something else, but this is especially important."[6] The tape of that conversation was made over two decades ago, and the time of the descendants has arrived. Let us address the question. In my opinion, Khrushchev was entitled to emphasize his role in the fall of Lavrentii P. Beria, but is this an appropriate subject in the context of a general discussion of the subject of reform? In Soviet reference works, social reform is defined as a societal transformation instituted by the ruling circles with the objective of resolving certain contradictions of socioeconomic and political life. It does not take much argument to prove that the arrest and condemnation of one of the leaders of the Party and government, a man who disposed of internal military and state security forces practically without any control, was indeed a mighty blow against the administrative-*punitive* sys-

---

[6]*Obnovlenie Rossii: Sbornik nauchnykh trudov prepodavatelei i aspirantov Rossiiskogo gosudarstvennogo gumanitarnogo universiteta* (Moscow, 1991), 95.

tem (*administrativno-karatel'naia sistema*) that arose under Stalin and that was the mainstay of his unlimited autocratic power. The emphasis on "punitive" is deliberate, to distinguish this administrative-punitive system from the administrative-*command* system (*administrativno-komandnaia sistema*), the former being the most reactionary manifestation of the latter.

In the late 1920s and early 1930s, illegal repressions became widespread in the Soviet Union. If a citizen was charged with planning or undertaking an act of terrorism, the investigation was limited to a period of ten days, the indictment was presented to the accused only twenty-four hours before trial, and the trial was held without the participation of either a prosecutor or a defense lawyer. Judicial appeals or petitions for pardon were not allowed, and the death sentence was carried out immediately. In 1937, the same procedure was applied in cases of wrecking and sabotage. Upon the initiative of L. M. Kaganovich, political cases were treated in the same fashion, and since there were so many of them, Molotov's proposal to pass sentences by lists was accepted. The lawlessness was such that, beginning in 1938, punishments were determined essentially by two individuals: Beria, as the people's commissar of internal affairs, and A. Ia. Vyshinskii, as the procurator of the Soviet Union. Similar teams functioned in the provinces.

During what for a long time was called the Great Patriotic War (1941–45), Stalin abolished many national autonomous regions and sent into exile, or even subjected to genocide, whole peoples, among them the Volga Germans, Crimean Tatars, Balkars, Chechens and Ingush, Kalmyks, and Karachais. Many Soviet soldiers who were taken prisoner by the Germans became victims of Stalin's arbitrariness at the end of the war. Finally, both the "Leningrad affair" of 1949 [in which a number of important Party officials were accused of being "enemies of the people" and were executed—ed.] and the "doctors' plot" of 1953 [in which several prominent physicians were charged with conspiring to kill a number of Party leaders—ed.] were organized along the same lines. It is interesting to note that popular memory links these crimes to this very day with the officials in charge of the People's Commissariat of Internal Affairs (NKVD), such as Beria and N. I. Ezhov. Even at the time when they held high posts, their names inspired fear and horror, but that is precisely what the Stalinist regime required.

Events following Stalin's death demonstrated anew the danger presented by the retention of past forms and methods of governing the Party and the state. The composition of the new leadership was quickly decided upon—on March 5, 1953, the day Stalin died. Approximately two-thirds of the members of the Presidium of the Central Committee that had been approved at the Nineteenth Party Congress in October 1952 had been new faces, the rest being Stalin's old collaborators. One can only guess at Stalin's purpose in creating such a leadership, from which he selected the membership of the political bureau (Politburo) of the Presidium as well as an even more select group of individuals. On the day of Stalin's death, the Presidium was cut down to ten full members and four candidate members. The full members were N. A. Bulganin, L. P. Beria, K. E. Voroshilov, L. M. Kaganovich, G. M. Malenkov, A. I. Mikoyan, V. M. Molotov, M. G. Pervukhin, M. Z. Saburov, and Nikita Khrushchev. Thus, the membership preceding the Nineteenth Congress was for all practical purposes restored. It would be naive to assume that this took place spontaneously, without preliminary agreement.

The leading posts in the Party and government were retained by men who had been Stalin's closest collaborators. Malenkov became chairman of the Council of Ministers and presided over the meetings of the Presidium of the Central Committee. The apparatus of the Central Committee, the secretariat, was headed by Khrushchev, who was accordingly relieved from his duties as first secretary of the Moscow regional and city Party committees. Formally, Khrushchev was merely one of the secretaries of the Central Committee, but as the only secretary who was also a member of the Presidium, he naturally assumed the leading role among them. Molotov regained the portfolio of foreign minister. Beria greatly strengthened his position by heading the Ministry of Internal Affairs, which combined the former ministries of Internal Affairs and State Security. Moreover, he was first deputy chairman of the Council of Ministers of the USSR. Bulganin took over the Ministry of Defense, with Georgii Zhukov, now returned to Moscow, serving as his deputy. Voroshilov became chairman of the Presidium of the Supreme Soviet of the USSR, replacing N. M. Shvernik, who took over the trade unions. Thus, all the key posts in the Party and government were monopolized by the entourage of the dead leader, people who had known each other well and for a long time.

On March 10, the day after Stalin's funeral, the Party Presidium met, chaired by Malenkov, who noted that "we've got great abnormalities here, much has been going on according to the line of the cult of personality [*sic*]," and he stressed that "we consider it necessary to stop the politics of the cult of personality."[7] Should one conclude from this that Malenkov took the leading role in raising this issue? There is no need to jump to conclusions or to imitate those authors who deduce the existence of serious differences of opinion or position from the pronouncements of different leaders.

The decisive role in the struggle for leadership was played not by words, which were nothing but camouflage, but by experience, energy, actions, and deeds. Beria, supported by the organs of state repression, had long striven for power but proved most vulnerable. On April 4, 1953, the newspapers disclosed that the investigation of the "doctors' plot" was being dropped (the official announcement of the "plot" had been published only a few months earlier, on January 13). The world was told that the accusations against the doctors were false and that the evidence supposedly proving their guilt had been extracted by impermissible and strictly illegal methods. All the accused were fully rehabilitated, and those who had falsified the results of the investigation were charged with criminal responsibility. The announcement aroused the interest of millions, but only a few knew the significance that the leaders of the Communist party attached to it. They had recently discussed and approved the text of the announcement, only to find it abruptly published by the Ministry of Internal Affairs, Beria's agency. In other words, Beria was deliberately and unceremoniously trying to take personal credit for the restoration of legality. This is how both Khrushchev and Bulganin interpreted it and how they told the story, in separate interviews, to Professor Ia. Etinger in the late 1960s.[8]

The writer Konstantin Simonov says in his memoirs that, soon after the case against the doctors was dropped, the members of the Central Committee were acquainted with documents pertaining to Stalin's role in the affair. Again, the idea was Beria's, and it was he who prepared the materials, as if to demonstrate that he was not involved in the affair or in Stalin's crimes generally. He also proposed that an amnesty be issued by a decree of the Presidium of the Supreme Soviet at the end of March.[9] The dictator-to-be was creating his new image.

His experienced rivals could not but see that the hour for decisive

---

[7]Tsentral'nyi partiinyi arkhiv (IML), *fond* 629, *opis'* 1, *delo* 54, p. 2 (hereafter cited as TsPA).
[8]Author's interview with Ia. Etinger in April 1990.
[9]Konstantin Simonov, *Glazami cheloveka moego pokoleniia* (Moscow, 1989).

steps had arrived. They knew Beria well enough to realize that any delay was tantamount to death. They also knew that he had a file on each one of them. It was easy to stop the reading of documents that had been prepared by the minister of internal affairs for the Central Committee, but how was one to stop the activity of the minister himself? At the April plenum of the Central Committee, Beria once again hypocritically called for observation of legality, completely ignoring his own responsibility for past crimes. He was also beginning to reassign cadres to his own advantage.

Enough material has been published by now to confirm that it was Khrushchev himself who, with the aid of the military, initiated Beria's arrest on June 26, 1953, and organized the entire risky enterprise.[10] The historians have not as yet explained the historical significance of this step, which was more than merely a heroic act in Khrushchev's biography. It proved to be an act of statesmanlike wisdom and political farsightedness, for it disclosed the organic connection between the system of the cult of Stalin and the routine practices of the punitive organs, which were a sort of subsystem of the cult, one of its foundations. The July plenum of the Central Committee confirmed this. Discussion of the report "On Criminal Anti-Party and Anti-State Actions of L. P. Beria" was on the agenda, but the meeting focused on the question of Stalin's personality cult, liquidation of its consequences, and democratization of Party and government. Only a few participants supported restoration of the past. The majority understood the necessity of correcting a situation that had allowed the Ministry of Internal Affairs to escape control by both Party and state, to usurp judicial functions, and to engage in large-scale illegal repressions.

The decisions of the July plenum have been extensively treated in Soviet and Russian literature. Historians unanimously view the liquidation of Beria and his closest aides, who were brought to trial, convicted by the Supreme Court of the USSR, and executed at the end of 1953, as an important step toward mass rehabilitation of unjustly condemned citizens and the restoration of the autonomy of many of the ethnic groups illegally exiled under Stalin. They also believe that there was an increase in the prestige of the Communist party and a certain degree of democratization of Soviet society as a result of these actions.

[10]See Strobe Talbott, ed. and trans., *Khrushchev Remembers* (Boston: Little, Brown, 1970), 321–41.

Many aspects of the question, however, have not been examined. How were these events, for example, reflected in the correlation of forces within the country's leadership?

KHRUSHCHEV'S ACCOMPLISHMENTS

The successful operation against the seemingly almighty dictator-to-be entailed the emergence of a new leader. In the language of chess, the loss of tempo led to the loss of initiative. This affected not only Beria but also his closest associate, Malenkov. Moreover, since the status of the security and internal affairs organs was being changed and since they found themselves under direct control of the top leadership of the Communist party, Khrushchev rose in an unprecedentedly short time to the highest level of power in the USSR. He was elected first secretary of the Party in September 1953. To be sure, this was still only 1953, and Khrushchev had much to comprehend and master in order to strengthen his position. Was the first secretary anticipating future troubles, and did he understand the blow that the incipient reforms would inflict on the very nature of Stalinism? Or was he simply continuing his struggle to become the sole leader?

But in the final account, what matters is not intentions but results. From this perspective, Khrushchev has entered history as the instigator and organizer of the unmasking of Stalin and Stalinism. Of course, from today's vantage point, it is easy to perceive his theoretical and political limitations, his adherence to the Stalinist model of socialism. This does not diminish Khrushchev's historical merits, however; the fact remains that he destroyed one of the mainstays of Stalinism: he put an end to mass repressions.

Later, Brezhnev would bring the head of the KGB back into the Politburo, and various steps would be undertaken against dissidence, along with other limitations on democracy. But these attempts to revivify the past only served to disclose the scope and impact of the first and historically most important reform, designed and realized under Khrushchev's leadership. The later years of the 1980s bear witness to this.

Many political scientists and commentators tend to view the events of the late 1980s and early 1990s as being connected with the revolutions in Eastern Europe, in countries that for almost half a century had followed in the wake of the Soviet Union. Given the character of their profession, historians call for broadening and deepening this initial analysis to place the current collapse of Stalinism in the context of underlying shifts that had already begun the destruction of the totalitarian regime during the period of the thaw, in order to improve our understanding not only of the inevitable limitations and contradictions of Khrushchev but also of the intertwining in his actions of the characteristics of reformer and revolutionary.

Liberation from fear has always aided the emancipation of man and of the spiritual and creative potential of society. So it was in the Soviet Union after 1953. Signs of extraordinary change became increasingly apparent. The introduction of coeducation in the schools, open access for all visitors to the Kremlin grounds, and New Year's celebrations in its palaces were the first sensations. Uniforms, until then mandatory, were abolished for miners and for officials in financial, communications, transport, and other institutions. The regularization of the workday in government and central offices also made a great impression. Until then, they had unofficially observed the routine usual for Stalin; he most often worked at night, and this, in turn, "detained" ministers and their apparatus, the workers in many institutions and enterprises, which presented problems for a normal lifestyle. Today, this may be viewed as a curiosity, but in the situation of a regime of personal power, things were seen differently. The return to normal hours was a sign of the recovery of the society as a whole. Unfortunately, we have not as yet sufficiently studied such subjects.

Scholarship has more fully analyzed the turn in foreign policy. The Korean war, where in one way or another the military forces of the United States and the Soviet Union came into conflict, was ended in 1953. In the next two years, Soviet leaders visited China and a number of other countries, and they managed to regularize the relationship with Yugoslavia. The signing of a peace treaty with Austria led to the evacuation of Soviet troops from that country. This unprecedented growth of diplomatic contacts came to be known as the "spirit of Geneva," as détente was then called, after the conference of Soviet, U.S., and other world leaders that was held there in 1955.

Soviet writers on foreign policy after 1953 invariably extolled the peacemaking efforts of Khrushchev, who always participated in major negotiations, meetings, and foreign travel with all the rights of a head of state (as leader of the Party, he was also a member of the Presidium of the USSR Supreme Soviet). This behavior was in striking contrast to Stalin's rigid course, based on the view that the two opposing world systems would inevitably engage in a military confrontation. Merely raising the possibility that another world war was not inevitable was in itself a significant event. The idea was proposed by Khrushchev and approved by the Party congress in February 1956. This was a major step in the direction of [Gorbachev's—ed.] "new thinking." It was followed by considerable reductions in the Soviet armed forces and by an agreement to prohibit nuclear tests in the atmosphere, in space, and under water.

Khrushchev did not doubt that, under conditions of the peaceful coexistence of capitalism and socialism, the latter would emerge victorious. He did not see the cuts in the military force as weakening the might of the USSR and its allies. Instead, the Warsaw treaty organization was created in 1955, uniting all the socialist countries in Europe except Yugoslavia.

The Soviet Union did not abandon direct support of national liberation movements in Africa, Asia, and Latin America. The stance taken by the Soviet Union during the Suez crisis in 1956 illustrates the reasons for this policy, which was by no means fortuitous. This is confirmed by Andrei Sakharov, who in 1955 witnessed a curious admission by a prominent Soviet official. The famous physicist, who was then involved in designing the newest nuclear weapon, was invited along with other scientists to attend a session of the Presidium of the Central Committee, but the meeting was delayed. An official emerging from the conference room said:

Please excuse the delay. Shepilov [the minister of foreign affairs] has just returned from his trip to Egypt, and they are finishing the discussion of his report. The issue is extremely important, and they are discussing a decisive change in the principles of our Middle Eastern policy. Henceforth we shall support Arab nationalists. The long-range goal is to undermine the existing relations between the Arabs, the United States, and Europe and to create an "oil crisis." This will cause trouble for Europe and make it dependent on us.[11]

We need to make allowance for the fact that this statement is based on Sakharov's memory; Shepilov himself probably would have spoken more diplomatically. However, it is no secret that Khrushchev often publicly promised to bury capitalism, and for this reason Sakharov's account is credible. It confirms the view that Khrushchev and the Party and state leadership were devoted to the traditions of the Bolshevik policy of struggle for victory on a world scale. In this respect, Khrushchev's views

[11]A. Sakharov, *Vospominaniia* (New York: Chekhov, 1990), 247.

had not changed. The contradiction in his behavior is obvious: on the one hand, decisive retreat from the former dogmas about the inevitability and intensification of conflict between the two world systems, and on the other, a pragmatic intention to use almost any possibility to weaken capitalism and undermine its foundations.

Khrushchev should not be indiscriminately praised or condemned. Could he have acted otherwise? Tradition required that he personify the theory and practice of the Party, the government, and the Soviet polity as a whole. Although he consciously turned to reformism, he was also the leader of the Party that for three decades had been shaped and ruled by Stalin. One must also take into account the fact that in many respects the West, too, subscribed to obsolete conceptions and conclusions. Perhaps the West was also not ready for compromise, and there were those in the West who were not eager to see the cold war end. The experiences of the second half of the 1980s and humanity's realization of the threat of thermonuclear catastrophe demand that we avoid simplistic answers, even if they concern events of nearly forty years ago.

It is from this perspective that we should study the agricultural boom that took place under Khrushchev's leadership between 1953 and 1958. An advance of such a magnitude had not been made in any five-year period before and has not been made since.

In the fall of 1952, Malenkov, presenting the Central Committee report to the Nineteenth Party Congress, announced that the grain problem had been resolved. But this was not true. State grain purchases were smaller in 1952 than in 1940, and they would be even smaller in 1953. Part of the state grain reserves had to be used to provide the population with bread, something that had not been done in 1940 or in any postwar year up to then. Yields were not increasing, and the number of cattle was much smaller than it had been on the eve of the war and even in 1928.

Khrushchev knew well the real situation in the countryside, and in July 1953 he proposed a discussion of steps to improve Soviet agriculture. Accordingly, in September 1953 he presented a report on agriculture to the Central Committee. The report evoked a remarkable response in the country. The objective of improving agriculture was described as a critical task in the development of Soviet society, one that could no longer be postponed. To be sure, the explanation of the deficiencies was trivial, and in this Khrushchev did not differ from his predecessors. However, the businesslike discussion of the proposed measures for agricultural progress produced an entirely different impression. For the first time, priority was given to the question of the material interest of the peasants in the results of their labors, and the issue of economic levers was given unprecedented attention. In addition, the new economic policy was marked by an increase in budgetary allocations for agriculture, capital investment to stimulate production on collective and state farms, a decrease in taxes on output, and cuts in the taxes levied on the private production of collective farmers. These measures helped to remove defects in the relationships between industry and agriculture that had characterized the previous period.

The considerable increase in financial assistance to the collective-farm peasantry was the most important innovation. Whereas in 1951–53 capital investment in agriculture was a bit more than one-fifth of that in industry, in 1954–58 it rose to almost one-third. More favorable terms of settling accounts with the machine and tractor stations (MTS) were introduced, to the advantage of the collective farms. Previously, payment in kind for the work of the MTS was based on a percentage of the estimated harvest, which usually was considerably higher than the actual harvest; now, firm rates were established that took into account actual crop yields and the peculiarities of various agricultural regions. The reduction in taxes on the household economy of the collective farmers also greatly improved their situation. Until then, taxes had been levied on income from individual agricultural activities (cattle raising, apiculture, horticulture), with the result that the more the collective farmer produced on his private plot, the more taxes he paid. Now, fixed rates were established per unit of the private plot.[12]

The most important factor, however, was the change in the policy of procurement and purchase prices, which had been an important tool in the hands of the state for channeling a considerable proportion of collective-farm income into its own coffers. Until 1953, procurement prices, the prices at which collective farms provided the state with compulsory deliveries, were extremely low, far lower than production costs. In many instances, they did not even cover the transportation costs incurred by

---

[12]["Private plot" is the customary English term, but it should be noted that the Russian term is *lichnoe khoziaistvo*, which does not carry connotations of private property (*chastnoe khoziaistvo*) or landownership. This distinction between personal use and private property was already present, as previous chapters in this volume amply illustrate, in the case of peasant landholding in prerevolutionary times. The distinction is also very relevant to post-Soviet political culture and current debates about privatization and private landownership.—Ed.]

a collective farm in the process of delivery. Purchase prices, the prices at which the collective farms sold a portion of their output above compulsory deliveries, were somewhat higher, but even they did not compensate the collective farms for their costs. These prices had been established in 1928 and remained practically unchanged until 1953, although retail prices greatly increased during that period. Thus, in 1927–28 procurement prices for grain were approximately 4–8 kopecks per kilogram, and in 1937–39 the price was 7.4 kopecks, while retail prices rose no less than tenfold over the same period. (Here and elsewhere, data are given in pre-1961 prices—i.e., before the currency reform.)[13]

These low prices, at times purely symbolic, could not stimulate the growth of such vital agricultural sectors as animal husbandry and horticulture. For example, the average procurement price of a kilogram of meat and suet was 22 kopecks. In 1953, a Central Committee plenum considerably raised procurement and purchase prices for potatoes and other vegetables and for products of animal husbandry; in the aggregate, these prices rose threefold between 1952 and 1959.

The significance of the agricultural reforms was that they equalized the terms of monetary and commodity exchange between the city and the countryside. The new procurement prices for agricultural deliveries to the state were extended not only to the public but also to the household economy of the collective farmers. This gave a material profit to the collective farms and the peasantry. Until then, all collective-farm output, though considered "commodity production," was not treated as such, and the dominant conception was that in the transition from socialism to communism there would be no need for the trading of commodities. A short time before his death, Stalin considered it necessary to reaffirm this postulate and to mandate its implementation in the economic practices of the collective farms.[14] In practice, this meant that the cost of agricultural production was completely disregarded.

The reforms in 1953 meant that commodity and monetary exchange would no longer be undervalued and that the relationship between the state and the collective farms would be based on production costs. Exchange between the city and the country began to follow the forms of commodity trading, taking these production costs into account. But it

[13][For additional information, see Alec Nove, *An Economic History of the USSR, 1917–1991* (London: Penguin, 1992), 397.—Ed.]
[14]Iosif V. Stalin, *Ekonomicheskie problemy sotsializma v SSSR* (Moscow, 1952), 93–94.

was not easy to overcome old habits. Until 1958, the principle of production costs was applied within the parameters of the economic relations between industry and agriculture that had largely been established during collectivization. After 1958, with the reorganization of the MTS, the character of these relations substantively changed.

In February 1958, the Central Committee decided to sell agricultural machinery to the collective farms and to transform the MTS into repair and technical stations. By this step, the work force of the collective farm would have a direct connection with the means of production: tractors, combines, and other machinery. The collective farm would be in control of its territory, abolishing the depersonalization of production that had existed when the MTS and the collective farm were masters over the same land.

Also in 1958, the government established a single system of purchase prices (except for differences established for different regions) and substantially changed the procurement process. Until then, the procurement system consisted of obligatory deliveries, payments in kind to the MTS, above-quota purchases, and purchases by contracts with collective farms. The state paid different prices to the collective farms for one and the same product, with obligatory deliveries receiving the lowest prices and above-quota purchases and contracts the highest. The MTS reorganization, the repeal of payment in kind to the MTS, and the establishment of unified purchase prices widened the sphere of commodity exchange between town and country. Included in this exchange was the machinery and the significant amount of output that had been previously taken as payment in kind by the MTS. The state began purchasing the entire agricultural output of the collective farm and selling to it all the requisite industrial goods and equipment.

But the practice of price formation manifested serious defects. In many instances, the prices, even taking into account regional variations, did not correspond to real production costs, and prices for some industrial goods (spare parts, fuel) were too burdensome for the many collective farms that were investing heavily in machinery.

Nevertheless, the situation in the countryside was quickly changing. Material incentives increased and became the means by which the complex knot of contradictions in the life of the collective farm could be gradually untied. As procurement prices rose and income and remuneration levels were increased, peasant interest in collective-farm work grew and collective-farm production went up.

The monetary income of collective farms more than tripled between 1952 and 1958. This permitted great increases in the funds available for capital investment and for labor remuneration. For the first time in some years, the collective-farm population increased, primarily the number of males. Between 1950 and 1953, the average annual size of the agricultural work force decreased from 30.7 million to 29.4 million individuals; during the following three years, from 1954 to 1956, it increased to 31.5 million.

The growth of economic incentives was combined with democratization of the life of the collective farm. The state, having granted greater economic rights to the collective farms, introduced a new system of planning that reduced the degree of centralization. The collective farms received the right to add to or modify certain norms of the law on collective farming, taking local conditions into account. Collective-farm assemblies began themselves to regulate the size of the private plots of their members, taking into consideration their labor contribution to the collective farm. The collective farms could now make decisions on such issues as organization of brigades and teams, work norms and remuneration, definition of brigade leaders' responsibilities, and evaluation of work. The very enumeration of these new rights—and the list is incomplete—helps us to understand how rigid, not to say cruel, the dependence of the collective farmers on the state had been. There was no future in such a relationship.

In the new conditions, after 1953, the voices of agronomists and agricultural engineers were greatly strengthened, too. At the end of 1940 the number of people with higher and specialized secondary education employed in agriculture was only 50,000; in 1953 it was 114,000; and in 1961 it reached 400,000. The composition of collective-farm leadership also qualitatively improved. In 1953, only 18 percent of collective-farm directors had completed higher or specialized secondary education; in 1962, such directors constituted 60 percent of the total.

A new era opened in the process of electrification of the countryside, which had barely begun before the war. In 1953, only 22 percent of all collective farms had electricity, but 49 percent did by 1958. Thanks to the virgin-lands campaign, the area of land under cultivation increased by 50 million hectares, almost by one-third, between 1953 and 1961. (Previously, it had taken almost fifty years to increase the area of land under cultivation by a similar amount.) The "conquest of the virgin lands" moved the center of gravity of grain production to the east, giving the western regions of the country an opportunity to increase the production of vegetables, industrial, and other nongrain crops.

The rapid progress of the village in this new stage of its evolution was especially remarkable in light of the prolonged stagnation of the preceding period. As is well known, the levels of agricultural economy of 1926–29 were not surpassed until 1950–53. Furthermore, this later growth took place primarily through the incorporation of Ukrainian, Byelorussian, and Baltic territories that contained 10 percent of the total arable land of the former Soviet Union. After 1953, progress was observed in all branches of agriculture. Between 1953 and 1958, gross agricultural output increased by one-third in comparison with the 1949–53 period. Agricultural procurements also rose. In 1960, grain procurement was one and a half times larger than in 1953; procurement of sugar beets, vegetables, and meat, more than two times; of milk, two and a half times. The whole country felt this progress.

It would be a great exaggeration, however, to characterize the measures undertaken in the Soviet countryside as a radical reform of the system of state and collective farms. In contrast to urban dwellers, collective farmers, as before, had no internal passports; they could not, as a rule, belong to trade unions; only a small proportion of the veterans among them had the right to a pension; and their monthly monetary income was several times smaller than workers' monthly salaries. We do not find in Khrushchev's speeches ideas or concepts pertaining to the development of commodity-market relations, individual farming, or private entrepreneurship. He remained a convinced supporter of the transformation of the collective-cooperative form of property into state property. That is how, following the late leader, he understood socialism. Progress in the countryside convinced him that his course was viable, especially as it was linked with the cleansing of Stalinist errors and of transgressions of legality.

Nevertheless, changes in the countryside gave hope and contributed to steps intended to raise the standard of living of the population. Especially important were the shortening of the workday, the introduction of a new pension system for industrial and white-collar workers in 1956, and a massive program of housing construction begun in 1957. By Khrushchev's admission, this was not easy to do, since many leaders were not ready for such steps. That is hardly surprising: Whole generations had been raised under the banner of the struggle for accelerated development, which emphasized heavy industry. From one five-year plan to the next, priority was given to increased production of coal, oil, and machinery. Everyone understood that housing was important, but money, time, and resources were always for some reason lacking. The principle that social needs were allocated only residual resources became the norm during the 1920s. Khrushchev was the first Soviet leader to try to change this policy. Within a short time, housing construction rose fivefold, and the pension system created during his regime proved adequate for a number of years.

However, these policies, sensible as they might have been, were still being implemented within the framework of the traditional administrative-command system for governing the Party, the economy, and society as a whole. One could understand why such methods were necessary to dispose of Beria. But the perestroika of agriculture was carried out in the absence of democracy. Similar methods were used in 1957 to institute councils of national economy (*sovnarkhozy*), to cut down the size of the army, and much else. And although popular initiative increased, and the Party congresses, plenums of the Central Committee, and sessions of the Supreme Soviet of the USSR were conducted regularly, the ultimate authority remained in the hands of the highest Party organ, which meant the first secretary. Khrushchev's reforms did not lead to the creation of a legal state.

THE "ANTI-PARTY GROUP"

These negative phenomena manifested themselves most clearly in the 1960s. In order to understand why, we must turn to the events of June 1957, when an attempt was made to remove Khrushchev from power. This attempt was organized by a group of members of the Party Presidium, with the old, convinced Stalinists such as Molotov, Malenkov, and Kaganovich playing the leading roles. They had soberly evaluated the process of democratization and realized that it held no promise of their retaining their former power; indeed, by this time all three already occupied secondary positions within the leadership. They were also aware of a definite dissatisfaction with Khrushchev on the part of a considerable proportion of the Party and government apparatus, and they knew that the Hungarian events of 1956 had alarmed conservative forces. To be sure, Khrushchev had acted in the spirit of Stalinist thinking, but they felt the need for a stronger hand. Nor did they fail to note Khrushchev's inconsistency in denouncing Stalin. His report, "On the Cult of Personality and Its Consequences," was presented at the end of the Twentieth Party Congress, but there was no discussion afterward. The text was read at Party meetings almost everywhere, but it did not appear in the Soviet press. (It was not published there until 1989.) On June 30, 1956, the Central Committee adopted a resolution on overcoming the cult of personality and its consequences. The name of Stalin was not mentioned in its title, just as it had not been mentioned in the title of Khrushchev's report. Stalin's role in fulfilling Lenin's behests was repeatedly discussed, but nothing was said about his participation in repressions, although this was unequivocally stated at the Twentieth Congress.

However, Khrushchev's opponents miscalculated the most important factor. Their names had already become odious to the majority of the Central Committee members, and Khrushchev received firm support. The minister of defense, Georgii Zhukov, and the head of the KGB, I. A. Serov, were among his supporters. Now that we have access to archival materials, we know the daily and hourly details of the Presidium's sessions. The attempt to remove Khrushchev and to appoint him minister of agriculture did not succeed, and the intervention of Central Committee members produced the convocation of an extraordinary plenum. The affair resulted in an entirely different outcome, as Molotov, Malenkov, Kaganovich, and those who voted with them, including the head of government, Bulganin, were denounced as an "anti-Party group."

At this plenum, individuals responsible for violations of legality and for derailing the process of rehabilitation of innocent victims after Stalin's death were condemned for the first time. Marshall Zhukov, and all the speakers following him, focused their attack on Molotov, Malenkov, and Kaganovich. Truly terrible documents were disclosed. In 1936, the total number of people executed was 1,138; in 1937, the figure was 353,074.[15] Between February 27, 1937, and November 12, 1938, Stalin, Molotov, and Kaganovich personally approved the death penalty for 38,679 individuals.[16] On one day alone, November 12, 1938, Stalin and Molotov sanctioned the execution of 3,167 persons.[17] On November 21, 1938, the NKVD presented a list of 292 persons, including former members of the Central Committee, former secretaries of regional and terri-

---

[15]AOI IML, no. 7051, p. 17.
[16]Ibid., p. 6. When materials like these were cited at the plenum, it is possible that the names of other persons involved, such as Mikoyan, Voroshilov, Andreev, and Khrushchev himself, were excised.
[17]Ibid.

torial Party committees, and former people's commissars and their deputies, who were being proposed for the death penalty. The list was reviewed by Stalin, Molotov, and Kaganovich, and 229 of the individuals were shot with their approval.[18] One document signed by Molotov and Kaganovich envisaged the extermination of some 44,000 Party workers whose names were listed.[19]

Many memoranda were found in the archives from Kaganovich and Malenkov, addressed to Ezhov, identifying specific persons to be arrested. It was reported that 1.5 million persons had been arrested between 1937 and 1939 and that 681,692 of them were shot.[20] In the fall of 1945, Bulganin, then the commissar of defense, submitted a proposal to send to concentration camps 126,000 Soviet officers who had been German prisoners of war, and to strip them of their rank. On October 22, 1945, Molotov ordered the proposal put into effect.[21] In 1950, Malenkov took an active part in establishing the so-called special (political) prison, where, in particular, many of those accused in the "Leningrad affair" were kept. Malenkov and Bulganin, together with Beria, later visited this jail and took part in the interrogations of the prisoners.

Confronted by the weight of evidence, the members of the "anti-Party group" began blaming each other; later, they blamed the supposedly extraordinary situation in the country and Stalin's orders. In the end, all expressed remorse, as had been done long ago by those whom they had wrathfully accused of Trotskyism, right-wing deviationism, and other sins. Did Khrushchev understand the true danger of repeating the Stalinist school's methods of struggle for power? He was himself a student from that school. Concluding the discussion, the first secretary stigmatized the "splitters" (*raskol'niki*) and portrayed them as the main culprits responsible for mass repressions.[22] As so often in the past, it was as if he were rehabilitating Stalin, although this was, of course, a game, the use of a trump card.

Time has confirmed the historical significance of the battle waged in June 1957. Khrushchev won, the actions of the "conspirators" were con-

---

[18]Ibid.
[19]TsPA (IML), f. 17, op. 57, d. 578, p. 18.
[20]AOI IML, no. 7051, p. 35.
[21]Ibid., p. 11.
[22][The term *raskol'niki* is exquisitely ironic in the context of the secular Marxism-Leninism of the Soviet political culture. It has a powerful religious and cultural connotation, for in tsarist times it was the official ecclesiastical term for the Old Believers, who left the Russian Orthodox church in the seventeenth century.—Ed.]

demned, and the majority of them, though not all, were removed from the Central Committee. Nobody, however, was expelled from the Party, despite some proposals to that effect. Much has been written about this plenum, but most attention has been paid to one issue: the defeat of the Stalinist faction. Many equally important aspects remain to be elucidated.

Khrushchev himself felt that the leadership struggle would continue, and he needed reserves. That is why there were no expulsions from the Party for the time being, and why Bulganin and Voroshilov, who participated in the conspiracy, nevertheless were kept at their posts. Their names were not even mentioned in the plenum's resolution. They would be retired later, and the active members of the "anti-Party" group would then be expelled from the Party. These tactics confirm the cunning and deftness of the victor, who knew how to soften the edge at the appropriate moment, to lower the tension, and even to gain a reputation as a kind leader. This was exactly how his teacher had acted in his time: first with Trotsky, then with Zinoviev and Kamenev, with Bukharin, and so on.

Historical experience demonstrates that he who adopts this course cannot stop himself. In order to solidify his power, Khrushchev later in that same year of 1957 abruptly removed Zhukov, who had provided him with great services in the arrest of Beria and the convocation of the extraordinary plenum. In 1958, at the age of sixty-four, Khrushchev added the job of chairman of the Council of Ministers of the USSR to his position of first secretary. As a result, the possibility of a collective leadership was sharply diminished, as was the scope for critical analysis of past experience and future prospects. Even before 1957, according to a tacit tradition, one rarely entered into an argument with the top leadership. The situation became worse after the 1957 plenum. Even the reasonable things said in the debate by the members of the anti-Party group were neglected: their references to the excessive haste and authoritarianism of the leader, to certain mistakes in agrarian policy, to the dubious slogan of overtaking the United States in agriculture in a few years.

KHRUSHCHEV'S LIMITATIONS

Khrushchev did not realize at once the consequences of his actions. Perhaps he was lulled by the progress in agriculture, the rise in the standard of living, the launching of sputnik, Gagarin's flight in space, and the victory of revolution in Cuba. There was also universal approval of his plans to erect in some twenty years the material and technical basis for communism in the Soviet Union. In retrospect, we can see other realities in these years. The swift agricultural advance that began in 1953 was over by the early 1960s. The replacement of the ministries by the sovnarkhozy did not produce the desired effect. Successes in foreign policy, such as "the spirit of Geneva," gave way to growing international tension (the collapse of the Eisenhower summit, the Berlin wall, the Cuban crisis). After the regional Party committees were divided into industrial and agricultural sections in 1962, the Party apparatus realized the danger that this would drastically weaken its powers. In short, Khrushchev's golden hour had passed.

In my opinion, the changes that Khrushchev wanted to introduce after 1961 cannot be viewed as reforms. Rather, these were frantic undertakings, hasty actions of the administrative-command system, imposed from above by antidemocratic methods. One still needs to elucidate the dynamics of the interrelationship between Soviet internal policy and the goal-oriented transition of the American economy onto the path of scientific and technical revolution that took place at the time. In practice, the Soviet Union, not having properly completed the process of industrialization, was taking upon itself the task of surpassing the United States in industrial output by 1970. Once again, adventurism was directing policy, and the outcome is well known.

The main lesson of the reforms of the era that began in 1953 and ended soon after the extraordinary plenum of the Central Committee in 1957 was that the creative potential of the Soviet people could be unleashed only in conditions of rejection of the Stalinist model, of emancipation of the village, of democratization in all spheres of the material and spiritual life of society. When this was being done decisively and soundly, taking into account the real potentialities of the country that had lived several decades under totalitarianism, progress was being made. Deformation of this course produced the opposite result.[23]

---

[23][Dorothy Atkinson commented that reform in Russia may well have been a self-defeating process, because economic and political reforms, which are interdependent, require systemic devolution of power, but a resolution of the crisis that necessitated the reforms in the first place appears possible only through a concentration of political power and authority. This observation is particularly pertinent in the light of developments since 1991.—Ed.]

Thus, it can be illuminating to juxtapose the beginning of Khrushchev's thaw with the first five years of Gorbachev's perestroika. If the cold war ended in the late 1980s, one must recognize that this was hinted at by the international contacts of 1953–59. One should also note that, whereas no more than one hundred thousand foreign visitors came to the Soviet Union in the 1920s and 1930s, the situation changed drastically after 1953. Five hundred thousand foreigners visited Russia in 1955, and the number soon rose into the millions. Glasnost, democratization, and the overthrow of the one-party system can be directly linked with the cessation of mass repressions in the 1950s. Finally, it is significant that many leaders of perestroika considered themselves as belonging to the generation of the Twentieth Party Congress. The experience of those years may well have helped them avoid the kind of conflicts that occurred at the plenum of 1957 and to contain the conservative forces, at least for a while.

In my view, perestroika's approach to the lessons of economic growth of the 1950s, however, has been much less successful. Under Khrushchev, top priority was given to the village, and agricultural progress played a key role in reinvigorating social and political life. The underestimation of this factor clearly complicated the progress of perestroika. The call for "acceleration," proclaimed in the spring of 1985, also proved to be an impediment. By 1990, talk of strengthening the administrative principle, of the need for a "strong hand," was widespread.

It is also worth noting that, just as knowledge of the past aids our understanding of the present, so the knowledge of the present helps us to comprehend the past. In the light of recent events, we can clearly see that Khrushchev could not have escaped the authoritarian and bureaucratic system that was established and had ossified under Stalin. He saw the history of that system through the eyes of his teacher, and when he affirmed in 1959 that socialism was fully and finally victorious in the Soviet Union, he only confirmed his fidelity to the past. He could hardly have imagined the inevitability of the collapse of the Stalinist model. But in the last analysis, the limitations and contradictoriness of even the best of Khrushchev's undertakings depended not so much on his personal qualities as a revolutionary leader as they did on the real conditions of a society that had found itself on a false path.

17

Perestroika: a revival of Khrushchevian reform or a new idea of socialist society?

GIULIETTO CHIESA

THE POSSIBILITIES OF CHANGE

The questions of the meaning and significance of perestroika have been raised many times, beginning in March 1985, and the different answers given to them reflect different evaluations of perestroika's roots and potentialities, of the real strategy of the reformers, and even of Mikhail Gorbachev's personality and psychology. These have been legitimate and essential questions, because the world faces a substantially new phenomenon, one that is difficult to measure by traditional standards. In the middle and late 1980s, many thought that to fail to transform peacefully what was, after all, a world power could have colossal and unpredictable effects on all aspects of international relations. At least, this was what the most qualified and impartial Western observers thought at the time.

This opinion, however, was not shared by the majority of observers, who stubbornly limited themselves to repeating, even after 1985, that any reform of the system was unthinkable. Either these observers contended that what was taking place was a structural paralysis of the "real," Stalinist socialism, or they invoked the failures of all the previous attempts to modernize Russia, or sometimes they combined the two interpretive strands. They reached, generally speaking, one of two types of conclusions: Either nothing new was happening (because nothing new, in principle, *could* happen in the Soviet Union) or the collapse of the system was inevitable (although perhaps it could be accelerated from without).

These currents of thought, however, located the collapse of the system in an indistinct and indefinable future. Andrei Amalrik was one of the few Sovietologists who tried to define a time frame. His book *Will the Soviet Union Survive until 1984?* predicted the wrong year, but the order of magnitude was substantially right, and this was not an accident; his was a rare case of a concrete analysis of the structural causes of the crisis. Another approach—which I define as an "ideological" one—by its very nature led to neglect of the analysis of the underground transformations that were in fact occurring in the society. Similarly, and for the same reason, a concentration of attention on the past, on Russian and Soviet history, on the long series of failures of the "revolutions from above," fails to take into account the dimensions and absolute novelty of the impact on Soviet society (no less than on all contemporary societies) of phenomena such as the development of mass media; the unavoidable fall (brought about by global communication) of barriers hindering the diffusion of knowledge; the long-term and contradictory effects of mass education and professional training; the uncontrollable proliferation of contacts with the external world; and changes in urban-rural relations.

I do not think that Fernand Braudel's perception of extreme slowness of alterations in the deep structures of history is contradicted by the visible accelerations that we have observed in the recent past. And yet many features of today's dynamics suggest that contemporary humanity faces growing difficulties in adapting itself to so frenetic a pace of change. One result of these difficulties is that individuals and communities, in a defensive reaction, try to shelter themselves in their "biological" time, accepting only partially the experience of "modernity" and rejecting all that they cannot "metabolize." Modern societies are involved in turbulent processes whose nature and breadth, exemplified by new technologies of unprecedented sorts, can produce whirls and spins far below the superficial foam. In other words, we must be very cautious about using analogies with previous reform attempts in Soviet and Russian history to deal with the present. How much of the character of the Russian peasant of Peter the Great's time has remained in the collective memory of the Russian people at the end of the twentieth century? We certainly can say that a conspicuous part of that heritage is still alive in the Russian soul. But if we should limit ourselves to that observation, we would deny ourselves an understanding of the reasons for the amazing rapidity of the democratic awakening in the Soviet Union during the late 1980s. This awakening was most likely an effect of a prolonged and sedimentary process that has not as yet been analyzed and that now is suddenly revealing its potentialities.

Finally, the effects of the "collapse of communism" on the external world, and thus on the whole system of international relations, have as yet fully to manifest themselves, much less to be properly analyzed. Already during the late 1980s, we found ourselves in the middle of an incredible, unforeseeable storm that overwhelmed all the preceding points of reference. Someone had overturned the chessboard, so that it was impossible to continue the old game, even if one could remember exactly where to put every single piece. Such an important researcher and scholar as Robert Conquest has admitted: "I and those in like case were on the record that the Soviet system was not viable. What took us by surprise was the speed of the collapse." Conquest went on: "Western Sovietology by and large failed and is failing to cope, in part because of a bent toward the academically respectable idea of 'objectivity' and avoidance of the 'judgmental,' in part because of an (equally academic) schematism. . . . Instead of an easily manageable, easily understandable set of non-urgent variables, what faced us was protean and unpredictable."[1] This was self-criticism on the part of a man who did not conceal but on the contrary brandished his own "long service as a hard-liner" and who indeed had been a good prophet in some cases.

In fact, the "collapse" theory has been confirmed by events. It would be difficult to find a more appropriate word with which to describe the events we have been observing in Eastern Europe and in the former Soviet Union. What was particularly unpredictable, and what astonished Conquest and many others, was that the collapse had been consciously decided upon by Soviet reformers. I understand that this is a contentious point, so let me respond immediately to the most probable objection: I do not believe that Gorbachev was particularly happy observing the rapid end of the socialist regimes in Eastern Europe. On the contrary, it was evident that the crisis was the end result of a dramatic and painful choice. The point to be made, however, is that a *choice* had indeed been made. And therein lies one of the elements of unpredictability: The Soviet leadership began—after a protracted internal political struggle—a gigantic strategic withdrawal, which affected every dimension of international competition and which was the result of a realistic assessment

[1]Robert Conquest, "The End of Global Tick-Tack-Toe," *Washington Post*, April 2, 1990.

of the correlation of forces, connected in turn with the internal needs of Soviet society.

The theory that the Soviet system was not reformable has been confirmed to a certain extent. Gorbachev was not "rectifying" the system or "reforming" it. As he had often stated, perestroika was a "revolution," and its aim was a "change of the system." Again, this means that the hard-liners were right. On the other hand, they were wrong in that the transformations did not take place "in spite of" and "against the will of" the Soviet leadership but were promoted by it (or rather by a part of it). The pronouncement of the end of the Communist monopoly of power had been decided upon by the Central Committee of the Communist Party. It would be correct to say that the Communist parties in Berlin, Prague, Bucharest, and Sofia were swept away by mass protests. But their sudden ruin had been coldly reckoned upon in advance when the Kremlin decided to withdraw from those regimes the last ideological, military, and organizational protections. The signal of the beginning of the end came in the summer of 1989, when Gorbachev gave his blessing to a Solidarity-led government in Poland.

In hindsight, it does seem that the Soviet Communist party—or, perhaps more precisely, the Party apparatus—represented the most tenacious opponent of change but was overwhelmed by popular pressure. At the same time, it cannot be denied that the chessboard had been overturned by a reformist Soviet leadership. Gorbachev began a revolution from above, but he had the courage to go on to promote a second revolution from below, "giving politics back to the Soviet citizens"—as he said in Krasnoiarsk—for the first time in Soviet history. The surprising result is that everything that was expected happened, but it happened in a way that nobody expected.

KHRUSHCHEV AND THE ERA OF STAGNATION

The question raised in the title of this essay can be given a preliminary response. After several years, perestroika progressed beyond a simple revival of Khrushchevian reform. Even if Gorbachev in 1985 was still, in many respects, a "Khrushchevian" reformer, eventually that was no longer the case. To be sure, Gorbachev and his supporters began with the economy, trying from the very beginning to link the discussion of the economic reform with the efforts of a quarter century before. By no means accidentally, the debates from 1985 to 1987—almost exactly repeating the Khrushchevian path—rapidly produced a "rehabilitation" of the New Economic Policy. Each time the situation in the Soviet Union became problematic, one could observe some kind of return to the first, fundamental crossroad at which Russian society found itself after Lenin's death. The ideas of those who were defeated in the late 1920s, especially Bukharin, came back to the forefront at the beginning of perestroika, exactly as they had emerged (only to be defeated again) during the first de-Stalinization under Khrushchev.

The two historical moments, however, were in many ways substantially different. For example, there was a profound difference between the socioeconomic contexts of the two eras. When Khrushchev became the "number one," the Soviet Union was still apparently in the middle of an exceptional economic development. The official outlook was positively euphoric, to the extent that Khrushchev sincerely believed in the possibility of overtaking the U. S. economy within approximately twenty years. Only a relatively small group of experts was aware at the time that the Soviet economy was beginning to reveal serious dysfunctions. The Party machine, the immense propaganda apparatus, still lived in complete tranquillity and propounded ideas about unlimited economic growth. The great majority did not perceive any kind of erosion. The crisis of the system began without consciousness of that fact. The machine was slowing down, but inertia gave an inaccurate perception of a continuing movement forward at the same pace.

In fact, Soviet growth began to reverse its trend in 1958. In the eight preceding years, the average annual rate of growth had been 7.1 percent; in the six following years, it was 5.3 percent. Some analysts, taking into account the unusually high growth rate up to 1958, were unfazed. But others noted that the reduction in the rate of growth was associated with a serious decrease in the productivity of labor and capital. Such signals indicated structural faults. An attempt by a Soviet economist to calculate the economic efficiency of the system showed that, whereas in 1952 every ruble of capital investment produced 62 kopecks of national income, in 1965 it produced only 53.2 kopecks, and in 1968 only 50.6. Between 1961 and 1965, the productivity of investment fell by 15 percent.[2] Many began to understand that the planning system put into place

[2]G. Khachaturov, in A. Rumiantsev and P. Bunich, eds., *Ekonomicheskaia reforma: Ee osushchestvlenie i problemy* (Moscow, 1969), as cited in Moshe Lewin, *Political Undercurrents in Soviet Economic Debates: From Bukharin to the Modern Reformers* (Princeton: Princeton University Press, 1974), 129.

by Stalin in the 1930s was proving incapable of running a complicated and gigantic economy. "Such an economic system, rigid from top to bottom," V. Nemchinov wrote prophetically in 1964, "is destined to slow down social and technological progress, and sooner or later it is destined to collapse under the pressure of the real processes of economic life."[3]

But a leadership composed essentially of "engineers" was incapable of a critical assessment of the situation. Their professional skills were largely technical in nature, and their personal experiences were those of second-rank Party leaders or military commanders during World War II. They could not imagine that a radical reform might be necessary for cultural and political rather than economic reasons. They even drafted, in 1961, a new Party program that envisaged spectacular social and economic progress, exactly at the moment when the relentless decline was beginning. They constituted a hostile environment to any real reform, and they were, in fact, the "cadres" who ousted Khrushchev and administered Party and state affairs during the "era of stagnation." The entire discussion around the so-called Kosygin reform involved only tinkering with the economic system, certainly not its replacement by another mechanism that would be radically different from the existing one.

Some reformers in the Khrushchev era did understand the necessity of deeper changes. But their influence—and in general, the influence of scientists and academicians—on the upper levels of the leadership was extremely limited. Moreover, they actually understood only the *objective technical faults* of Stalin's planning system and the unavoidable decline that these faults would produce in the coming decades. But Khrushchev's de-Stalinization, the liberation of millions of prisoners from the camps, and the end of forced labor and of absolute terror introduced new, unexpected factors in the process of decline, factors that rapidly became the dominant ones.

In other words, the first real undermining of the Stalinist system was produced by essentially *political* decisions. Unwittingly, Khrushchev opened Pandora's box. Once the "administrative-command system" was deprived of the political ingredient of terror, it revealed itself incapable of functioning. The decline of the economic indicators was simply the visible evidence of the progressive reduction of fear. The conclusion,

---

[3]V. Nemchinov, "Sotsialisticheskoe khoziaistvovanie i planirovanie proizvodstva," *Kommunist*, 1964, no. 5: 76.

which is only superficially paradoxical, is that the Stalinist-Soviet model was essentially a *political* one, without any autonomous economic content. The so-called economic laws of socialism were merely political rules implemented through the use of other political rules. Without terror, the administrative-command system was shown to be a total fiction, even though it endured for some decades. It continues to display a kind of residual vitality to this day, but that is the natural result of the slow, contradictory processes by which fears and terrors only gradually lose their grip on human minds.

Soviet reformers, however, would reach this conclusion only thirty years later, during the process of perestroika. In Khrushchev's time, if we exclude some clairvoyant economists, even the most outspoken radicals were still ready to accept the principle of central planning. Most of them were convinced of the necessity of maintaining some degree of centralism, differences arising only over what degree was necessary for state planning and over the ways of defining it. They rejected the erratic behavior of central management and pleaded for "scientific criteria." In other words, they criticized not central planning per se but the existing administrative-command system and its absolute domination by the center. Obviously, we have to recognize that the discussion was still largely encoded and that open competition among cultural and theoretical schools of thinking was still far away. It was to Khrushchev's credit that he favored a certain openness, but he was unable to understand and use professional scholarly advice. To a certain extent, however, the positions taken by the scholars also reflected the real level of knowledge. To be convinced of this, it is sufficient to recall the idea of "optimal planning" developed by the economical-mathematical school, which suggested amplifying the center's control capacities through a new "feedback" system capable of transmitting a sufficient and immediate flow of information so as to produce rational decisions.

Today, one may consider these discussions as largely outmoded and even naive. Already in the mid-1960s, however, many reformist economists acknowledged that "Stalinist planning" was not real planning, that it grossly challenged all productive rationality, that it proceeded in uncontrolled fits and starts, that it did not have any self-regulating mechanism, that political decisions continuously modified "scientifically defined" objectives, that it created enormous productive capabilities that then were not used, that it produced huge surpluses of goods that nobody wanted to buy, and so on. Many economists understood that a transition to an intensive economy, a rational use of resources, and a new economic mechanism would have required a combination of markets and planning.

In effect, the discussion was stopped at this point. Khrushchev's fall in October 1964 signaled the beginning of the creeping restoration of the core political content of the administrative-command system. However, an open restoration of terror was already impossible, and the Brezhnev leadership was incapable of putting that option into action. The decline of the system proceeded, therefore, substantially uncontrolled. That was the meaning of "stagnation."

This second attempt (after NEP) to define an idea of socialism in which markets, planning, and a certain degree of political openness could coexist also failed (Bukharin, of course, had envisioned only a temporary coexistence, whereas the post-Stalin reformers were ready to accept a strategic, long-term coexistence). This fact had tremendous political and psychological consequences inside and outside the Soviet Union, resulting in a widely accepted notion that any change would be impossible. The eighteen years of the Brezhnev era can be considered as a "triumph of ideology." This was ideology in the strictly Marxist meaning of the concept as "false consciousness," as a system of values elaborated by a ruling class to justify its own behavior and leading role and to convince the majority of the population not only that the rulers were "the best," but that they were in harmony with the common interest of society. A thick layer of this kind of "ideology"—designed as a substitute for terror—covered the whole society and the leadership itself.

The propagandistic requirement of hiding the weakness of the system, evidence of which was increasing with each passing year, together with the phobia of encirclement, created an infinite series of "optical illusions." Despite producing an image of success on the outside, they boomeranged upon themselves inside the country. Society found itself prisoner in a labyrinth of distorting mirrors, where the choice was either to believe what one saw, fully aware that everything around was false, or not to believe in anything at all. Tens of thousands of cadres pretended to believe, but millions of citizens simply refused to accept what they were constantly being told. Brezhnev's regime repeated Stalin's regime, covering an authoritarian substance with socialist trappings. It pretended to explain and mitigate the poverty of the present by pointing to the "inevitable" conquests of the future, and to explain the existence and justify the repression of both internal and external enemies, as well as the lack of liberty (attributed to the democratic "immaturity" of the people). It was designed to account for the de facto social inequality, the corporatization of the society as a whole, and the hierarchical distribution of privileges and goods. Soviet citizens, generation after generation, were instructed to behave on the basis of the official system of a "dual truth." The effects of this ideological system over a long period of time turned out to be disastrous. Applied on a large scale to Party and state relations, it led to a progressive paralysis.

A society in this condition cannot grow. The Soviet leadership, imprisoned in the network of secrets that it itself had created, was deprived of the necessary input of correct information on the actual state of the country. The political system, built as a "channeler" of orders and campaigns from the top down, represented—with the soviets nominated by the Party and ratified in an electoral farce to which the citizens were periodically subjected (another, and not a minor, element in the alienation of the populace under the system of "dual truth")—yet another blind alley, unsuitable for supplying the leadership with any real description of the popular mood. Brezhnev and his comrades did not want to face the risk of leaving the labyrinth, or were unable to do so, or perhaps simply did not understand what their situation was. What they did perceive, and acutely so, was the danger of losing their power, and they fought with all their might against any "revisionist" possibility.

GORBACHEV'S REVOLUTION

Contravening the idea of an omniscient KGB (but confirming that the KGB was the best-informed organization in the country), it was its chairman Iurii Andropov who recognized in 1983 for the first time that the leadership and the Soviet scientific community lacked sufficient knowledge of the actual state of affairs in the country and even had no clear idea of what kind of "socialist society" they were leading. He wrote, "It is impossible not to recognize that we are delaying in the face of the exigencies posed by the present level of material, technical, social, and cultural development of society."[4] As yet, however, the elements of Soviet leadership that were trying to seize power in order somehow to

[4]*Kommunist*, 1983, no. 3. This was an essay written on the occasion of the centennial of Marx's death.

change the situation had reached only some very preliminary conclusions about the nature of the crisis. It is not surprising that even observers from the outside encountered difficulties in drawing a reliable picture of the situation, a situation that, despite outward appearances of stability, was rapidly changing. Change had already occurred after the Twentieth and Twenty-second Party congresses, though without any real planning, and this change took place on the threshold of a deep crisis.

Gorbachev—and, before him, Andropov—came to power with that enormous ideological burden on his shoulders and an awareness that there was a need rapidly to introduce substantial changes and that the window of opportunity to "salvage the salvageable" was, by then, quite narrow. The formula with which Gorbachev succeeded in being elected general secretary of the Party in March 1985 was "there is no other way"—a cry of alarm so loud it convinced even the most conservative and the most recalcitrant. But we know, because it has been revealed on several occasions by Gorbachev himself, that he did not then understand the true extent of the economic and social crisis or, consequently, in what direction and at what speed to proceed in the colossal attempt to overcome it. It is probably for these reasons that perestroika started essentially as an attempt at economic reform, resuming, after twenty-five years, the economic program outlined by Khrushchevite economists in the 1960s, which was buried by the Brezhnevite restoration. Gorbachev's first catchwords were those of "acceleration" (*uskorenie*) and "transition to the intensive phase" of the economy. Yet in the year and a half that followed the April plenum of 1985, it could be argued that Gorbachev's proposals were essentially a rehashing of previous efforts.

It soon became apparent, however, that simple implementation of the Kosygin reform would have been both impossible and useless: impossible, because the margins that had been present twenty-five years previously no longer existed—labor, raw materials, energy, and funds were scarce, extremely expensive, difficult to reach, "in the wrong place," or completely obsolete—and useless, because the existing socioeconomic situation would no longer respond to the traditional solicitations. At that point, in early 1987, a radical change took place, perhaps the most important in the years of perestroika, since it carried within itself the embryo of a possible "mutation." This was when Gorbachev, in his report to the plenum of January 1987, explicitly enunciated the need for political reform. This was the turning point with respect to the heritage of

Khrushchev, even if, ironically, it coincided with Khrushchev's rehabil-itation.[5] However, it was Khrushchev the de-Stalinizer who was being rehabilitated, not Khrushchev the economic reformer, with his regional economic councils (*sovnarkhozy*) and his championing of corn as the solution to the problems of agriculture.

The new fact was that the most advanced reforming nucleus of the Soviet leadership had finally understood that no economic reform of the Soviet system would be possible unless the political structures were changed. Gorbachev recognized that the roots of the economic and social crisis that had brought the Soviet Union to zero economic growth in 1982 did not lie solely in the years of Brezhnevite "stagnation." They were deeper, reaching into the 1920s, to the "deformation" of socialism produced by Stalin, to the separation of socialism from democracy. Here, Gorbachev's position for a brief moment coincided with Khrushchev's, but then it immediately diverged, taking a completely new direction. The administrative-command system was now seen as not only an economic mechanism, a structural base (to use Marxist terminology) relatively in-dependent of the political-institutional superstructure. It did not concern only the style of state planning or the "production relations"; rather, it permeated the entire system of social and political relations. The nation-alization of the means of production had turned into the nationalization of society in its entirety. The individual, his material and intellectual production, his rights and his individual aspirations, had been sucked into a mechanism in which the state was everything and civil society must not and could not exist. Hence, it was impossible to reform the system only economically; real reform had to involve the political sys-tem. Indeed, if the political system was not involved from the very be-ginning, any attempt at economic reform would fail. In other words, *economic reform was political reform.* In the Soviet system, the two terms were synonymous. Without democratizing the country, pere-stroika could not be carried out.

In this way, Gorbachev provided a new perspective, different from all past approaches, on how to resolve a crisis in Soviet society. Probably, at the very beginning, he believed in the possibility of remaining inside the ideological framework. But it soon appeared that one could not stop with Stalin in the search for the origins of the crisis. When Gorbachev

[5]This moment marks, at the same time, a cleavage within the Andropov team, which had elected Gorbachev and begun perestroika.

arrived at the conclusion that there could be no socialism without democracy, at the same time, and independently of his awareness of the global implications, he began to delegitimize the ideological structure of Leninism and the practices that led to the one-party system. It was Gorbachev who initiated the destruction of the monopoly of power of the Communist Party.

Here again emerges the substantive difference between Khrushchev and Gorbachev. The former never put into question the power of the Party and its role as the sole ruling force in society. He was aware that the Party apparatus was thoroughly pervaded by Stalinism, but his objective was to replace one type of cadres with a more democratic type, and that was all. He certainly never intended to threaten the political structures through which the Party apparatus exercised its power. He criticized the "cult of personality" as a "deformation," as an "excess" of despotic dictatorship and political terror, and as a violation of Party rule. In other words, the target of his criticism was the "superstructural" part of Stalinism. The very term "cult of personality," devoid of any concrete structural content, reveals the limits of Khrushchevite de-Stalinization. What provoked the criminal degeneration of the leader and of an immense army of killers subject to his orders? What produced the deformations of the socialist society? Khrushchev did not answer, even if he was inexorable in denouncing Stalin's crimes. It seems to me that—besides the tremendous force of threatened interests, which militated against any real change—his inability to answer was a result of an ossified theory, by then incapable of analyzing real situations.

Gradually, as he discerned the depth of the social and economic crisis, Gorbachev perceived how formidable were the obstacles to its solution. He understood that significant opposition to perestroika was arising within the Party and state apparatuses, hostile to any reduction of their power and privileges. Even when faced with the danger of an impending social collapse, this "power bloc" actively resisted change. Gorbachev thus found himself caught in a contradiction: He was the leader of the Party that was proclaiming the advent of perestroika, but at the same time the Party apparatus revealed itself as the principal obstacle to perestroika's realization. At first, Gorbachev denied this fact, asserting that there was no "political opposition to perestroika."[6] But there is no doubt that he already had a clear idea on the matter at the beginning of 1987.[7]

---

[6] See the interview in *L'Unità*, May 20, 1987.

[7] For an analysis of the events preceding the January plenum, see Giulietto Chiesa and Roy

It is impossible to interpret Gorbachev's behavior without taking into account this hypothesis. He decided to "use" that contradiction without resolving it.

In other words, Gorbachev implicitly formulated a crucial question: How would it be possible to modify the system—which was already incapable of functioning—while maintaining one-party rule and, moreover, the rule of the very party that was directly responsible for the catastrophic situation? He would resolve the question with a complex tactic that he faithfully followed during his years in power:

1. Maintain, as long as possible, the unity of the leadership, in order to avoid the risk that the conservatives might cement an alternative alliance.

2. Take into account that, as perestroika developed, the political struggle would escalate and it would be impossible to avoid collisions regarding the pace, rhythm, and rapidity of transformations. However, it would be necessary to prevent those collisions from degenerating into permanent factions.

3. Keep within the leadership all the members disposed to compromise, even if they represented different political tendencies. Only those who proved to be absolutely hostile and potentially dangerous would be expelled.

4. Weaken progressively the power of the apparatuses, subjecting them to continuous pressure from above and—through glasnost—to a permanent and growing control from below.

5. Undertake the necessary replacements of cadres without public disgrace. Those who had to leave should be persuaded to do so, perhaps to quit "voluntarily," maintaining all their privileges.

6. Weaken the apparatuses without producing collapse. The process must be controlled and gradual. If the danger of collapse should arise, it might even be necessary to intervene, supporting the apparatuses and protecting them from popular pressure.

With these guidelines in mind, it is possible to interpret all the most significant episodes of the political struggle in the Soviet leadership after 1985. Gorbachev did not win all the battles. Sometimes (despite the

Medvedev, *La Rivoluzione di Gorbachev* (Milan: Garzanti, 1989), 99–136. The English-language edition is Roy Medvedev and Giulietto Chiesa, *Time of Change: An Insider's View of Russia's Transformation* (New York: Pantheon, 1989).

superficial impressions), he was even defeated. More frequently, a compromise was reached between conservatives and reformers. It should be emphasized here that this does not imply that this tactic was destined to achieve victory; on the contrary, it faced increasing difficulties in dealing with shifts in the correlation of political forces in Russian society, and, as we know now, it ultimately failed. It worked very well, however, in the first phases of perestroika, when the political struggle was essentially "at the top," and until the revolution descended "from above" onto the shoulders of Soviet society.

The tactic began to show serious defects when glasnost and democratization reached a "critical mass" and put in motion autonomous processes, uncontrollable from the center or from above. The political leadership of the Party unwillingly became involved in bitter clashes provoked by "external" protagonists. Some of them—national movements, informal organizations, new political parties, and individual figures like Boris Yeltsin—became powerful and influential. Under these new conditions, the search for compromises became more difficult with each passing day. In turn, these collisions produced serious conflicts within the Party leadership,[8] ultimately leading to the coup of August 1991.[9]

Gorbachev, therefore, went much further than Khrushchev. His principal target—when he understood the real dimension of the crisis—was the *Stalinist system* as a totality of political and economic structures. As we have already noted, he did not reach this conclusion at the very beginning but only gradually. Initially, Gorbachev was not entirely outside the framework of Stalinism, and he found his way only in the process of perestroika. But there is no doubt that he clearly perceived, early on, the necessity of a second and deeper phase of de-Stalinization. In June 1986, he wrote, "Our economy is fully disorganized and we find ourselves only at the beginning of the road. Really at the beginning. And if somebody thinks that we can restructure the situation in one or two years, he is really a naive man!"[10] Gorbachev himself revealed toward

[8]Solidarity within the Politburo was jeopardized, for example, by the tragedy in Tbilisi on the night of April 8, 1989. The work of the two special investigators, T. Gdlian and N. Ivanov, and their fight against Egor Ligachev also threatened Politburo unity. Gorbachev, on both occasions, avoided making personal statements, giving free rein to public discussion. But this gave the impression that he was excessively impartial, or even was protecting corruption among Party officials, thus diminishing his popularity in the country.

[9]For an analysis of the August coup and the events surrounding it, see Giulietto Chiesa, *Cronaca del Golpe Rosso* (Milan: Baldini & Castoldi, 1991).

[10]Chiesa and Medvedev, *La rivoluzione di Gorbachev*, 21.

the end of 1989 how difficult and complicated was the transition: "While, during the first steps, we thought that the question was essentially that of correcting some limited deformation of the social mechanism and of improving the system, which was the result of decades of experience and by and large was reliable enough, now we speak of the necessity of a radical restructuring of the entire social edifice—from the economic base to the superstructure."[11]

Moreover, Gorbachev possessed a culture and a political experience very different from those of the previous generation. He was at once a man who had passed through the entire *cursus honorum* of the apparatus and had learned all of its secrets, and a man continuing the effort at change that had occurred during his youth and that he had seen defeated. One cannot overlook the fact that the beginning of perestroika is connected with the names of individuals who were active during the Khrushchev era, the so-called generation of the sixties (*shestidesiatniki*). Gorbachev and his closest advisers seem to have assiduously sought out the many intellectuals, academicians, and political functionaries who had been shunted for almost two decades to obscure offices and institutes and to remote embassies: Anatolii Cherniaev, Georgii Shakhnazarov, Aleksandr Iakovlev, Fedor Burlatsky, Egor Iakovlev, Iurii Kariakin, Evgenii Ambartsumov, Ivan Frolov, Nail Bikkenin, Evgenii Primakov. All of them were men with the same sorts of experiences and from the same stock, even if they had gone through Brezhnevism with different fortunes and different degrees of adaptation.

There is a need for further research on the influence of dissent on the ideas of perestroika, especially the influence of a particular kind of dissent—"state dissent," as displayed by the Czechoslovak Communist party in 1968. Gorbachev, not by accident, surrounded himself with men all of whom had been, in different ways, defeated during the 1960s, men who, having been punished, demoted, and cast aside, nevertheless refused the temptation to become dissenters or to emigrate. These men did not lose the connections among themselves or with the long list of exiled people. It seems to me that men like these helped Gorbachev to broaden his ideas beyond the boundaries of his previous experience as a Party apparatchik. The "revolutionary" character of perestroika appears to be in part the result of this kind of indirect influence, surprisingly mixed with the sincere idea of a "return to Lenin." In this sense, Gorbachev

---

[11]"Sotsialisticheskaia ideia i revoliutsionnaia perestroika," *Pravda*, November 16, 1989.

remained an iron man of the apparatus, an integral politician who never lost sight of his tactical and strategical aims. As we have tried to explain, he could not tell the truth, at least not all of it and not too suddenly. If he had done so, he would have risked being ousted immediately by the same interests that had defeated Khrushchev.

In this sense, too, Gorbachev demonstrated that he had carefully studied Khrushchev's experience and defeat. However, he was not simply a cold-blooded tactician and a refined pragmatist. He seems to have understood (and in this sense he represented a complete mutation in the experience of the Soviet Communist party) that social processes are slow in their essence and that it is a mistake to attempt to control them with short cuts. Nor can democratization—and he has repeated this many times—be ordered by state mandate. There are unavoidable steps that must be followed; there is a school of democracy that everybody should have the time to attend; there is the need to learn the complicated procedure of a discussion among different positions, expressed without constraint. Finally—and this, in my opinion, was one of the most prominent characteristics of Gorbachev's conception of perestroika—he constantly bore in mind the fact that always and everywhere (but particularly in Russia, and in the Soviet Union) popular pressure is not necessarily destined to assume democratic forms and produce democratic results.

Certainly Gorbachev defined himself as a communist throughout his years in power. But his communism of January 1985 was very different from that of the early 1990s. The Soviet leader worked within a framework of part Marxism and part Leninism, yet he moved outside the ideology of "Marxism-Leninism." The idea of "interdependence" that he unveiled at the Twenty-seventh Party Congress was light-years beyond the Khrushchevian idea of "peaceful coexistence among states with different social systems." On this course, Gorbachev would somberly proclaim the superiority of "general and human" over "class" interests, and he would no longer consider the individual rights of citizens to be subordinate to those of the state or inferior to those of the collectivity. He would arrive at the endorsement of the "rule-of-law" state as a permanent juridical-institutional form, as an essential element of *any* democratic society, including those that would eventually build socialism.

It was quite difficult to detect any organic conception of socialism in Gorbachev's pronouncements at the time, and, as already indicated, he was "sincere" only to a certain extent. From another perspective, he had repeatedly changed his ideas—for instance, regarding political pluralism—to meet the needs of the situation. Within a few months, Gorbachev changed his point of view almost completely, beginning with a strenuous defense of the leading role of the Party (to be precise, he used political more than ideological arguments, and he emphasized the Party's "unifying role" as an antidote against dangerous centrifugal tendencies) and ending with a full recognition of the possibility of political pluralism and a multiparty system. Nevertheless, his vision entailed a reduction in the political power of the Party, an increase in that of the soviets, and a hybrid economic system with elements of both planning and markets, adapted to the realities of a society that had lived for sixty years in conditions of total state ownership of the means of production.

This was not an "organic solution" to the problems of Soviet society. Gorbachev's actions and ideas resembled a first approximation, although with a clear enough tendency: the prospect of a new multinational, federative state, with a special social-democratic regime, characterized by a high level of state economic control, dictated by the obvious exigencies of a redistribution of national wealth in a country highly differentiated economically, socially, and culturally.

In the sphere of foreign policy, Gorbachev, proposing a "new thinking" based on interdependence, abandoned forever the ideas of a world revolution and of an "inevitable" victory of communism. The new model he envisaged embraced practically the whole sphere of international relations: its methodology, the behavior of states and individuals, the system of rights and institutions, the use and purpose of armed forces, tactics and strategies in regional conflicts, and so on. His goal was to integrate the Soviet Union into the world market, to involve it in a network of economic, political, and military relations and commitments with the outside world, and to transform it into an interlocutor completely different from the one the world had known in the previous decades.

Whether Gorbachev's plans and intentions were realistic is by now a moot question. What we can conclude, however, in retrospect, is that perestroika implied an idea of society that was completely different from the other models that had been experimented with during the seventy-year existence of the Soviet Union. Khrushchev and Lenin—not just Stalin—appear to be incompatible with perestroika's direction and evolution, which, on the theoretical plane, seem more related to the elaborations of the Second International and to the ideas of European Marxists and socialists at the time when they were opposing Lenin's and

Stalin's experiments, both before and after World War II. There is another enormous difference between Khrushchev's and Gorbachev's eras: Hungary in 1956 and Czechoslovakia in 1968 were the last manifestations of a concept of world communism that would be erected through the export of revolution. Autumn 1989 marked the end of any idea of "world revolution" and the beginning of an attempt at world interdependence, characterized by the deideologization of international relations and a recognition of the interests of all the protagonists, great and small alike. Does the recent past then mark the end of history? That seems unlikely, even in Hegelian terms. Like T. S. Eliot, I prefer to say that "to make an end is to make a beginning. The end is where we start from."

18

Khrushchev and Gorbachev—similarity and difference: commentary

ROBERT V. DANIELS

The preceding chapters establish a historical background that allows us to perceive significant differences between the administrations of Khrushchev and Gorbachev, particularly differences in the extent and accomplishment of each leader's reform effort. In considering these differences, I should like to focus primarily on the political context of each man's consolidation of power as a base for reform and the eventual outcome of this consolidation.

I have been working for many years with a concept that I call "the circular flow of power" as a model for understanding the personal power and control exercised by Soviet leaders. Through use of the appointive power of the general (or first) secretary and the apparatus of the central secretariat, a Soviet leader controlled the appointments of Party secretaries at the regional, provincial, and district levels and through them manipulated the nominally democratic committee and conference structure of the Party at the local level. From this power base, he stage-managed the national Party congresses and secured the automatic and unanimous approval of the Central Committee slate he had chosen. This configuration of the slate was carefully arranged according to what Gorbachev called "the schedule of allocations"—a secret rule by which Central Committee seats were allotted to the various functional components of the bureaucracy in accordance with their importance. Thus, after passage of a sufficient period of time, a general secretary could control the whole circuit of power within the system and dictate the composition of the Central Committee, which, in turn, would confirm him as general secretary. This system was, of course, created by Stalin in the course of his rise to power in the 1920s and was reapplied each time a major succession occurred in the Soviet regime.

Khrushchev used his powers as first secretary to restaff the lower apparatus in order to ensure his control of the central organs, and he controlled the circular flow of power from 1953 through the Twentieth Party Congress in 1956 and the crisis of the anti-Party group in 1957. This crisis enabled him to capitalize on the system and to appoint his own people to the Party Presidium as well. Indirect evidence indicates, however, that in the winter of 1959–60, before the U-2 incident of May 1960 and the dramatic reorganization of the secretariat that followed, the neo-Stalinists—Brezhnev, Suslov, and Kozlov—in effect broke into the circular flow of power and took control of appointments away from Khrushchev. From that time on, Khrushchev's enemies steadily tightened their control over the Party apparatus while leaving him to flounder at the policy level. This disruption of the "circular flow" perhaps explains some of the erratic behavior and "hare-brained schemes" of Khrushchev's later years, as he tried to outmaneuver the neo-Stalinist opposition in a system in which he had lost ultimate control. Here I underscore my agreement with Vitalii Lel'chuk's distinction between Khrushchev's later reform efforts and his earlier, more radical and energetic ones.

Brezhnev did not really need to use the circular flow upon his assumption of power; he simply took advantage of what had been accomplished during the latter part of the Khrushchev era. The frequency of removals and replacements of regional Party secretaries was very low during his tenure, although cumulatively over his eighteen years in power these replacements amounted to a substantial restaffing of the apparatus with relatively young people. It was precisely these younger people, in my opinion, who were the basis of reformist successes between 1982 and 1985.

After the death of Brezhnev, however, Andropov immediately began operating the circular flow again, stepping up the renovation of the apparatus. Under Chernenko, it slowed down once more, this time practically to a standstill. Gorbachev put the system to work for himself very intensively in his first year, from 1985 until the Twenty-seventh Party Congress in 1986, in order to eliminate Brezhnev's appointees and put in his own people. His success in doing so was facilitated by the fact that the Brezhnev appointees represented the old, postpurge generation.

They had been in office as a generation for decades and by the 1980s were either dying or sufficiently decrepit to provide a ready justification for their removal.

As Gorbachev began to succeed by using the old system, however, he faced a problem: As people rise in the *nomenklatura,* their interest in maintaining the old system becomes firmer. Younger people who might have seemed to be reformers when they were appointed as regional first secretaries of the Party and as Central Committee members became more and more conservative and failed to remain reliable supporters of re-form. I believe that Gorbachev perceived this phenomenon and indicated its danger in the intriguing meeting that he held with leading writers just prior to the June 1986 congress of the USSR Writers' Union. At that meeting, Gorbachev complained that perestroika was going badly, that the bureaucracy was blocking him at every turn, and that the reformers needed the help of the writers. The unofficial (samizdat) version of this discussion concludes with Gorbachev's comment that "our enemies"—meaning Western Sovietologists—"are writing that the apparatus broke the neck of Khrushchev, and they are saying that the apparatus will break our neck, too." I think this represents Gorbachev's realization that he could not use the apparatus either as a basis of personal power or as an instrument for instituting reforms from above, but that instead he needed to broaden his power base and find forces that would support him in what has been called, if you will, "civil society."

I believe the real origin of systematic glasnost, of Gorbachev's deci-sion to unleash the press, was precisely his predicament within the sys-tem. His choice in favor of glasnost then led him into an extraordinary series of political steps. He tried to appeal to the rank and file of the Party against the apparatus in the elections to the Nineteenth Party Con-ference in 1988 but failed to make much headway and was unable to force the conference to make the basic leadership changes that he wanted. This experience of confronting the apparatus—knowing, surely, what had happened to Khrushchev—convinced Gorbachev that he had to establish a completely new base of power. I would agree with those who argue that Gorbachev did not intend to abandon the Party when he embarked on perestroika. Rather, he subsequently discovered that the only way he could survive personally, or implement the reforms he be-lieved essential for the country, was to find another source of support and authority. This exigency led him to experiment with electoral poli-tics and a genuine parliamentary body, changes by which Gorbachev undid not only the Stalinist system of politics but the Leninist system as well, however much Lenin continued to be quoted.

By virtue of the circumstances of the resistance that he faced, and because of the existence of a far more modern, urbanized, and better-educated population than that of Khrushchev's time (a development for which Brezhnev should receive some credit), Gorbachev was able to create a new power base and effectively mobilize new sources of support for reform, above all the Soviet press. I think we must recognize that, at this point, the differences of degree between Khrushchev and Gorbachev as reformers became qualitative and fundamental. With that in mind, I would tend to side with those scholars who see the reforms of Khrushchev and Gorbachev as deserving distinct analytical approaches.

━━

19

The reformer's dilemma—damned if it's reform, damned if it's revolution: commentary

WILLIAM TAUBMAN

Before discussing the Khrushchev era as a period of reform in Soviet history, I should like to address the broader issue of reform versus revolution. I shall attempt first to pinpoint the relationship between the two, at least as far as it applies to the Khrushchev and Gorbachev eras (although the distinction may apply to the nineteenth century as well) and then to examine three possible determinants of the outcome of reform under the two leaders: the party-state, the nature of society, and what may be called, following Linden's example, the personality of the emperor.

There are, I believe, three possible approaches to defining reform and revolution. The first makes the distinction in terms of the actor who is doing the reforming or "revolutionizing." If the action comes from above and is instituted by the regime or the leader, it is more likely to be considered as reform; if the action comes from below, it is more likely to be considered as revolution. The second approach focuses on the means, or perhaps the pace, of change: Reform is nonviolent and revolution is violent, or reform is gradual and revolution precipitous. One can immediately imagine exceptions to both of these approaches. The third approach, that used by Emmons in his analysis of tsarist reform, defines reform as change within a given system and revolution as a change of the system itself. In my opinion, this is the most useful definition.

Now let us relate this understanding of reform and revolution to the Khrushchev and Gorbachev periods. Linden concludes from his study of Khrushchev that reform of the Soviet system was impossible, and he raises the issue of whether a reform prince can change a regime without at the same time putting himself out of power. Chiesa argues that Gorbachev attempted not to rectify or reform the system but to transform it through the revolution of perestroika. Yet the very idea of revolution raises the specter of reform spinning out of control. It is tempting to conclude that reform cannot work very well precisely because it is merely reform, that reform will work only when it is no longer reform, but revolution. But if revolution means a new leadership and even a new regime, why would any leader embark upon reform? Any leader who did so would surely meet, and in Soviet history did meet, resistance prompted in part by the danger that the reform process would prove uncontrollable and would turn into revolution.

We saw this resistance to spiraling reform/revolution appear under Gorbachev, and it strikes me that one might characterize the fate of reform at the end of the nineteenth century in the same manner. Several authors in this volume claim that the key to the failure of reform in the late nineteenth and early twentieth centuries was that it did not go far enough and embark upon real democratization. Others write of the constraints exerted on reform by the empire, suggesting that thoroughgoing reform was impossible without first dismantling the empire. These arguments seem to reinforce my conclusion about reform in the Soviet system: Reform may not work until it goes beyond reform and becomes a change of the system, which is exactly what real democratization and an end to the empire would have represented. This understanding of reform makes it very unattractive for a political actor to embark on the road to reform, for it would put him in a no-win situation: He is damned if it remains reform and damned if it becomes revolution.

Turning now to the three possible determinants of the outcome of reform in the Soviet Union under Khrushchev and Gorbachev—the party-state, the nature of society, and the personality of the emperor—let us examine how these determinants have changed over time. The party-state has been discussed extensively in the preceding chapters, and it is clear that the *nomenklatura* operated under both Khrushchev and Gorbachev to thwart reform. However, there was a fundamental difference between the apparatuses confronting the two leaders. The Khrushchev/Brezhnev leadership had been catapulted into high office as the beneficiaries of Stalin's purges and as a single generation. Looking at biographical data, one discerns that Stalin actually liquidated everyone over the age of thirty-five who had occupied a leadership position in the

Soviet Union, with the exception of a handful of cronies. Practically no one born before 1902 figures in the leadership after 1953; they simply are no longer alive. The members of the beneficiary generation, which Sheila Fitzpatrick describes as the "newcomers" (*vydvizhentsy*),[1] were trained as tough young men in their twenties to take over when the purges ended, and Khrushchev had to contend with them until they died. The demographic fact of that peculiar, long-lived leadership generation makes for a fundamental difference between the 1950s and 1960s, on the one hand, and the 1980s, on the other.

To be sure, under Gorbachev, there was still the problem of the apparatus replicating itself, like a kind of political DNA, with the younger people promoted within the apparatus turning out to be uncomfortably similar to the older generation in their attitudes. But the most fundamental change with respect to the apparatus in the late 1980s was made by Gorbachev's decision to switch his primary political base from the Party to the state. In my opinion, he was unreasonably criticized at the time by many radical reformers, who saw him amassing personal power when in fact he was trying to make himself immune to any attempted conspiracy on the model of 1964. As the putsch of August 1991 showed, he did not succeed in this endeavor, but the deeper reason for his fall was the very fact that he encouraged the transformation of reform from above into a revolution from below.

As for the scope of change in Soviet society since Khrushchev, Chiesa draws our attention to the changes in city-country relations, urbanization, mass education and professional training, the growth of mass media, and the proliferation of contacts with the external world. Chiesa's enumeration of these changes reminds me of the argument made by Moshe Lewin, who has suggested that the real change in Russian or Soviet society came after Khrushchev—not in the 1880s, not in 1917 or the 1920s, not even in the 1950s, but only in the 1960s and 1970s, with the creation of a middle class and of, in effect, a civil society.[2] At this point, however, I would raise a warning flag. One must ask whether Soviet society of the 1960s and 1970s was indeed a civil society or whether it was still a mass society. The concept of "mass society" has been described by Hannah Arendt and William Kornhauser, among oth-

[1]See, for example, Sheila Fitzpatrick, *The Russian Revolution, 1917–1932* (Oxford: Oxford University Press, 1982), 129–34, 159–60.
[2]Moshe Lewin, *The Gorbachev Phenomenon* (Berkeley: University of California Press, 1988), chap. 3.

ers, as a society insufficiently characterized by the development of inter-mediary groups standing between the state and primary groups and individuals.[3] These intermediary groups prevent the state from being overwhelmed by the masses but at the same time prevent the masses from being mobilized by new totalitarian movements. I think the question of whether the Soviet Union was still a "mass society" remains open.

Finally, let us consider the personality of the emperor. Linden describes Khrushchev's origins and his inability to escape them, which he seems to attribute to Khrushchev's training and experience in the Stalin-ist apparatus, and he writes of Khrushchev as a kind of true believer in Soviet ideology, although he also refers to Khrushchev's "personal identity." It seems to me, however, that if we are really interested in personality in the way Robert Tucker has been interested in the personality of Stalin,[4] we have to go beyond examination of Khrushchev's Stalinist roots. In my opinion, Khrushchev had a much more complicated personality than that of a simple "newcomer"—a personality that undermined his activities, his position, and, in the end, the cause of reform itself. Some of these issues are raised by Lel'chuk and are an invitation to psychobiography.

If the subsurface elements of Khrushchev's personality were indeed related to his "hare-brained schemes" and hence to his downfall, one is forced to ask whether Gorbachev was really all that different. On the surface, Gorbachev's personality stands in considerable contrast: far more stable, more tolerant of criticism, less prone to adventurous forays. At least it seemed so, yet as time passed, Gorbachev increasingly appeared vulnerable to the very same character flaws as Khrushchev had been. I am tempted, therefore, to assert that, in spite of the fact that Gorbachev was a different kind of person, endowed with a personality more conducive to furthering the cause of reform, the changes that he encouraged in society, combined with the lack of change in the party-state, doomed him in the end.

[3]Hannah Arendt, *The Origins of Totalitarianism* (New York: Harcourt, Brace, 1951); William Kornhauser, *The Politics of Mass Society* (New York: Free Press, 1968).
[4]Robert C. Tucker, *Stalin as Revolutionary, 1879–1929: A Study in History and Person-ality* (New York: W. W. Norton, 1990), and *Stalin in Power: The Revolution from Above, 1929–1941* (New York: W. W. Norton, 1990).

Part V

The past, the present, and the future

20

Perestroika and the role of representative institutions in contemporary Soviet politics

SERGEI B. STANKEVICH[1]

I should like to draw your attention to some fundamental features that, in my view, characterize perestroika as a truly peaceful revolution. I must apologize for not submitting a written text of my presentation, but our political life is so intensive that, unfortunately, it is practically impossible to combine it with any sort of serious scholarship. It is quite likely that my participation in this conference will be the swan song of Sergei Stankevich as a historian.

Five years have passed since the beginning of perestroika, and this is a sufficiently significant historical interlude to allow us to attempt to identify some of its systemic features. Furthermore, perestroika manifests not only temporal duration but also relatively wide spatial distribution and variety. We can compare the course of events in the USSR with what has happened and is happening in the countries of Eastern Europe, in order to reach more substantively founded conclusions. In my view, a peaceful, antitotalitarian, and antibureaucratic revolution is taking place in both Eastern Europe and the Soviet Union. It represents a single phenomenon, albeit with several variants, in which the first stage is the modernization of the regime, and the second, the regime's transformation. The first stage is characterized by attempts to adapt the existing order to changed historical realities but without affecting its foundation.

[1][Sergei Stankevich was a deputy mayor of Moscow and a member of the Supreme Soviet in May 1990, and he later became a presidential counselor in the Yeltsin government. Although his views have evolved since the time of the conference, Stankevich's analysis of the political situation in the Soviet Union and of perestroika's prospects is presented here as a historical document, a primary source reflecting the perspective of a prominent member of the democratic movement in Russia at the time.—Ed.]

The second stage involves truly radical transformations that affect the economic, legal, and political foundations of the society.

Within this general type, there are substantial differences among the various countries involved. For example, in Czechoslovakia and East Germany the transition to transformation was direct, and it is easy to understand why. In Czechoslovakia the stage of modernization was largely completed in the late 1960s, and in East Germany a powerful accelerating factor was the interaction with neighboring West Germany. In Poland, there were repeated attempts at modernization, and the effort to embark on transformation at the beginning of the 1980s was halted by force. After martial law was lifted, the [new] point of departure was already the second stage, the transformation of the regime, which is also proceeding in an intensive fashion. The stage of modernization thus far has not been completed in Bulgaria, but it is apparently approaching completion. Hungary represents the special case of a gradual transmutation of modernization into transformation, where everything proceeded relatively smoothly, in an evolutionary way—mainly, by the way, because of the unique role played by the ruling party, which de facto assured the fluidity of transition.

In the Soviet Union, we have a very variegated situation. In some republics, even the modest attempts to modernize the regime may be merely ephemeral. I have in mind, above all, the Central Asian republics. The Baltic republics turned out to be quite advanced, and they have already embarked upon transformation. As far as the core areas of the Soviet Union are concerned, especially Russia, the tasks that should be resolved at the stage of modernization have unfortunately not been completed: tasks such as elementary improvement of the economy; the realignment of cadres; a critical rethinking of the past; elaboration of the programs of action for the perestroika of society; accumulation of material resources; the clearing away of purely political impediments; and the creation of the legal foundation necessary for the functioning of society in this new stage, primarily freedom for the mass media and guarantees of property rights. None of this, unfortunately, has been completed.

Yet the historic segment of time that could have been devoted to the modernization of the regime in order to accomplish a smooth transition to transformation has been exhausted. Thus, perestroika finds itself now in a rather difficult situation. Time has been wasted. It has already been noted at this conference that this has been a certain distinguishing characteristic of all Russian reformers: their fateful delay, their inability to outstrip events, their incapacity for transcendent political thought. All of this has been encountered in the process of perestroika. And now, when it is patently obvious that we must proceed from modernization efforts, which have reached a blind alley, to transformation—alas, we are faced with the fact that forces that should be leading this sort of transition have proved incapable of doing so. The fact of the matter is that transformation is integrally linked with rather painful and unpopular measures, such as the lifting of controls over most prices, allowing inefficient enterprises to go bankrupt, and enduring a significant decrease in the overall standard of living of the population for at least a ten-year period.

Naturally, only a very popular government can undertake steps that are so unpopular. Unfortunately, the leaders (*lidery*) of perestroika have not only wasted time, but they have also lost a considerable amount of their popularity. The result is that the people are now unwilling to tolerate painful measures from this particular group of leaders. The May 1, 1990, demonstration that many of you may have seen [on television] or at least read about in the press accentuated this crisis of confidence. Thus, the distinctive paradox of the current stage of perestroika is that in order to move ahead, the leadership must receive a new infusion of trust when the past stock has been nearly exhausted and the measures that must be undertaken will diminish it even further.

What is apparently needed here is some sort of substitution, an intervening replacement of the team. Naturally, the ideal scenario would be for the Communist party to retreat into opposition. This would produce an abrupt outburst of social energy and immense expectations addressed to the new government, which would permit it to take unpopular measures, as has happened in Poland. Unfortunately, what distinguishes the Communist parties from other political parties, with rare exceptions, is that for them the goal of retaining power has become an end in itself. Even in theory, and even temporarily, any loss of power is impermissible. Thus, the possibility of using that reservoir of energy inherent in the realignment of political parties does not exist in the given situation. However, I have a strong feeling that at least some steps in this direction are inevitable. I have in mind the resignation of President Gorbachev from the post of general secretary and the appointment of a non-

Communist to the office of prime minister, who would then probably form a coalition government. Without these steps, a successful transition to the stage of transformation is highly doubtful.

In turn, this raises some questions concerning the political system. The Congress of People's Deputies, a rather unique political institution, was conceived in accordance with the traditions, albeit somewhat modernized, of estate representation. An excessive application of the principle of representation was the [guiding] idea behind the congress. The congress was convened not to make decisions but rather to represent the entire spectrum of public opinion and to include all social groups and all categories, not in proportion to their numerical representation in the population but in accordance with some sort of preconceived plan. Groups that were more moderate and more loyal to the central authority were supposed to predominate and to exert a restraining influence on the congress as a whole. The result was a distinctive all-union forum, where one could listen to a variety of voices and simultaneously—having, as it were, the society in miniature before oneself—test out the political plans of the leadership on this model of public opinion. In that sense, the first Congress of People's Deputies [May 25 to December 12, 1989—ed.] played an immense role. It really was a shock to public consciousness and irreversibly changed it. From the point of view of the political education of the people, those few days were worth many years. However, already beginning with the second session of the congress, the historic task of this institution was played out. The congress was politically powerless and too easily controlled. Once the interest in political debate began to wane, the congress began to discredit the very idea of democracy. Because devotion to democracy lacks deep roots among a considerable proportion of the people, easy enchantment with the new democratic institutions alternates with equally easy disappointment in them.

On the other hand, the Supreme Soviet has undergone a remarkable evolution. This development once again confirms the need for very precise political analysis. Let me provide an example. When the first congress elected the Supreme Soviet, Iurii Afanasiev made his famous reference to the "Stalinist-Brezhnevite" character of the Supreme Soviet. The Inter-Regional Group of deputies, which later assumed the role of a parliamentary opposition, decided that its chief slogan would be, "No power to the Supreme Soviet." The Inter-Regional Group wanted to transfer as many of the Supreme Soviet's prerogatives as possible to the

Congress of People's Deputies, which it regarded as less conservative and less manipulable. However, subsequent events proved the opposite.

The Supreme Soviet has undergone a major evolution over the past year, but the extent of that evolution should not be overestimated; the Supreme Soviet is not as yet a real, functioning parliament (*parlament*). Nevertheless, the degree of its evolution is readily apparent. By the very logic of the legislative process, having to work together from early morning to late evening over legislative drafts, needing to seek compromise because the voters invariably demand a constant stream of new statutes, individuals—even when they had diametrically opposed convictions and personal animosities—gradually found it possible to collaborate, even if only on a limited range of issues.

In this way, the parliament was gradually being built as an institution. This process is not as yet finished, but it must be said that the Supreme Soviet is presently the most workmanlike institution of the political system, and it is slowly becoming an increasingly independent one. Its most significant effort to acquire independent political authority took place during a debate on the question of presidential powers. The initial version of the law on the presidency granted the president very extensive powers, but eventually many of the Supreme Soviet's prerogatives were successfully defended. Both prior to and during the debate, numerous correctives that strengthened the status of the Supreme Soviet, albeit still insufficiently, were successfully introduced into the draft bill. Nevertheless, in comparison with the original text, this was a very important compromise. In the future, I believe that the Supreme Soviet will evolve in the direction of a system of checks and balances—to be sure, probably not in its classical version but, like everything that takes place among us, in some specifically Russian variant.

In connection with this, I rest my greatest hope about the next stage of perestroika on the following chain of developments. The Supreme Soviet, greatly pressured by obviously impatient voters, who are continually and increasingly presented with opportunities to influence their deputies, is ready to adopt some very significant legislative measures. Rather radical versions of the law on entrepreneurial activity are currently under consideration, and the tax-reform legislation is also promising. A law on freedom of the press and of the other mass media is under consideration; it has been completed and awaits only a final debate. It was on the agenda several times, but political maneuvering has prevented its being brought up. However, judging by the mood of the

Supreme Soviet, the legislators are fully determined to pass this law before the end of the current session. A law on political parties and civic organizations is also coming up.

On the one hand, these steps create a new legal environment for entrepreneurship, and, on the other, they present a political opportunity to buttress all of these changes and to make them more profound. In this way, the Supreme Soviet is ready to provide needed opportunities on the federal (*federal'nyi*)—that is, the union—level, while at the same time the legislative organs of the union-republics are also beginning to function, and they will most likely proceed further than the Supreme Soviet in this direction. They were relatively recently elected under new circumstances, and they reflect much more accurately the contemporary correlation of forces in the republics and the society. This will provide a very powerful stimulus to the transition to transformation at the republican level.

Finally, there is one more level, the level of towns and of urban municipalities (*munitsipalitety*). A real democratic breakthrough took place at that level during the most recent elections. The coalition that calls itself Democratic Russia gained a majority in the city soviets of Moscow, Leningrad, Gorky, and Sverdlovsk. According to our calculations, almost twenty major cities in the Russian federation alone are controlled by Democratic Russia. This is an increasingly radical level [of political life—ed.]. It opens the way for the cities (starting with Moscow and Leningrad) to become seed beds for the development of the most modern forms of entrepreneurship. Moreover, it would permit, on the one hand, the strengthening of the overall position of the democratic coalition in the country, because it would mark the transition from agitation by slogans to convincing the people by using political power to produce real results. On the other hand, it would also permit further extension of trust in the reformist course. President Gorbachev would be able to say, "Look here, we are proposing a package of radical economic measures, and this is a reliable package because the steps being proposed by us are already functioning in Moscow and Leningrad, and you can see the truth of this with your own eyes."

In conclusion, let me stress once again that we are presently at the point of transition from modernization to transformation and that this is, indeed, a decisive moment for perestroika.

21

Glasnost in Russia and the USSR:
the 1860s and the 1980s

IURII M. BATURIN[1]

Reform is the sort of thing that, once it gets going, there is nothing you can do about it.

M. E. Saltykov-Shchedrin

One of the first comparative studies of glasnost—to be sure, for a briefer period than is covered in this conference—was conducted by the nineteenth-century Russian poet Vasilii Kurochkin, who in one of his poems demonstrated how in three years "baby glasnost" was transformed into a mumbling old woman.[2] The approach proposed here is systems analysis, diametrically opposed to the method of poetry. I have condensed the theoretical portion of my paper, preserving only enough to demarcate the limits of my study and to delineate its terminology. The latter is especially important for an author who wants to avoid misunderstandings, such as occur when his words are made to express more than he intends to say.

[1][Iurii Baturin was one of the authors of the draft laws on the press and on the archives then under consideration by the Supreme Soviet, and he has been actively involved in Russian politics under Yeltsin. This chapter is Baturin's summary of his remarks at the conference, and it reflects the nature and vocabulary of contemporary Soviet political discourse and the debates over freedom of the press during the late 1980s.—Ed.]

[2]Vasilii S. Kurochkin, "Glasnost' 1859 goda i glasnost' 1862 goda," in his *Stikhotvoreniia, stat'i, fel'tony* (Moscow, 1957), 153–54. [The poem is a satirical account of two incidents. The first, which took place in 1859, grew out of the arrest of a well-known ethnographer; it was given wide publicity in the press and was perceived as the first public (*glasnyi*) protest against police arbitrariness. The second, in 1862, concerned the arrest of another individual; though the affair was similar, the treatment in the press was much more discreet.—Ed.]

The function of a political or economic system is to control a nexus of political or economic relations. A system is functional when it is characterized by the conditions that are necessary and sufficient to ensure its operations. There are two kinds of functional conditions: (a) real (existing) conditions and (b) desirable (programmatic) conditions. The reform of a system may be viewed as a conversion of its real initial functional state into a desirable functional state. In this paper, I shall be focusing on only one functional aspect, glasnost.

Let us first analyze and compare the initial real functional states of the systems of the 1860s and of the 1980s. They manifest the same five characteristics. The first is an extreme degree of bureaucratization. The Russian bureaucracy of the 1860s strove mightily to seize in its hands control over all aspects of social existence. "What kind of control over ministerial power was possible, and what kind of accountability could there be for it, as well as for the administration subordinated to it, given the network of connections and solidarity of interests of our bureaucracy?" wrote the historian S. P. Pokrovskii. "For successful control, one needed light and glasnost, but they were lacking in our government at the time. The dark curtain of official secrecy carefully protected the arbitrariness of the bureaucracy, and under this heavy shroud, a stifling atmosphere smothered every living creature or honorable striving, even if it arose in individual personalities."[3]

The society was completely isolated from government policy. For example, it was considered "better to maintain secrecy than [to adopt] glasnost" in budgetary and fiscal matters. "It is impossible to speak under such conditions of any sort of legality in financial outlays, while the harm inflicted on the state budget by this secrecy is obvious. The state budget is not trusted at all, either inside the country or by foreign governments, for which Russia is a poor credit risk because our budgets are kept secret."[4] This passage so well describes the situation of the early 1980s that, if it were not for the citation, hardly anyone would doubt that what was being discussed was the USSR of the era of perestroika.

It is equally instructive to compare the degree of bureaucratization of tsarist Russia and of the contemporary Soviet Union. The Soviet bureaucracy historically originated in the administrative-command system of War Communism, which was gradually transformed into an appa-

---

[3]S. P. Pokrovskii, *Ministerskaia vlast' v Rossii: Istoriko-iuridicheskoe issledovanie* (Iaroslavl, 1906), 288–89.
[4]Ibid., 328–29.

ratus for the extraordinary administration of the economic, social, and cultural life of the country. The transition to this form of administration was justified by the goal of solving in as short a time as possible the whole complex of problems that arose in connection with such conditions as economic collapse, famine, and the need for a cultural revolution. On the surface, this goal corresponded to the needs of society, but it was being pursued by authoritarian methods that ultimately resulted in the corruption of democratic values and ideals. The equality of citizens under the law was replaced by the equality of citizens before the arbitrariness of the political authority. The bureaucracy successfully veiled itself in democratic forms and systematically strove to persuade the public that the socialist bureaucracy was the only possible bureaucracy. The state so submerged the society that it—the state—became incapable of performing all the functions that it had taken upon itself. The fact that bureaucratization had reached dangerous proportions was even admitted officially.[5]

The second characteristic common to the systems of the 1860s and the 1980s is the absence of democratic traditions. In this regard, the situation in the Soviet Union has already been sketched out in the preceding discussion of bureaucratization. Things were no better in monarchical Russia. As far as glasnost was concerned, for example, nothing could be "published for public information" without police permission.[6]

The third characteristic is the presence of a crisis situation. In nineteenth-century Russia, the crisis was provoked by the military defeat after the fall of Sevastopol in the Crimean War. New ideas began to gain favor in government circles: "Thoughts that must be hidden cannot be controlled or debated and, therefore, as a result, may become dangerous much more easily. . . . They may lead to systematic opposition and even without journalistic articles and despite any censorship attain significance, weight, and influence in society. . . . One should fear the actions and consequences of compulsory silence."[7] The acute crisis in the USSR was quite obvious, and, just as in the past, it was decided to open the "spigot" of glasnost.

The fourth characteristic is a mighty and harsh censorship. The Rus-

---

[5]See *XIX Vsesoiuznaia konferentsiia Kommunisticheskoi partii Sovetskogo Soiuza, 28 iunia—1 iulia 1988 goda: Stenograficheskii otchet* (Moscow, 1988), 2: 145.
[6]*Pamiatnaia kniga politseiskikh zakonov dlia chinov gorodskoi politsii* (St. Petersburg, 1856), 129 (art. 26).
[7]As cited in Vladimir Rozenberg and V. Iakushkin, *Russkaia pechat' i tsenzura v proshlom i nastoiashchem* (Moscow, 1905), 73.

sian censorship statute forbade criticism not only of the government but also of any "authorities" subject to it (that is, the bureaucracy itself), "in order not to weaken the respect due to them" (art. 166) or to diminish [the subjects'] "feelings of devotion, loyalty, and voluntary submission" (art. 167). It was forbidden to make any "proposals concerning change in any aspect of state administration or in the rights and privileges [of the population]" (art. 169) until such time as the government itself undertook such steps. The statute further declared that, even if no policy issues were considered, "articles concerning state administration may not be published without the approval of the ministry whose jurisdiction is affected" (art. 141). Such topics could not be addressed either "directly" or "indirectly" (art. 168). It was strictly forbidden to publish "historical excerpts and judgments that by form of expression of recounted events or by reference to other circumstances contained therein manifest an unfavorable attitude toward . . . the government" (art. 180). Such prohibitions extended also to the sphere of foreign policy (art. 171).[8]

The bureaucratic apparatus strove by all means to protect itself from any impartial judgment; the law provided that "no reproaches [were] permitted, even if indirect, against the government's or lawful authorities' actions and regulations, whatever the hierarchical level of such authorities."[9] In order to prevent "discussion of state and political questions," articles on Russian history had to be written "with extreme caution and only with greatest moderation."[10] Censors were strictly enjoined "not to allow into print expressions hinting at the strictness of censorship."[11]

This last provision vividly reminds one of an incident that took place in the eighties of our century. Addressing the editorial board of a very respectable Soviet journal, the representative of the Chief Administration for the Protection of State Secrets in the Press (Glavlit), attached to the Council of Ministers of the USSR, spoke against any publication on the subject of censorship "since it might lead the reader to think that censorship of the press might exist among us."[12] Strange as these words

---

[8]See *Sbornik postanovlenii i rasporiazhenii po tsenzure s 1720 po 1862 god* (St. Petersburg, 1862), 125–96.
[9]Ibid., 250.
[10]Ibid., 240.
[11]Ibid., 244.
[12]Quoted in M. Fedotov, "Bol'she svobody—vyshe otvetstvennosti," in *Glasnost': Mneniia, poiski, politika* (Moscow, 1989), 166.

were, none of the journalists present even cracked a smile. Nor was the censor trying to be funny; his institution was protecting state secrets, and it just so happened that the existence of preliminary censorship was a state secret in the USSR. Moreover, the very fact that the law on Glavlit (in contrast to the tsarist censorship statute) was not published makes one suspect that the Glavlit censors and the Soviet bureaucracy in general adhered closely to the mentality of the mid-nineteenth century—the censorship realities of both periods are so congruent. Similar censorship conditions produced the same outcome: samizdat. There are no differences in principle between the samizdat of the nineteenth century and that of the twentieth.

Finally, neither then nor now were there the necessary juridical guarantees or any mechanism for legal defense in matters of censorship.

Proceeding now to the analysis of desirable functional states, it is apparent that in both cases the goal was to get out of the crisis situation. But the repression of glasnost led to the absence of any accurate information about the existing state of affairs. That is why in 1859, the Council of Ministers recognized that "disclosure in newspaper and journal articles of existing disorders and abuses may prove useful in that by this means the government may receive information independent of official sources and in that some of this news may be used to verify official reports and to undertake appropriate measures as necessary."[13] In other words, it turned out that glasnost was useful for acquiring information and new ideas needed for drafting a program of action. The same condition occurred in the USSR after 1985.

It should be noted that the concept of glasnost was rather nebulous ("fuzzy" [this English word is used in the original—ed.]). A conceptualization of glasnost akin to the contemporary one had been formulated already in the 1860s and referred to the human right to express one's opinion regarding governmental measures and institutions and to enjoy freedom of speech and of the press. However, this understanding of glasnost was not enshrined in law either then or now.[14]

The way in which the two systems actually functioned also manifested great similarity. In 1862, the Chief Administration of Censorship was abolished, and jurisdiction over censorship was transferred to the Min-

---

[13]Rozenberg and Iakushkin, *Russkaia pechat'*, 76.
[14][For a discussion of the concept of glasnost in the era of the Great Reforms, see W. Bruce Lincoln, *In the Vanguard of Reform: Russia's Enlightened Bureaucrats, 1825–1861* (De Kalb: Northern Illinois University Press, 1982), chap. 6.—Ed.]

istry of Internal Affairs, with the introduction of the Temporary
Censorship Regulations of May 12, 1862. There were only thirteen regulations in this act, and they filled less than two pages of text. The third
and fourth of these regulations were:

In evaluating works and articles dealing with imperfections of our existing laws,
publication is to be permitted only of specialized, scholarly works, written in a
tone appropriate to the subject and concerning only such laws whose inadequacies have already been manifested in practice.
    In discussions of shortcomings and abuses of the administration, publication
of personal names and exact titles of places and institutions is not to be permitted.[15]

These regulations remind one very much of the limits on glasnost in
early perestroika. If one also takes into account discussions of what
should be done with Glavlit, during legislative drafting of the law on
state secrets, then the real conditions of the system's functioning appear
as almost identical, too.

Finally, let us address the programmatic conditions of the system's
functioning. Here, finally, one finds differences. In 1860, the issue was
limited to changes in censorship legislation; in 1987, the question of legal
guarantees of glasnost was placed on the agenda. In the 1860s, glasnost
gained ground only through memoranda submitted "upstairs" and
through journalistic publications (including those printed as samizdat).
As perestroika advanced, one encountered "alternative" legislative proposals regarding the sphere of communications (draft legislation on the
press, on the archives, and so on). As a consequence, the statute on the
press that was adopted not only abolished censorship but also proclaimed freedom of the press. In addition, a formal decision was made
to draft a statute on the citizen's right to information.

Thus, the baby glasnost, while still not a teenager, continues to flourish, and we shall yet see much from it. Saltykov-Shchedrin wrote, "For
some time we have been discovering our own America. This America is
our past. . . . There are people who even argue that this is not even the
past, but very simply our present that refers to itself in the past tense
out of delicacy."[16] Although analogies are often deceptive, they are the
least of things that lead us to delusion.

[15]*Sbornik postanovlenii*, 469.
[16]M. E. Saltykov-Shchedrin, *Sobranie sochinenii* (Moscow, 1965–77), 9: 385–86.

22

Reform and revolution: commentary

BLAIR A. RUBLE

In reviewing the various periods of reform in Russian and Soviet history analyzed in this book, certain points of consensus emerge concerning the reform process itself. These points may not be universally accepted by historians and political scientists, but they nevertheless give us a basis for coming to some general conclusions about reform in Russia. The first point of consensus appears to be that one must distinguish between reform and revolution. We have repeatedly had to consider this distinction, and it seems that the most commonly held view is that reform is change within a system, whereas revolution is the change of a system. We have identified examples of reform and revolution from both above and below in Russian and Soviet history. There appears to be the broadest consensus that the Great Reforms of the 1860s were instances of reform from above and that Stalinism was a case of revolution from above, and the least consensus on whether the New Economic Policy (NEP) constituted an era of reform at all. Precisely what NEP was, and whether one can include it in a discussion of reform in Russian and Soviet history, has not, I believe, been resolved. There is also considerable disagreement as to whether the perestroika of the late 1980s represented reform or revolution and as to whether the impulse for reform under Gorbachev came from above or below. In his commentary in the next chapter, Robert Tucker proposes that there have been five revolutions in Russia in the twentieth century: those of 1905, February 1917, October 1917, 1928, and the Gorbachev era. (Among those of us who view the last period as revolutionary rather than reformist, the apparent consensus is that 1987 was the year in which reform became revolution.)

If Tucker is right, then the twentieth century, despite deep continuities with the past, has been a century of revolutions for Russia.

The second point of consensus about the process of reform appears to be that Russian development is uneven, moving forward in fits and starts. Reform in Russian society seems to have a cyclical nature, with periods of stagnation followed by frantic efforts to catch up with the West (or with the world), and those followed by counterrevolution. This cycle seems to have trapped Russia and prevented it from achieving what is seen as "normal," or Western, development. Some thinkers discount the existence of these cycles, others point out that Western development may be neither normal nor even, but I have the distinct impression that most specialists on Russian and Soviet history and politics have had their views shaped by this cyclical image, even if only as an idea to react against.

The third point of consensus is that Russian and Soviet history has been marked by an unresolved tension between a highly centralized, imperial state and the regional, national, and social differentiations within it. The failure to resolve this tension is generally attributed to Russia's inability to generate a civil society and a law-based state. Although some believe that a law-based state was beginning to emerge in the early twentieth century and others see the beginnings of civil society in the Gorbachev era, I believe there is consensus in the profession that Russia has never produced a fully formed civil society or law-based state and that this failure is related to the difficulties of reforming Russian society. Furthermore, it appears that the emergence of the nationality issue during the period of perestroika and the subsequent dissolution of the Soviet Union following the revolution of August 1991 are causing us to reconsider the problem of centralization and differentiation in prerevolutionary history as well, forcing us to reevaluate its imperial context. Perhaps the real question, then, is whether the Russian and Soviet imperial systems were viable, whether they could ever have been successfully reformed, given their multiethnic character.

What we see in Russian and Soviet history is a story of reform and revolution played out in a diverse but noncivil society and an autocratic state, against the backdrop of constant challenges from abroad. Russia strives to be something like the West, although it searches out its own path in order to avoid the fate of the Ottoman Empire, or India, or China. This fear of falling onto the wrong path is apparent whatever the period of reform; only the negative model that Russia seeks to avoid seems to change.

Four sets of issues are, in my opinion, inseparably linked to the process of reform in Russian and Soviet history. The first set comprises the issues of citizenship, the law-based state, and civil society; the second, the relationship between the economic performance and relative international strength of Russia, on the one hand, and the impulse for reform on the other (i.e., Russia's place in the world); the third, center-periphery relations within a far-flung multinational empire; and the fourth, the relevance of the October Revolution—or, did 1917 matter?

As to the first set of issues: Whether one chooses to highlight the absence of a constitutional framework, an inadequate culture of active citizenship, or the lack of intermediary groups and institutions within the polity, there is a strong sense that both reform and revolution in Russia eventually lose momentum because of the failure to establish rules of political life that mediate between state and society. There have always been alternative visions of the rules of the game, and there have even been concrete legislative proposals spelling out these alternatives, but in the end these alternative visions lose out to central authority. One is forced to ask: What are the historical causes of this pattern? Under what conditions can Russia break out of this cycle? What is the role of *lichnost'*, or individual personality, in perpetuating or breaking the cycle? What is the role of *fortuna*, or fate, in this process? Did the revolution of 1928, if we agree to call it a revolution, somehow throw Russian society back to a previous period in its history, in which case the 1980s were just a replay of the 1860s? Or was there continuous development through 1928 toward the emergence of a law-based state and a civil society? Many contributors to this volume note that as one moves forward in Russian history, the social basis of support for a civil society grows. That basis of support was seemingly stronger under Gorbachev than it had ever been before in Russian history. Did the revolution of August 1991 break the cyclical nature of reform in Russia because of the growth of civil society up to that point? Will a law-based state emerge in Russia? I believe that as we find the answers to these questions, we will have a more precise understanding of the process of reform in Russian and Soviet history.

Russia's place in the world presents a second set of issues closely intertwined with the problem of reform. A recurring theme in this book is that Russian rulers are eventually forced to undertake programs of change as a consequence of their empire's falling behind the outside world in terms of economic performance and technological innovation. This retardation poses a direct threat to the position of Russia as a great power, both objectively and subjectively. Falling behind the world is a matter of cultural prestige as well as of objective military and economic strength.[1] In considering the relationship between the Russian defeat in the Crimean War and the Great Reforms of the 1860s, for example, or between the economic failures of the centrally planned Soviet economy and the advent of Gorbachev, we need to specify the extent to which the integrity of the Russian state depends on its remaining a great power. We must ascertain the answers to such key questions as: Why has Russia been unable to sustain innovation and economic development? Why can't Russia keep up? How can one evaluate the relationships between such external forces and the domestic impulse for reform?

The third set of issues linked to reform are those connected to center-periphery relations within a far-flung empire. We have recently witnessed the collapse of the Soviet Union, a diverse multinational state whose dominant central authority was challenged and finally defeated by strong centrifugal forces on the periphery. The tension between these forces seems to conform to a long-standing pattern, not only with respect to problems of nationality within the empire but also with respect to a hierarchy or competition among regions within Russia itself. Siberian separatism, for instance, is an example in which regionalism rather than nationalism or national liberation seems to be at stake. The state system that has prevailed in the face of the center-periphery struggle is one that is both underinstitutionalized and hyperinstitutionalized. The Russian, and later the Soviet, state was underinstitutionalized in the sense that governmental institutions, particularly at the local level, did not have the resources to fulfill their obligations, and it was hyperinstitutionalized in the sense that the state attempted to encompass under its aegis and to control all social and human activities. It was a state that tried to eliminate all space for autonomous activity by its citizens. One is forced to ask whether there are any cases in Russian history of reform, or of revolution for that matter, where this imbalance was broken and the pattern

---

[1][John LeDonne observed that there were eras in imperial Russian history—for example, the reigns of Peter I, Catherine II, and Alexander I—when reforms took place against the background of relatively successful foreign and military policy (rather than of defeats, as in the Crimean War, the Russo-Japanese War, or the conflict in Afghanistan) and did not create social or political problems to the extent they seemed to do after 1861. They were the work of a reasonably permanent, stable, and successful ruling class. The reforms that followed policy failures, however, brought into question the legitimacy of the elite's rule and did provoke turbulence. Thus, the connection between domestic and foreign policy may cut either way.—Ed.]

of simultaneous underinstitutionalization and hyperinstitutionalization gave way to an alternative model, perhaps that of civil society. Indeed, is that what is occurring today in Russia and the newly independent states that once constituted the Soviet Union? Would various reforms in Russian history have been more "successful," if one may use the term, had the Russian state not been a multinational empire? How do we account for the failure of imperial Russian and Soviet society to generate social autonomy? Or does a tradition of autonomy in fact exist?

Finally, in any discussion of reform and revolution in Russian history, one must ask, Does 1917 matter? I am struck by the way in which the very tone of discussion and analysis changes as one moves into the Soviet period. I am unsure about why this happens, but it may be because different sources are used in documenting imperial Russian and Soviet reform efforts, and even different research methods and different rules of evidence. There do seem to be certain eternal verities in Russian culture, such as egalitarian values, an aversion to private property, and an idiotic resort to censorship. Do these continuities imply that 1917 is not as important as it might otherwise seem? Or do we talk about the Soviet period in a different way because we are dealing with a different object of study, one that has fundamentally changed from what it was in tsarist Russia? Perhaps this difference in approach really says something about us: that, in fact, we use a different prism when dealing with the Soviet period, one fitted with different ideological mirrors. Now that we have seen the end of the Soviet period, will we begin to analyze it within the same context, the same framework, as we analyze imperial Russian history?

These are some of the issues that remain unresolved. As we follow the development of the fifteen former Soviet republics into sovereign national states and, most especially, as we monitor the evolution of Russia—a Russia freed of the burden of empire—these issues will continue to deserve contemplation. I believe that scholars who focus on the relationship of society to the process of change and reform, calling attention not just to reform from above but also to what is happening below, go right to the heart of one of the unresolved issues of the Russian reform tradition. This issue will undoubtedly remain at the center of Russia's development as a sovereign national state.

23

The fifth Russian revolution: commentary

ROBERT C. TUCKER

I believe we must consider the reforms initiated by Gorbachev, the reforms that led to the revolution of August 1991, as the fifth revolution in modern Russian history. The first was, of course, the revolution of 1905, the second and third were those of February and October 1917, and the fourth was Stalin's revolution of the 1930s. I consider it essential for analytic purposes to recognize that two revolutions took place during the Soviet period prior to Gorbachev. The entire period from October 1917, perhaps even from February 1917, through 1921, including the Civil War, was the first revolution of the Soviet period, during which the new revolutionary order began to take shape. To place this period in a broader Russian historical context, it might be conceived of as a new *smuta*, a new Russian Time of Troubles, like the one at the beginning of the seventeenth century. Just as, at that time, one dynasty came to an end and a new one came to power, in 1917 the new dynasty was that of the Bolsheviks, and a new period of Russian history began. This revolution was followed by the New Economic Policy (NEP), which in turn, beginning in 1928, was succeeded by another revolutionary transformation. Stalin called collectivization a "revolution from above"; I would extend the concept to encompass not simply collectivization but all the processes that took place during the 1930s—processes in both internal and external policy—and that continued through 1940 or 1941. It seems to me that this second Soviet revolution, Stalin's revolution, transformed the new order that emerged after the Bolshevik victory of October 1917, despite the elements of continuity and the fact that a change of regime was never proclaimed. Stalin's contention was always that his course was simply the fulfillment

412

of Lenin's revolution. Stalin's revolution, however, was in many ways contrary to Lenin's.

After the hiatus of NEP, Russian history resumed in a strange way as a rerun of earlier history, not just as a counterrevolution in the normal sense, where there is a return to a static status quo ante. It was a return to a process of development similar to the process of development epitomized by the Russian historian Vasilii Kliuchevsky in his observation about the seventeenth century and the Petrine revolution from above: "The state swelled while the people wasted away." The central fact of Stalin's revolution from above is that it went back deep into the Russian past and restored a great deal of tsarism: the statification of society, a centralized bureaucracy, and much of the traditional political culture. This was a restoration not of the immediate tsarist past, that of the late nineteenth and early twentieth centuries, however, but of the tsarist past dating back to the seventeenth century. Specifically, it meant the restoration of serfdom, of corvée (*barshchina*), or something very close to it, within the framework of the collective farm; of the internal passport system; and of forced labor—though on a scale that tsarist Russia had never seen and could never have imagined. The essence of the Stalinist institution of labor camps was an enormous expansion of traditional *katorga,* or convict labor. Finally, the Stalin revolution restored *samoderzhavie:* the autocracy, forged in the terror of the late 1930s. Of course, technically Stalin never became known as tsar, but he nevertheless was a new tsar-autocrat, and in the course of this development he transformed the ruling Bolshevik party. The Bolshevik Party became what Stalin had described in 1921 as an "order of swordbearers of the Soviet state," one part of Stalin's phalanx of support. It was no longer the Communist party that had existed under Lenin or in the post-Lenin 1920s.

It seems to me that we cannot begin to consider the problems of reform in Russian and Soviet history without recognizing this fourth revolution. We gain three insights by assuming that a revolution did indeed occur in the 1930s and that it was the second revolution of the Soviet period. First of all, this assumption helps us to understand the depth of change that began under Gorbachev and has continued since August 1991. If there is resistance from below to a radical reform of Russian society, for example, the continued adherence of many people— peasants and others—to the leveling tradition (*uravnitel'naia traditsiia*), it is safe to assume that this resistance is not simply the result of Soviet institutions but can be traced back for hundreds of years into Russian history. Viewing resistance to radical reform as a long-standing historical trend allows us to appreciate the depth of the difficulties that faced the Gorbachev reformers.

The second insight permits us to see that the agendas for reform and change in the 1860s and the 1980s had certain common features, as Baturin so ably demonstrates in his contribution. By this I mean the absence of glasnost in the early part of both periods and the way in which glasnost appeared in both periods, including the term itself. It is inconceivable that these phenomena could have repeated themselves a century after the 1850s and 1860s if what intervened in the twentieth century was not a throwback to the tsarist era. It is only in the light of this hypothesis that we can explain the startling analogy between these two reform periods.

Finally, recognition of the intervening fourth revolution is extremely important if we are to resolve the analytical problem of whether or not Gorbachev was a reformer. The Stalin revolution's restoration of tsarism enabled Gorbachev to come forward as a reform leader and to propose to do away with deformations ascribed to Stalinism and the Stalin period on behalf of a Leninism that had existed in the 1920s. It is at this juncture that I, like all contributors to this volume, feel we must distinguish between reform and revolution. I choose to think about this difference in terms of political culture. All countries have a political culture with certain ideals, paradigms, and cultural patterns or principles, as well as commonly accepted political practices. Oftentimes, the practices deviate from the principles. A reform leader may be a pragmatic leader, but in many cases he is someone to whom the principles are very dear and who, therefore, finds deviant practices intolerable and wants to change them. A classic example of this kind of reform leader in American political culture is Martin Luther King, Jr., who accepted the Supreme Court's 1954 decision banning segregation in the schools and sought to extend that principle to transportation, lunchrooms, and society as a whole. Wherever segregation appeared, it was held to be contrary to the constitutional principle enunciated by the Supreme Court, and consequently the deviant practice had to be changed; in short, segregation had to be abolished. This was the root of the civil-rights movement that emerged in the 1950s in the United States, with King at its head.

I believe we can apply this kind of analysis to all post-Stalin reform efforts in the Soviet Union, including those of Khrushchev. In his secret speech to the Twentieth Party Congress, Khrushchev said that Stalin's dictatorship, Stalin's terroristic despotism, violated what he called the "Leninist norms of collective leadership," and it was on those grounds that he condemned Stalin. He thus emerged as a reformer in the sense in which I use the term. Similarly, Gorbachev, an heir of the Twentieth Party Congress, came forward in the mid-1980s as a reform leader, proclaiming the need to modify deviant practices—excessive centralism and many other aspects of the Stalinist order that continued to exist at the time—on behalf of certain Leninist principles. We find him, for example, going back to NEP and suggesting that the departures of the Stalin period from NEP were erroneous, and using NEP as a guide to the directions in which Soviet society should proceed in the late 1980s.

The fact that two revolutions had occurred in the Soviet period meant that Gorbachev could argue against elements of Soviet political culture of the mid-1980s on the grounds that they deviated from certain paradigmatic Leninist norms of the Bolshevik Revolution and therefore ought to be abandoned or radically altered. I agree with those contributors to this volume who compare Gorbachev to Khrushchev. I also agree with those who assert that Gorbachev did not begin as a revolutionary. The principles of the existing order, at least those that can be traced to the time when that order was established, were and perhaps always remained valid for Gorbachev. He believed, however, that practices that deviated from these founding principles could and should be changed, so in this sense he was a reformer.

I believe that, as has been pointed out repeatedly in preceding contributions, the strength of resistance to Gorbachev's reforms was very great. Not surprisingly, the tsarist system as reconstituted in the fourth revolution reasserted the principle of bureaucratic centralism. I recall that in 1947, during the celebration of the eight-hundredth anniversary of the founding of Moscow, Stalin issued a statement glorifying the rise of centralized Russian statehood (*russkaia gosudarstvennost'*) and proclaimed this centralization to be an ideal norm of Russian political culture. In 1988, that ideal still prevailed as far as the Soviet regime was concerned. Once efforts began to build up the local soviets and institute a new system of elections, it became obvious that these reforms would grant localities an autonomy that they had not hitherto enjoyed, and still did not possess as late as 1988.

What happened to the early reform efforts of Gorbachev? As Chiesa's excellent chapter demonstrates, it was clear to Gorbachev by 1987 that in order to effect economic change—change in the political-economic culture, as it were—it would be necessary to change the political system. And in order to change the political system, it would be necessary for the movement for reform from above to become a movement supported from below. Thus, Gorbachev took certain steps to encourage a movement from below in order to advance the reform process that he had initiated from above. Yet the movement from below soon went its own way, often pursuing goals undoubtedly contrary to those that Gorbachev and others working with him had hoped to pursue. In some republics, this movement from below erupted into interethnic tension; in others— the Baltics, for example—it erupted into movements for secession from the Soviet Union. Furthermore, the movement from below quickly assumed forms that differed from those supported, or even anticipated or hoped for, by Gorbachev when he moved in the direction of political reform at the January 1987 plenum of the Communist Party Central Committee. Little by little, a situation of fluidity was created in Soviet society that pushed the reformer from above reluctantly into the position of a revolutionary from above. This reluctant revolutionary had to espouse far-reaching proposals for reform of the political system, culminating in the formation of the presidential system and the repeal of article 6 of the Soviet constitution and thereby of the Party's monopoly of power. All this led to the revolution of August 1991 and the dissolution of the USSR.

Under Gorbachev, a revolutionary process that might be described as a transition from a party-state to a governmental state appeared to be taking place in the Soviet Union. Stankevich argues that the movement for reform that began in the Soviet Union in 1985 was at first a movement to modernize the system but then became a movement to transform the system. I would say, rather, that it began as a movement to reform the system but that it did reach the stage of transformation—the fascinating, exciting, and hopeful stage that we witnessed in the years 1989 through 1991.

The question that confronts us now, as we consider what happened to Russia in this century—this strange, violent, unprecedented century— is the question of where Russia is now in her history. It is not in 1990 or in 1992, I believe, but somewhere at the beginning of the twentieth century, if one looks at historical as distinguished from chronological time, although, of course, one needs to make allowances in this interpretive scheme in order to account for real differences. I am struck by the fact that references have been made to the "inertness" of the masses both at the time of the Stolypin reforms and in the countryside at the present time. I am impressed by the emergence of a variety of new political groups and parties in contemporary Russia and by the manifold signs of a new Russian Time of Troubles, like the one that began in 1917.

In turn, this raises another question: whether one can take a more hopeful or less hopeful view of the future. That is, should one expect the ultimate outcome to be the same as the tragic outcome that occurred after the early years of this century, when things were moving forward in a very constructive way with the emergence of the Duma and other developments? It is of course very difficult to make any prediction, but it is worthwhile to consider the matter. One must hope that at least there will not be another war, and that is terribly important, because World War I was a crucial factor in the failure of the outcome of the reform process of the early 1900s. I do not think that there will be a war, and that is one reason to expect that the current reforms in Russia will be successful.

But success will not be easily achieved, for there is also the factor of what could be termed spiritual difficulty. Chiesa observes that it would have been much easier now if reforms had begun thirty or thirty-five years ago, because conditions were in many ways better economically for the success of a reform effort in the Khrushchev period than they are now. I would go even further. I happened to be living in Moscow in 1945, a time when Americans were able to meet and talk with Russians, and I can say from my own personal memories of that time that, even if the terms were not known or used with their current meanings, the Russian people were waiting even then for real perestroika, glasnost, and democratization. During the years between 1941 and 1945, their own leadership, which under Stalin "talked" to the people by putting rumors into circulation, had encouraged this hope. Once the war was over, the people expected that this time was coming. On May 9, 1945, as Victory Day was being celebrated in Red Square, I heard one Russian shout, "Now it's time to live!" But it was not to be. It was time to resume five-year plans, and it was time for the cold war to develop, and it was then that the country went into a spiritual crisis. In a sense, therefore—and this is the most tragic thing one can say—perestroika came, in 1985, forty years later than it should have come. That means, unless I am mistaken, that there is a deep tiredness in the people, a spiritual obstacle to reform. And yet, on the side of hope for a more constructive and promising historical outcome, Russian society has in many ways become a more modern society, a better-educated society—all the things that social historians have been telling us about—and these are factors in favor of success.

24

The return to normalcy: commentary

THEODORE TARANOVSKI

The relationship of reform and revolution in modern Russian history is inescapably tied to the question of the historical significance of 1917. A historian approaches such issues with considerable trepidation, since they involve matters not only of professional and intellectual conviction but also of personal preference and values. Knowledge of the past informs the present, but the present also informs the past, and together they define our hopes and anticipations for the future. Of course, 1917 matters: The October Revolution decisively shaped the past three-quarters of a century of Russian history. And yet, in light of what has been happening since 1985, it increasingly appears that in the long run 1917 will not matter, or at least it will matter much less than we have been prone to believe.

For decades, both Western and Russian historians have consciously and perhaps unconsciously looked at the evolution of Russian history as a prelude to the revolutions of 1917 and the establishment of the Soviet regime. The totality of the Russian past becomes a mere long prologue to the Soviet period, an ascending trajectory; and the natural tendency has been to explore those patterns, traditions, and events that have contributed to this particular outcome. As a consequence, historians and Sovietologists have tended to accentuate those interpretations and characteristics of Russian historical experience that have differentiated Russia from Western Europe, because the victory of communism in 1917 seemed to validate them. Autocracy, serfdom, economic and social backwardness, religious and cultural differences, and ideological hostility and ethnic prejudice, which were especially prominent in the nineteenth and twentieth centuries and characterized Russians and West-

ern Europeans alike,[1] have been featured at the expense of those aspects
of the Russian past that reflect the common experience of the European
civilization that Russia shares with the West. Nor has much attention
been paid to the phenomena of Russian history that parallel Western
experience without necessarily being genetically related. Comparative
history (especially political, legal, or institutional) that places Russia
within the context of European civilization, reasonably well developed
in prerevolutionary Russia and adhering to the traditions of nineteenth-
century scholarship, has been relatively neglected in American historiography, which favors professional specialization and cross-disciplinary
expertise and is pursuing a different set of research agendas.

For example, the significance of the fact that Russian civilization was
a Christian one, sharing significant theological norms (which entail
moral and legal norms as well) with the West, has often been neglected
in discussions of the nature of Russian culture.[2] The fact that those nineteenth-century epigones of German idealism, the Slavophiles, and other
Russian intellectuals have subscribed to the idea of the dualism of Russia
and the West is something that should be analyzed, not taken for
granted. More relevant to the question of reform is what can be termed
a discounting of the liberal tradition in Russian political culture and
public life. This tends to minimize the significance of those evolutionary
processes that were leading toward the formation of civil society and
constitutional government in the Russian Empire, especially after 1861.[3]
The fact that these tendencies were defeated in 1917 makes understandable but not justified, *pace* Robert Tucker, the predominant emphasis
on the totalitarian impulse in both Russian history and Soviet life. The
judicial reform of 1864, for one, was a significant step in the direction
of the rule of law in Russia and brought the Russian Empire closer to

---

[1]See John H. Gleason, *The Genesis of Russophobia in Great Britain: A Study of the Interaction of Policy and Opinion* (Cambridge, Mass.: Harvard University Press, 1950).
[2]See, for example, Donald W. Treadgold, *The West in Russia and China,* vol. 1, *Russia,
1472–1917* (Cambridge: Cambridge University Press, 1973), esp. xxii–xxiii.
[3]The most blatant example of this tendency is Edward L. Keenan, "Muscovite Political
Folkways," *Russian Review* 15 (1986): 115–81, which, with its focus on schematized
archetypes of Muscovite and Soviet history, dismisses the significance of the imperial
period in Russian history. To put this into some sort of perspective, the Kievan period of
Russian history (862–1242) was much longer than either the Muscovite or the imperial,
and the imperial period (technically 1721–1917, but usually seen as beginning ca. 1690)
was as long as the Muscovite (ca. 1450 to ca. 1690) and was chronologically equivalent
to the entire history of the United States as a sovereign nation.

the Western ideals of good government and an equitable society. Moreover, the Russian administration of justice between 1864 and 1917, whatever its defects, was superior in defending civil rights by comparison with the tribunals of revolutionary communism. Tsarist Russia was not totalitarian, and that is a fundamental distinction from the Soviet era.

Recent events, however, have brought some of these traditional assumptions into doubt. Perestroika ushered in an era of what promised to be Gorbachev's version of the Great Reforms, but it ended in his deposition, although the real revolution may be yet to come. What we have been witnessing is not only the beginning of something whose ultimate outcome we cannot predict but also the end of something—the end of the Bolshevik Revolution of 1917 and of the Stalin revolution as well.

While it is dangerous to become excessively fascinated with what the French term *la longue durée*, it may be instructive to glance at the pattern of revolutions in modern European history. As we approach the present, European revolutions, like modern war, seem to grow more all-encompassing in scope and intensity; the repercussions and aftershocks also appear progressively greater and longer lasting. Only the religious wars of the early modern period are comparable to modern revolutions in their ideological and physical violence. Thus, the English Revolution may be said to have started in 1640 and to have involved largely the sphere of elite politics, although the religious element played an important role. The Glorious Revolution of 1688 brought the crisis to an end and set the stage for the subsequent peaceful evolution of the British state and society. The French Revolution began in 1789 and did not exhaust itself until the establishment of the Third Republic in 1870. It can even be plausibly argued that in the United States the revolutionary principles of American political and social organization as enunciated in 1776 were not fulfilled until the Civil War and Lincoln's Emancipation Proclamation.

The Russian Revolution of 1917 was perhaps the most violent and most profound political and social transformation in modern European history, and its revolutionary utopianism found a fitting climax in Stalinist totalitarianism. But such revolutionary zeal, with its transformative vision of the future, cannot maintain itself indefinitely and ultimately must make peace with the frailty of the human condition. Since the revolutionary utopia cannot be realized, it must be compromised, although this can also be said of most reform efforts, whose maximum goals likewise are never attained. The revolution's accomplishments, however, are eventually integrated into the framework of the past. In turn, they set the stage for future historical developments.

This process of completion and stabilization may be observed in Russia today. The Russian Revolution of 1917 is ending in the 1990s. Its end is marked by the collapse of Marxism-Leninism as an ideology, of Stalinism as a system of government, and of the Soviet Union as an empire. It is also marked, I believe, by a certain reversion to the evolutionary patterns of late imperial Russia: the recovery of Russian cultural traditions, political liberalization, the growth of civil society, and movement in the direction of a market economy. Of course, the experience of the years since 1917 precludes return to, or repetition of, the past. Nevertheless, the new Russia is likely to regain its place in the European state system in the sense in which it had enjoyed it during the eighteenth and nineteenth centuries. It may still be a distant cousin or a poor relation, but it will be a recognizable member of the family.

This is not to say, of course, that one should sanguinely anticipate the future. Revolution, civil war, social conflict, and economic collapse are as characteristic of modern European history as what are usually perceived as the progressive features of Western civilization are. It behooves us to recall that both communism and fascism were products of Western civilization. Russia, by rejoining the community of European nations, may benefit from the association, but that does not guarantee it an escape from the hazards that lie ahead. What it is likely to avoid, however, is a return to the Soviet past, which separated Russia from Europe in the twentieth century.

Be all of this as it may, reform also matters and has mattered in Russian history. Tsarist reform may not have succeeded, but all success is relative. In 1861, peasants who had been serfs became free human beings. In 1906, the Russian Empire became a constitutional monarchy, though in embryonic form. Is it reasonable to argue that this did not matter? Reform in the past, however, has usually been imposed from above, and there is a curious parallel here with revolution, which also often begins with a crisis at the top, whether in the France of 1789 or the Russia of 1917. Neither under the tsars nor in the 1920s or the 1950s were the people consulted about their interests and desires. Tsarist bureaucrats with their paternalism and Marxist revolutionaries with their utopianism dominated and managed society the way they saw fit.

This, too, has been changing. The recent conjunction of a reform impulse from above meeting and cooperating with pressure for reform from below, which is quite atypical of most past reform efforts,[4] gives us hope that the cyclical pattern of reform in modern Russian history may finally be transcended.

[4]The early twentieth century, especially the decade from 1902 to 1911, also represents an atypical conjunction, this time of reformist and revolutionary impulses, which resembles the late 1980s and the early 1990s and does not fit easily into any model of reform in Russian history. It may well prove to be an exception that is highly relevant to the analysis of present-day Russian politics.

About the editors and authors

BORIS V. ANAN'ICH is a senior researcher at the Institute of History of the Russian Academy of Sciences in St. Petersburg. He has published extensively on the economic and financial history of Russia in the late nineteenth and early twentieth centuries and is the author of *Rossiia i mezhdunarodnyi kapital, 1897–1914* (1970) and *Rossiiskoe samoderzhavie i vyvoz kapitalov* (1975) and coauthor of *Krizis samoderzhaviia v Rossii, 1895–1917* (1984).

IURII M. BATURIN is a senior researcher at the Institute of State and Law of the Russian Academy of Sciences in Moscow and a member of Boris Yeltsin's government. He has written on legal issues for both scholarly and popular audiences and was one of the drafters of the law on the press and other mass media, which was adopted by the Supreme Soviet of the USSR in 1990, and of the law on archives and archival affairs.

JOSEPH BRADLEY is associate professor of history at the University of Tulsa, specializing in nineteenth- and early twentieth-century Russia. He is the author of *Muzhik and Muscovite* (1985) and *Guns for the Tsar: American Technology and Small Arms Industry in Nineteenth-Century Russia* (1990).

VALENTINA G. CHERNUKHA is a senior researcher at the Institute of History of the Russian Academy of Sciences in St. Petersburg. She has written extensively on the internal politics of the Russian autocracy in the nineteenth century; her publications include *Krest'ianskii vopros v pravitel'stvennoi politike Rossii* (1972), *Vnutrenniaia politika tsarizma s serediny 50-kh do nachala 80-kh gg. XIX v.* (1978), and *Pravitel'stvennaia politika v otnoshenii pechati 60–70-e gody XIX veka* (1989).

GIULIETTO CHIESA is the special correspondent for Russia and Eastern Europe for the Italian newspaper *La Stampa*. Formerly a correspondent for *L'Unità*, he has spent many years in Moscow. He is the author of *Cronaca del Golpe Rosso* (1991), an account of the attempted coup in August 1991, and coauthor, with Roy Medvedev, of *Time of Change* (1989). He is a former Fellow of the Woodrow Wilson International Center for Scholars.

ROBERT V. DANIELS is professor emeritus of history at the University of Vermont. His publications include *The Conscience of the Revolution* (1960), *Red October* (1967), *Russia: The Roots of Confrontation* (1985), *Is Russia Reformable?* (1988), and *Year of the Heroic Guerrilla* (1989). He is a former Fellow of the Woodrow Wilson International Center for Scholars.

BEN EKLOF, associate professor of history at Indiana University, has a strong interest in the social history of Russia. He is the author of *Russian Peasant Schools: Officialdom, Village Culture, and Popular Pedagogy* (1986) and *Soviet Briefing: Gorbachev and the Reform Period* (1989). He is a former Fellow of the Woodrow Wilson International Center for Scholars.

TERENCE EMMONS is professor of history at Stanford University. His publications include *The Russian Landed Gentry and the Peasant Emancipation of 1861* (1968) and *The Formation of Political Parties and the First National Elections in Russia* (1983).

DANIEL FIELD, professor of history at Syracuse University, specializes in nineteenth-century Russian history and is the author of *The End of Serfdom* (1976) and *Rebels in the Name of the Tsar* (1976).

PETER KENEZ, professor of history at the University of California at Santa Cruz, has research interests in the revolutionary and early Soviet period. His publications include *Civil War in South Russia, 1918* (1971), *Civil War in South Russia, 1919–1920* (1977), and *The Birth of the Propaganda State* (1985). He is a former Fellow of the Woodrow Wilson International Center for Scholars.

AVENIR P. KORELIN is a senior researcher at the Institute of History of the Russian Academy of Sciences in Moscow. He is a specialist in Russian social history on the late imperial period and the author of *Dvorianstvo v poreformennoi Rossii* (1979) and *Sel'skokhoziaistvennyi kredit v Rossii v kontse XIX–nachale XX v.* (1988).

VITALII S. LEL'CHUK is a senior researcher at the Institute of History of the Russian Academy of Sciences in Moscow and the author of a number of books on Soviet history, including *Industrializatsiia SSSR: Istoriia, Opyt, Problemy* (1984) and *Nauchno-tekhnicheskaia revoliutsiia i promyshlennoe razvitie SSSR* (1987).

CARL A. LINDEN is professor of political science at George Washington University and the author of *The Soviet Party-State* (1983) and *Khrushchev and the Soviet Leadership, with an Epilogue on Gorbachev* (1966; rev. ed., 1990).

DAVID M. MCDONALD, assistant professor of history at the University of Wisconsin–Madison, has research interests in prerevolutionary politics and foreign policy. He is the author of *United Government and Foreign Policy in Russia, 1900–1914* (1992).

DAVID A. J. MACEY is associate professor of history at Middlebury College and the author of *Government and Peasant in Russia, 1861–1906* (1987). His research interest is in prerevolutionary political and social history.

PEGGY MCINERNY received an M.A. in Soviet studies from the Nitze School of Advanced International Studies of the Johns Hopkins University. She is currently editor at the Kennan Institute for Advanced Russian Studies of the Woodrow Wilson International Center for Scholars.

DANIEL T. ORLOVSKY, professor of history at Southern Methodist University, has research interests in prerevolutionary and early Soviet history and is the author of *The Limits of Reform: The Ministry of Internal Affairs in Imperial Russia, 1802–1881* (1981).

ALFRED J. RIEBER is professor of history at the University of Pennsylvania. He is the author of *Stalin and the French Communist Party* (1962) and *Merchants and Entrepreneurs in Imperial Russia* (1982), and he is the editor of *The Politics of Autocracy: Letters of Alexander II to Prince A. I. Bariatinskii* (1966). He is a former Fellow of the Woodrow Wilson International Center for Scholars.

BLAIR A. RUBLE is director of the Kennan Institute for Advanced Russian Studies of the Woodrow Wilson International Center for Scholars and a political scientist with a particular interest in Soviet local politics and

Russian urbanization and cityscape. His publications include *Soviet Trade Unions* (1981) and *Leningrad: Shaping a Soviet City* (1990).

SERGEI B. STANKEVICH is a state counselor and adviser to Boris Yeltsin's government. He was a deputy in the Congress of People's Deputies and the Supreme Soviet and a deputy mayor of Moscow. A specialist in the history of the United States, he began his career at the Institute of General History of the Academy of Sciences in Moscow.

THEODORE TARANOVSKI, professor of history at the University of Puget Sound, has research interests in the politics of the Russian autocracy and the ideology of its bureaucracy. He has served as research associate and acting program secretary of the Kennan Institute for Advanced Russian Studies of the Woodrow Wilson International Center for Scholars (1988–90).

WILLIAM TAUBMAN is professor of political science at Amherst College. His publications include *Governing Soviet Cities* (1973) and *Stalin's American Foreign Policy* (1982), and he is the coauthor with Jane A. Taubman of *Moscow Spring* (1989).

ROBERT C. TUCKER is professor emeritus of political science at Princeton University. His publications include *The Marxian Revolutionary Idea* (1969), *The Soviet Political Mind* (rev. ed., 1971), *Stalin as Revolutionary, 1879–1929* (1973), *Political Culture and Leadership in Soviet Russia* (1987), and *Stalin in Power, 1929–1941* (1990). He is a former Fellow of the Woodrow Wilson International Center for Scholars.

NEIL B. WEISSMAN, professor of history at Dickinson College, has research interests in early twentieth-century Russian and Soviet history. He is the author of *Reform in Tsarist Russia: The State Bureaucracy and Local Government, 1900–1914* (1981).

LARISA G. ZAKHAROVA is professor of history at Moscow State University. She has published extensively on nineteenth- and early twentieth-century Russian history and is the author of *Zemskaia kontrreforma* (1969) and *Samoderzhavie i otmena krepostnogo prava v Rossii, 1856–1861* (1984).

Index

Abaza, A. A., 79, 82
administrative-command system, 371–73, 376, 402–3
Adzhubei, Nikita, quoted, 331, 345
"Aelita," 263
Agrarian Law Code, 161–62
agrarian reform: agricultural dysfunction and, 139–47; consequences of, 154–62, 184–89; Council of Ministers and, 175–77; Duma responses to, 175–79, 181–82; economic goals of, 50–51, 185–87; economic reform linked to, 171–72; gentry and, 74–75, 101, 105, 113, 168–69; preconditions for, 164–80; Stolypin's program for, 43, 148–54, 180–83
Agricultural Congress, 229–30, 234–35
agricultural production, 142–43, 330, 358–59
Agronomists' Congress, 229–30
Aksakov, Ivan S., 78
Alexander I, reforms of, 56–60, 93
Alexander II, Great Reforms of, 29, 38–39, 46–54, 60–77, 85, 103–22
Alexander III, counterreforms of, 77–83, 95, 122–24
All-Russian Congress of Administrative Workers, Second, 280
All-Russian Congresses of Cooperatives, 216–17, 219–21, 223, 230, 232
All-Russian Extraordinary Committee for the Liquidation of Illiteracy (VChK/lb), 258
All-Union Congress of the Union of Soviet and Commercial Employees, Eighth, 306–7
allotment land, redemption of, 43, 49, 105, 108, 113–18, 141–48, 150–52, 154–57
"alternativity," 37–38, 103–5
Amalrik, Andrei, 367
Ambartsumov, Evgenii, 380

Andropov, Iurii, 322, 341, 374–75, 385–86
antibureaucratic campaigns: circumstances leading to, 293–99; discourse of, 309–10; during NEP, 290–310; rationalization phase of, 299–301; Regime of Economy phase of, 301–6; self-criticism and purge phase of, 306–9; Stalinism and, 292, 347
anti-Party group, 360–63, 385
anti-Semitism, 88
Artisans' Congress, Second, 216–17, 228–29
assassinations, 77, 90, 121–22, 153; attempted, 73, 112, 120
Austria, 70
autocracy: Asiatic principle of, 29–32; crisis of, in early 20th century, 190–211; personal styles in, 195–96; police under, 265–70; political subculture of, 129–36; reactions of, to reform, 59–60, 64–65, 93–95, 119–22, 161; see also names of individual autocrats
"Autocracy and the Zemstvo," 197

Bariatinskii, A. I., 74
Barsukov, N., 345
"Bear's Wedding, The," 263
Beissinger, Marc, quoted, 292
Bekhteev, S. S., 178
Belgium, 98
Bell, The (Kolokol), 66
Beloborodov, A. G., 273
Berdyaev, N. A., 262
Beria, Lavrentii P., 346–51, 360, 362–63
"Better Fewer, but Better," 295
Bezobrazov, A. M., 194–95
Bezobrazov, V. P., 62, 63
Bikkenin, Nail, 380
Bliummer, P. L., 64
Bloody Sunday, 133

Bludov, Dmitry N., 32
Boldyrev, M., 277
Bolsheviks, 326; censorship by, 252–54,
  261–64; civil war and, 252–60; cultural
  policies of, 252–58; intellectual
  background of, 248–52; police reform
  by, 270–79; white-collar, 298–99
Borodin, D. N., 226, 231
Brezhnev, Leonid: autocratic ideology of,
  335–36, 340–41, 385–86; Khrushchev
  overthrown by, 320, 331; stagnation
  under, 373–74
Bukharin, Nicholas, 301
Bulganin, N. A., 348, 349, 361–63
Bulgaria, 396
Bunge, Nicholas Kh., 63, 79, 81–88,
  90, 123
bureaucracy, *see* antibureaucratic
  campaigns; bureacratization; liberal
  bureaucracy; white-collar workers
bureaucratization, 402–3
Burlatsky, Fedor, 344, 380

Can the Bolsheviks Retain State Power?,
  271
censorship, 63–64, 403–6; Bolshevik, 252–
  54, 261–64; congresses and, 215–25;
  under reform of 1865, 71, 76
Central Committee, 348, 350, 361
Central Control Commission (TsKK), 284,
  290, 295, 304–5
Central Executive Committee of Soviets,
  252–53
Cherkasskii, Prince V. A., 48, 107, 121
Chernenko, Konstantin, 341, 385–86
Cherniaev, Anatolii, 380
Chernyshevsky, Nicholas, 61
Chess Club, 63
Chicherin, B. N., 61
Chief Administration for the Protection of
  State Secrets in the Press (Glavlit), 404–
  5
Chief Committee on Peasant Affairs, 104,
  114
Chief Committee on the Organization of
  Village Society, 117
"circular flow of power," 384–87
Citizen, The, 208
collective farms, 355–59
collectivization, 39; antibureaucratic
  campaigns during, 292, 306–9
Commissariat of Enlightenment
  (Narkompros), 258, 262
Commissariat of Finance, 287
Commissariat of Health, 285, 287
communes: attempted dissolution of, 43,

151–52, 154–57; landholding by, 83,
  88, 106–7, 123, 141; survival of, 106,
  108, 116–17, 144–48, 160
communism: collapse of, 368–69;
  Gorbachev's influence on, 374–83;
  Khrushchev's influence on, 319–36
Communist Party: anti-Party group
  within, 360–63; Gorbachev reform of,
  397–98; police reform by, 270–88;
  power struggles in, 346–51
concentration camps, 362
Conference of Physicians' Assistants,
  Second, 229
Congress of People's Deputies, 321, 398–
  99
Congress of Representatives of Municipal
  Government, 224
Congress of Retail Employers, 233
Congress on Alcoholism, 216, 218, 222,
  225–27, 231, 233
Congress on Fire Insurance, 234
Congress on Livestock Insurance, 234
Congress on Prostitution, 221, 231–32
Congress on the Family, 221–22
Congresses of Factory Physicians and
  Representatives of Factory Industry,
  216–17, 222
congresses of organizations: censorship of,
  215–25; division in, 227–32;
  politicization of, 224–27; resolutions
  drafted by, 220–22, 225–27; surrogate-
  parliament status of, 232–36
Conquest, Robert, quoted, 368
Constantine Nikolaevich, Grand Duke,
  99–100, 111–12; Great Reforms and,
  61, 68, 72, 102, 117
constitutional monarchy, 183; *see also*
  constitutionalism
constitutionalism, 77, 93–96, 133–34,
  183; resistance to, 119; Speransky
  and, 57; united government and, 190–
  211
Contemporary, The (Sovremennik), 61
*Contemporary Situation in Russia and the
  Estate Question, The*, 80
Council of Ministers, 99; agrarian reform
  and, 175–77; creation of, 119–22;
  reform of, 190–200; Stolypin
  chairmanship of, 200–206, 210; Witte
  chairmanship of, 190–202, 208, 210
Council of State, 58, 70, 72
counterreforms, 77–83, 95, 122–24
Crimean War, outcome and consequences
  of, 32, 47, 60–61, 94, 98–99, 132, 238,
  403
Czechoslovakia, 380, 383, 396

Decembrist movement, 31–32, 59–60
de Gaulle, Charles, 339–40
Delianov, I. D., 82
democratization, 67–70, 76, 360, 376, 379, 381, 400
desiatina defined, 142
"developed socialism," 335
Dobroliubov, Nicholas, 61
"doctors' plot," 347, 349
Dolgorukov, P. V., 64
Duma: and agrarian reform, 175–79, 181–82; dissolution of, 148; establishment of, 34, 56, 58, 72, 92; operation of, under Nicholas II, 191, 193, 198–99, 208, 210–13
Durnovo, P. N., 204

East Germany, 396
economic reforms: agrarian reforms linked to, 171–72; 19th century, 82–83, 87–89, 99, 111–12
Editorial Commission for Review of Peasant Legislation (1902–4), 145–46, 172–74
Editorial Commissions (1859–60), 54, 66, 106–16, 120, 123, 131
Eidel'man, Natan, 27–45; concept of continuity and, 39–42
Elena Pavlovna, Grand Duchess, 63, 107
emancipation, 46–52, 58–59, 94, 100–124, 140–41, 165–66
Emancipation Act, 63, 106, 110–11, 117, 123
entrepreneurship, 87, 92, 400
environmental issues, 312
era of stagnation, 369–74
Ermolov, A. S., 170
"Europeanism," 228–29
Ezhov, N. I., 347, 362

Fadeev, Rostislav A., 78, 82, 84
famine, 84
Filaret, Patriarch, 134
Frank, S. L., 262
Free Economic Society, 216
Free Russian Press, 100
freedom of assembly, 214–24
French Revolution, 55, 93, 337, 339–40
Frish, V. E., 268
Frolov, Ivan, 380
Fundamental Laws, 197–99, 209, 212–13

Gagarin, Prince Pavel, 33, 114
Gagemeister, Iu. A., 62
Geiden, Count D. F., 232

gentry, 69–72; agrarian reform and, 74–75, 101, 105, 113, 168–69; and landownership, 50, 104, 106, 108, 115, 142; political representation of, 118–19
Gentry Land Bank, 142–43
Germany, 396
Gerschenkron, Alexander, quoted, 40, 42
Getty, J. Arch, 291–92
glasnost: 19th-century, 32–33, 63–64, 95, 100–101, 106, 114–15, 401–6; 20th-century, 365, 379, 386, 401–6
Glotov, V., 344
gold standard, 67, 88
Golos (The Voice), 240
Golovnin, A. V., 61, 64, 65, 98, 121; salon of, 169, 178
Gorbachev, Mikhail: Khrushchev compared with, 375–77, 384–91; perestroika and, 39, 44, 369, 374–83; political ideology of, 381–82; as reformer, 397–98, 414–16; Soviet principles renounced by, 128–29, 320–22, 339, 341
Goremykin, I. L., 89, 177, 209–11
Gorky, Maxim, 260
Gosizdat (State Publishing House), 259, 262
Great Patriotic War, 347
Great Reforms: approaches to, 65–77; consequences of, 52–54, 115–24; counterreforms to, 77–83, 95, 122–24; goals of, 50–52; legislative acts of, 105–15, 165–66; preconditions for, 45–50, 60–65, 98–103
Great Terror, 291
Grigor'ev, Dr. N. I., 226
Gromeko, S. S., 73
Grzhebin, 260
Guchkov, A. I., 224
Guide to Political Economy, A (Politiko-ekonomicheskii ukazatel'), 63
Gurko, Vladimir I., 170, 172–79

Haxthausen, Baron August von, 98
Herald of Europe (Vestnik Evropy), 81, 235–36
Herzen, Alexander, 64, 66, 73, 100
home brewing, 280–83
hooliganism, 281–83
Hungary, 360, 383, 396

Iakovlev, Aleksandr, 380
Iakovlev, Egor, 380
Iakovlev, Ia., 307
Iatsynevich, A. I., 231
ideocratic principality, 336–41

Ignat'ev, N. P., 79, 85
imperial manifestos, 66, 90, 99, 122, 145, 190
Imperial Public Library, 104
Imperial Russian Geographic Society, 48, 63, 102
Imperial School of Jurisprudence, 169–70
industrialization, antibureaucratic campaigns during, 301–9
intelligentsia, 249–50
"Intelligentsia and Socialism, The," 249–50
"Introduction to the Code of State Laws," 57
Ivan the Terrible, 30

Journal of Landowners (Zhurnal zemlevladel'tsev), 61
Judicial Reform of 1864, 48, 56

Kaganovich, L. M., 347, 348, 360–63
Kaledin, A. M., 253
Kalinin, M. I., 273, 306–9
Karakozov, Dmitry, 112, 121
Kariakin, Iurii, 380
Katkov, Michael N., 79–82, 88, 122–23
Kavelin, K. D., 61, 107, 121
Kennan Institute for Advanced Russian Studies, 2–6
KGB, 345–46, 351, 361, 374
Khrushchev, Nikita: agricultural reforms of, 354–60; anti-Party group and, 360–63, 385; economic dysfunction under, 370–72; Gorbachev compared with, 375–77, 384–91; limitations of, 333–36, 363–65; and Marxism, 325–33; peacemaking efforts of, 352–53; political identity of, 319–25; power struggle of, 346–51; reevaluation of, 342–46, 365; reform attempts by, 325–36, 340; Stalin denounced by, 322–24, 328–29, 332–33, 338–39, 360–61, 414–15; Stalinism and, 321–22, 351, 376–77
Khrushchev, Sergei, 345
Khvesin, T., 272
King, Martin Luther, Jr., 414
Kiselev, I., 277
Kiselev, P. D., 60
Kliuchevsky, Vasily, 336, 413
Kokovtsev, V. N., 93, 192, 205–9
Komsomol, 258, 330
Korf, Modest A., 32
Kosunovich, L., 269

Krasin, Leonid B., 295–97
Krivoshein, A. V., 154, 158, 176
Kryzhanovskii, S. E., 191, 211
kulaks, 309–10
Kulomzin, A. N., 79, 90
Kuskova, E. D., 221

Labor Code, 276
land captain, 167, 179
landless emancipation, 104–5, 113
landownership: communal, 83, 88, 106–7, 123, 141; and gentry, 50, 104, 106, 108, 115, 142; and peasants, 71, 86, 108, 116–18, 174–79, 181
Lanskoi, Sergei S., 32–33
Laue, Theodore von, 313
Le Nord, 98–99
Lenin, V. I.: antibureaucratic campaigns of, 290–310; censorship by, 253–54, 261–64; Marxism and, 326–27, 337–38, 340; police reform initiated by, 270–79; political ideology of, 251–52, 271, 293–95
"Leningrad affair," 347, 362
Letters on the Contemporary Condition of Russia, 78, 79, 88
Levshin, A. I., 62
Lewin, Moshe, 390
liberal bureaucracy, 49, 101–2, 105–15
Librarians' Congress, 234
List, Friedrich, 78, 87
literacy, 126n2, 258–59, 268, 275–76, 314
Liubimas, A., 274
Liubimov, D. N., 89
local government reform, 86; *see also* zemstvo
Loris-Melikov, Michael T., 53, 68; "constitution" of, 33, 112, 121; reforms of, 75–77, 79, 91, 131
Losskii, N. O., 262
Lunacharsky, A. V., 258, 263–64

Machiavelli, Niccolò, 319n1
machine-tractor stations (MTS), 330, 355, 357
Makarov, A. A., 207, 268, 274
Maklakov, N. A., 207–8
Malenkov, G. M., 322–23, 326, 348–49, 351, 354; anti-Party group and, 360–63
Manasein, N. A., 82
Marx, Karl, 340
Marxian princes, 319–41
Marxism, Khrushchev and, 325–33

Marxism-Leninism, 250–52, 326–27, 337–38, 340
Mel'gunov, N. A., 61
"Memorandum on the Organization of Judicial and State Institutions in Russia," 57
Mensheviks, 253–54, 261
Menshikov, A. S., 104
Merezhkovskii, D. S., 262
Meshcherskii, V. P., 90, 194, 208
Migration Office, 151–52
Mikhailov, M. L., 73
Mikoyan, A. I., 322–23, 348
militia, *see* police
Miliutin, Dmitry A., 61, 65, 79, 104, 239
Miliutin, Nicholas A., 32, 50, 104; liberal-bureaucracy leadership by, 107, 109, 111–16, 121; quoted, 54, 62, 102
Miliutin, V. P., 253
Ministry of Internal Affairs, 71, 90, 102, 111; congresses and, 217–18
Mirovich, Zinaida, 218
Molotov, V. M., 323, 326, 347–48, 360–63
monarchical initiative, 109
Mongol invasion, 29–30, 35
Moscow Printers' Union, 231–32
Moskovskie vedomosti (Moscow News), 81, 240
Mossukno, 302
multinationalism, 410–11
Murav'ev, N. V., 194

Nabokov, D. N., 82
Napoleon I, 337
Narkompros (Commissariat of Enlightenment), 258, 262
national liberation movements, 353
National System of Political Economy, The, 87
nationalism, 87
Naval Ministry, 61–62, 72, 111
New Economic Policy (NEP): antibureaucratic campaigns during, 290–310; criticisms of, 311–15; introduction of, 34–35, 260–64; police-reform policies during, 272–88
New Peasant Statute of 1856, 105
Nicholas I: reign of, 32, 48, 60, 85, 93–94; foreign policy of, 98
Nicholas II, 124; Council of Ministers reform by, 190–211; Duma operation under, 191, 193, 198–99, 208, 210–13; peasant reforms and, 147; quoted, 91
Nikolai, A. I., 82

Nikol'skii, A. P., 176–77
1905 revolution, 34, 91–93, 116, 174, 267, 412; consequences of, 190–210, 212–36
1917 revolution, 34–35, 247–48, 252, 270, 412, 421–22; consequences of, 252–64, 270–89, 293–99
Nizier-Vachot, Philippe, 194
Nogin, V. P., 253
nomenklatura, 326, 332, 335, 386, 389
Novoe vremia (New Times), 233
Novosil'tsev, Nicholas N., 31, 58–59

October Manifesto, 194, 198–99, 212, 234–35
Octobrists, 174–75, 179
Oldenburg, S. F., 256
"On Agrarian Communities with Allotment Landownership," 148
"On Criminal Anti-Party and Anti-State Actions of L. P. Beria," 350
"On the Cult of Personality and Its Consequences," 360–61
"On the Immutability of Autocracy," 122
"On the Intelligentsia," 249–50
Openkin, L., 344
Ordzhonikidze, G. K., 301–2, 304; quoted, 305–6
Orlov, A. V., 61
Orlov, I. F., 104
Orlov, M. F., quoted, 55
"Orthodoxy, Autocracy, and Nationality," ideology of, 60, 93–94
Ostrovskii, M. N., 79
Osvobozhdenie (Liberation), 235

Panin, Nikita, 193
Pan-Slavism, 78, 81
Pares, Bernard, 192
party congresses: 14th, 304; 15th, 297–98, 301; 16th, 301; 19th, 348, 354; 20th, 322, 328, 343, 375, 385; 21st, 329; 22nd, 328–29, 331, 343, 375
passport system, 67, 83, 88
Pavlov, P. S., 231–32
Pazukhin, A. D., 80, 122
Peace of Paris, 99
Peace of Portsmouth, 194
Peasant Land Bank, 123, 142, 145–51, 155, 157, 160, 166, 174–76, 179, 181
peasants: bureaucratization of, 300; civil rights of, 150–52; emancipation of, 46–52, 58–59, 94, 100–124, 140–41, 165–66; landownership by, 71, 86, 108, 116–18, 174–79, 181; migration of, 83,

88, 146–47, 157–58; population of,
158; redemption of allotment land by,
43, 49, 105, 108, 113–18, 141–48,
150–52, 154–57; self-government by,
50–51, 109
penal system, 313–14
People's Commissariat of Internal Affairs
(NKVD), 347; police-reform
implementation by, 271–88
People's Commissariat of Transportation,
302
People's Commissariat of Workers' and
Peasants' Inspectorate (Rabkrin), 284,
290, 295, 299–301, 304, 306
perestroika, 39, 44; glasnost as
precondition for, 401–6; Khrushchev
reevaluated during, 342–46, 365;
opposition to, 377–78; peacefulness of,
395–400; roots of, 366–83
Perestroika and New Thinking, 344
Pervukhin, M. G., 348
Peshar-Deshan, P. I. (Pechard-Deschamps),
58
Pestrzhetskii, D. I., 178
Peter I, reforms of, 30–31, 55
Petersburg Union of Agriculturists, 63
Petrine reforms, 30–31, 55
Pirogov Congresses, 229
Pisarev, Dmitry, 61
Pius IX, Pope, 98
Plehve, Viacheslav K., 89–90, 145–46,
170, 172, 195
Plekhanov, G. V., quoted, 124
plenums, 344, 346, 350, 364, 375
Pobedonostsev, Constantine P., 78–80, 89,
130, 196
Pogodin, M. P., 61, 100
Pokrovskii, S. P., quoted, 402
Poland, 396
police *(militsiia):* Bolshevik reform of,
270–79; consequences of reform of,
279–89; specialization within, 274–75;
training of, 275–77; in tsarist era, 265–
70
Polish revolt of 1863, 64, 78, 107, 120
Politburo, 333–36, 340–41, 348–50
Political Economy Society, 63
Polovtsev, A. A., 198
population, 158
Posthumous Memorandum (Bunge), 84–88
Presidium, *see* Politburo
prices, 355–57
Prigradov-Kudrin, A., 273
Primakov, Evgenii, 380
private property, *see* landownership
procurement prices, 355–57

prohibition, 280–83
Provincial Committees, 101, 104, 105,
114
Provisional Government, 53, 256
publishing industry, 259–63
purges, Stalinist, 291, 306–9, 338, 347–
48, 361–62, 389–90

rationalization campaign, 299–301
Razuvaeva, N., 344
redemption of allotment land, 43, 49,
105, 108, 113–18, 141–48, 150–52,
154–57
reforms: agrarian, 43, 46–50, 74–75, 77,
101, 105, 113, 139–62, 164–89;
Alexander I and, 56–60, 93; Alexander
II and, 29, 38–39, 46–54, 60–77, 85,
103–22; Alexander III and, 77–83, 95,
122–24; autocratic reactions to, 59–60,
64–65, 93–95, 119–22, 161; Bolshevik,
270–79; censorship, 71, 76; Constantine
Nikolaevich and, 61, 68, 72, 102, 117;
Council of Ministers and, 77–83, 95,
122–24, 175–77, 190–200; Duma
responses to, 175–79, 181–82;
economic, 82–83, 87–89, 99, 111–12,
171–72; "from above," 97, 140, 173,
331, 340, 390, 416; "from below,"
213, 416; gentry and, 74–75, 101, 105,
113, 168–69; Gorbachev and, 397–98,
414–16; Great, 45–54, 60–83, 95, 98–
103, 105–24; judicial, 48, 56; key
elements of, 237–42; Khrushchev and,
325–36, 340, 354–60; Lenin and, 270–
79; Loris-Melikov and, 75–77, 79, 91,
131; NEP and, 272–88; Nicholas II
and, 147, 190–211; NKVD and, 271–
88; Peter I and, 30–31, 55; police, 270–
89; revolution versus, 388–91, 407–11;
Stolypin's program for, 34, 43, 51,
148–54, 179–83; taxation, 67, 71, 77,
83, 166; Valuev's proposals for, 68–72,
74–75, 94, 113–14, 133; Witte and, 83,
88–90, 92–93, 123–24, 131; zemstvo,
106, 109, 122–23
Regime of Economy campaign, 301–6
Reutern, M. Kh., 61, 71, 99, 111–12, 120
revolution: "from above," 31–32, 38–39,
128, 163, 243, 291, 367, 369, 412;
"from below," 43, 48–49, 97, 390;
Gorbachev's, 374–83; modern Russian,
412–18; of 1905, 34, 91–93, 116, 174,
267, 412; of 1917, 34–35, 247–48, 252,
270, 412, 421–22; reform versus, 388–
91, 407–11; *see also names of
individual revolutions*

"Revolution from Above" in Russia, 27–45, 125–26; "lessons" in, 35–36, 127
Rittikh, A. A., 170, 172–79
Rosenberg, William, 312
Rossiia (Russia), 233
Rostovtsev, Iakov I., 32, 105, 130
Rozmirovich, E., 300
Russian News (Russkie vedomosti), 81
Russian Technological Society, 238
Russian Thought (Russkaia mysl'), 82
Russian Word, The (Russkoe slovo), 61, 235
Russo-Japanese War, 89, 90, 93, 202, 238
Russo-Turkish War, 78
Rykov, A. I., 253

Saburov, M. Z., 348
St. Petersburg Women's Mutual Aid Society, 216
Sakharov, Andrei, 353
salons, 62–63
Saltykov-Shchedrin, M. E., 101, 406
Samarin, Iu. F., 107, 108, 117, 121
samizdat, 405
Sazonov, S. D., 202
"scientific communism," 335
Scientific Organization of Labor (Nauchnaia organizatsiia truda, NOT) movement, 290, 299–300
"second peasant reform," *see* Stolypin, Peter A.
self-criticism campaign, 306–9
Semenov, P. P., 54
Semenov-Tian-Shanskii, V. P., 112
Semichastnyi, Vladimir, 345–46
serfdom, 29–32; *see also* peasants, emancipation of
Serov, I. A., 361
Shakhnazarov, Georgii, 380
Shuvalov, Count Peter A., 68, 73–75, 130, 133
Shvanebakh, P. Kh., 202
Shvernik, M. M., 348
Smirnov, N. P., 81
Society for Mutual Land Credit, 63
Society for the Encouragement of Russian Industry and Trade, 238
"Society for Workers' Welfare," 74
Sol'skii, D. N., 191–93
Solzhenitsyn, Alexander, 325n7
Sonderweg, 240–41
Special Conference on the Needs of Agriculture, 89, 123–24, 145–46
Speransky, Michael, 31, 48, 50, 56–59
sputnik, 364

Stalin, Josef: antibureaucratic campaigns of, 301–9; collectivization and, 39; Khrushchev's view of, 322–24, 328–29, 332–33, 338–39, 351, 360–61, 414–15; purges under, 291, 306–9, 338, 347–48, 361–62, 389–90
Stalinism, 243, 413–14; antibureaucratism and, 292, 347; Khrushchev and, 321–22, 351, 376–77
State and Revolution, 293
State Planning Commission, 286
State Political Directorate (GPU), 278
State Publishing House (Gosizdat), 259, 262
"Statutory Charter of the Russian Empire," 58
Stein, Baron Heinrich Friedrich vom, 59
Stishinskii, A. S., 178
Stolypin, Peter A.: agrarian program of, 34, 43, 51, 148–54, 179–83; Council of Ministers chairmanship of, 200–206, 210; policy consequences of reforms of, 154–61, 184–89; revolution of 1905 and, 92–93
Strelianyi, Anatolii, 344
Sukhomlinov, V. A., 207
Supreme Council of the National Economy (Vesenkha), 304
Supreme Soviet, 398–400
Suslov, Mikhail, 335
Sviatopolk-Mirskii, Prince Peter, 90–91

Tambov Provincial Committee, 116
taxation, 287; peasant burden of, 143; reform of, 67, 71, 77, 83, 166
Teachers' Congress, 234
Technical Society, 216
Temporary Regulations, 213–16, 218–19, 406
Teodorovich, I. A., 253
"Third of June System," 204
Third Section, 68, 73
"Thoughts of a Russian," 62, 69
"Three Meshchanskaia Street," 263
Tolmachev, V., 280, 284–85
Tolstoi, Dmitry A., 79, 122, 135, 167
Tolstoy, Leo, 220
Tomskii, M. P., 309
Tracy, Destutt de, 337
Trade Union Congress, Fifth, 302
Trezvost' i berezhlivost' (Sobriety and Thrift), 231
Trotsky, Leon, 249–50, 327; and support of censorship, 263
Tsion (Cyon), I. F., 81
Turgenev, Nicholas I., 59

Turkey, 78, 120
Tyrkova, A. V., 221

Unified State Political Directorate (OGPU), 285
Union of Medical and Public Health Workers, 304
Union of Mineworkers, 303
Union of Soviet and Commercial Employees, 299, 302–3, 306–7
united government, 90–211
United Nobility, 174–75, 178–81
Unofficial Committee, 59
Uvarov, S. S., 60

Valuev, Peter A., 61–63; reform proposals of, 68–72, 74–75, 94, 113–14, 133
Vannovskii, P. S., 79
Vernadskii, I. V., 63
Vestnik politsii (Police Herald), 268–69
Vestnik promyshlennosti (Herald of Industry), 240
Vestnik trezvosti (Herald of Sobriety), 226
Viazemskii, Peter A., 58–59
Vlasov, V., 283–84
Von-Anrep, A. K., 231–32
Vorontsov-Dashkov, Illarion I., 78, 79, 82, 84
Voroshilov, K. E., 348, 363
Vyshinskii, A. Ia., 347
Vyshnegradskii, I. A., 83, 123

War Communism, 248, 259, 273, 278, 402–3
West Germany, 396
What Is to Be Done?, 251–52, 337–38

white-collar workers, 302; NOT movement and, 300; purges and, 306–9; scapegoating of, 298–99, 306
Will the Soviet Union Survive until 1984?, 367
Witte, Sergei Iu.: Council of Ministers chairmanship of, 190–202, 208, 210; economic-policy reforms of, 83, 88–90, 92–93, 123–24, 131; peasant landownership and, 145–47, 174–77
women, 226–27, 229–30
Women's Congress, First, 216, 218–19, 221
Worker-Peasant Militia, 271
Workers' Control movement of 1917, 296
World War II, 347
Wrangel, Baron E. V., 62
Writers' Congresses, First, 216–18, 220, 230

Yeltsin, Boris, 379
Young Communist League (Komsomol), 258, 330
Yugoslavia, 352–53

Zaitsev, P., 275
Zamiatnin, Dmitry N., 32, 61
Zarudnyi, Sergei, 32
Zelenyi, A. A., 61
zemstvo: counterreforms and, 122–23; creation of, 169; elections to, 79, 118–19; reform of, 106, 109, 122–23; representation in, 51, 94, 112–14
Zhenotdel, 258
Zherebtsov, N. A., 61
Zhukov, Georgii, 330, 348, 361, 363
Zubkova, E., 344